Competing Jurisdictions

Afrika-Studiecentrum Series

in collaboration with SAVUSA (South Africa – Vrije Universiteit – Strategic Alliances)

VOLUME 6

Competing Jurisdictions

Settling land claims in Africa

Edited by

Sandra Evers
Marja Spierenburg
Harry Wels

BRILL
LEIDEN · BOSTON
2005

This book is printed on acid-free paper.

Photo on cover: Harry Wels

Library of Congress Cataloging-in-Publication Data

Competing jurisdictions : settling land claims in Africa / edited by Sandra Evers, Marja Spierenburg, Harry Wels.
p. cm. — (Afrika-Studiecentrum series, ISSN 1570-9310)
Selected papers from a conference held in September 2003 at the Vrije Universiteit Amsterdam.
Includes bibliographical references and index.
ISBN 90-04-14780-2 (pbk : alk. paper)
1. Land tenure—Africa—Congresses. 2. Land reform—Africa—Congresses. 3. Land use, Rural—Government policy—Africa. 4. Right of property—Africa—Congresses. 5. Land titles—Africa—Congresses. 6. Commons—Africa—Congresses. I. Evers, Sandra. II. Spierenburg, Marja. III. Wels, Harry, 1961- IV. Title. V. Series.

HD966.C66 2005
333.3'16—dc22

2005050842

ISSN 1570–9310
ISBN 90 04 14780 2

PRINTED IN THE NETHERLANDS

Contents

List of tables *vii*
List of figures *vii*

INTRODUCTION – COMPETING JURISDICTIONS: SETTLING LAND CLAIMS IN AFRICA, INCLUDING MADAGASCAR *1*
Sandra Evers, Marja Spierenburg and Harry Wels

1 COMMUNAL TENURE 'FROM ABOVE' AND 'FROM BELOW'. LAND RIGHTS, AUTHORITY AND LIVELIHOODS IN RURAL SOUTH AFRICA *21*
Ben Cousins and Aninka Claassens

2 LAND TENURE REFORM IN SOUTH AFRICA: A FOCUS ON THE MORAVIAN CHURCH LAND IN THE WESTERN CAPE *55*
Lungisile Ntsebeza

3 CONTESTATION, CONFUSION AND CORRUPTION: MARKET-BASED LAND REFORM IN ZAMBIA *79*
Taylor Brown

4 'WE FOUGHT THE WAR TO RETURN TO THE OLD WAYS'. CONFLICTS ABOUT LAND REFORMS IN DANDE, NORTHERN ZIMBABWE *103*
Marja Spierenburg

5 FRACTIONATING LOCAL LEADERSHIP: CREATED AUTHORITY AND MANAGEMENT OF STATE LAND IN ZIMBABWE *129*
Bill Kinsey

6 FIRST-COMERS AND LATE-COMERS: THE ROLE OF NARRATIVES IN LAND CLAIMS *157*
Carola Lentz

7 STATE FORMATION, ACCESS TO THE COMMONS AND AUTOCHTHONY AMONG THE BERBERS OF THE MIDDLE ATLAS, MOROCCO *181*
Bernhard Venema

8 LAND AND THE POLITICS OF IDENTITY. THE CASE OF ANYWAA-NUER RELATIONS IN THE GAMBELLA REGION *203*
Dereje Feyissa

9 TRUMPING THE ANCESTORS: THE CHALLENGES OF IMPLEMENTING A LAND REGISTRATION SYSTEM IN MADAGASCAR *223*
Sandra Evers

10 THE STRUGGLE FOR LAND RIGHTS IN THE CONTEXT OF MULTIPLE NORMATIVE ORDERS IN TANZANIA *243*
Rie Odgaard

11 TRADITIONAL ADDITIONAL AUTHORITIES IN UGANDA AND THE MANAGEMENT OF LEGISLATIVELY DECENTRALISED FOREST RESOURCES *265*
Frank Muhereza

12 PARTICIPATIVE APPROACHES AND DECENTRALIZED MANAGEMENT OF THE SAMORI FOREST IN THE BAYE MUNICIPALITY, MOPTI REGION (MALI) *289*
Bréhima Kassibo

13 INSIDERS OUT: FOREST ACCESS THROUGH VILLAGE CHIEFS IN SENEGAL *315*
Sagana Thiaw and Jesse Ribot

14 FIGHTING OVER CRUMBS? SMALL VALLEYS IN WEST AFRICA AS A NEW LOCUS OF LAND *333*
Mayke Kaag

List of contributors *353*
Index *359*

List of tables

5.1 Domains of perceived authority I *140*
5.2 Existence of administrative and enforcement mechanisms *141*
5.3 Social identities and access to common pool resources I *142*
5.4 Social identities and access to common pool resources II *143*
5.5 Autonomy and control of resources *143*
5.6 Domains of perceived authority II *144*
5.7 Village heads' declared methods of dealing with violations involving natural resources *145*
5.8 Decision-making powers I *146*
5.9 Decision-making powers II *147*
5.10 Decision-making powers III *148*
8.1 Land, population and political claims in the GPNRS *214*
8.2 Political representation in the GPNRS council *215*
8.3 Allocation of managerial posts in the GPNRS *216*
8.4 The ethnic profile of the civil servants in the GPNRS *216*
8.5 Demographic composition of the GPNRS *217*

List of figures

3.1 Distribution of customary and state lands in Zambia (adapted from Van Loenen 1999) *82*

Introduction – Competing jurisdictions: Settling land claims in Africa, including Madagascar

Sandra Evers, Marja Spierenburg and Harry Wels

Conference on competing jurisdictions in land management

In September 2003, over twenty-five scholars from Africa, the United States, and Europe gathered at the Vrije Universiteit Amsterdam to tackle the issue of competing jurisdictions in land management. The conference was organised to serve as a forum for exchanging ideas and a platform for future research. The main goal was to develop a comprehensive overview of land claim settlement in Africa. Papers covered a variety of geographical locations in Africa, including Madagascar. Subjects included land disputes resulting from competing jurisdictions, the role of social identity in land claims, emerging alliances between local actors and regional, state, or international bodies in connection with land access issues (natural resource management), and analyses of the social and cultural repertoires used to create these alliances.

The conference was organised by the Department of Culture, Organisation, and Management (COM) and the Department of Social and Cultural Anthropology (SCA) of the Vrije Universiteit Amsterdam. It was financed by the Interchurch Organisation for Development Co-operation in The Netherlands (ICCO), the World Resource Institute from Washington D.C., and the Faculty of Social Sciences of the Vrije Universiteit Amsterdam.

A selection of the leading papers delivered at the conference appears in this volume. These papers discuss the following sub-themes addressed at the conference: Narratives and cultural repertoires; land as the basis for identity, democracy and decentralisation; theories of property; social relations and property; property and the issues of violence, power, and authority.

The various chapters of this book are primarily written from an anthropological perspective. This predominance does not imply that the authors contributing to this volume do not have a keen eye for the 'political economy' of their research settings.

The issue of land in Africa

Securing access to land and other natural resources is the key to sustaining the livelihoods of millions of Africans across the continent. From a political point of view, African states naturally considered control of these resources a priority, for a large part as a tool to ensure authority over the African populace (Mamdani 1996; Benjaminsen and Lund 2003). The theme of access to natural resources has also received plenty of attention from the North, which began in colonial times. Colonialism 'allowed Europeans to impose their image of Africa upon the reality of the African landscape' (Anderson and Grove 1987: 4), that was '(…) often completely out of touch with local realities' (Broch-Due and Schroeder 2000: 12). According to the latter, this detachment of (Western) representations from local realities '(…) has been carried into the contemporary age' (*ibid.*). This might partly explain the continued abundant attention paid by Western scholars to issues of land, and especially land tenure, in Africa, as well as the prominent place on the agenda that is accorded to land issues in the 'development business' (see for an excellent annotated bibliography on land issues in Africa, with an emphasis on its relation to poverty and development, Palmer 1997). Many of the (Northern) narratives on land and other natural resources in Africa were, and often still are represented in the popular media as quite bleak, with doom-laden predictions about retreating forests, ongoing desertification, soil erosion, species extinction as well as resorting to other 'declinist' terminology (Beinart and McGregor 2003: 1).

More recently, however, both colonial and current developmental narratives about land and other natural resources in Africa have increasingly been challenged, especially from within the emerging field of environmental history (Beinart and McGregor 2003; Dovers, Edgecombe and Guest 2002; Leach and Mearns 1996). These challenges have mainly taken the form of looking anew at historical (colonial) records and data, and examining 'the moral and cultural filters through which concepts about the natural world have been passed in different times and places' (Beinart and McGregor 2003: 2).

Environmental historians increasingly turn to cultural studies and literary criticism for inspiration and for concepts to reflect on their 'moral and cultural filters' (*ibid.*: 5). In literary criticism, particularly in the field of post-colonial studies, Edward Said, Gayatri Spivak, and Homi Bhabha, have led the debate within the broader context of a deconstructivist paradigm. Post-colonial theory offers a whole range of concepts on which to reflect and discuss one's own position in relation to the subject(s) under study (Ashcroft *et al.* 2000). We will return to this theme of self-reflexivity later in this introductory chapter, especially in relation to policy and advocacy, which is an important undercurrent of this volume.

Competing jurisdictions over land

For centuries, Africa has been characterised by pluralistic land tenure systems, consisting in different forms of state tenure, private tenure, and communal tenure. The state generally retains residual 'ultimate ownership', while private tenure is often effected through rights of usufruct. Land tenure systems nevertheless vary considerably and in many cases, central and local power structures are engaged in struggles for control of land. Where strategies are employed to foster the incorporation of local communities into the wider fabric of society, this is often with the intent of diminishing the relative power of local institutions (Venema and Van den Breemer 1999). Land tenure is a key issue in this arena (Toulmin and Quan 2000). Land tenure can be defined, following Barrow and Murphree (2001: 29) as '(…) the rights of secure, long-term access to land and other resources, their benefits, and the responsibilities related to these rights'. These rights, in turn relate to terms like 'ownership, property, proprietorship and entitlement' (*ibid.*). It is important to note in the context of this edited volume that the term 'tenure' includes a 'temporal dimension' (*ibid.*: 30). This means that rights of tenure are 'rarely, if ever, absolute' (*ibid.*). This observation provides an important key to this particular volume, because it implies an ongoing process of competition over these rights in terms of legitimising narratives and counter-narratives that challenge those narratives, the very topic of this book.

One of the recurrent themes recently has been the development of a relationship between land and social / ethnic identity in Africa (Berry 1989; Ranger 1999; Evers 2002; Spierenburg 2003). Mamdani (1996) argues that in many parts of Africa, this relation was forged under colonialism, when Africans could only claim rights to land from the state on the basis of their alleged membership of an (ethnic/'tribal') group, and by referring to 'ancestral ties to the land'. Both Mamdani (1996) and Vail (1989) argue convincingly that 'tribes' were constructed through this process, rather than being a primordial locus of identity formation. Land in those areas set aside for Africans was to be administered through communal tenure, which, together with territorial land claims based on references to the ancestors, is often presented as reflecting 'authentic' pre-colonial forms of land tenure (Bruce and Migot-Adholla 1994). A number of authors, however, have argued that 'communal tenure' is a colonial construct as well (Le Bris *et al.* 1982; Cheater 1990; Ranger 1993; Mamdani 1996; see also below).

There are at least two issues that complicate matters of autochtony (from the Greek, literally 'sprung from the earth, soil') significantly. The first is the high degree of mobility of many Africans (De Bruijn, Van Dijk and Foeken 2001; Andersson 2002). The complex processes of incorporation of local communities in the colonial and post-colonial state and the ensuing legal pluralism pertaining to land more often than not has resulted in tensions between 'newcomers' and those who consider themselves 'locals' (Evers 2002; Lentz 2003; Spierenburg 2004). A second complicating factor is the heritage of the so-called settler colonies, where a racially skewed distribution of land leads to conflicts and questions concerning the identity of white landowners. Can white Southern Africans, both Boer and Brit, ever be considered African in the sense of 'sons of the soil'? If we are to believe President Robert Mugabe of Zimbabwe this is definitely not the case (Blair 2002: 169-86). Both President Thabo Mbeki from South Africa as well as President Sam Nujoma from Namibia seem to support him in his definition of who is and who is not 'indigenous' to the region.

There are authors who argue that the aesthetic aspects of land and landscape played a particularly important role in white identity construction (Grove 1987; Wels 2003; Draper *et al.* 2004) and created a sense of 'locality and belonging' (Lovell 1998). Grove, for instance, provides the example of the missionary John Croumbi Brown, who went to South Africa as colonial botanist, bringing with him'a Scottish intellectual tradition which was at that time [1862] [was] nurturing a splendid neo-Romanticist school of landscape painting (...) The connection between the development of a conservation policy in the Cape and the Scottish Romanticist proclivities of Brown was a significant one' (Grove 1987: 29; see also Grove 1997). This perspective basically argues for acknowledging and recognising that both white and black *African* social identities are based on claiming a relationship with the land (see also Ranger 1999).

The process of white identity construction, however, was often made possible by raw power politics (Levering Lewis 1988; Wesseling 1992). European colonial powers superimposed a European style administration and jurisdiction upon Africans, but also laid claims to natural resources such as ivory, copper, gold, timber, diamonds, and cocoa not to mention land (Pakenham 1991), often in the form of property rights that formed the basis for exclusion. Furthermore, owners of property also perceived (and often still do perceive) that they were entitled to political control of the people to whom they allowed access to their property, for example, through leases. Property rights and political control over people generally go hand in hand. In colonial Southern Rhodesia, for instance, policies were introduced to try to value land on the assumption that attaching monetary value to the land in relation to its potential agricultural productivity would stimulate productivity. Although it is was explicitly stated that '(t)he creation of a market for land does not necessarily imply a system of private ownership of land' (Yudelman 1964: 114), it usually turned out that way and by implication this gave political control over local people and labour in terms of granting them access (see for a critical study of this process Rutherford 2001). Licences were granted to private, predominantly European, interests for the purpose of developing and marketing resources. In certain colonies, the political and economic power of such interests often exceeded the power of the colonial state. This was particularly true in Southern Africa, Kenya, and the (Belgian) Congo, where land was appropriated, then reallocated under a variety of land grants to settlers of European descent or (chartered) companies (see for an example from the Congo, Depelchin 1992; examples in Southern Africa, Thomas 1996; Rotberg 1988; Newitt 1995; 1999; examples from Kenya, Bates 1989).

During the 1960s, the European powers engaged in the process of decolonisation. Some of the newly formed states (particularly socialist regimes) nationalised natural resources and private companies. States with a more market-based orientation or mixed economies also asserted considerable control over ownership, as well as the control and allocation of land and land titles. The centralisation of control over resources was commonly to the detriment of local (often kinship-based) land tenure systems (Hesseling 1996). Centralisation could only be accomplished by 'simplifying' locally developed complex patterns of land tenure and land use, often involving multiple use, with multiple owners using different tracts of land for different purposes during different periods of time (Scott 1998). It also entailed the simplification of local authority structures. The complexities of kinship practices, which were often central to local land tenure practices, as well as references to religious rites and concepts pertaining to these practices, were often ignored (Van der Klei 1985).

Since the late 1980s international monetary organisations such as the World Bank, in addition to other donor agencies and NGOs, have been promoting decentralisation within a larger context of democratisation. Decentralisation often seems to be donor-driven, but in fact many African countries have a long history of swinging back and forth between decentralisation and (re)centralisation (Ribot 2000; Spierenburg 2003). The international community has put the introduction of multi-party democracy high on its agenda, resulting in the creation of elected councils and committees at several levels and the constitution of new actors claiming authority in land issues. All these processes show an ongoing concern with the question of how land tenure should be administered locally. Systematic attempts to abolish communal tenure and undermine the authority of its associated 'traditional guardians of the land' (chiefs, local religious leaders) have often been followed by a corresponding reaction to reinstate communal tenure. This political and economic uncertainty is compounded by a plethora of local and national (state) institutions disputing authority over land, that is, competing jurisdictions over land (Juul and Lund 2002).

Hence, land use is not subject to just any single, cohesive body of legal concepts and rules, but to plural normative systems (Hesseling 1996: 102). State law, 'traditional' law, and religious law may all apply to land use and land tenure. Hesseling (1996: 102) and Von Benda Beckmann (1991: 78) add another form of regulation which is relevant to this volume, namely 'project law' (see Kassibo, in this volume). Sometimes the various normative systems result in competing claims to land. In other cases they are combined into hybrid forms of local regulation, made up of elements of different systems (Von Benda Beckmann 1991: 78). In this book we look at the processes through which various actors draw upon a range of, often competing, jurisdictions in their attempts to settle land claims. We use the word processes here intentionally, since, as most chapters will demonstrate, conflicts over land are seldom resolved permanently.

A narrative approach

Some have argued that Post-Modernism brought an end to the grand or meta narratives (Lyotard 1984: 37). That is to say that all embracing explanatory models for social reality, such as functionalism, are no longer accepted. Differentiation, diversity, and fragmentation are now the rule. In other words, general (hi)stories have come to be replaced by very localised and personalised narratives and stories (Ellis and Flaherty 1992). Narratives, as part of the broader category of rhetorical figures, originated 'as a humanistically inspired reaction against an all too far-reaching rationalism, which regards language as something second to logical content' (Alvesson and Sköldberg 2000: 89). It was a scientific paradigm shift that fits almost perfectly into the ethnographic tradition within anthropology in the tradition of fieldwork (Malinowski) and interpretative anthropology (Geertz). Geertz' 'doing ethnography' (1973) became increasingly considered to be telling stories with a narrative framework, including a beginning, a middle, and an end, linked in a certain plot (Bruner 1986: 140-1). It is therefore not surprising that literary criticism, and other forms of art, became an important source of inspiration for anthropologists and social scientists in general (Kloos 1990; Cosgrove and Daniels 1988: 4).

If we link this general narrative approach to the issue of competing jurisdictions over land, in whatever form of expression it is presented and with all its implications for the (strategic) use of rhetoric devices and shared cultural repertoires, it becomes clear that we are talking about who has constructed and produced the most convincing story to tell in terms of legitimisation and processes of in- and exclusion (compare Nauta's narrative about local South African land sector NGOs representing the 'grassroots people' 2001: 147-83; see also Broch-Due and Schroeder 2000). It also means that protest against one story line almost always takes the form of a counter-narrative, an opposition (with serious possibilities for contamination by opposites, see below). A story can therefore never be interpreted in isolation. It is inherently linked to multiple other narratives in the arena. Good and bad cannot be easily discerned in such situations of constantly mutating complicities. For a better understanding, the various narratives should be deconstructed and dissected to reveal their constituent elements.

Important in this respect is the concept of memory. Memory is fraught with difficulties. It is a concept that conflates with other concepts like nostalgia and processes of remembering. Central to the problem of memory are questions like: Whose memory are we talking about? What is memorised? For what particular reasons? In the context of post-colonial Africa these are highly relevant questions. Narratives of colonial nostalgia are, for instance, having to compete with several state and personal counter-memories, leading to an arena of '*politicised* memories' (Werbner 1998: 15). 'Memory narratives' are social constructions that are produced and linked to power and interests (Simpson 1998: 220) and are therefore 'constantly updated to suit present needs' (Cole 1998: 105). Nevertheless, Werbner argues that despite the obvious politicisation of memories 'the political cannot be meaningfully studied apart from the moral' (Werbner 1998: 15) because generally human rights and injustices are at stake (see also Falk Moore 1998). Politicised memory should therefore lie 'at the very heart of postcolonial studies' (Werbner 1998: 15). South Africa can be taken as a clear example of how, for instance, the 'official memory' of the apartheid state was 'sanitised' in the period leading up to the change of government in 1994. Between 1990 and 1994 huge volumes of public records were destroyed in an attempt to keep the apartheid state's darkest secrets hidden (Harris 2002: 135). 'Politics of archiving' (Hamilton 2002: 209) can be considered a sub-category of the 'politics of knowledge' in which memory is actively created and destroyed, depending on the broader configurations. This brings us to our own position concerning processes of knowledge production in the next section.

Scholarship and advocacy

Scholarship naturally involves critical analysis, deconstructing, and occasionally the outright rejection of existing theoretical approaches. Nevertheless, the practical and temporal constraints of policy formulation also require a broad understanding of the historical processes which have led to current paradigms. Some commentators have drawn a boundary between scholarship and policy, even though the two are not necessarily mutually exclusive. Choices have to be made, but not in a decisional or historical vacuum. Beinart and McGregor appear to view the conundrum as a 'Catch-22' situation, as they find it necessary to state in their introduction that they have not written 'a book about policy' (Beinart and McGregor 2003: 2). Although understandable and legitimate, it also seems a rather artificial separation between scholarship and influencing policy or straightforward advocacy. Considering scholarship in the social sciences as able to be 'neutral' in the political and policy sense of the word seems rather naïve from a social constructivist perspective. If we accept that '(…) (S)ocial facts , including native points of view, are human fabrications, themselves subject to social inquiry as to their origins. Fieldwork constructs now are seen by many to emerge from a hermeneutic process; fieldwork is an interpretative act, not an observational or descriptive one' (Van Maanen 1988: 93). We acknowledge that the social sciences are not neutral or objective. Should we not then go a step further and acknowledge that in terms of policies and politics we are not neutral either? This question led to some debate at the conference from which this volume derives. Some of the authors contributing to this book argued that not all research should be aimed at policy making, that we have some fundamental issues to address that may not easily translate into policy making or advocating. Others, in contrast, have been involved in advocacy and policy relevant research for quite some time and feel that we have a moral obligation to analyse and contribute to the development of policies pertaining to land use and land tenure, since these affect the lives of the people among whom we do research so much.

In this book many authors have, often implicitly, sided with people who previously were or still are rather oppressed and marginalised, and whose strategies and counter-narratives have not been recognised in the arena of competing jurisdictions over land in Africa. In that sense many authors in this book are 'judgemental' and, often implicitly, try to suggest options for policy formulation that attempt to address the needs of the less powerful in society more adequately. In that process they often oppose current policies and policy formulations. But taking this seemingly moral high ground is not without its own complications and problems. There is an inherent danger in this approach that we would like to put forward on the basis of Derrida's discussion (1976; 1989), applied in Sanders (2002: 8-11 and 201), on '(…) complicity – [or] the foldedness or "contamination" of oppositional pairs (…)'(*ibid.* 2002: 9). The basic argument is that '(w)hen opposition takes the form of a demarcation from something, it cannot (…) be untouched by that to which it opposes itself. Opposition takes its first steps from a footing of complicity'. In a way oppositionality 'is parasitic on that to which it opposes itself' (*ibid.*: 9 and 10). Therefore every choice for opposition is choosing for a certain type of contamination. This paradox of opposition and resistance means that '(…) responsibility is sharpened. No longer can the intellectual

(...) simply proclaim his or her opposition. Complicity has to be acknowledged, and, when a strategy of demarcation is adopted, responsibility assumed for choosing "between ... terrifying contaminations"' *(ibid.*: 10). A further complicating factor in this moral arena, and paradox, is that the intellectuals or advocates often do not speak or write about themselves, but that they suggest that they speak on behalf of others; that they give some sort of voice to the marginalised they have chosen to represent in their work. We realise that we use concepts that have strong and basic moral connotations to make our argument, but they might shed some new light on certain research processes related to competing jurisdictions. Two types of (theoretical and methodological) reflections are required on the basis of the above: How far are we as various authors in this book contaminated by that which we try to oppose? And secondly: How sure can we be about our voice-giving capabilities? These questions have a broader relevance than this book.

On the basis of Derrida's observation described above, we could ask ourselves whether we are parasitic on that which we try to oppose. The answer to that question could perhaps be summarised as follows: Many if not most conceptualisation, categorisation and theorising on the issue of land in Africa is done by academics or people from the development business, in many cases from the developed world. If they side with the less-fortunate, that is, oppose certain policies and practices that (seem to further) marginalise certain categories of the less-powerful people in the arena of land, at the same time the researchers and practitioners are part and parcel of this process, that is, participating in and making a living on the basis of what is going on which they try to oppose. But in how far do we dare to acknowledge our parasitic status? Do we have the courage to use this strong wording to describe what we do, and how do we cope with it and take our responsibility accordingly? In South Africa, for example, these were fundamental questions for the Truth and Reconciliation Commission (TRC), chaired by Archbishop Tutu, in order to indicate the possibility of a joint future for all South Africans after Apartheid. The TRC report is quite clear on this by choosing to follow Hannah Arendt's notion of 'the banality of evil'. Although the terms 'parasitic' and 'contamination' connote the darker side of human interaction, they certainly do not apply only to the extremes of human behaviour. Most of the time they refer to the banality of everyday routines, of which we are no longer aware, but that in their own small and tiny ways contribute to the perpetuation of the status quo and the injustices that come with it. It is more in this context that concepts like parasitic and contamination should be placed and understood according to the TRC. Following this line of argument it pleads, 'for a heightening of personal responsibility, which, paradoxically, would mean not washing one's hands but actively affirming a complicity, or potential complicity, in the "outrageous deeds" of others' (*ibid.*: 3). Only this acknowledgement could further the process of reconciliation and ultimately lead to a common future for all South Africans, according to Desmond Tutu (Tutu 1999).

For some of us how to cope with it means primarily taking the 'dare to be dirty'-approach, that is, we dare to discuss openly and explicitly issues in the communicating domains of the social sciences and research on the one hand and political and power debates on the other. We should have the courage to write that we are not politically neutral and that we would like to contribute to a policy process through which the position and livelihoods of the formerly disadvantaged groups might improve. We acknowledge wholeheartedly that there are no easy answers to these issues and that we would like to postpone moral judgements about the ideas and convictions we oppose as much as possible, although this might be difficult in the context of political debates. We should also try to cope with the idea of intellectual complicity by investing in an extensive reflection process where it concerns our research material along the lines suggested by Alvesson and Sköldberg. 'The whole idea of reflexivity, as we see it, is the very ability to break away from a frame of reference and to look at what it is *not* capable of saying' (2000: 246).

Alvesson and Sköldberg's suggestion that we focus on what we are 'not capable of saying' could be linked to Spivak's argument in the field of literary criticism, on the impossibility of speaking on behalf of others, especially the 'subaltern', a concept of crucial importance to post-colonial studies. Spivak develops her argument in 'Can the subaltern speak?', in which she basically problematises the claim of academics like Foucault and Delleuze, or intellectuals in general, that they can represent, or are able to give voice to, the disenfranchised. In their effort to try and let the subaltern speak for themselves, academics efface their roles as intellectuals according to Spivak (1988: 292). She makes particular note of the impossibility of Western feminist writers speaking for 'Third World' women: '(…) the subject of exploitation cannot know and speak the text of female exploitation even if the absurdity of the non-representing intellectual making space for her to speak is achieved' (*ibid.*: 289). What Spivak does in her argument is highlight 'the limitations of applying European theories of representation to the lives and histories of disempowered women in the 'Third World'. Unless western intellectuals begin to take the aesthetic dimension of political representation into account, Spivak argues that these intellectuals will continue to silence the voice of subaltern women' (in Morton 2003: 58). In other words, 'Spivak is certainly sceptical about the political benefits to be gained from the benevolent western radicals speaking for postcolonial subjects' (*ibid.*: 127). She not only makes her point for Third World women in literary criticism. In analysing the rewriting of Daniel Defoe's *Robinson Crusoe* by J.M. Coetzee in his book *Foe*, for instance, there are several attempts made by a person named Susan Barton to teach a man called Friday to communicate in English. In Coetzee's book, Friday is not able to speak because his tongue has been removed by slave traders. Therefore Susan Barton tries to teach him how to write in English. She fails dismally. In Spivak's interpretation Friday can be seen as an 'agent of withholding in the text' (Spivak 1991: 172). She 'suggests that Friday's agency lies in his refusal to be represented. By doing so, Spivak emphasises [once more, now by analysing Coetzee's book] that Coetzee draws attention to the limitations of postcolonial representation as an effective vehicle for political change' (Morton 2003: 123).

In a revealing article on English landscape painting, Prince starts with a reproduction of a painting of an English landscape drawn by a Chinese painter, Chiang Yee, in 1936, entitled 'Cows in Derwentwater'. 'The painting looks strange, not because it is incorrect in detail, but because it fails to reproduce images we have learned to associate with English Lakeland scenery' (Prince 1984: 4). The famous Australian writer David Malouf, has said in an interview with a Dutch newspaper that if he had to write about the consciousness of Aboriginals, no matter how much research he were to put into it, the resulting narrative would undoubtedly be considered not-authentic (Vloet 2001). Narrators around the world seem to be strongly influenced by 'spirits of place' (Brown 2001). In the social sciences, especially in the disciplines of anthropology and history, many European and other Western-born and trained scientists have written about locality and belonging in the African context. We, the editors, belong to that tradition. Many of the contributing authors of this volume are scientists from Africa (but often trained in a Western discourse of science). With such a mixture of perspectives, both Western and African, the interesting meta-question that underlies this volume and which only the reader can answer by reading 'between the lines' is whether the narratives in this book show similarities and differences in relation to spirits of place. In addition to the critical debate about representation in post-colonial studies, which we have presented above, we add this observation on landscape painting, through which we want to indicate how precarious knowledge production and construction is and how (ultra) modest its producers should be about claiming any close proximity to certainty. In other words, we (only) add our (politicised) narratives on land, and the constructed memories inherent in them, to the ongoing processes of policy making and competing jurisdictions over land in Africa.

Outline of the book

This book can be roughly divided into three parts. The first part describes various attempts by governments to control land use and land tenure through programmes of land reforms. Together the chapters provide an overview of colonial influences on local land use and tenure, and the resulting legacy that post-Independence governments had to deal with. This part sets the scene for the second part of the book, which discusses the increasing importance of narratives about autochthony, about 'first-comers' and 'late-comers' in local competing claims on land, which result from colonial and post-colonial national land legislation. In addition, the chapters discuss how people derive their identity from land. The third part of the book explores the apparent resurgence of so-called traditional authorities in the management of land, often in a context of national policies of decentralisation.

The land reform programmes analysed in the first section of the book range from the redistribution of land to redress racially skewed access patterns to programmes aimed at reorganising land use practices within communal areas. The first chapter, by Ben Cousins and Aninka Claassens, is to a large extent based on actual advocacy work that the Programme for Land and Agrarian Studies (PLAAS) from the University of Western Cape, South Africa, is doing on land issues, particularly on communal land tenure systems in South Africa (see our discussion on academic and advocacy work earlier in this introduction). This chapter was written when Ben Cousins and his colleagues had just fought a long and bitter battle in the South African parliament over the Communal Land Right Bill in the second half of 2003. This recent experience resonates through the chapter, which results in a vibrant text pleading and arguing for social justice for the rural poor in the field of communal land tenure. Its political positioning and a positive choice for South Africa's rural poor is a refreshing angle in the usual arena of academic restraint, and a fitting contribution to an edited volume focused on *competing* jurisdictions over land in Africa. Also in this chapter, as in the other chapters in this section of the book, the often controversial role and position of local authorities is highlighted and central to the chosen political economy approach and analysis.

The second chapter, by Lungisile Ntsebeza, addresses a hitherto ignored but highly relevant and interesting problem: How should issues of restitution and redistribution concerning land owned by churches be addressed? Ntsebeza analyses local views on the pros and cons of the restitution of church land in South Africa. The third chapter, by Taylor Brown, analyses Zambia's market-based programme for land reforms. Given the high hopes that institutions like the World Bank project onto such land reforms in terms of the contribution these allegedly could make to economic growth and equity, Brown's critical analyses of the effects of Zambia's programme makes interesting reading. The fourth chapter, by Marja Spierenburg, describes the implementation of internal land use reforms in a communal area in Zimbabwe. Between the mid-1980s and the year 2000 (when the first farm invasions occurred), the post-Independence government quickly shifted its focus from land redistribution to the reorganisation of the communal areas, adopting policies that showed striking similarities to Rhodesian land use policies. Spierenburg describes the role of spirit mediums in resisting the land reforms. The fifth chapter, written by Bill Kinsey, discusses very recent developments in the so-called resettlement areas of Zimbabwe, former 'European' land that had been redistributed among African farmers shortly after Independence. In these areas, farmers had to (re)create village communities under circumstances that differed from those in the communal areas. Kinsey describes the effects of the recently introduced Traditional Leaders Act.

In the second section of the book the contributing authors analyse narratives constructed around 'first-comers' and 'late-comers' within the context of multiple jurisdictions over land. In the first chapter of this section Carola Lentz describes how narratives – recounting the immigration of one's ancestors into the area, the establishment of the settlement, and subsequent property transactions – play a decisive role in legitimising land claims. She maintains that even the forcible appropriation of land is usually narrated as a voluntary cession by the previous owners. In conflicts over land or political allegiance connected with land ownership, the contestants inevitably present different versions of the settlement history to buttress their own case. Even under modern property regimes, narratives, like those presented in court cases, are crucial to legitimising claims. Drawing on case studies from northern Ghana and southern Burkina Faso, the chapter explores the role of narrative in asserting, defending, and contesting land claims. In the following chapter Bernhard Venema discusses how Berbers and newcomers in the Moroccan Middle Atlas competed for access to the commons, the outcome of which has been shaped by processes of state formation. Formerly, newcomers could settle and farm only by being adopted into the Berber community. This continued during the first phase of the Protectorate, which maintained customary law and traditional management. During the second phase, capitalistic enterprises created a land and labour market leading to the privatisation of land and the undermining of customary law. After independence, national legislation was introduced and government officials became the guardians of ancestral lands. However, the local population and their leaders asserted their Berber identity by resisting the new legislation and restricting access to land by newcomers. The chapter by Dereje Feyissa also focuses on narratives, but through an analysis of the meaning of land in identity formation among contemporary Anywaa and Nuer in Ethiopia. They are engaged in a social struggle which is becoming increasingly violent. At the heart of the conflict lie the multiple meanings attached to and the growing political significance of the land. At a symbolic level, the Anywaa landed identity discourse collides with the Nuer mobile identity discourse. As an economic resource, a specific land type (riverine land) has become an object of struggle, and, in the context of institutionalised ethnicity, land has become a strategy of political entitlement. Where the Anywaa invoke autochthony in the struggle for cultural identity and as an ideology of political entitlement, the Nuer have relied upon a scheme of interpretation and creative strategies of entitlement that counter Anywaa exclusionary practices. The resolution of the dispute is increasingly influenced by extra-local political processes. Sandra Evers' chapter focuses on identity formation based on land in the Malagasy context. For the Betsileo people of the extreme Southern Highlands of Madagascar, land plays a vital role in social relations. It is the main source of subsistence. It serves as a sign of visible wealth, and as an instrument of exclusion. In a country where poverty is widespread, and where outlying regions are little influenced by the hand of central government, land is the principal avenue to power. And, finally, because one must have land to possess a tomb, it is the *sine qua non* of a successful passage into the Hereafter. The chapter outlines how the *tompon-tany* ('master(s) of the land') control access to and management of land in rural Madagascar. They generally do not register their land claims. Tombs are deemed to constitute sufficient evidence of title, since the Malagasy believe tombs are geographical markers of family origin in a particular region. This naturally raises potential disputes between claims based on local tenure practices and the national land title system, which the Malagasy government is currently trying to overcome with new legislation, a policy which is in direct conflict with the historical supremacy of the ancestors. Rie Odgaard analyses the effects of an increasing land scarcity in some parts of Tanzania. Looking at land rights from the perspective of social relations and as results of processes of negotiation in the context of the multiple normative orders existing in Tanzania, her chapter shows that some groups, for example, women and pastoralists, are generally less favourably positioned than other groups in the struggle to defend their rights to land. Changing gender relations and the special land use system practised by the pastoralists are identified as the major factors influencing this situation.

Attempts made by various African governments to decentralise management powers over natural resources to traditional local authorities is the common theme in the chapters in this third section of the book. This also is true of Uganda, the subject of the first chapter in this section, where the government decentralised management of natural resources to district and sub-county level in a 1993 statute. Frank Muhereza approaches the issue from a primarily juridical perspective and sketches a detailed account of government's meandering attempts to achieve decentralisation. His case study of the Masindi District in Uganda shows that, as in many other instances in Africa, a policy of decentralisation is often followed by acts and regulations that can in effect be interpreted as part of processes of re-centralisation, after which (re)-decentralisation is attempted once more. Furthermore and almost inevitably, in the process, decentralisation favours certain institutions, authorities, and individuals to the detriment of others, making it a very uneven, and as a result very competitive process where formal policies and informal practices become intertwined. A good example of this is where Muhereza shows how the government's objective of curtailing the illegal harvesting of timber in forest reserves by decentralising the monitoring and policing to local authorities of the Forest Department and the private sector is completely counterproductive, because colluding with the illegal pit-sawyers earns local communities a nice, and much needed, income.

In their chapter Sagane Thiaw and Jesse Ribot concentrate on two cases in southeast and east Senegal, West Africa, where village chiefs hold the legal authority for allocating forest access. Interestingly enough, in the two cases they present in this chapter, chiefs particularly favour outsiders in allocating access, despite the vehement and consistent protests of insiders, namely community members. As village chiefs are dependent on the goodwill and trust of the village people for their position, the villagers should consequently be able to exert considerable local pressure on the decisions of to whom to grant and from whom to withhold forest access. Why do village chiefs nevertheless favour outsiders in these two cases? How are they able to resist the protests of their own people? Thiaw and Ribot try to find an answer to these intriguing questions, based on empirical research done in 2002.

Senegal, but this time the southern central part close to the Gambian border, also features as a case study in the next chapter by Mayke Kaag. She shows a fascinating development in which local communities, particularly the women, have started to develop small valleys which used to be virgin bush or were only used as cattle tracks, into arable agricultural land. A creative form of agricultural entrepreneurship in a context of land scarcity and an uneven distribution of resources. Because there is no formal allocating framework for this type of land, these developments show a creative mix of informal and formal settlements between the local entrepreneurs and the various traditional authorities dealing with land. It is fascinating to study how this new development will be either incorporated into existing structures of land management or will require new structures of governance with the consequences it will have for generating new configurations of power where the entrepreneurs will have to compete for their own space, both literally and figuratively speaking.

References

ALVESSON, M. and K. SKÖLDBERG (2000) *Reflexive methodology. New vistas for qualitative research*, London, New Delhi: Sage Publications.

ANDERSON, D. and R. GROVE (1987) The scramble for Eden: Past, present and future in African conservation, in: Anderson, D. and Grove, R. (Eds), *Conservation in Africa. People, policies and practice*, Cambridge: Cambridge University Press, pp. 1-12.

ANDERSSON, J.A. (2002) *Going places, staying home. Rural-urban connections and the significance of land in Buhera district, Zimbabwe*, Ph.D.-thesis, Wageningen Agricultural University.

ASHCROFT, B., G. GRIFFITHS and H. TIFFIN (2000) *Post-colonial studies. The key concepts*, London: Routledge.

BATES, R.H. (1989) *Beyond the miracle of the market: The political economy of agrarian development in Kenya*, Cambridge: Cambridge University Press.

BEINART, W. and J. MCGREGOR (Eds) (2003) *Social history and African environments*, Oxford: James Currey; Athens: Ohio University Press; Cape Town: David Philip Publishers.

BENJAMINSEN, T.A. and C. LUND (Eds) (2003) *Securing land rights in Africa*, London: Frank Cass.

BERRY, S. (1989) Access, control and use of resources in African agriculture: An introduction, *Africa*, 59(1): 1-6.

BLAIR, D. (2002) *Degrees in violence. Robert Mugabe and the struggle for power in Zimbabwe, London*, New York: Continuum.

BRETTELL, C.B. (Ed.) (1993) *When they read what we write. The politics of ethnography*, Westport (Connecticut): Bergin and Garvey.

BROCH-DUE, V. and R.A. SCHROEDER (Eds) (2000) *Producing nature and poverty in Africa*, Stockholm: Nordiska Afrikainstitutet.

BROWN, J. (2001) *Spirits of place. Five famous lives in their English landscape*, London: Penguin Books.

BRUCE, J.W. and S.E. MIGOT-ADHOLLA (Eds) (1994) *Searching for land tenure security in Africa*, Dubuque: Kendall / Hunt.

BRUNER, E.M. (1986) Ethnography as narrative, in: Turner, V.W. and Bruner, E.M. (Eds) *The anthropology of experience*, Urbana, Chicago: University of Illinois Press.

CHEATER, A.P. (1990) The ideology of 'communal' land tenure in Zimbabwe: mythogenesis enacted?, *Africa*, 60: 188-207.

CLIFFORD, J. and G.E. MARCUS (Eds) (1986) *Writing culture. The poetics and politics of ethnography*, London, Berkeley: University of California Press.

COLE, J. (1998) The uses of defeat: Memory and political morality in East Madagascar, in: Werbner, R. (Ed.) *Memory and the postcolony. African anthropology and the critique of power*, London, New York: Zed Books, pp. 105-25.

COSGROVE, D. and S. DANIELS (Eds) (1988) *The iconography of landscape. Essays on the symbolic representation, design and use of past environments*, Cambridge: Cambridge University Press.

DE BRUIJN, M., R. VAN DIJK and D. FOEKEN (Eds) (2001) *Mobile Africa. Changing patterns of movement in Africa and beyond*, Leiden: Brill.

DENZIN, N.K. (1997) *Interpretive ethnography. Ethnographic practices for the 21st century*, London, New Delhi: Sage Publications.

DEPELCHIN, J. (1992) *From the Congo Free State to Zaire (1885-1974). Towards a demystification of economic and political history*, Dakar: CODESRIA Book Series.

DERRIDA, J. (1976) *Of grammatology*, translated by Gayatri Chakravorty Spivak, Baltimore: John Hopkins University Press.

DERRIDA, J. (1989) *Of spirit: Heidegger and the question*, translated by Geoffrey Bennington and Rachel Bowlby, Chicago: Chicago University Press.

DOVERS, S., R. EDGECOMBE and B. GUEST (Eds) (2002) *South Africa's environmental history. Cases and comparisons*, Athens: Ohio University Press; Cape Town: David Philip Publishers.

DRAPER, M., M. SPIERENBURG and H. WELS (Eds) (2004) African dreams of cohesion: Elite pacting and community development in transfrontier conservation areas in Southern Africa, *Culture and Organization*, 10(4): 341-53.

ELLIS, C. and M.G. FLAHERTY (Eds) (1992) *Investigating subjectivity. Research on lived experience*, London, New Delhi: Sage Publications.

EVERS, S. (2002) *Constructing history, culture and inequality: The Betsileo in the extreme southern highlands of Madagascar*, Leiden: Brill.

FALK MOORE, S. (1998) Systematic judicial and extra-judicial injustice: Preparations for future accountability, in: Werbner, R. (Ed.) *Memory and the postcolony. African anthropology and the critique of power*, London, New York: Zed Books, pp. 126-51.

GEERTZ, C. (1973) *The interpretation of cultures*, New York: Basic Books.

GROVE, R. (1987) Early themes in African conservation, in: Anderson, D. and Grove, R. (Eds), *Conservation in Africa. People, policies and practice*, Cambridge: Cambridge University Press.

GROVE, R. (1997) Scotland in South Africa: John Croumbi Brown and the roots of settler environmentalism, in: Griffiths, T. and Robin, L. (Eds) *Ecology and empire. Environmental history of settler societies*, Keele: Keele University Press, Pietermaritzburg: University of Natal Press.

HAMILTON, C. (2002) 'Living by fluidity': Oral histories, material custodies and the politics of archiving, in: Hamilton, C., Harris, V., Taylor, J., Pickover, M., Reid, G. and Saleh, R. (Eds) *Refiguring the archive*, Cape Town: David Philip.

HARRIS, V. (2002) The archival sliver: A perspective on the construction of social memory in archives and the transition from apartheid to democracy, in: Hamilton, C., Harris, V., Taylor, J., Pickover, M., Reid, G. and Saleh, R. (Eds) *Refiguring the archive*, Cape Town: David Philip.

HESSELING, G. (1996) Legal and institutional incentives for local environmental management, in: Marcussen, H.S. (Ed.) *Improved natural resource management – The role of formal organisations and informal networks and institutions*, Occasional paper 17, Roskilde: International Development Studies, pp. 98-134.

JUUL, K. and C. LUND (Eds) (2002) *Negotiating property in Africa*, Portsmouth, NH: Heinemann.

KLOOS, P. (Ed.) (1990) *True fiction. Artistic and scientific representations of reality*, Amsterdam: VU University Press.

LEACH, M. and R. MEARNS (Eds) (1996) *The lie of the land. Challenging received wisdom on the African environment*, The International African Institute in association with Oxford: James Currey, Portsmouth (N.H.): Heinemann.

LE BRIS, E., E. LE ROY and F. LEIMDORFER (Eds) (1982) *Enjeux fonciers en Afrique noire*, Paris: Karthala.

LENTZ, C. (2003) 'This is Ghanaian territory!': Land conflicts on a West African border, *American Ethnologist*, 30(2): 273-89.

LEVERING LEWIS, D. (1988) *The race to Fashoda. European colonialism and African resistance in the scramble for Africa*, London: Bloomsbury.

LOVELL, N. (Ed.) (1998) *Locality and belonging*, London, New York: Routledge.

LYOTARD, J.F. (1984) *The postmodern condition: A report on knowledge*, Manchester: Manchester University Press.

MORTON, S. (2003) *Gayatri Chakravorty Spivak*, Routledge Critical Thinkers, London: Routledge.

NAUTA, W. (2001) *The implications of freedom. The changing role of land sector NGOs in a transforming South Africa*, unpublished Ph.D. thesis, Vrije Universiteit Amsterdam, The Netherlands.

NEWITT, M. (1995) *A history of Mozambique.* London: Hurst and Company.

NEWITT, M. (1999) The late colonial state in Portuguese Africa, *Itinerario*, 23(3/4): 110-22.

PAKENHAM, TH. (1991) *The scramble for Africa, 1876-1912*, London: Weidenfeld and Nicolson.

PALMER, R. (1997) *Contested lands in southern and eastern Africa. A literature survey*, an Oxfam Working Paper.

PRINCE, H. (1984) Landscape through painting, *Geography*, 69(1), no. 302.

RANGER, T.O. (1993) The communal areas in Zimbabwe, in: Basset, T.J. and Crummey, D.E. (Eds) *Land in African agrarian systems*, Madison: University of Wisconsin Press.

RANGER, T.O. (1999) *Voices from the rocks. Nature, culture and history in the Matopos Hills of Zimbabwe*, Harare: Baobab, Bloomington and Indianapolis: Indiana University Press, Oxford: James Currey.

ROTBERG, R.I. (1988) *The founder. Cecil Rhodes and the pursuit of power*, Oxford: Oxford University Press.

RUTHERFORD, B. (2001) *Working on the margins. Black workers, white farmers in postcolonial Zimbabwe*, Harare: Weaver Press, London: Zed Books.

SANDERS, M. (2002) *Complicities: The intellectual and apartheid*, Pietermaritzburg: University of Natal Press.

SIMPSON, A. (1998) Memory and becoming chosen other: Fundamentalist elite-making in a Zambian Catholic mission school, in: Werbner, R. (Ed.) *Memory and the postcolony. African anthropology and the critique of power*, London, New York: Zed Books, pp. 209-28.

SPIERENBURG, M.J. (2004) *Strangers, spirits and land reforms. Conflicts about land in Dande, northern Zimbabwe*, Leiden: Brill.

SPIERENBURG, M.J. (2003) Natural Resource Management in the Communal Areas: From centralisation to de-centralisation and back again, in: Darnolf, S. and Laakso, L. (Eds) *Zimbabwe, twenty years of independence. From liberation to authoritarianism*, Basingstoke, New York: Palgrave (MacMillan), pp. 78-103.

SPIVAK, G.C. (1988) Can the subaltern speak?, in: Nelson, C. and Grossberg, L. (Eds) *Marxism and the interpretation of culture*, Urbana: University of Illinois Press, pp. 271-313.

SPIVAK, G.C. (1991) Theory in the margin: Coetzee's *Foe* reading Defoe's *Crusoe / Roxana*, in: Arac, J. and Johnson, B. (Eds) *Consequences of theory: Selected papers of the English Institute, 1987-88*, Baltimore: John Hopkins University Press, pp. 154-80.

TOULMIN, C. and J. QUAN (Eds) (2000) *Evolving land rights, policy and tenure in Africa*, London: IIED / Natural Resource Institute.

TUTU, D. (1999) *No future without forgiveness*, London: Rider Books.

THOMAS, A. (1996) *Rhodes. The race for Africa*, Harare: African Publishing Group.
VAIL, L. (Ed.) (1989) *The creation of tribalism in southern Africa*, Berkeley, Los Angeles: University of California Press.
VAN DER KLEI, J. (1985) Agricultural modes of production and the beginning of labour migration among the Diola of Senegal, in: Van Binsbergen, W. and Geschiere, P. (Eds) *Old modes of production and capitalist encroachment*, London: Kegan Paul International.
VAN MAANEN, J. (1988) *Tales of the field. On writing ethnography*, Chicago: University of Chicago Press.
VENEMA, B. and J. VAN DEN BREEMER (Eds) (1999) *Towards negotiated co-management of natural resources in Africa*, Hamburg: LIT Verlag.
VLOET, C. (2001) Geluk is de triomf van de geest [Translation: Happiness is the triumph of the mind], *NRC Handelsblad*, 7 December 2001.
VON BENDA BECKMAN, F. (1991) Legal uncertainty and land management, in: Savenije, H. and Huijsman, A. (Eds) *Making haste slowly*, Amsterdam: Royal Tropical Institute, pp. 75-88.
WELS, H. (2003) *Private wildlife conservation in Zimbabwe. Joint ventures and reciprocity*, Leiden: Brill.
WERBNER, R. (1998) Beyond oblivion: Confronting memory crisis, in: Werbner, R. (Ed.) *Memory and the postcolony. African anthropology and the critique of power*, London, New York: Zed Books, pp. 1-17.
WESSELING, H.L. (1992) *Verdeel en heers. De deling van Afrika 1880-1914* [translation: Divide and rule. The partition of Africa 1880-1914], Amsterdam: Uitgeverij Bert Bakker.
WILSON, R.A. (2001) *The politics of truth and reconciliation in South Africa. Legitimizing the post-apartheid state*, Cambridge: Cambridge University Press.
YUDELMAN, M. (1964) *Africans on the land. Economic problems of African agricultural development in southern, central and eastern Africa, with special reference to Southern Rhodesia*, Cambridge (Mass.): Harvard University Press, London: Oxford University Press.

1

Communal tenure 'from above' and 'from below'. Land rights, authority and livelihoods in rural South Africa

Ben Cousins and Aninka Claassens

Introduction

This chapter discusses struggles over land rights, authority, and livelihoods in communal tenure systems in South Africa from the colonial era through to the present, with a particular focus on the changing character of state policies in relation to these systems. This sets the scene for a discussion of current debates on tenure reform policy in the communal areas of the ex-Bantustans, and on the Communal Land Rights Bill in particular.

A political economy approach, that locates questions of land tenure in a wider social context of unequal class relations articulated with political power and forms of state rule, is adopted. Three major themes are pursued in this analysis: (a) the role of land tenure in rural livelihood systems; (b) the content and strength of rights within communal systems; and (c) institutional arrangements for land administration. The latter are often the site of a complex politics over competing claims for jurisdiction over land allocation and land conflicts. In relation to all three themes, the view 'from below', (that is, of the mass of rural people), is contrasted with the view 'from above' (that is, of the holders of political and economic power).

Communal tenure, in the past and in the present, is shown to have two faces – one revealing advantages for ruling (or aspirant) elites, and one revealing key strengths for the rural poor – although these broad groupings are not homogeneous, but internally differentiated in various ways. Contrasting perspectives result in very different policy prescriptions, and precisely which policies happen to be implemented depends on the outcome of struggles between contending interest groups. This has been the case in times past, and is still the case today, as revealed in controversies over the Communal land Right Bill.

What is 'communal tenure'?

Most land tenure systems in Africa are still 'communal' in character, although, as Bruce (1988) points out, this is in some respects a misnomer, since it is taken to imply common ownership of *all* resources and collective production, which is rarely the case. What 'communal' generally means is a degree of community control over who is allowed into the group, thereby qualifying for an allocation of land for residence and cropping, as well as rights of access to the common property resources used by the group. Groups often restrict alienation of land to outsiders, and thus seek to maintain the identity, coherence, and livelihood security of the group and its members.

In these systems allocations of residential and arable land usually result in strong and secure rights for individuals or families, the household being the basic unit of production. Families and larger clusters of households sometimes also have preferential rights to some common pool resources such as water points, or areas of dry season grazing. The result is that 'communal tenure' systems are *mixed* tenure regimes, comprising bundles of individual, family, sub-group, and larger group rights and duties in relation to a variety of natural resources.

The overall character of communal tenure is that rights to land and natural resources are *shared and relative*, with *flexible boundaries* between a variety of social units, but nevertheless conferring *high levels of security of tenure*. Relative rights are nested within a hierarchy of social and administrative units or levels. Okoth-Ogendo (2002: 2) puts it thus:

> (...) the [African] Commons are managed and protected by a social hierarchy (…) the family, the clan and lineage, and the community (…) are decision-making levels designed to respond to issues regarding allocation, use and management of resources comprised within the Commons on the basis of scale, need, function and process.

Western ideas about property tend to equate it with 'ownership', and even more narrowly, with private ownership. Western legal systems often do not recognise non-Western systems of property rights, and this has been widely used to discriminate against indigenous land rights holders.

One important difference between Western and non-Western systems of property is the degree of exclusion involved. Key features of private property and the 'ownership' model are clearly defined (often surveyed) physical boundaries between areas of land, unambiguous definitions of who has what kinds of rights and who does not, and the exclusion of non-owners. As Peters (1998) points out, this is not necessarily the case with non-Western systems, where inclusivity and the 'right not to be excluded' are often core features.

These tenure systems are ubiquitous in Africa, where, despite rapid rates of urbanisation, the majority of households still derive the bulk of their livelihoods from land-based activities (cropping, livestock production, and natural resource harvesting). Common property resources make a vital contribution, providing grazing and browsing for livestock, water for domestic use, livestock and irrigation, habitats for wildlife (yielding food, cash, and medicines), building materials, medicinal plants, fuel, edible plants, and raw materials for tools and handicrafts. The role of communal tenure systems in securing access to these resources is often under-estimated (Cousins 2000).

Thus communal tenure systems in all their diversity must be understood in terms of their embeddedness within social relations, the manner in which they articulate with characteristic modes of production and livelihood, and the central role of political authority in their day-to-day 'administration'.

Historical dynamics: Communal land tenure under colonial rule, segregation, and apartheid

Conquest and incorporation of African polities in South Africa by the colonial state brought the imposition of new forms of authority, law and economic organization, and the subordination of indigenous forms of land tenure and governance. Over two centuries whites took possession of the bulk of the land, and state policies attempted to mould African livelihood and land tenure systems to the needs of the dominant classes. These policies were actively resisted by rural communities, in high profile rebellions or less obviously in 'hidden struggles' of various kinds (Beinart and Bundy 1987). Both kinds of struggle shaped policies and their outcomes.

Subordination of indigenous land rights was achieved in two main ways. Firstly, African 'reserves' were created, at first as a way of containing resistance to dispossession, and later as reservoirs of cheap labour for the emerging capitalist economy. The reserves also facilitated the creation of a system of indirect rule, in which traditional leaders undertook local administration on behalf of the colonial state. Some core elements of the indigenous tenure systems survived, but the governance and land administration components in particular were severely distorted. Those leaders who collaborated with the colonial state tended to wield their power in support of their personal and political interests. Some chiefs led resistance to domination, and were then deposed by government officials as a result (Mbeki 1964; Levin and Mkhabela 1997: 156; Mamdani 1996: 195-6).

Secondly, many Africans continued to live on white-owned land outside the reserves, and for decades remained the main agricultural producers on that land, either as sharecroppers or as labour tenants. The new owners were either speculators or Boer farmers unable to use much of the land productively. As capitalist agriculture slowly took root in the countryside, African producers were gradually stripped of their rights to engage in farming and transformed from being sharecroppers or labour tenants into highly exploited farm workers (Morris 1976).

Variations in colonial land tenure policy: Individualisation, reserves, indirect rule, and community purchases

Within this overall pattern there were many regional variations in policies and their impacts, detailed in a comprehensive overview by Delius *et al.* (1997).[1] In the Cape Colony, for example, various measure attempted to restructure land tenure and to provide individual titles. The Native Locations and Commonage Act of 1879, for example, allowed the Governor to divide land in the Ciskei into individual 'quitrent' titles with areas reserved as communal grazing. Quitrent was originally a system under which some settlers had been granted titles to land by the Dutch East India Company, later converted into freehold titles. Quitrent appeared to offer 'the dual advantage of modernising African societies and generating revenue for the state' (Delius 1997: 10). But the quitrent system was extended to Africans in a diluted and discriminatory form – no conversions to freehold were allowed, and a key condition was that the title-holder could not alienate his land without permission (Ntsebeza 2003: 147).

The response was disappointing to policy makers. In 1881 an official report pointed out the widespread failure by reserve occupants to take up their titles, in part because of reluctance to pay the costs of survey and titling. Many original grantees had died but their heirs had not taken steps to transfer lots into their own names. Many quitrents had not been paid for years, plots had been abandoned or given away without official sanction, and houses had been built on the commonage. One of the reasons for this state of affairs, according to the Surveyor-General, was a 'preference for tribal or common tenure' (cited in Delius *et al.* 1997: 10). The Cape Commission on Native Laws and Customs of 1883 reported that 'in several of the frontier districts the mass of the inhabitants (…) although legally subject to Colonial law, had only been nominally so: And to a very large extent they are still

---

[1] Limitations of space mean that only a superficial summary can be provided here.

actually under their traditional laws and usages' (cited in Delius *et al.* 1997: 10).

In the Transkei the courts applied customary law, and the existing land tenure was allowed to continue to operate largely as before. However, a new system of land administration was imposed, headmen being appointed within wards or locations. They were responsible for allocating land, subject to confirmation by a magistrate. This system was first introduced in the Ciskei in the 1850s to keep the influence of potentially rebellious chiefs under control.

The Glen Grey Act of 1894 also sought to introduce a system of individual tenure, at first only in the Glen Grey district in the Ciskei, but later extended to districts in the Transkei. By the 1930s a deeds registry in Umtata held over 50,000 titles. The act was portrayed as modernising and 'assimilationist', but in fact sought to reduce the size of individual arable lands and thus facilitate the supply of migrant labourers to the newly established gold-mining industry. Married men were entitled to only one arable plot, and only title-holders were entitled to graze their livestock on the commonage. Security of tenure was not very strong – titles could be revoked for rebellion, conviction for theft, non-beneficial occupation, and non-payment of quitrent or surveying costs. Allotments could not be mortgaged, leased, subdivided, or sold. Only one male heir could inherit the plot, rendering other male heirs landless. Title-holders did not qualify for the Cape franchise.

As with quitrent, the new system did not operate in the manner anticipated by the policy makers. Boundaries of cultivated lands were not observed, with survey beacons torn down or ignored; the distinction between arable and commonage land became blurred as landless family members ploughed areas of the commonage; and transfers through inheritance were often not registered.

Some social groupings, albeit a minority of the rural population, remained in favour of individual title. Ntsebeza (2003) analyses the early twentieth century struggles by the holders of freehold land in Xhalanga district to resist the diminution of their rights to the restricted terms of quitrent, partly because this would mean the loss of their rights to vote. There was a distinct class character to this struggle, since those who had been allocated farms in the district by the colonial authorities were drawn from the ranks of Mfengu 'loyalists', who were also largely educated, 'school' rather than traditionalist, 'red' people (*ibid.*: 168). A larger proportion of residents were hut tax-payers who cultivated land but held no title, or applicants for land (*ibid.*: 159).

In Natal, by contrast, individualisation of land rights was not pursued. The British accepted recommendations by a commission of enquiry that customary law be recognised and chiefs be used for local administration. This meant that pre-existing systems of land tenure would continue.

Attempts were made to give chiefdoms jurisdiction over clearly defined territories, but in reality boundaries were ill-defined and members of different chiefdoms intermingled, leading to conflicts. Only on mission stations was individualisation of land tenure attempted, but even here only a minority of converts accepted the offer of individual title.

In the Transvaal, a relatively weak Boer state and determined resistance by Africans meant that for much of the nineteenth century 'competing systems and conceptions of land rights co-existed in varying degrees of tension and conflict' (Delius *et al.* 1997: 24). On the basis of somewhat shaky 'agreements' with local chiefs, the trekkers distributed land between the Vaal and the Limpopo. Over time individuals accumulated massive holdings, and vast holdings were held for speculative purposes by land holding companies by the end of the nineteenth century. Holdings included large areas of African settlement and independent chiefdoms.

There were debates about establishing reserves for African settlement, but none were designated until after 1881. To secure their independent land rights many Africans had no choice but to attempt to purchase farms and become landowners themselves. Since only white burghers could buy land, many African communities requested missionaries to purchase farms on their behalf, using money collected by the chief from cattle sales or the wages of migrant workers. After 1881 a Native Location Commission was established to reserve land for 'Native tribes'. Africans were now allowed to acquire land but this would have to be registered in the name of the Commission (later the Superintendent of Natives). Although the boundaries of African land were established through market transactions or administrative fiat, internally the land tenure systems continued to operate along customary (that is, communal) lines (*ibid.*: 31).

Increasing state regulation of communal tenure

The 1913 Land Act was intended to lay the basis for a 'segregationist social order' in the newly established Union of South Africa. It did not create the reserve system so much as entrench the existing locations and overall distribution of land. The Act was a holding measure while the Beaumont Commission developed recommendations for a permanent land dispensation. The scheduled 'native areas' covered seven per cent of the land area of the country, but Africans actually occupied a much larger area.

There were long delays in the making of policy, and the impasse created a need to allow African land purchases outside the scheduled areas, which was possible if the Governor General gave his approval. Land so acquired was held in trust by the Minister of Native Affairs, and had to be effected on a 'tribal' basis rather than as a purchase as community or a partnership.

The 1936 Land and Trust Act added another six per cent of the country to the area in which Africans would be allowed land rights. A body called the South African Native Trust was established, in which all crown land set aside for 'native occupation' would be vested. The Act also allowed regulations to 'prescribe the conditions on which natives may hire, purchase or occupy land held by the Trust.' and to control soil erosion. The Native Affairs Department was determined that land purchased by the Trust, in order to be allocated and occupied by Africans, 'will not be ruined by malpractices'. Proclamations followed in 1939 that allowed the department to declare betterment areas, in which stock numbers could be assessed and surplus animals culled.

Regulations were passed that drastically reduced tenure security. Land holders' rights to transfer or bequeath land were limited, the size of allotments was set, and women's land rights were severely circumscribed. As Delius *et al.* comment, 'access to land depended upon the whims of white officials and strict observation of a host of regulations', and there was 'a reduction in the scope for flexibility and diversity in land holdings which had characterized 'customary' systems' (1997: 38). Resentment of this pattern of intensified state intervention in land tenure helped provoke major rural revolts (as in Sekhukhuneland and Pondoland) from the 1940s to the early 1960s (Chaskalson 1987). Trust land was also used by the state to accommodate the victims of forced removals or farm evictions from the 1950s onwards.

Large numbers of farms purchased and long-settled by Africans became known as 'black spots'. They were targeted for forced removals when apartheid policies were implemented after 1950. Often operating systems of communal tenure within their boundaries, these areas also accommodated large numbers of evictees from farms, usually as tenants, partly due to the continuing strength of an African 'land ethic'. The high population densities that resulted often led to severe strains on the tenure system (TRAC 1992).

The drive towards uniform approaches and increased levels of state interference in the operation of communal tenure systems was evident in the Native Administration Act of 1927. Africans were to be governed in a distinct domain legitimated by 'custom' and chiefly rule, but control was exerted from above. The Governor General, as 'supreme chief of all natives in the provinces of Natal, Transvaal and the Orange Free State' could recognise or appoint anyone as a chief or headman and define the boundaries of any tribe or location.

The Bantu Authorities Act of 1951, coming on top of betterment planning and authoritarian regulation of land rights under Trust tenure, was the last straw for many rural residents, and a key factor in the rural rebellions of the 1950s (Mbeki 1964). It involved the establishment of Tribal Authorities. The version of 'traditional rule' imposed was highly authoritarian, 'stripped of many of the elements of popular representation and accountability which had existed within pre-colonial political systems and which had to some extent survived within (...) the reserves' (Delius *et al.* 1997: 39). Many chiefs used their new-found powers and reduced accountability to allocate better quality land to themselves and their supporters, and to demand higher payments for allocations. Tenure security and the legitimacy of customary systems were thus further weakened.

Proclamation R.188 of 1969, issued under the powers vested in the State President (formerly the Governor General) under the Native Administration Act and the 1936 Land Act, was intended to regulate the operation of land tenure in black areas in greater detail. Two forms of tenure were defined – quitrent for surveyed land and 'Permission to Occupy' (PTO) for unsurveyed land. Severe limitations on the content of the rights of holders were laid down, for example, one man – one lot; restrictions on plot size; a rigid system of male primogeniture to govern inheritance; non-recognition of female land rights (Budlender and Latsky 1991). Officials were given extensive powers to appropriate land and to cancel quitrent titles and permissions to occupy. Chiefs and headmen undertook the task of allocation, agricultural officers surveyed the boundaries of sites and fields, and magistrates issued the PTOs. Registers of permit-holders were kept at the magistrate's offices.

In the Bantustan era large areas of land occupied by blacks (including, in the Transvaal in particular, a large number of purchased farms) were transferred to the jurisdiction of 'self-governing territories' and many communities were placed under the jurisdiction of government-recognised chiefs and Tribal Authorities. The governments of the Bantustans often passed laws to regulate the operation of land tenure systems yet more, but none undertook fundamental reforms of the prevailing legal and administrative regimes.

Communal tenure, migrant labour, and capitalist development

High levels of state interference in and regulation of 'traditional' tenure systems in the colonial era and in the subsequent decades of white minority rule emerge clearly in this brief historical overview. Interventions took two very different forms: (a) largely unsuccessful attempts were made to create forms of individual title and do away with communal tenure, which was seen as backward and constraining of capitalist-style development and enterprise; and (b) the dominant type of intervention was a policy of preserving communal tenure, with chiefs and headmen playing key roles in land administration, but increasingly under the direct supervision of government officials. Communal land rights were increasingly circumscribed and limited by government regulations. A distorted and legally insecure form of communal tenure resulted.

What were the underlying motivations of these policies, and what were the wider political and economic dynamics that informed them? These are issues of ongoing controversy and debate. Three strands of thought will be summarised here.[2] Firstly, Wolpe (1972) and others (for example, Hendricks 1992) have argued that early processes of capitalist accumulation depended upon the maintenance of pre-capitalist relations of production in the reserves. Traditional social and economic relationships provided a significant proportion of the means of reproduction of the migrant labour force, through agricultural production together with a range of 'social security' functions (for example, care of the young, the aged, the sick, and 'resting' migrants). This meant that employers could pay wages to migrants that were significantly lower than they would have to have been if workers and their families had been permanently resident in urban and mining centres. Access by migrants to both agricultural production and social service functions depended on the preservation of networks of reciprocal obligation between migrants and family. This is why the state recognised African law and custom, enhanced the powers of chiefs, and accepted the existence of communal tenure.

However, the rough equilibrium between production, distribution, and social obligation in the reserves was fragile. The absence of male migrants, together with growing population pressure, led over time to impoverishment of the reserve economy, and a decline in its capacity to contribute to the reproduction of the work force. At the same time, a number of workers began to be permanently urbanised, with reduced access to rural social networks. Both factors led to increased levels of conflict over wages. According to Wolpe, apartheid polices developed by the Nationalist government after 1948 were a response to this political challenge, and the function of the reserves was now 'exercising control over a cheap African industrial labour force in or near the 'homelands', not by means of preserving the pre-capitalist mode of production, but by the political, social, economic and ideological enforcement of low levels of subsistence' (Wolpe 1972).

Hendricks (1992) puts forward similar arguments. In his view, government-sponsored communal tenure bore little resemblance to the pre-colonial system, and was severely 'distorted'. It allowed the 'maximum occupation of land' in the reserves which was congruent with territorial segregation and proletarianisation, facilitated the political authority of a co-opted chieftaincy that functioned as agents of social control, and sought to

---

2 Arguments on these questions are complex and wide-ranging, and at the heart of long-standing debates on the political economy of capitalist development in South Africa. Only a simplified and condensed version can be presented here.

'insidiously create tribalism in the form of bogus mini-nationalisms' (*ibid.*: 77).

Mamdani (1996) stresses the political rather than the economic significance of communal tenure. He suggests that across Africa policies of indirect rule and the creation of native reserves created a 'bifurcated' state. Power in urban areas was characterised by the discourses and institutions of civil society, citizenship rights and the separation of powers; but in rural areas by community, custom and the fusion of powers in a unitary traditional authority. Communal tenure rather than private property was deemed the appropriate system for holding land. Traditional authority, based in part on control over land, constituted a 'decentralised despotism' of subjects ruled by chiefs. These measures considerably lowered the cost of colonial rule.

Mamdani also discusses democratic struggles against the 'clenched fist' of repressive traditional authority. These took the form of a 'civil war within the tribe', and as in the South African cases he cites (for example, the Witzieshoek, Sekhukhuneland and Pondoland revolts) could involve violence against collaborationist chiefs. Notions of the accountability of chiefs to the community at large were often invoked in the course of these struggles: 'A chief is a chief by the people' (*ibid.*: 195). Thus,

> … the customary was never a single, non-contradictory whole. Not only the Native Authority but also many peasant movements spoke the language of the customary. For every notion of the customary defined and enforced by the state, one could find a counter notion with a subaltern currency. A democratic appreciation of the customary must reject embracing modernism or traditionalism. As a start, it needs to disentangle authoritarian from emancipatory possibilities (Mamdani 1996: 299).

In a third line of argument, Beinart (1982) asserts that social change in rural social formations and the trajectory of class formation in South Africa was not determined solely by the needs of capital or the state, but was moulded in part by the internal character of these societies, and the active responses by their members to larger processes. In a detailed study of Pondoland, he describes how capitalist penetration was met with tenacious resistance when it threatened communal access to land and resources, since these forms of independent livelihood provided rural people with a defence against loss of control over their lives. Communal tenure and the ethic of 'universal access' to land also constrained emerging class differences between rich and poor peasants, peasants and proletarians. Beinart argues that the specific form taken by proletarianisation in South Africa (migrant labour) arose from the internal dynamics of rural society as much as from state policy. Similarly, the retention of communal tenure is explained in part by the pressure that the people and chiefs maintained on the state. The interests of chiefs and the people in protecting access to rural resources coincided to a degree, and 'the chiefs could, on some issues, serve as a spearhead of popular opinion. It was partly for this very reason that the state found it necessary to incorporate them into the administrative hierarchy' (*ibid.*: 6).

In this discussion the two faces of communal tenure are clearly revealed. On the one hand, the retention of a form of communal tenure facilitated cheap labour policies and cost-effective control of rural populations from above; on the other, systems of communal land rights underpinned independent land-based livelihoods, and facilitated resistance to policies of exploitation and external control, and were therefore often actively defended by rural communities. Rural struggles sometimes showed the 'emancipatory possibilities' of invocations of custom and community (Mamdani 1996). Chiefs were caught between these contending forces, and played different roles in different times and places in response to local political realities.

The legacy of colonial and apartheid policies

By the early 1990s a range of problems afflicted communal tenure systems in rural South Africa, and these persist today, forming the backdrop to contemporary policy debates and struggles. Central to these are unresolved questions of jurisdiction and authority, the key actors being: (i) elected local government; (ii) traditional authorities; and (iii) a range of interest groups at community level who are in favour of land administration being the responsibility of either local government, *or* traditional leaders, *or* democratically elected local committees. At present land administration is a 'messy matrix' of institutional relationships characterised by ambiguity, confusion, uncertainty, and ongoing power plays, which contributes in large part to insecurity of land tenure within communal areas (Cousins 1997; Claassens 2001).

The fundamental legacy of past interventions in systems of communal land rights is the second-class status of these rights in law, which provides few protections from arbitrary decisions by those wielding authority over land allocation or land use. Underlying historical rights of occupation have never been adequately recognised in law, and are still not acknowledged by bodies such as provincial departments or local government authorities. Closely linked to the weak legal status of black land rights is the overcrowding and forced overlapping of rights that derives from South Africa's history of conquest, forced removals and evictions. While some accommodation between original residents and new arrivals often took place in the apartheid years, when both groups resisted forced removals, latent tensions over land rights have emerged strongly since the advent of democracy.

A consequence of past policies of control from above is the partial breakdown of the legitimacy of group systems of land tenure. One manifestation of the malaise is corruption and abuse of authority by chiefs and Tribal Authorities (Levin and Mkhabela 1997; Ntsebeza 1999), sometimes challenged by civic organisations or local residents' associations, which can lead to a vacuum in legitimate authority. Communal tenure is also subject to internal pressures for individualisation in some areas – from aspirant entrepreneurs who seek titles as collateral for bank loans, from women who cannot own land in their own name under 'traditional' tenure and seek greater security through titling, and in areas near towns and cities where an informal land market already exists (Cross 1998).

Tenure insecurity is increased by the near-collapse of land administration systems in the former homelands, where magistrates no longer play a role in land matters. PTOs are not issued in some areas, in others the procedures followed are *ad hoc* and unclear, and registers are often not kept up-to-date (Turner 1999). In peri-urban areas that are nominally under traditional tenure, as well as in some densely settled rural areas, it is not uncommon to find shack lords allocating land in return for cash and warlords building a power base through control over land. Discrimination against women in the allocation of land and the holding of rights is a fundamental feature of tenure systems in most of rural South Africa (Meer 1997).

Lack of clarity on land rights is constraining the improvement of infrastructure and service provision in rural areas, and there are tensions between local government bodies and traditional authorities over the allocation of land for development projects (for example, housing, irrigation schemes, business centres, tourist infrastructure). It constrains the effective management of common property resources, which are the key to rural livelihoods. Other problems include constraints on investment in smallholder irrigation schemes; poor performance of agricultural projects; underutilisation of arable land; and tensions over mineral rights or benefits from mining on communal land.

How widespread are these problems? The available evidence (for example, analysis of 61 cases brought to the Department of Land Affairs between 1995 and 1999 – see Cousins 1999) suggests that tenure-related problems receive recognition only when the underlying lack of clarity in respect of legal status is brought to the fore by development planning or investment projects on communal land, such as Spatial Development Initiatives (Kepe 2001), or within land reform programmes such as restitution or redistribution (Lund 1997). It may be the case that the majority of occupants of communal land have a degree of *de facto* tenure security, because existing systems, many of them now informal as a result of the breakdown of administrative systems, work reasonably well on a day-to-day basis. However, there is also evidence that these systems are failing to facilitate efficient use of arable land (for example, through sharecropping or land rental) and that lack of clarity is negatively affecting management of common property resources (Turner 1999).

Tenure insecurity in the communal areas of South Africa thus takes two forms: (a) a relatively small number of high profile cases where conflicts and contestations over land rights and competing jurisdictions are explicit and obvious, and (b) a larger number of chronic, low-profile situations where lack of clarity and certainty are constraining land-based livelihoods, but no immediate threat to occupancy and use is evident.

The contemporary livelihoods context

These problems within communal tenure systems occur in a context in which rural poverty appears to be deepening, despite improved service provision, infrastructural development and public works programmes implemented by the post-apartheid government. Over seventy per cent of the country's poorest people still reside in rural areas, and over seventy per cent of all rural people are poor (May 1998). The deepest levels of poverty are found in the former homelands, where about thirty per cent of the country's population lives, and where communal tenure systems predominate. A realistic assessment of the current realities of rural livelihoods in these areas, and the constraints and opportunities they present,[3] acknowledges:

- the high degree of dependence on non-rural income, including pensions or other state grants, and migrant wage remittances;
- high population densities, some landlessness, and a large proportion of households without livestock;
- weak or absent support systems for agriculture and other land-based livelihoods, together with constrained access to input or output markets; consequences include under-cultivation and lack of interest in farming by the youth;
- food insecurity at household level, resulting in widespread under-nutrition;
- rising levels of unemployment in the formal sector and continuing insecurity and low levels of income in the informal sector mean that migration to urban areas is not the sole answer to rural poverty;
- movement between rural and urban areas is not all one-way: Some unemployed workers are returning to rural areas looking for new livelihood opportunities;
- although poverty is widespread, the rural population is socially differentiated and pockets of (relative) wealth and privilege exist;

[3] For empirical evidence in support of these conclusions, see Shackleton *et al.* 2000; Kepe and Cousins 2002; and De Swardt 2003.

- despite the highly adverse conditions, land-based livelihoods (including use of natural resources held in common) are significant for many poor rural households.

These realities mean that the most important rationale for communal tenure reform today, from the perspective of the majority of the rural population, is poverty reduction and the promotion of sustainable rural livelihoods. This echoes arguments made for other parts of Africa (Toulmin and Quan 2000), despite evident differences with countries to its north (for example, higher levels of urbanisation and dependence on non-farm income in South Africa). These differences should not be over-emphasised, however. Analysts such Bryceson (2000) have drawn attention to the profound transformations in livelihood systems in most parts of Africa over the past two decades. Byceson refers to these transformations as de-peasantisation or de-agrarianisation, but notes that 'African rural dwellers … deeply value the pursuit of farming activities. Food self-provisioning is gaining in importance against a backdrop of food price inflation and proliferating cash needs' (*ibid.*: 5).

Research reveals that many rural South Africans desire a tenure system that facilitates widespread and secure access to land and resources, to underpin multiple livelihood strategies (Claassens 2003; Cross 1992; Marcus *et al.* 1996). Clearly, however, a fundamental problem in these areas is the very high population density resulting from the history of conquest, 'native reserves', and forced removals described above. Urbanisation is not a realistic solution in the short to medium term, and part of the answer is surely a large-scale programme of land redistribution to correct the extreme inequality in land holdings. Tenure reform must seek to complement such a programme and address the tenure issues that inevitably arise on newly redistributed land.

Tenure reform in South Africa after 1994

Between 1994 and 1998 tenure reform carried out by the newly created Department of Land Affairs (DLA) focused mainly on securing the rights of labour tenants and farm workers, as well as creating a new form of legal entity for holding land rights in common. Since 1998 the main focus has been reform of communal tenure, both in the former 'Coloured' reserves and in the former African 'homeland' areas.

Post-apartheid tenure reform, 1994-1998

Between 1994 and 1998 laws and programmes to secure the tenure rights of labour tenants and farm workers were actively pursued (see Box 1). In addition, legislation passed in 1996 allowed for the formation of Communal

Property Associations (CPAs) as a mechanism for group land holding. These were intended primarily for use by beneficiaries of land restitution and redistribution programmes, and designed as an alternative to trusts, which were seen as allowing too much control to trustees as opposed to members of land-holding groups. CPAs and trusts take full private ownership of land, on behalf of their members, and are governed by constitutions.

Box 1: Key tenure legislation since 1994

- *Land Reform (Labour Tenants) Act 3 of 1996* – protects the land rights of labour tenants on privately owned farms and provides a process whereby such tenants can acquire full ownership of the land they occupy. Labour tenants are largely concentrated in Mpumalanga and KwaZulu-Natal.
- *Communal Property Association Act 28 of 1996* – a new legal mechanism whereby groups of people can acquire and hold land in common, with all the rights of full private ownership. CPAs have been established by groups receiving land under both restitution and the redistribution programme. By late 2002, a total of about 500 CPAs had been registered.
- *Interim Protection of Informal Land Rights Act 31 of 1996* – intended as a temporary measure to secure the rights of people occupying land without formal documentary rights, pending the introduction of more comprehensive reform. In the absence of such legislation, the Act has been extended annually and remains in force.
- *Extension of Security of Tenure Act 62 of 1997* – protects occupants of privately owned land from arbitrary eviction and provides mechanisms for the acquisition of long-term tenure security. Experiences have been mixed: Some cases of illegal eviction have not come before the courts and few permanent settlements have been approved to date.
- *Transformation of Certain Rural Areas Act 94 of 1998* – provides for the repeal of the *Rural Areas Act 9 of 1987* that applied to the twenty-three so-called Coloured reserves in the Western Cape, Northern Cape, Eastern Cape and Free State. Deals primarily with the control of commonage land but also provides for the transfer of township land to a municipality.

Source: Lahiff 2001

Group titles have been issued to over 500 CPAs and community land trusts, but many of these are now dysfunctional. Constitutions have been poorly drafted and often misunderstood by members, and the rights of members (especially in relation to land and resource use) are often ill-defined. Members have often retained ties to their original communities, rather than seeing themselves as belonging to the new social entity. In some cases traditional leaders have contested the authority of elected trustees, and in others elites have captured the benefits of ownership (Cousins and Hornby

2002). A policy lesson often drawn is that the main problems in CPAs and trusts derive from inadequate government supervision of and levels of support to these groups.

The Land Rights Bill of 1999

Since 1998 the major focus of attention in tenure reform policy has been a new law to provide improved security of tenure in communal systems, and thus give effect to the Bill of Rights (sec 25 (6)):

> A person or community whose tenure of land is legally insecure as a result of past racially discriminatory laws or practices is entitled, to the extent provide by an Act of Parliament, either to tenure which is legally secure or to comparable redress.
>
> Key concerns have once again been the nature of the rights to be created in the new law, the vexed issue of jurisdiction over land administration, and the question: 'Who will benefit from reform?'

Drafting of a Land Rights Bill (LRB) was initiated in early 1998. It attempted to embody the principles of tenure reform set out in the White Paper on Land Policy of 1997 and provide full recognition of the underlying land rights of people who occupy areas registered as 'state land' in the Deeds Registry. The land rights specified in the LRB were thus to be vested in the members of group systems, not in institutions such as legal entities, the chieftaincy or Tribal Authorities. From the distinction between ownership and governance set out in the White Paper flowed the result that group members have the right to choose which institution should manage and administer land rights on their behalf. Group systems had to provide 'bottom line' protections for their members, consistent with constitutional principles of democracy, equality (including gender equality), and due process. In situations of overlapping and contested rights, transfer would only take place after a rights inquiry, with the government providing incentives to local stakeholders to negotiate solutions, mainly in the form of funds for additional land to relieve overcrowding.

At first policy was based on a paradigm of transferring ownership from the state to its rightful owners. However, experience in a number of test cases revealed inherent difficulties (Claassens 2000), and as a result the 1999 LRB did *not* adopt a 'transfer of title' paradigm. One major difficulty arose in relation to defining the 'unit of ownership' in communal areas: Should land be transferred to 'tribes', or 'nations', often consisting of hundreds of thousands of people, or to wards, or to villages, or to groups at Tribal Authority level? Vesting land ownership in the larger group could make it difficult for smaller groups to make meaningful decisions about land within their own localities; conversely, vesting rights at the local level might deny some rights inherent in the larger group. These questions derive from the nested and hierarchical character of land rights in communal systems. The test cases provided important lessons in relation to the processes involved in land transfers. Investigation and consultation with the prospective rights holders was necessarily resource intensive, intricate, and time-consuming. They showed that the prospect of transfer triggers intractable conflicts: '(…) the irrevocable nature of land transfer is an effective alarm clock for latent social tensions' (Claassens 2000: 254).

As a result of these difficulties, the drafters of the LRB moved towards a paradigm based on statutory rights which are secure but do not convey full ownership. The law would create a category of protected rights, for which the majority of those occupying land in the former 'homelands' would qualify. Rights holders would be the key decision makers on matters related to their land, and derive the full benefit from its use or transfer. The Minister of Land Affairs would continue to be the nominal owner of the land, but with strictly delimited powers. Her ownership would be an 'empty shell', with high content statutory rights held by the occupants.

These protected rights would be vested in the individuals who use, occupy, or have access to land, but in group systems these rights would be subject to those shared with other members, that is individual rights would be relative to 'group rules', as decided upon by the majority of members. These in turn would require the definition of the boundaries of the group – also a key difficulty, as pointed out above, for the 'transfer of ownership' paradigm. The solution proposed in the LRB was as follows:

> (…) 'boundaries' must be seen as flexible. In other words, the boundary of the group would be determined with reference to who (which group of people) is affected by the particular decision. Thus, if the decision is about a change in grazing practice then the people affected by the change must be consulted, not the entire 'tribe' (Claassens 2000: 255).

Protected rights, defined by statute, would thus confirm in law the rights of the 2.4 million households (the *de facto* rights holders), occupying and using land in the communal areas of South Africa, without having first to resolve, in each and every case, disputes over the extent of rights. The possible content was set out in the LRB and allowed for rights to occupy and use land, to bequeath, transact and mortgage the right, to benefits from the land, and to evict others. To balance individual and group rights, and to maintain a necessary element of flexibility, a local process of defining or limiting the specific detail of the content of rights would have to take place.

The LRB established the right of those with protected rights to choose or create their own preferred local institution for the purpose of managing land rights. Where existing local institutional structures were able to meet certain criteria (for example, majority support), they would be accredited by government, but were thought to require ongoing support from government in order to carry out their functions (Cousins 1997; Sibanda 2000). This would be through Land Rights Officers, who would help rights holders enforce their rights and assist (and monitor) accredited structures.

There is a constitutional imperative for the state to provide tenure security or 'comparable redress' to those whose tenure was made insecure as a result of previous policies, for example, forced removals and the overlapping rights that resulted. The LRB attempted to provide a mechanism for unpacking these situations through recognition of legitimate claims, albeit of differential strengths, and allowing for 'tenure awards' to protected rights holders who cannot all be accommodated on the same land, commensurate with their rights (Makopi 2000). Awards were envisaged as involving a combination of the confirmation of the occupation rights of some rights holders together with compensation or additional land for others.

The Communal Land Rights Bill of 2002

In June 1999 a new Minister of Agriculture and Land Affairs took office,[4] and work on the LRB was stopped. The minister's view was that the LRB was too complex, that it would be too costly to implement, and that it assumed that a 'nanny state' would protect people's rights on their behalf. She was in favour of a law that transferred title of state land to 'tribes', that gave a key role in land administration to traditional leaders, and that did not require such high levels of institutional support to rights holders. In her view ordinary people, including women, should take greater responsibility for protecting their rights themselves.

Following several false starts a Communal Lands Rights Bill (CLRB) was drafted and discussed at a national conference in Durban in 2001. This third draft included several provisions that appeared to privilege traditional leaders, for example it allowed 'traditional communities' operating under 'customary law', as well as authorised representatives (chiefs), to be recognised as 'juristic persons' for the transfer of state land in full ownership. This pleased the traditional leader lobby at the conference, but was seen by many other delegates as highly problematic, sparking heated debates.

In August 2002 the CLRB was published for public comment, and many civil society organisations sent submissions to government. Critical articles on the CLRB appeared in the media, initiating a public debate on communal tenure reform for the first time since 1994. At the same time a civil society

---

4 Thoko Didiza, formerly Deputy Minister.

grouping initiated a project[5] to promote awareness of the Bill amongst affected communities in five provinces, and to assist them to express their views on tenure problems and on the CLRB proposals. In this period the government made no attempt to convene community consultation processes, but met several times with traditional leaders.

The August 2002 draft provided for 'transfer of title' of communal land from the state to its current occupants. Complex procedures for transfer include a rights inquiry, community meetings, and adoption of community rules on tenure. Registration of these rules converts the community into a 'juristic person' capable of owning land, yet crucially, there must be agreement about the size, nature, and boundaries of what and who will constitute the 'community' that will hold the land title. Once the rules are registered a land administration committee can be elected, made up of community members.

Traditional leaders must be on the committee in an *ex-officio* capacity, but cannot comprise more than twenty-five per cent of members. This has been controversial: Groups such as the Congress of Traditional Leaders of South Africa (Contralesa) argue for the transfer of title to traditional authorities, on the basis that they have always held land rights in trust for their communities, and that they are not inherently undemocratic and unaccountable.[6] This lobby objects vehemently to the 'twenty-five per cent' rule.

Civil society organisations as well as many members of rural communities expressed highly critical views of the CLRB (Claassens 2003). The key flaw identified in the bill was the underlying paradigm of a transfer of freehold title, requiring clear boundaries to be drawn between communities. This could open up and exacerbate boundary disputes and ethnic differences. In addition, transferring title will effectively 'privatise' communal land. Since government refuses to provide services and infrastructure on privately owned land, the effect will be to insulate poor rural areas from local government development programmes. This would force rural people to choose between ownership rights and development. The procedure for transfer of title is long-winded and intricate,[7] and until transfer occurs the status of

---

5 The project was organised by the National Land Committee (NLC) and the Programme for Land and Agrarian Studies (PLAAS) at the University of the Western Cape. Partners include NLC affiliates, the Trust for Community Outreach and Education, the Legal Resources Centre, the Transkei Land Service Organisation, the Legal Entity Assessment Project, and others.

6 Patekile Holomisa, 'Resolving communal land rights a vital link in reform process', *Business Day*, May 21, 2003.

7 Over thirty administrative steps were required before title could be transferred to a community, requiring a minimum of twelve months (and the likelihood that bureaucratic slippage would result in delays of at least two years).

people's existing rights to occupation and use remains unclear. In addition, women's land rights are not adequately provided for.

Civil society submissions generally approved of the provisions for awards of alternative land as a form of comparable redress for tenure insecurity, citing the need for tenure reform to contribute in a significant manner to land redistribution 'beyond the thirteen per cent' of land allocated to black South Africans in the past. They would, however, like this aspect of the CLRB to be strengthened somewhat, with fewer discretionary powers for the Minister to decide whether or not the comparable redress processes should be instituted.

The limits imposed on traditional leader representation on land administration committees was welcomed by some civil society organisations as a victory for democracy, but others were concerned that this measure does not in itself deal adequately with the problem. This was due to the fact that it was unclear what impact this rule would have in areas where traditional leaders are contested, or in areas where land administration functions are undertaken by traditional leaders who have significant support.

Alternatives to the approach adopted in the CLRB were discussed in community meetings and proposed by civil society critics (Claassens 2003). One approach would be for the new law to recognise existing occupation and use rights and give them the status of secure property rights, without waiting for a time-consuming and expensive process of transfer of title to which the government is unwilling to devote sufficient funds or create capacity for. Measures to secure individual rights could be complemented by mechanisms to support management of common property and other land matters of common concern. People would participate in community processes as stakeholders with guaranteed rights. The rights of women would need to be explicitly provided for. This approach would require ongoing support from government officials to rights holders and to local land administration bodies, as one component of a coherent programme of rural development. These proposals are somewhat similar to the approach taken in the 1999 Land Rights Bill.

Amendments and debates in 2003

In response to mounting civil society criticism, the Bill was amended in several drafts between August 2002 and October 2003. In April 2003 the South African Local Government Association, representing all the country's local government bodies, asked for a legal opinion on the powers granted to land administration committees in the Bill. This opinion expressed concerns that a 'fourth tier of government' was being created, and indicated that the privatisation of communal land via titling, and the difficulties this would create around service provision by local government, was another potential problem with the Bill. In response, a June 2003 draft of the Bill introduced the provision that a 'communal general plan' (that is, a land-use plan) must be registered with the Surveyor-General prior to any transfer of title. This would allow the Minister to reserve part of the land to the state, for the provision of infrastructure and municipal services, and it was hoped that this would be a solution to the service provision problem.

Other changes resulted from attempts to shorten the Bill, and many provisions were now to be dealt with in separate sets of regulations. Civil society critics pointed out that a critical omission now was the absence of community consultation on whether or not they desired a transfer of title, or on the form and content of land rights. The Minister was given sweeping powers of determination in relation to a range of key decisions, including the boundaries of the land to be transferred to 'communities'. A continuing problem was the lack of clarity on how the different processes set out in the Bill (for example, the drawing up of the communal general plan, the rights enquiry, the drafting of community rules, the making of determinations by the Minister) relate to one another, and in what sequence these different processes were supposed to occur. On the other hand, the Bill still does not recognise the complexity and onerous nature of the land administration tasks (registration, recording, land use and development planning, dispute resolution) to be carried out by local committees, and did not provide for a dedicated system of government support to committees.

In a presentation to the Deputy Minister of Land Affairs and senior officials in July 2003, community members pointed out that women's land rights were not adequately secured by the Bill. For example, it provided for the registration of existing rights, which are generally vested in men, without any proviso that women's rights should be asserted or registered. Earlier sections banning discrimination in community rules had disappeared. Concerns were also expressed that the status of people's land rights prior to transfer and registration remained unclear and hence potentially insecure; this called into doubt the constitutionality of the Bill.[8]

Government drafters paid little heed to these concerns. A thirteenth draft of the Communal Land Rights Bill, similar in all important respects to the June 2003 version, was approved by Cabinet in early October 2003, and published in the *Government Gazette*. Notice was given that the Bill would be debated in parliament within a matter of weeks. However, within days another version was submitted to and approved by Cabinet, one that contained a highly contentious new provision. This was in relation to the land administration committees that the Bill required all communities to establish in order to 'represent the community owning communal land' and which

---

[8] See requirements to create tenure security in Section 25(6) of the Bill of Rights, quoted above.

would have 'ownership and administrative powers conferred on it by the rules of the community'.[9] The new clause stated that where a community has a 'traditional council', the functions and powers of the land administration committee 'must be performed by such a council'.[10]

This provision cross-referred to the Traditional Leadership and Governance Framework Bill (TLGFB) then being debated in parliament's portfolio committee on local government. This Bill (subsequently adopted by the House of Assembly on 11 November 2003, and thus now an Act) sets out to clarify the long-unresolved issue of the roles and powers of traditional leaders and their relationship to local government (Murray 2004). The Act provides for the establishment of 'traditional councils', sets minimum requirements with which such councils must comply, and lists the functions of traditional leaders and councils. These functions are fairly 'soft' (Murray 2004: 11), including such roles as 'facilitating development'. However, they include the wider function of 'administering the affairs of the traditional community' (including in relation to land).

The final version of the TLGFB required that forty per cent of the members of the traditional councils be elected and that thirty per cent should be women, and these are seen by government as 'transforming' traditional leadership to bring them into line with the country's democratic dispensation. The Act also contains a provision for a transitional arrangement which deems existing Tribal Authorities, created in terms of the Bantu Authorities Act of 1951, to be traditional councils, and gives these Authorities a year to 'transform' (but without any specified sanctions should they fail to do so).

The proposal that land administration committees be traditional councils wherever these existed was greeted with jubilation by the traditional leader lobby, and considerably reduced their unhappiness over the 'softness' of the somewhat vaguely defined powers conferred on them by the TLGFB. Control over land has long been seen to be the material basis of the power of traditional authorities (Levin and Mkhabela 1997; Ntsebeza 1999; Mamdani 1996) and their reaction to the new legislation would appear to confirm this diagnosis. In contrast, the new clause was met with dismay by NGOs and community groups, provoked considerable public controversy, and became one of the key aspects of the Bill that was debated in parliamentary portfolio committee hearings in November 2003.

Civil society groupings saw the new clause as the imposition of structures dominated by non-elected traditional leaders, undermining fundamental democratic rights. According to a press release, the clause 'deprives rural

---

9 According to Section 25.3 of the Communal Land Rights Bill of 8 October 2003, these had to include allocating new rights to land, registering such rights, maintaining registers and records of rights and transactions, liaising with municipalities, resolving disputes, and other functions.

10 Section 22.2 of Communal Land Rights Bill of 8 October 2003.

people of the right to choose who will administer their land rights'. The press statement pointed out that the Bantu Authorities Act, which established Tribal Authorities and gave them considerable power over rural communities, was prime apartheid legislation designed to secure rule from above, and had provoked rural revolts across South Africa in the 1950s (Mbeki 1964). Together with the sweeping powers of determination given to the Minister, this lack of choice over how a land administration committee should be composed gave the Bill an authoritarian character at odds with the strong emphasis on democratisation of communal tenure in previous policy documents (for example, the 1997 White Paper on Land Policy).

NGOs and community groups were also angry that so little consultation with rural communities had taken place, and that the new clause on traditional councils had been introduced so late in the process. It seemed to them that the Bill was being rushed through parliament at the last possible moment because of wider political dynamics and 'deal-making' before the upcoming general election of April 2004. According to Murray (2004: 15), three issues appeared to underlie the government's willingness to accommodate traditional leaders: The need to avoid pre-election violence in KwaZulu-Natal,[11] the fact that traditional leaders are perceived to command votes in rural areas; and the need for government to work with traditional structures in delivering services to rural people, given the real weakness of elected local government in many rural municipalities. Murray speculates that another reason may have to do with culture and identity, since 'many South Africans are in search of a political culture that feels less imposed than the one we inherited from our colonial rulers' (*ibid.*: 16).

The character of the portfolio committee hearings and subsequent passage of the Bill through parliament confirmed the suspicion that a political decision to pass the Bill had been made at the highest levels of the ANC. Concerted opposition to the Bill from the ANC's partners in the Tripartite Alliance, the Congress of South African Trade Unions (Cosatu), and the South African Communist Party (SACP), and from within the ANC itself (for example, its members on the Joint Monitoring Committee on the Status of Women) did not lead to a postponement of this clearly controversial piece of legislation until after the election, when more debate and consensus building could have occurred.

Parliamentary debates

A total of thirty-five submissions was made to public hearings on the Bill called by the portfolio committee on Agriculture and Land Affairs, in the last

[11] Pre-election violence in KwaZulu-Natal had marred both the 1994 and 1999 general elections.

two weeks of November 2003. These included thirteen submissions by community groups,[12] and twelve by NGOs.[13] Other bodies which presented submissions were two statutory bodies (the Commission for Gender Equality and the Human Rights Commission), a committee of parliament itself (the Joint Monitoring Committee on the Status of Women), the trade union federation Cosatu, two academic research institutes,[14] the Coalition of Traditional Leaders, and the railways parastatal Spoornet. Of these, thirty-two submissions were highly critical of the Bill on a variety of grounds, and were unanimous in calling for its withdrawal and a fresh start. Only three submissions were in favour of the Bill, those by Spoornet, the traditional leader lobby, and that of the Bafokeng Royal Nation (a 'community group' represented by their monarchy, and aligned to the traditional leader lobby).

The critics argued that the Bill was deeply and fundamentally flawed, and was probably unconstitutional in a number of respects. In addition to the criticisms summarised in previous sections, the following arguments were made:[15]

- The nature and content of the 'new order rights' to be created in the Bill are not clearly defined, and instead the Minister of Land Affairs is given wide and sweeping powers to determine these rights on a discretionary basis.
- The Minister is not explicitly required by the Bill to define land rights in a manner consistent with the Bill of Rights, and leaves decisions on equal land rights for women to the discretion of the Minister.
- The wide discretionary powers given to the Minister to make determinations on a range of issues central to the security of people's land rights are probably unconstitutional, insofar as the Bill of Rights requires the law to define clearly the extent of the land rights to be secured. No clear criteria and factors to guide the Minister's decisions are provided, and few opportunities to either participate in making these crucial decisions or to challenge them are provided in the Bill.
- The measures in the Bill for achieving gender equality in relation to land rights are weak and unconvincing and are likely to be overridden by the

---

12 The NLC/PLAAS consultation project provided support for community groups and NGOs to prepare their submissions through joint workshops to discuss the Bill and its implications. Different views emerged on some key issues (for example, the role of chiefs), and broad consensus on others; the project did not attempt to resolve differences and the principle that diverse views could be held was accepted by all participants in these workshops.

13 The NGO grouping included the South African Council of Churches, the Legal Resources Centre, and the Women's Legal Centre, in addition to land activist organisations such as the National Land Committee and many of its affiliates.

14 The Programme for Land and Agrarian Studies (PLAAS) from the University of the Western Cape, and the Centre for Applied Legal Studies (CALS) of the University of the Witwatersrand.

15 Most civil society submissions can be found on www.uwc.ac.za/plaas.

provision that traditional councils dominated by traditional leaders will allocate land, and can do so on the basis of custom. In addition, many of the 'old order rights' which the Bill seeks to secure, such as Permits To Occupy (PTOs), are vested exclusively in men, and their upgrading to registered 'new order rights' will be at the expense of the informal use and occupation rights of women.

- The Minister will make determinations on who has land rights, on what these land rights will be, and on the boundaries of the 'community' that will have ownership of communal land transferred to it, and will be guided by the report of a land rights enquirer. However, the people whose rights are to be decided in this manner have no right to view or challenge the report that the enquirer sends to the Minister, and no opportunity to agree or disagree with a decision to transfer title. The terms of community participation in the land rights enquiry are not made clear. There are no provisions that ensure that people will have a real choice over the nature of their tenure system or the content of their land rights.
- Communities are required to adopt community rules to govern land use and administration, that will set out who can hold new order rights, but there is no requirement that the community must agree to the content of these rules, and no procedure for adopting these rules is provided. In addition, the Minister may impose a standard set of rules on a community (as adapted by the Minister) should a community fail to adopt a set of rules.
- The constitutional requirement that tenure legislation provide for comparable redress in the event that land rights cannot be secured due to overlapping rights (see Section 25(6) of the Bill of Rights) is not met in the Bill, which devotes only two clauses to this issue, and does not define the extent of such redress nor provide any clear basis for doing so. Once again, the Minister has wide discretionary powers, and no guidelines are provided to direct Ministerial decisions.
- Democratic and accountable institutions for land administration are not provided for in the Bill.
- The Bill undermines the existing property rights of communities who own communal land historically, or through trusts and Communal Property Associations; many of the latter have had their land restored to them through the restitution component of the land reform programme, and many do not support or recognise traditional leaders who were imposed on them in the apartheid era.
- It is thus clear that the fundamental principle that the holders of land rights should have the democratic freedom to select a land administration body of their choice (a principle set out clearly in the White Paper on Land Policy of 1997) has been violated in the Bill.
- Despite attempts in the Bill to address the problem of municipal service delivery on communal land transferred from the state into private ownership by communities (for example, Section 37), the problem will remain where undivided blocks of land are transferred, since in South African law on the ownership of infrastructure (for example, water pipes) and buildings (for example, schools) attaches to the owner of the underlying land.

- Where the land for development is excluded from transfer of title, long delays in compiling a communal general plan will result while detailed and long-term land-use planning is carried out, far in advance of any development actually taking place, and without clear guidelines from the Integrated Development Plan for the area. In many cases such long-term planning will be seen to be inappropriate and untimely and will probably not happen at all.

In addition to questions of substance, most submissions were highly critical of the non-consultative nature of the process through which the Bill had been developed. The memorandum to the Bill claimed that a total of fifty consultative workshops had been held, in conjunction with civil society organisations. These involved 'traditional leaders and their communities, the National House of Traditional Leaders, the Coalition of Traditional Leaders, Contralesa and the Ingonyama Trust Board'. However, NGOs and community representatives expressed their scepticism, said they were unaware of such meetings, and called on the government to release details of the dates and location of such meetings. Members of Parliament requested such information, and on the final day of the portfolio committee's deliberations a large file said to contain these details was given to the chairman of the committee. No summary was made available, the file was not available to the public, and civil society suspicions that these meetings were largely fictitious were not allayed.

Another contentious issue was the financial implications of the new law. The memorandum to the Bill stated that the annual costs of implementation were estimated to be R68 million, but portfolio committee members queried this, and the Director-General of Land Affairs admitted that it was a 'guesstimate' only and that there was no solid basis for this amount.

Amendments, public controversy, and passage of the act

As the final parliamentary session of 2003 came to a close, the portfolio committee deferred further discussion of the Bill until January 2004, the Department of Land Affairs commissioned legal opinions on the constitutionality of the Bill, and officials began to draft amendments. The portfolio committee met in late January to discuss these as well as the financial implications and other unresolved issues (such as the composition of Land Boards) and eventually approved an amended Bill. This went to the National Assembly in mid-February, in the final two-week session of parliament before electioneering began. The amended Bill was then passed by both the National Assembly and the National Council of Provinces, and at the time of writing[16] is awaiting the signature of the President before it becomes law.

[16] In May 2004.

Before its final passage through parliament, the Bill continued to be dogged by controversy and intense behind-the-scenes lobbying, over issues of both substance and procedure.

Amendments sought to address a number of issues. On the question of women's rights, one amendment provided that 'old order rights' are deemed to be held by all spouses in a marriage, not by the husband alone. However, no provision was made for securing the current use and occupation rights of single women (widows or unmarried women), and no requirement that land administration committees allocate land on the same basis as men was inserted. The Women's Legal Centre raised doubts about these amendments, and their attorney, Sibongile Ndashe, said that the status of women married under customary law was still legally in question.[17]

Other amendments also sought to address potential challenges on constitutional grounds. Rewording of certain sections attempted to create greater certainty that Section 25(6) of the Bill of Rights (requiring clear definition of the extent and content of 'security of tenure') were being effected, but may still not be adequate, according to lawyers from the Legal Resources Centre. Amendments were also made in relation to decisions and determinations of the Minister. For example, a land rights enquiry must seek to establish the majority views of a community, and these must inform the making of community rules. However, critics pointed out that there was still no requirement that majority consent was necessary for the decision to transfer title, or when a land administration committee is established, or prior to the Minister reserving part of communal land for state use. One amendment stated that the Minister may not make a determination on land rights until outstanding disputes have been resolved, but no definition of dispute or clarity on who determines whether or not a dispute exists is provided.

The final version of the law also contains a definition of 'land administration committee' that avoids specifying that it will be a traditional council in all areas where these exist. However, the law still does not specify clearly that an alternative structure (such as an elected committee) may administer communal land, and is open to competing interpretations.

Departmental officials told the portfolio committee that the real costs of implementing the law would probably be seven or eight times higher that the original estimate of R68 million, that is, closer to R500 million, but could still not provide a detailed breakdown of costs. Opposition MPs sharply criticised government for 'such an incredible discrepancy'.[18]

There was also controversy over whether or not the Bill should have been tagged as a 'Section 76' Bill, requiring further hearings by the National Council of the Provinces. The constitution requires this of laws affecting functional areas of concurrent competence between national and provincial

---

[17] *Mail and Guardian*, January 30, 2004.

[18] *Cape Times* January 27, 2004.

governments, of which traditional leadership is one, but land is not. In the end the Bill was *not* re-tagged and was passed unanimously by both houses of parliament.

Unprecedented public interest in the passage of the Bill saw wide media coverage, editorials calling for it to be scrapped or 'substantially amended',[19] angry articles by gender activists,[20] and a statement by the Gender/Council for Gender Equality that it had 'taken an executive decision to challenge the bill constitutionally'.[21] It is likely that legal challenges to the law will be also mounted in due course by public interest lawyers acting on behalf of some of the communities that presented submissions to parliament.

The traditional leader lobby was also outspoken in public – but in support of the new law. Patekile Holomisa, an ANC MP and chair of Contralesa, wrote that 'the bill confirms the long-standing historical fact that African land belongs to the African communities jointly with their African traditional leaders. The three entities – land, people, traditional leaders – are inextricably bound together'.[22] However, a critic of the Bill pointed out that the law could 'cut the nexus that keeps traditional leaders responsive to their 'subjects' (…) control over land administration provides traditional leaders with a guaranteed power and resource base, regardless of whether their 'subjects' support them or not'.[23] Controversy over the role of traditional leaders in land administration continues to rage.

Conclusion: The future evolution of communal systems of land rights in South Africa

Informing the politics of tenure reform policy are competing understandings of the three key aspects of communal tenure that this chapter has emphasised: Livelihoods, rights, and institutions. In relation to livelihoods, the view 'from above' is that communal areas and the livelihoods they support are marginal to the mainstream economy and hardly worth investing in. Lip service is paid in speeches and policy documents to notions of rural development and poverty reduction, but derisory budgets for programmes of

---

19 'The wrong direction', *Cape Times,* January 29, 2004; 'Land Bill turns back the clock', *This Day*, 30 January, 2004.

20 'Parliament gives rural women a raw deal', Pregs Govender, *Sunday Times*, 15 February, 2004.

21 'United front to oppose controversial land bill', *Sunday Independent*, 29 February, 2004.

22 'Chiefs bill gives pride of place to traditional leaders and customs', Patekile Holomisa, *Business Day*, 11 February, 2004.

23 Aninka Claassens, 'Land rights bill gives excessive power to traditional leaders and erodes women's rights', *Cape Times*, 19 February, 2004.

economic development belie these statements. This explains why the Communal Land Rights Act does not contain meaningful provisions for ongoing, dedicated support for local land administration.[24] Also important, however, is the dominant neo-liberal view that state expenditure, including that on developmental support, must be kept in check. In the view 'from below', land-based livelihoods, even though they are constrained and inadequate, are more significant than policy makers acknowledge, and should be a key focus for programmes of local economic development aimed at poverty reduction in rural areas.

In relation to land rights, the view 'from above' is that only land titling (that is, private ownership) provides adequate tenure security – but forms of group title must be made available, as well as individual title, given the strong rural demand for a community-based form of tenure. Interest groups in favour of titling include emergent commercial farmers, businessmen, chiefs (on condition that titles are issued to tribes or Tribal Authorities), and, occasionally, women (some of whom feel that freehold can best provide land rights free from the constraints of patriarchal traditions). The strongest demand from the ground, however, is for security of the rights of families and individuals, within a system that secures access to common property. This need not take the form of titling.

Land administration systems that are based on local institutions such as elected committees are viewed as cheap and cost-effective by policy makers, and attractive in the context of dominant neo-liberal doctrines of development. The view from below also stresses the importance of local institutions, but with far more emphasis on their potential to be accountable and responsive to people's needs. Proposals to build on institutional arrangements that already exist make sense to both sides, but community calls for adequate funding and support by government for local institutions, as well as for greater clarity on the relationship between land administration committees and local government, stand in stark contrast to the minimalist provisions of the CLRB.

Most controversial remains the issue of traditional authority and its role in communal tenure regimes. Political deals may have informed the rapid progress of the Communal Land Rights Bill through parliament, but the long-term prospects for this institution are in doubt. At stake are some of the fundamentals of South Africa's proud new democracy, as Murray (2004: 18) points out:

> It may be possible to marry the idealised notions of an older, different democratic order eulogised as an intrinsic part of an original, untainted, form of

---

[24] It also helps explain the tiny national budget for land reform, and the shift in the LRAD redistribution programme to assisting 'emergent' black commercial farmers (Cousins 2002).

> pre-colonial traditional leadership with the requirements of a modern, democratic state. But such an amalgamation should not be the product of either short-term horse trading or transparently sectional interests for whom tradition is little more than a shield from the demands of democratic accountability. We must guard against the possibility that a new order revelling in its emancipation from (neo)colonial rule will abrogate its responsibility to its citizens in the name of a new Africanisation. The danger is that settlement with the lobby of traditional leaders will be a smokescreen for the failure to implement democracy where it really matters: At grassroots, in the material conditions of the ordinary existence of women and men.

When the CLRA is implemented, possible consequences and impacts are that:

- insufficient funds are allocated for its implementation on a significant scale;
- a few successful and high-profile land transfers take place, to large and powerful groups (like the Bafokeng Nation), or to groups where chiefs dominate the decision making and the transfer process can be manipulated to their own advantage;
- in some cases where people apply for transfer, conflicts over boundaries and community membership erupt, and lengthy and expensive rights inquiries are instituted that do not yield viable solutions;
- a long queue of applicants for transfer builds up, the non-availability of dedicated officials is constraining implementation on a significant scale;
- the gap between *de facto* and *de jure* realities remains as wide as at present for the majority of communal area residents.

The African experience of tenure reform has largely been one of ineffective law and policy, in which interventions have failed to bridge the gap between *de facto* and *de jure* realities and tension and conflict over competing jurisdictions persist. This has arisen partly from inadequate funding or weak state capacity, both underpinned by lack of political will, but another reason is the persistent lack of understanding by policy makers and legislators of the realities of African systems of land rights (Okoth-Ogendo 2002). However, although usually ineffective, state interventions are not simply ignored – the confusion that results is often used by elites as an opportunity to feather their own nests (Peters 2002). They are the clear winners, and the losers are usually the poor and desperate. Despite the many differences between South Africa and other African countries, this danger clearly exists here too.

A key lesson from history, as well as from the wider African experience, is that organised pressure from below is the essential condition for alternative and emancipatory policies of tenure reform. Although no strong, independent civil society or political organisations have emerged in rural areas in recent decades, the post-apartheid era included, embryonic social movements such as the Landless People's Movement (LPM) may be the harbingers of change. It is clearly too early to pronounce on just how widespread is support for the LPM, or how effective it is in organisational terms, but there is no doubt that the LPM's calls for an end to farm evictions and for real progress in land redistribution have resonated widely in rural areas (Cousins 2004). A sustained effort at linking land NGOs, the LPM and community members in communal areas who are unhappy about the thrust of the CLRA could see real pressure being exerted on government in relation to tenure reform as well as other aspects of land reform policy.

References

ALDEN WILY, L. and S. MBAYA (2001) *Land, people and forests in eastern and southern Africa at the beginning of the 21st century*, Nairobi: Natural Resources International and The World Conservation Union.

BERRY, S. (1989) Social institutions and access to resources, *Africa*, 59(1).

BRUCE, J.W. (1993) The variety of reform: A review of the recent experiences with land reform and the reform of tenure, with particular reference to the African experience, in: Marcussen, H.R. (Ed.) *Institutional issues in natural resource management*, Roskilde, Denmark: International Development Studies, Roskilde University.

BRUCE, J.W. and S.E. MIGOT-ADHOLLA (Eds) (1994) *Searching for land tenure security in Africa*, Washington: The International Bank for Reconstruction and Development.

CLAASSENS, A. (2000) South African proposals for tenure reform: The draft Land Rights Bill, in: Toulmin, C. and Quan, J. (Eds) *Evolving land rights, policy and tenure in Africa*, London: International Institute for Environment and Development and Natural Resources Institute.

CLAASSENS, A. (2001) *'It is not easy to challenge a chief': Lessons from Rakgwadi*, Research Report no. 9, Cape Town: Programme for Land and Agrarian Studies, University of the Western Cape.

CLAASSENS, A. (2003) *Community views on the Communal Land Rights Bill*, Research Report no. 15, Cape Town: Programme for Land and Agrarian Studies, University of the Western Cape.

CLAASSENS, A. (2004) Land Rights Bill gives excessive power to traditional leaders and erodes women's rights, *Cape Times*, 19 February.

CHASKALSON, M. (1987) Rural resistance in the 1940s and 1950s, *Africa Perspectives*, New Series, 5 and 6: 47-59.

COUSINS, B. (1997) How do rights become real? Formal and informal institutions in South Africa's land reform, *IDS Bulletin*, 28(4): 59-68.

COUSINS, B. (1999) *The economic benefits of tenure reform*, Mimeo: Submission to Senior Management meeting, Department of Land Affairs, 11 June.

COUSINS, B. (2002) Controversy and consensus in South Africa's Land Reform Programmme, paper presented at World Bank Regional Workshop on Land Issues in Africa and the Middle East, Kampala, 29 April – 2 May.

COUSINS, T. and D. HORNBY (Eds) (2002) *Leaping the fissures: Bridging the gap between paper and real practice in setting up common property institutions in land reform in South Africa*, Occasional Paper no. 19, Cape Town: Programme for Land and Agrarian Studies, University of the Western Cape.

CROSS, C. (1998) Reforming land in South Africa: Who owns the land? *Proceedings of the International Conference on Land Tenure in the Developing World*, UCT.

CROSS, C. (1992) An alternate legality: The property rights question in relation to South Africa Land Reform, *South African Journal of Human Rights*, 8(3): 305-33.

DELIUS, P. (WITH R. KINGWILL and M. CHASKALSON) (1997) *A historical investigation of underlying rights to land registered as state owned*, a report commissioned by the Tenure Reform Core Group, Pretoria: Department of Land Affairs.

DEPARTMENT OF LAND AFFAIRS (DLA) (1997), *White Paper on South African Land Policy*, Pretoria: DLA.

DE SWARDT, C. (2003) *Unravelling chronic poverty in South Africa: Some food for thought*, paper presented at the International Conference on Chronic Poverty, Manchester, 7-10 April.

GOVENDER, P. (2004) Parliament gives rural women a raw deal, *Sunday Times*, 15 February.

HOLOMISA, P. (2004) Chiefs bill gives pride of place to traditional leaders and customs, *Business Day*, 11 February.

HOLOMISA, P. (2003) Resolving communal land rights a vital link in reform process, *Business Day*, 21 May.

IIED (1999) *Land tenure and resource access in West Africa: Issues and opportunities for the next twenty-five years*, London: International Institute for Environment and Development.

KEPE, T. (2001) *Waking up from the dream: The Wild Coast SDI and the pitfalls of 'fast track' development*, Research Report no 8, Cape Town: Programme for Land and Agrarian Studies, University of the Western Cape.

KEPE, T. and COUSINS, B. (2002) *Radical land reform is key to sustainable rural development in South Africa*, Policy Brief no 3, Cape Town: Programme for Land and Agrarian Studies, University of the Western Cape.

LAHIFF, E. (2001) *Land reform in South Africa: Is it meeting the challenge?*, Policy Brief no 1, Cape Town: Programme for Land and Agrarian Studies, University of the Western Cape.

LAVIGNE DELVILLE, P. (1999) *Harmonising formal law and customary land rights in French-speaking West Africa*, IIED Issue Paper no. 86, June, London: International Institute for Environment and Development.

LEVIN, R. and S. MKHABELA (1997) The chieftaincy, land allocation and democracy, in: *'No more tears': Struggles for land in Mpumalanga, South Africa*, Trenton: Africa World Press.

LUND, C. (1998) *Law, power and politics in Niger. Land struggles and the rural code*, Hamburg: LIT Verlag.

MAKOPI, S. (2000) Awards to provide security of tenure and comparable redress, in: Cousins, B. (Ed.) *At the crossroads: Land and agrarian reform in South Africa into the 21st century*, Cape Town: Programme for Land and Agrarian Studies, University of the Western Cape and National Land Committee.

MAMDANI, M. (1996) *Citizen and subject: Contemporary Africa and the legacy of late colonialism,* Princeton, N.J: Princeton University Press.

MAY, J. *et al.* (1998) *Poverty and inequality in South Africa*, Durban: Praxis Publishing.

MEER, S. (1997) (Ed.) *Women, land and authority: Perspectives from South Africa*, Cape Town: David Philip.

MOORE, S.F. (1998) Changing African land tenure: Reflections on the incapacities of the state, *European Journal of Development Research*, 10(2): 33-49.

MORRIS, M. (1976) The development of capitalism in South African agriculture: Class struggle in the countryside, *Economy and Society*, 5(3).

MORTIMORE, M. (1999) *History and evolution of land tenure and administration in West Africa*, IIED Issue Paper no. 71, May 1997, London: International Institute for Environment and Development.

MURRAY, C. (2004) *South Africa's troubled royalty: Traditional leaders after democracy*, Law and Policy Paper 23, Canberra: Federation Press in association with the Centre for International and Public Law, Faculty of Law, Australian National University.

NTSEBEZA, L. (1999) *Land tenure reform, traditional authorities and rural local government in post-apartheid South Africa*, Research Report no. 3, Cape Town: Programme for Land and Agrarian Studies, University of the Western Cape.

OKOTH-OGENDO, H.W.O. (2002) *The tragic African commons: A century of expropriation, suppression and subversion*, Occasional Paper no. 24, Cape Town: Programme for Land and Agrarian Studies, University of the Western Cape.

PETERS, P. (1998) The erosion of commons and the emergence of property: Problems for social analysis, in: Hunt, R.C. and Gilman, A. (Eds) *Property in economic context*, Monographs in Economic Anthropology, no. 14, Lanham, New York, Oxford: University Press of America.

PETERS, P. (2002) The limits of negotiability: Security, equity and class formation in Africa's land systems, in: Juul, K. and Lund, C. (Eds) *Negotiating property in Africa*, Portsmouth, NH: Heinemann.

QUAN, J. (2000) Land tenure, economic growth and poverty in Sub-Saharan Africa, in: Toulmin, C. and Quan, J. (Eds) *Evolving land rights, policy and tenure in Africa*, London: International Institute for Environment and Development and Natural Resources Institute.

SANSOME, B. (1974) Traditional economic systems, in: Hammond-Tooke, W.D. (Ed.), *The Bantu-speaking peoples of Southern Africa*, London: Routledge/Kegan Paul.

SHACKLETON, S., C. SHACKLETON. and B. COUSINS. (2000) The economic value of land and natural resources to rural livelihoods: Case studies from South Africa, in: Cousins, B. (Ed.) *At the crossroads: Land and agrarian reform in South Africa into the 21st century*, Cape Town: Programme for Land and Agrarian Studies, University of the Western Cape and National Land Committee.

SHIPTON, P. and M. GOHEEN (1992) Understanding African landholding: Power, wealth, and meaning, Introduction, *Africa*, 62(3).

SIBANDA, S. (2000) Proposals for the management of land rights in rural South Africa, in: Cousins, B. (Ed.) *At the crossroads: Land and agrarian reform in South Africa into the 21st century*, Cape Town: Programme for Land and Agrarian Studies, University of the Western Cape and National Land Committee.

TRAC (Transvaal Rural Action Committee) (1992) *Botho Sechanbeng. A feeling of community*, Johannesburg: TRAC.

TURNER, S. (1999) *Land rights and land administration in the Herschel and Maluti Districts, Eastern Cape*, Occasional Paper no. 10, Cape Town: Programme for Land and Agrarian Studies, University of the Western Cape.

WOLPE, H. (1972) Capitalism and cheap labour power in South Africa: From segregation to apartheid, *Economy and Society*, 1(4): 425-56.

2

Land tenure reform in South Africa: A focus on the Moravian Church land in the Western Cape[1]

Lungisile Ntsebeza

Introduction

The South African Constitution requires that South Africans whose tenure of land is legally insecure because of past racially discriminatory laws or practices are entitled to either tenure, which is legally secure, or to comparable redress. In the brief history of land tenure reform in South Africa since the advent of democracy in 1994, the focus has been on farm-dwellers and rural residents in the former Bantustans. Legislation has already been promulgated with respect to farm-dwellers and tenants. A protracted and complicated legislative process to establish an appropriate law that will ensure land tenure security for residents in the rural areas of the former Bantustans was, at least for the moment, finalised when the Communal Land Rights Act was signed by the South African President in July 2004.

A category of people that has not received similar prominence is composed of residents living on mission stations, which are established on land that is legally owned by various churches. As with farm-dwellers and rural residents in the former Bantustans, people on mission stations have lived in these areas for long periods of time without any clarity as to their land rights. But unlike rural residents in the former homelands and farm-dwellers, the

1 I would like to thank the Surplus People Project in Cape Town for allowing me to use material from an evaluation I did for them.

post-1994 land reform programme is not precise about the land rights of these people. It is also not clear, I argue, whether it is the duty of government to clarify these land rights.

This chapter deals with this group of people. It does so by taking a brief historical look at how churches got involved in land matters, and the problems they encountered with residents on their land with specific reference to the late 1980s and early 1990s. The chapter goes on to examine how churches have responded to pressures for land reform on their land both before and after 1994. At the same time, the chapter will outline the South African land reform programme and its attempts to deal with residents on church Land. The case study of two mission stations of the Moravian church in the Western Cape, Goedverwacht and Wittewater, will be used to examine the difficulties and complexities of trying to understand the land rights of residents in mission stations and what land tenure reform conceivably means for them. In this context, I will also reflect on the current and possible uses of land in these two cases.

Church and land reform

Background

Current efforts towards fundamental reform on church land need to take into account two critical factors: The manner in which the church acquired land, on the one hand, and the relationship between the church, as the registered owner of the land, and residents on its land, on the other. The manner in which the church obtained land and the relationship with its constituency, especially those on church land are fraught with controversy and the subject of continued reinterpretation and contestation.[2] These factors cannot be divorced from colonial conquest and the dispossession of indigenous people in South Africa of their land since the European settlement in the Cape in 1652.

Missionaries played a dubious role in this colonial process. Their main pre-occupation, it appears, was to convert the indigenous people to Christianity and acquiring land in order to establish mission stations. While the process of acquiring land for mission stations might have rendered indigenous people landless, church land later provided some degree of tenure security for the simple reason that it was not easy for the state to evict indigenous people on church land. As Marais has noted, the few 'Hottentot'[3]

---

[2] See Surplus People Project and the Legal Resource Centre (2000) 'An inventory and description of the historical acquisition of Moravian Church Land: A report compiled for the Moravian Church of South Africa', p. 1.

[3] This is a derogatory term referring to the Khoikhoi, the indigenous people in the Western Cape at the advent of colonialism in the seventeenth century.

kraals in the Western Cape that survived the colonial process were 'missionary institutions' (1957: 109-11; see also Surplus People Project and Legal Resource Centre 2000: 6).

According to Roux (1964), missionaries initially encountered hostilities from the Dutch colonialists in the Cape. Colonialists were opposed to the spreading of Christianity to the Khoikhoi whom they saw as mere labourers, not significantly different from slaves. However, Roux goes on, this attitude changed when the Dutch discovered that mission-trained Khoikhoi were, in his words, 'industrious, obedient, respectful to the white man and willing to accept without question his inferior position in a patriarchal society' (1964: 25).

The acquisition of land by the church differed from case to case. In some instances, land was bequeathed to the church, subject to certain conditions. For example, the land of the first mission institution to be established in the Cape in 1737 at Genadendal was granted to the Moravian church by the colonial government as a concession. This was also the case with other pieces of land that were granted later.[4] In cases such as the Karwyderskraal farm in the Cape, land was bequeathed to the Moravian Church, with the specific condition that 'the church may on no account sell the farm and all monies derived from whatever source must be kept for improving the farm or for the church on it'.[5] In other cases, the church bought the land. There are also instances where land that was purchased by blacks was registered in the name of the church. The reason for this was that it was illegal for blacks to register land in their name (Mbenga 1998).

Given the various forms of land acquisition, the question as to who owns church land has been unclear, to say the least. With regard to land that the colonial government granted as concessions, the land was later taken away from the church in terms of Act 29 of 1909 and declared a 'Coloured Rural Area', similar to the Native Reserves that were created for Africans in the nineteenth and twentieth centuries. Land that was bought by Africans but registered in the name of the church, for example, land bought by the BaFokeng group, was later transferred to the Minister of Land Affairs (Mbenga 1998). It would appear, therefore, that land which the church held in trust, and did not purchase, was later taken away from it.

At face value, it would seem that the issue of ownership of land was less contentious where the church purchased land. Yet, this is far from being the case. This is particularly the case with mission stations. At stake here are the property rights of residents on these mission stations. The critical question is whether residents on mission stations are co-owners of the land or not. In strict legal term, it appears they are not. The land is registered in the name of the 'church'. This immediately raises another question as to how to define

4 Surplus People Project and the Legal Resource Centre, 2000: 6.

5 Quoted from Surplus People Project and the Legal Resource Centre, 2000: 1.

the church. One way of responding to this question is to consider where decision-making lies with regard to the administration of church land. Here it seems clear, from the case study of the Moravian church that the church structure is hierarchical and the congregation and residents on the land are often excluded from decision-making processes.

As will be seen below, the exclusion of residents from decision-making processes has been and is being challenged. Indeed, the residents on the Moravian church land in Goedverwacht and Wittewater, for example, contend that they should be co-owners of the land. Their argument is that their forefathers either contributed to the purchase price of the land, and/or that their forefathers and subsequent generations made various forms of payment towards rates and the general improvement of the land to the church. Under the circumstances, they conclude that they have made a contribution to the purchase price to warrant upgrading their status to that of ownership of the land (see also Marais 1957; Strassberger 1969). These contestations and claims gained momentum in the dying moments of the apartheid regime.

The church debates

At the height of forced removals during the apartheid era, some churches joined forces with the regime and forcibly removed residents from mission stations.[6] For example, the Moravian church forcibly removed amaMfengu from their land in the Clarkson. In terms of the Deed of Grant of 1841, the land was registered 'on behalf of and in trust for the Fingoes (…)'.[7] Despite this, the residents were forcibly removed and relocated to Keiskamahoek in the Ciskei in 1982. By the early 1990s, some of these communities approached various non-governmental organisations (NGOs) for assistance in claiming their land rights on mission stations.[8] For example, amaMfengu approached the Legal Resources Centre in 1990,[9] while communities in Bethanie and Elandskloof in the Western Cape approached the Surplus People Project (SPP).[10]

It is worth noting that the above struggles took place against the backdrop of the broader anti-apartheid campaign which had, by the late 1980s and early 1990s, shifted to the countryside too. In response, some prominent church leaders felt called upon to identify with the anti-apartheid movement.[11] The South African Council of Churches (SACC) took a bold initia-

6 For an account of removals in this period, see Platzky and Walker 1985.

7 See Surplus People Project and the Legal Resource Centre, 2000: 4.

8 See introduction to a SPP report on a 'Mini-Workshop' held 1994.

9 See 2000/1 Annual Report of the Legal Resource Centre, pp. 24-7.

10 SPP report on a 'Mini Workshop' held in June 1994.

11 Telephone interview with Graham Philpot of the Church Land Project, 7 February 2003.

tive and urged member churches to return the land they occupied unjustly to the rightful owners (Khanya College 2000). This was resolved at a conference that was held in Rustenburg in 1990 in what became known as the Rustenburg Declaration. Missing in the Declaration, though, were the mechanics as to precisely how this objective would be achieved.

The debate on church land was taken a step further in a 'Mini-Workshop' that was organised by the Surplus People Project (SPP) on 27 and 28 June 1994, two months after the advent of democracy in South Africa.[12] The main aim of the workshop was 'to develop an understanding of what is happening on church land and to motivate the church to address the development of its land'. Representatives from the major churches attended the workshop. There were also community representatives from Bethanie and Elandskloof, academics and NGOs working with communities on church land.

What seems to have emerged at the workshop was that participants were not clear on crucial details about church land. For example, there was no clarity about the amount of the land each church owns, the history of the land, including how it was acquired, and how the land was utilised. In cases where there were residents on church land, it was not clear what the total number of people on the land was, their skill levels, the infrastructure, the land potential and land rights of residents, and how secure they were. The issue of land rights included the question of decision-making, whether residents on mission stations were included or not. A typical example was whether residents participated in decisions around the lease of church land to commercial farmers or not.

For these reasons, the workshop decided, amongst other measures, on an audit of church land to bring greater clarity on the above issues. The need for an audit was made all the more urgent when it was established at the workshop that even church representatives were ignorant about what was happening on church land.[13]

Participants later proposed that an ecumenical Church Land Policy Forum be established to allow different churches to share their experiences and develop a common approach to land and resource management. Given the limited capacity of the churches, the workshop resolved that the churches should consult with NGOs and other agencies in the development sector. A 'conference continuation' task team was set up to 'continue networking with each other regarding church land issues'. This included working towards a more representative follow-up conference.

The conference, referred to as the 'Summit on the Effective Utilisation of Church Land', was organised by the National Land Committee (NLC) and the SACC on 4-6 November 1997. The conference produced a 'Framework

---

12 Details about this workshop are from the SPP report.

13 This raises strong suspicion and concern that church land was and is under-utilised or unutilised.

of a Church Land Policy' of which the main principles included the restoration of land held by the church to the dispossessed and landless, and the provision of land for people to live on, produce on and to re-affirm their identity on. The Framework was subsequently presented to and accepted by church leaders in the same month. They committed themselves to taking the Framework to their respective churches 'for further discussion and possible adoption by the denomination'.[14]

Despite the above promising start, little had been achieved by the end of 2004. Activists on church land such as Philpot attribute lack of progress partly to the fact that declarations and resolutions passed at the above meetings/conferences were not binding except, possibly, to those who were in attendance. The gatherings were ecumenical, comprising different churches. In addition, according to him, few church leaders attended the 1997 conference organised by the SACC and NLC.[15] Philpot even doubts that churches had committed themselves to any policy in writing. According to him, 'churches are scared of policy, rather talk principles'. Philpot has also indicated that the SACC representative stopped attending meetings after 1997, apparently as a result of staff shortages resulting from retrenchments.

No exhaustive audit of church land has been done. Some churches, like for example the Moravian Church, have done their audit, while others have not. This means that as at the time of writing this chapter in 2004, there is not enough information to bring clarity to the issues raised at the 'mini-workshop' in 1994, which led to the decision to embark on an audit of church land. In particular, it is still not possible to establish the area of church land. Despite this, there is a widely held view that the total size of church land is significant.[16] According to some estimates, the church owns almost seven per cent of all land in South Africa.[17]

The fact that no exhaustive land audit has been completed also makes it difficult to know how church land is currently used, including its potential use by residents. The rest of the chapter focuses on land reform on Moravian Church land in the Western Cape, with specific reference to two mission stations: Goedverwacht and Wittewater. As will be seen below, a land audit

---

14 Surplus People Project, 'Church Land Project proposal – 1998-2000', p. 3.

15 Telephone interview with Graham Philpot of the Church Land Project, 7 February 2003.

16 See special edition on Church and Land, *Bulletin for Contextual Theology in Africa*, 5(3), September 1998 (delayed until October 1999). According to an SPP report on a 'Mini Workshop' held in June 1994, '(o)nly the Moravian and the Evangelical Lutheran Churches have a full audit of all the land owned by the Church. The other Churches were at various stages of completing audits although most had little understanding of their land holdings'.

17 See Land Reform Policy 68/1999. I am in possession of an electronic version of this document.

of this church has been done and some research conducted which give us clues of some of the dynamics around church land.

The case of the Moravian Church

Background

When churches took up the issue of land reform in the early to mid-1990s, the Moravian Church participated in discussions. The church was involved in the 1990 Rustenburg conference referred to above. According to the Reverend Mr. Meyer, the Deputy-President of the Western Cape Provincial Board of the Moravian Church and the person who represented the church, the Reverend Mr. Wessels, signed the Rustenburg Declaration. The church also participated in the Mini-Workshop that was put together by SPP in 1994. According to Meyer, his church had been grappling with the issue of transferring land to residents on Mission stations long before the transition to and advent of democracy in South Africa. The main reason, he gave was that the church was no longer in a position to run and manage the mission stations:

> The Church struggled to maintain the mission stations. We did not have resources. We were no longer getting money to administer the mission stations. Money that was available was for development, but not infrastructure. The thinking was that it was not the task of churches to run business and villages.[18]

What Meyer did not mention, though, was the fact that, as has been shown above, the Moravian Church was also under pressure from some of its communities to embark on land reform by either returning land to dispossessed residents or clarify the land rights of residents[19] At the advent of democracy in South Africa in 1994, the Moravian Church had around eighty congregations and a membership of approximately 30,000 people. The membership consisted mainly of Afrikaans- and Xhosa-speaking people, with the Afrikaans-speaking communities mainly based in the Western Cape, and the Xhosa-speakers in the Eastern Cape.[20] The documented total area of land held by the Moravian Church was 57,160.074 ha. This was around 1999, when the Surplus People Project and the Legal Resources Centre conducted a land audit. A substantial amount of the land, 52,466.200 ha is in the Western Cape, while the rest is in the Eastern Cape (3,686.451

[18] Interview, Landsdowne, 20 February 2003.

[19] It was unfortunately not possible for me to interview more people within the church in order to obtain a more representative view.

[20] See Paul Swart's input, 10 July 2000.

ha) and Northern Cape (1,007.423 ha) (Surplus People Project and Legal Resources Centre 2000: 13).

With the establishment of democracy in South Africa in 1994, organisations such as the Legal Resource Centre which, as seen above, assisted communities on church land in their land rights struggles, started exploring ways in which church land could be incorporated into the post-1994 South African land reform programme. This programme follows the theme of the South African Constitution, which, amongst other matters, guarantees security of land tenure for all South African citizens. As indicated in the introduction, a critical question that arises is how should the land rights of residents on mission stations be defined. Church land is private land, similar to commercial farms. In this regard, church land cannot be equated to so-called communal land, where land is legally owned by the state. At the same time, an unknown, but perhaps significant, number of South Africans reside on church land without any clarity about the nature of their land rights. Hence, to a certain extent, residents on church land are in pretty much the same position as dwellers on commercial farms. There are also some similarities between those living on church land and those living in the communal areas of the former Bantustans in the sense that despite the fact that they built their own houses which they rightly regard as their own, their legal status is unclear (see Philpott 1998: 4).[21]

Government position on church land

Whereas the question of the security of tenure of dwellers on commercial farms and residents in the communal areas were obvious targets for the Department of Land Affairs (DLA) in its policy development, the evolution of state policy for church land was slow to emerge. The reason for this was that DLA did not regard church land as different from the property of any other private landowners in South Africa.[22] It was only after a series of discussions and negotiations with the Legal Resources Centre and the Moravian Church that DLA drafted an agreement on land reform on the Moravian Church land. This agreement, called the Genadendal Accord, was signed on 22 October 1996 between the Moravian Church and DLA. According to Meyer, 'we both decided to accelerate land reform. DLA promised to help with the land reform process'.[23]

In terms of the Genadendal Accord, DLA and Moravian Church committed themselves to, *inter alia*, the following goals: Promote security of tenure at the mission stations; address land-related problems, basic needs and

---

[21] See also Khanya College (2000) and Legal Resources Centre and Legal Resources Trust (2000/1).

[22] See Land Reform Policy 68/1999. I am in possession of an electronic version of this document.

[23] Interview, Landsdowne, 20 February 2003.

the development potential of communities; and effect institutional reform for the establishment of appropriate systems of local governance. However, other than agreement on principles, no clear-cut policy was formulated.

It took DLA more than three years to come up with a policy position on church land. This was in the form of 'Proposals for the development of a flexible engagement strategy on dealing with the church as a substantial landowner'.[24] This document was developed by the Land Reform Policy Committee, submitted by the Directorate of Tenure Reform in DLA and was approved by the Minister on 20 March 2000. Its key objective was:

> To clarify and communicate the application of the existing policies of the Department to church-owned land and the rights of various groups and individuals residing on or occupying such land, thereby removing any obstacles that might prevent the church from engaging with the land reform programme. This is intended to lay the basis for the church to make a more informed and direct contribution to land reform, to the extent that it is guided by its ethical concern for social justice.

In other words, the document did not seek to formulate new policy, but was intended more to point out how existing policy could be adapted to facilitate land reform on church land.

According to the document, one piece of legislation that could be used to implement land reform on church land is the Extension of Security of Tenure Act (ESTA). This Act was introduced to ensure the tenure security of farm workers. In essence the Act protects the rights of people who reside on private land but have received express or tacit consent to occupy the land. The long-term objective of ESTA is that occupiers will acquire independent land rights. These would include rights of ownership to land, either on-site, that is have a portion of the farm alienated to the farm-worker, or off-site, meaning alternative piece of land. The land rights could also be in the form of long-term leases. The residents are entitled to apply for state assistance or subsidy either in the form of the Settlement/Land Acquisition Grant (SLAG) administered by the DLA, or the Housing Subsidy administered by the Department of Housing. These grants are in the form of once-off payments of R16,000. Beneficiaries, defined as households, could use the grant to acquire and develop land on the open market. The grants were specifically designed for households with a monthly income of not more than R1,500.00 per household. Residents on church land who are either unemployed or earn R1,500.00 or below could hereby explore this route to obtain residential land, including the land they occupy on church land.

Those interested in buying church land for agricultural production could make use of the land redistribution component of the South African land

---

[24] See Land Reform Policy 68/1999. I am in possession of an electronic version of this document.

reform programme. In this regard, the church would be viewed as any other private landowner or farmer. Residents could apply for assistance through the Settlement Planning Grant and, as from 2001, the Land Redistribution and Agricultural Development Programme (LRAD).

The Land Reform Policy document also addressed the procedure that could be followed in the event the church decided to donate the land. Here, the issue was whether the church would be expected to pay donation taxes or not. In this regard, the document clarified the position by arguing that, since churches are viewed as Section 21 companies or non-profit organisations in terms of the South African Income Tax Act, they are automatically exempted from paying the donation tax. Irrespective of the manner in which the land was acquired, residents on church land would, according to the document, still qualify for the subsidy/grant as outlined above.

An issue that the Land Reform Policy document could not resolve that is relevant to the purposes of this chapter was the state provision of services on mission stations. The question arises as a result of the fact that church land is technically private property. Consequently, local government and municipalities treat these stations in the same manner as they would treat private land such as commercial farms. In a nutshell, local government and municipalities do not offer services on privately owned freehold land. Hitherto, the churches provide most of the services that would ordinarily be rendered by municipalities. These services include provision of water, sanitation and infrastructure development.

Land reform on Moravian Church land in the Western Cape: 1996 to 2003

The above account of land reform on church land, including that of the Moravian Church, suggests a somewhat radical shift from an initially church- and NGO-driven land reform in the 1980s to mid-1990s, to a state-led land reform process. The signing of the 1996 Genadendal Accord was a significant landmark. NGOs seem to have lost the initiative particularly after the 1997 conference referred to above, when resolutions taken at that conference were never vigorously pursued.

It is worth noting the broader context of land reform in South Africa. Following the political negotiation process which took place in South Africa in the early 1990s, leading to the first democratic elections in 1994, there was an agreement among participants, including the ANC, that land reform in South Africa would be market-led. For the ANC, the majority party in post-1994 South Africa, this represented a fundamental shift from its policy during the liberation struggle. This policy was based on the principles of its 1955 key document, the Freedom Charter. On the question of land, the Freedom Charter was very clear that the land belongs to all, and that it would be a national asset after liberation. However, in its 1994 election manifesto, the Reconstruction and Development Programme (RDP), the ANC endorsed a market-led land reform approach, as opposed to nationalisation of land as promised in the Freedom Charter. If the RDP was still cautious in its embrace of neo-liberal principles, the Growth, Employment and Redistribution (GEAR) programme that was launched in 1996 was forthright in its endorsement of a macro-economic approach which 'was unabashedly geared to service the respective prerogatives of national and international capital and the aspirations of the emerging black bourgeoisie' (Greenberg 2003: 46; see also Marais 1998).

I would argue that the market-led land reform programme in many ways provided the Moravian Church with a golden opportunity to rid itself of the administrative burden and cost of running the mission stations, while at the same time opening up a morally acceptable vehicle for the church to raise income from the sale of the land. Following the Genadendal Accord, the Moravian Church, focused on resolving the issue of land rights of its residents through the land reform programme, in particular, as will be seen below, the possibility of selling land. This approach would push some of the possibilities such as the church donating land that were part of the debates in the early to mid-1990s into the background.

Through its Provincial Board, the Moravian Church reworked its constitution so as to accommodate the principles of the South African land reform programme. In particular the reworked constitution addressed the question of securing land tenure for residents plus sorting out governance issues around decision-making. A central principle of the South African land reform programme with regard to governance is that decision-making structures should be constituted along democratic lines. On 5 July 1998, the Provincial Synod, the highest decision-making structure, adopted the 1996 Genadendal Accord as part of its constitution and also agreed to amend its constitution to facilitate the land reform process (Meyer 2001). The amendment included the endorsement of a Coordinating Committee for the Moravian Church Land Reform project that was established in 1997. The committee consisted of representatives of the Moravian Church, DLA and the Legal Resources Centre (LRC). This Committee was later expanded in 1998 to include the Surplus People Project and representatives from the mission stations. A crucial omission was that the Synod did not give the Provincial Board powers to alienate land to residents on mission stations. It was critical that the church adopted a resolution around these tenure issues for residents on mission stations to access government grants and subsidies for housing and land reform. In this regard, the Legal Resources Centre, in consultation with the church authorities and residents, prepared a resolution for the 2001 Synod meeting.

Although the Synod by and large supported the resolution, there was a condition that the Provincial Board should only alienate residential land to residents on mission stations. This would make it possible for residents to access housing subsidy grants. At face value, this meant that agricultural land would remain the property of the church. However, from the interview with the Reverend Mr. Meyer, it appears as if there is room for the church to reconsider its position in the long run. According to the Reverend Mr. Meyer:

> The agricultural land for now will not be transferred. Land reform is to take place in phases. Agricultural land will be leased either to the legal entity or residents in their individual capacities. However, we realise that agricultural land would improve the livelihood of residents. In this regard, the leased land would benefit not only the church but also the mission stations. There will be an agreement on how the income will be divided. The Provincial Board's idea is a fifty-fifty split, but this has not been discussed with the residents. In the long run, say after fifteen years, the Constitution can be amended. Ownership of land (village land and not agricultural land) will be passed to the legal entity.[25]

It is worth noting that the residential and garden land that would be transferred to residents on mission stations would not be donated. The land would be sold. The Reverend Mr. Meyer drew a distinction between the sale of residential plots and agricultural land. Residential plots would be sold at a nominal price:

> Our principle is not that of merely giving. We are not making money on the transfer of residential land and plots, this is not a money-making device. The land must be bought from the church at a nominal price. This price will be determined by the Provincial Board. The church is thinking in terms of a percentage of the grant which may work out at about R1500.00 per household.[26]

For agricultural land, though, the principle would be different. The land would be sold at market-related prices. The Reverend Mr. Meyer justified the sale of agricultural land at market-related prices thus:

> With agricultural land we will consider a market-related price. We will be losing an asset that supports the church. We would invest this in other properties. The agricultural land would definitely be a business transaction. At this stage, we may or may not give a percentage to the village. The big question facing the church would be how to continue running the church without an income. At the moment, the church is not running the mission stations profitably. We are at the moment re-organising the property portfolio of the church. We are currently running our church at a loss. We entered into contracts with communities two years ago. We are not getting any income from agricultural land. Income goes to the mission stations. We struggle from day-to-day. The church is running on an overdraft. This is the reason why we cannot merely hand over. We need income to function. Overseas grants are not meant to pay for projects and salaries.

---

25 Interview, Landsdowne, 20 February 2003.

26 Interview, Landsdowne, 20 February 2003.

The Reverend Mr. Meyer was very eager that state-led land reform on mission stations be expedited. As early as 2001, he was emphasizing that the Moravian Church 'wants to bring the process with the help of DLA to a satisfactory conclusion for all parties involved'.

It must be noted though that it is not only the church that is concerned with the delays. Residents who are supportive of land reform on mission stations are also impatient:

> This process is taking too long. People get disenchanted. It's affecting a lot of things: People can't get subsidies because the land does not belong to them. People want to farm and they can't get subsidy either and are reluctant to invest in land that is not theirs. Outside investors don't want to invest until the landownership issue has been resolved. People put their lives on hold, the land reform process has to be finalised.[27]

The interviewee blamed DLA for the delay. He alleged that a consultant to steer land reform had not been appointed as of the beginning of 2003. Furthermore, the terms of reference had not even been formulated.

However, as of the end of 2003, the transfer of even the residential plots, let alone agricultural land, had not taken place in mission stations such as Goedverwacht and Wittewater.

Delays and problems regarding land reform in mission stations: The cases of Goedverwacht and Wittewater

One question that presents itself is why the delay in transferring land to residents on mission stations? Furthermore, what do residents themselves understand by land reform and how it is perceived?

Budgetary constraints seem to be one of the main reasons for the delay in transferring residential land to residents. The Western Cape Provincial Land Reform Office (PLRO) that is supposed to process the transfer of residential plots in the mission stations is confronted with a real budget problem. According to the PLRO projections, the *Western Cape alone would require a capital budget of at least R1.5 billion per annum* to meet the DLA Minister's target of transferring thirty per cent of land within fifteen years.[28] Yet, the 2003/4 national budget for land reform, *the highest so far, amounted to about R1,6 billion, a mere forty-nine per cent of the total national budget* (my italics). This budget, which almost equal to what the Western Cape

[27] Interview with David Cornelius, Goedverwacht, 9 February 2003.

[28] See Western Cape Land Reform Implementation Strategy 2003-2015 (Final Draft), p. 9.

alone would require to meet its targets, falls far below the required amount needed to meet the current government target.

There are, however, other problems with land reform on church land that should be noted. A major problem which surfaced during interviews was the provision of services, particularly who should pay for them. This concern, as will become clear below, must be seen against the background of the privatisation of critical services such as water and electricity under the macro-economic framework of the post-1994 South African state, and how this negatively affects the poor who often cannot pay for these services and end up either not getting them or losing their property to cover debts they cannot pay.[29] To illustrate these complexities, I will draw on the case studies of Goedverwacht and Wittewater mission stations.

Residents on these mission stations are divided on the question of land reform on church land between those who support the state-led initiative and those who do not. There seems to be a class character to the divisions, with the less affluent, mainly pensioners, opposed to land reform and the more affluent in support of it. As will be seen, sceptics see land reform as a Trojan horse that would rob them of even the limited land rights they have. The issue of the role of the municipality, particularly the question of taxes seems to be the bone of contention.

In Goedverwacht, which is the more affluent of the mission stations, the majority of the people who were interviewed seemed to support the land reform programme. We have seen in the above quote from David Cornelius that they were impatient with the slow pace of land reform. Those who are happy with land transfer are divided yet again between those who support the current position of the Moravian Church that only residential land and small plots be transferred, and those who want all the land, including agricultural land, to be transferred. Cornelius was a strong advocate of the group that wants all the land to be transferred. In his words: ‘We tasked DLA (Sue Middleton) and Legal Resources Centre (Kobus Pienaar) to negotiate on our behalf for the handover of all the land, including the agricultural land. Some residents seem to be happy that property such as the Church, the manse and the school remain part of the church land, but not agricultural land’.

Linked to the question of transfer of land is another issue: Should the Moravian Church sell and/or lease land to the residents? Some residents feel that even if the Moravian Church bought the land in the first instance, residents have paid taxes over years to the church and are of the view that the land should be handed over to them without any payment. In the words of one resident: ‘Give land back to the people’.[30] Some even question the

---

[29] See Desai 2002 for a dramatic account of this phenomenon.

[30] Meeting with some members of the Goedverwacht Land Reform Committee, 30 August 2002.

legitimacy of the church in taking unilateral decisions to sell and/or lease land without consulting residents on mission stations. One resident complained: 'currently, the church can sell agricultural land without consulting us. They are selling land now to white farmers'.[31] On the church's proposal to lease agricultural land to residents, one resident protested: 'It is not economic empowerment to lease land to us'.[32]

There was however a minority of those interviewed who viewed the church as having 'protected us from the apartheid government' by not evicting them. Hence, 'we are grateful to the church'. Although acknowledging that there was/is 'racism in the church',[33] they felt that the *status quo* was much better than land reform. Some people felt that they 'pay a standard tax and people fear that with municipalities they will be severely taxed'. The other fear was that with land reform, there would be an influx of other churches/denominations. Land reform was linked to freehold title, with the implication that houses could be sold to anyone, including outsiders, with serious implications for crime, for example.[34]

Compared with Goedverwacht, there seemed to be a visible element of resistance to the transfer of land to residents in Wittewater. The Secretary of the Overseers' Council, the governing body in Wittewater, was particularly opposed to land reform. According to him, the main problem was the lack of adequate feedback about the land reform process. Above all, the question of the role of the municipality and taxes seemed to be worrying the secretary:

> Our community is not well informed. Meetings are not attended. People feel that the church should do what they want to do. My view is that we are not interested in land reform. We prefer the current, to be under the church and pay rent to the church. I would prefer this; to stay under the banner of the church. People need to be informed and implications should be clearly stated, including implications if municipality gets involved. There is an unemployment rate of over sixty per cent in the area. How am I going to pay the municipality? The church rate is much more bearable and affordable. It's our own source. People have lost their RDP houses, as they cannot afford to pay taxes.[35] Or they sell their houses. This I

---

31 Meeting with some members of the Goedverwacht Land Reform Committee, 30 August 2002.

32 Interview, Goedverwacht, 9 February 2003.

33 Meeting with some members of the Goedverwacht Land Reform Committee, 30 August 2002.

34 Cornelius conceded that there was petty crime and a drug problem in the area. He attributes this to 'globalisation'. The perception, though, is that outsiders may aggravate the current crime levels and residents would lose the cohesion that makes them deal with problems as a group.

35 RDP refers to the Reconstruction and Development Programme, an election manifesto of the ANC in 1994 which promised, *inter alia*, housing for all – see African National Congress 1994. The SLAG grant discussed above is a mechanism poor people use to acquire houses.

> heard from people in Piketberg. The church protects us at least from losing our property.[36]

The Secretary contrasted the municipality with the church, especially on the question of how these two institutions dealt with people who were in arrears with their taxes. According to him, the church, unlike the municipality, is under severe moral pressures not to evict people who fall behind their rates and taxes, and it is this that makes some residents on mission stations prefer the church rather than accept land reform. As he puts it:

> We can't take people to court without going to the Provincial Board. People do not pay. There is an outstanding amount of about R63,000.00. Some people are paying, but others not. We haven't terminated the water service as yet. We are also looking at the socio-economic situation of people, most of whom are seasonal workers, working for up to nine months in a year.

The Secretary conceded that residents should pay a reasonable amount of taxes. 'We have to teach our community that you can't get things for nothing. Some households owe over R3000.00'. He strongly argued that the *status quo* should be maintained. According to him, they as residents have the experience to run mission stations. The secretary felt that they could negotiate with the church about its financial crisis:

> The Provincial Board should be transparent about its financial position. Provincial Board goes with land reform because they are going to earn money. Why can't government give us subsidy under the church? The municipality would not be involved. We will continue providing services for ourselves. The church must listen to us as the community. We hold very few meetings. Most communication is written. The church should call a meeting and explain about its financial crisis to the people. A survey is necessary within the community.[37]

The secretary's attitude towards land reform is best captured in his following philosophical formulation:

> Land reform promises life from king to pauper. Under the municipality, things would radically change. We are the church. Why did they sign the Accord? Derrick Hanekom and our president signed the Accord. The community was never consulted before the Accord was signed. Implications were never explained. Only the bright side was presented. The feelings of the people were never tested. But we are happy with the system. We have tenure security. The church is lenient.[38]

---

[36] Interview, 22 February 2003.

[37] Interview, 22 February 2003.

[38] Interview, 22 February 2003. Derrick Hanekom is the former (1994-1999) Minister of Land Affairs.

A survey of the views of the Moravian mission stations on their views regarding land reform needs to be conducted. The views expressed by the secretary have, as seen in the case of Goedverwacht, been expressed in various, perhaps less articulate ways. In the further interviews I conducted over two days in Wittewater, I came across similar views. This is despite my suspicion that the secretary may, given his status in the community, have influenced quite a number of people. I was quite aware of this and ensured that I obtained the independent views of the interviewees as far as possible. My knowledge of Afrikaans came in handy as most of the answers were in Afrikaans or a mixed version of Afrikaans and English.

What became clear was that most of the fears about land reform came from the poorer sections of the community, especially those who relied on social grants as the following shows:

> If land is transferred to us, what will happen to the payment of services and taxes. As pensioners, where do we get money as pensioners? The other fear is that outsiders would invade us. Our mission rights should be protected. At the moment the church is protecting us. There is crime, but controllable. We will be evicted by the municipality. Also, things were not properly explained. I don't want land reform here. I prefer the *status quo*. I'm currently paying R100.00 per month. We do not see any advantage with land reform. Rich people may want land reform, but there are many old people on a pension here. Land reform will definitely bring hardship. It is not liberating.[39]

Even those who wanted land reform had their reservations. For example, a community member, Oom Koos, expressed his views thus: 'Yes, I know about land reform, it involves change of ownership. There's good in the project. I'll choose land reform. At the moment, we can't get loans from banks. However, more information is required. But I do not have fears for the future'. A choir-master, Theo de Klerk, who was also not involved in any land reform structure, indicated that it was a good move on the part of the church to hand over land to them. He had heard about land reform in a meeting that was organised by SPP. However, he had his fears and concerns:

> We do not have enough information. The church and SPP should come and inform us fully about the programme. Not enough information is made available to us. The meeting took only an hour. What can you do in an hour? They told us that there was no turning back. We need more information and documentation. More meetings need to be held with the local committee. We were told to form a land reform committee, and nothing has happened.[40]

---

[39] Interview, 23 February 2003. The interviewee, an old woman, did not want her name to be disclosed.

[40] Interview, 23 February 2003.

In a nutshell, the main fear of the poor is loss of property through evictions by the municipality in the event they fail to pay municipal taxes. This is assuming that the municipality would provide services on mission stations after the transfer of land, especially to a group entity such as the Communal Property Association. We have seen above that municipalities are not keen to provide services on privately held land.

It is worth recalling the position of the Moravian Church on land reform. The church wants to transfer land, a point that the Reverend Mr. Meyer emphasised so much. He was not unaware of the concerns of the residents, especially the poorer sections of the population. Despite this, he was emphatic that his church is determined to go ahead.

> It is now up to DLA. We are ready to transfer land tomorrow. Some people are fearful of the process. They pay a small amount; some don't even pay that. They pay less than R100 per annum. We are struggling to get accurate information from the Overseers Councils. But the church is determined to divest land. We can't run mission stations anymore. We are waiting for DLA to appoint a consultant. The terms of references for the consultant have already been drafted. DLA's target is to complete the land reform process in this area in 2003.[41]

Church land in South Africa: Which is the way to go?

A question that the above quotation raises, especially in the context of the concerns expressed by the poorer sections of residents on mission stations is whether the state-led land reform is the only route available for the Moravian Church and other churches in the broader sense to pursue. This question should be understood within the context of the debates in the 1990s raised earlier on in this chapter involving the churches and land-based NGOs, in particular the 'Framework of a Church Land Policy' adopted at the 'Summit on the Effective Utilisation of Church Land' that was organised by the National Land Committee (NLC) and the SACC on 4-6 November 1997. As indicated, the keys principles of a Church Land Policy entailed the restoration of land held by the church to the dispossessed and landless, and the provision of land for people to live on, produce on, and to re-affirm their identity on. The Moravian Church was among the delegates to this conference. The question is why it is not considering these principles given the problems of the state-led land reform programme. Why is the Moravian Church not considering donating land to residents on its land without mediation by the state, especially as there seems to be no evidence that it is currently utilising the agricultural land?

---

[41] Interview, Landsdowne, 20 February 2003.

Church land activists such as Graham Philpott have suggested 'a need to question the fundamentals of land reform'. He says:

> I don't believe the notion of the Moravian Church that there is no alternative to the economic position they find themselves in. There are alternatives. The church has to keep its moral commitment and justice. There is a tension between this (the moral dimension) and financial constraints. What is the difference between the church and commercial farmers? What is the church commitment to the agrarian question? There is a need to ensure that those on land can benefit substantially on the land. The church has to grapple with this. This is their constituency. The issue is not merely the settling of debt, but creating and rebuilding communities. The church is not just a land-owner like a commercial farmer, the church has an added responsibility/obligation.[42]

Philpott's argument is that the church should conduct 'some internal scrutiny', particularly its 'managerial capacity'. He raised the following questions: 'how are they conducting their financial affairs? What got them into debt? What are the underlying causes? Is selling assets the solution? What is the long-term strategy?' Philpott's view was that '(…) selling land impoverishes the poor. It is not a good management option, nor is it morally defensible'.[43]

In many ways, Philpott raises some of the central questions of the NGO- and church-driven land reform initiative of the early to mid-1990s. For example, the key question in the 1994 mini-workshop was whether it is moral for the church to make profits, especially out of land that it is either not utilising or is under-utilising. As already stated, there is little evidence to suggest that the Moravian Church in the Western Cape is currently utilising its land in a productive manner.

There are two critical issues that debates and the interviews I conducted have not clarified regarding church land and its residents: Form of landholding and land use. The issue around landholding is whether the land should be held individually or collectively, or in a combination of both, where residential land could be privately held and productive land be held collectively or administered by the state.

Land use can be productively explored if one were to split it into land for residential purposes and productive land, land that can be used for agricultural and livestock production purposes. It struck me during interviews that the primary concern of residents in at least the two case studies was land for residential purposes. This category of land includes a small vegetable garden. It is possible to make the bold generalization that every resident on the mission stations wants residential land.

---

42 Interview, 26 February 2003.
43 Interview, 26 February 2003.

The same, however, cannot be said about land for agriculture and livestock. Interviewees indicated that not everyone is committed to agricultural production. It was interesting to note that some of those who strongly felt that all land, including agricultural land, should be transferred to them, turned out to be not interested in agriculture. The return of land seemed to be a symbolic, if not a political stance. Some residents are old, while others are workers and work-seeking. Others, such as Cornelius are entrepreneurs, exploring projects to do with tourism and guesthouses. But there were residents who expressed interest in the agricultural land. The key problem they raised, though, was lack of resources, in particular financial support to buy implements. This is where, in my opinion, the state could come in.

In sum, how church land should be held in the event of transfer, how it should be used, and what potential the land has to enhance the quality of life of residents are issues that need urgent attention. Unfortunately, this falls beyond the scope of this chapter.

Conclusion

There is little doubt that the issue of defining the land rights of residents on mission stations is complex and complicated. The central question seems to be how precisely the notion of land ownership should be understood when it comes to the church. Is the church a landowner in the same way farmers own their land? Should the principles guiding land redistribution in terms of the South African land reform programme apply to the church? How can the dilemma that the Moravian Church in particular is facing of having to deal with financial constraints in a context where they own land be resolved? How should residents hold their land after transfer? How will the land be used?

This chapter has attempted to examine the above questions by situating the plight of residents on mission stations within the historical context of how churches became involved in land matters, the problems they encountered with residents on their land with specific reference to the late 1980s and early 1990s and how churches have responded to pressures for land reform on their land both before and after 1994. The case studies of two mission stations of the Moravian Church in the Western Cape, Goedverwacht and Wittewater, have been used to illustrate some of the difficulties and complexities of trying to understand the land rights of residents in mission stations and what land tenure reform conceivably means for them.

More specifically, the chapter has shown that the South African land reform programme has not specifically addressed the question of the land rights of residents living on mission stations that are legally owned by various churches. These residents have, like farm-dwellers and rural residents in the former Bantustans, lived on mission stations for long periods of time without any clarity about their land rights. Yet, the South African Constitution is very clear that South Africans whose tenure of land is legally insecure because of past racially discriminatory laws or practices are entitled to either tenure which is legally secure or to comparable redress.

The chapter has traced two land reform processes on church land, one led by NGOs and some churches with its origins in the pre-1994 period, on the one hand, and the state-led land reform programme that was introduced after the advent of democracy in South Africa. The key features of the NGO- and church-driven initiative were the need to establish the history of the land, including how it was acquired, how the land was utilised, the land potential and land rights of residents, and how secure they were. The chapter has shown that most churches were ignorant of what was happening on their land something that strengthened the urgency of an audit. This necessitated the need to develop a church land policy following the guidelines as laid out in the 'Framework of a Church Land Policy' adopted at the 'Summit on the Effective Utilisation of Church Land' that was organised by the National Land Committee (NLC) and the SACC on 4–6 November 1997 referred to above.

The post-1994 state-led land reform programme, on the other hand, is market-driven and one of its legs, the land redistribution component, provides that the state would purchase land for purposes of land reform for landless communities. When pressure was put on the Department of Land Affairs to clarify its policy on church land, the department, it has been shown, argued that existing policies and laws on land reform could be used for purposes of land reform.

It has been demonstrated in the chapter that the Moravian Church initially straddled between the two processes, eventually committing itself to the state-led initiative. The chapter has shown that the church has for some time before 1994 grappled with the problem of managing its mission stations and contending with financial problems they were encountering. It has been argued that economic considerations seem to be central to its eagerness to transfer mission stations to residents. In this regard, the church has, in particular since 1996, vigorously pursued the state-led land reform programme. This is despite the fact that the Moravian Church endorsed the NGO- and church-led initiatives that were based on a totally different basis than the market-led land reform of the state.

The chapter has shown that land reform in the Moravian Church mission stations is at a standstill mainly as a result of budgetary constraints. However, the case studies of Goedverwacht and Wittewater have added another dimension to church land. It has been demonstrated that the majority of those interviewed in Goedverwacht and Wittewater have some doubts about land reform. The poor, that is, those on a pension in particular, do not want land reform. The question of the role of the municipality after land transfer, and how the municipality would deal with taxes and service charges, in particular, how it would deal with arrears, seems to be the main reason why land reform is questioned. In short, the fear of the poor is that municipalities will evict them from their land, something that the church, presumably on moral grounds, found difficult to do.

The key question with regard to land reform on church land appears to be whether the state-led and market-driven land reform programme should inform the land policies of the church or not. This chapter expresses strong reservations about this strategy and suggests that the role of the state could perhaps be at the level of providing support for residents in a situation where the church would have donated the land to those dwelling on its land.

References

AFRICAN NATIONAL CONGRESS (1994) *The reconstruction and development programme: Policy framework*, Johannesburg: Umanyano Publications.

DESAI, E. (2002) *We are the poors: Community struggles in post-apartheid South Africa*, New York: Monthly Review Press.

GREENBERG, S. (2003) Land reform and transition in South Africa, *Transformation*, 52: 42-67.

KHANYA COLLEGE (2000) *The land reform process in South Africa*, Johannesburg: Khanya College.

LEGAL RESOURCES CENTRE AND LEGAL RESOURCES TRUST (2000/1) *Annual Report*, Cape Town: Legal Resources Centre.

MARAIS, H. (1998) *South Africa, limits to change: The political economy of transformation*, London: Zed Books.

MARAIS, J.S. (1957) *The Cape coloured people 1652-1937*, Johannesburg: Witwatersrand University Press.

MBENGA, B. (1998) *The acquisition of land by Africans in the Western Transvaal, South Africa: The case of the BaFokeng of the Rustenburg District, 1902-1931*, Paper presented to the African Studies Association of America, 29 October-1 November.

NTSEBEZA, L. (2003) *Report on the church land project*, Report prepared for the Surplus People Project, Cape Town.

PLATZKY, L. and C. WALKER (1985) *The surplus people: Forced removals in South Africa*, Johannesburg: Ravan Press.

ROUX, E. (1964) *Time longer than rope: A history of the black man's struggle for freedom in South Africa*, Madison: University of Wisconsin Press.

STRASSBERGER, E. (1969) *The Rhenish Mission Society in South Africa 1830-1950*, Cape Town: Struik.

WESTERN CAPE PROVINCIAL LAND REFORM OFFICE (2003) *Western Cape Land Reform Implementation Strategy 2003-2015 (Final Draft)*, Cape Town: Department of Land Affairs (Provincial Office).

Documents kept in the resource centre of the Surplus People Project (SPP), observatory, Cape Town (author has copies)

SURPLUS PEOPLE PROJECT AND LEGAL RESOURCES CENTRE (2000) *An inventory and description of the historical acquisition of Moravian Church Land*, Report compiled for the Moravian Church of South Africa, November.

SWART, P. (2000) *Input presented by the Moravian Church: 10 July 2000 meeting between the South African Church Leaders and the Minister of Agriculture and Land Affairs.*

3

Contestation, confusion and corruption: Market-based land reform in Zambia

Taylor Brown

Introduction

This chapter explores the politics of 'customary' land tenure, land reform, and traditional leaders in Zambia. In Zambia, as elsewhere in southern Africa, the government at the behest of donors has implemented market-based tenure reform legislation. This legislation aims to improve the security of land tenure and to promote development through investment. The chapter shows how complex, indeterminate, and contentious this tenure reform has been on the ground – particularly in relation to the ninety-four per cent of Zambian land that is held in 'customary' tenure. It explores the ways in which local, national, and even international elites have been able to secure private title to 'customary' lands. In so doing, the chapter demonstrates the malleability of tenure reform. It also highlights the changing roles of traditional leaders and provides insights into the character of the Zambian state and its administration – particularly at a local level.

Land reform has long been at the heart of efforts to promote rural development. From the end of the Second World War, through decolonisation and into the early 1980s, the dominant approach to land reform was redistributive. In an effort to redress past inequalities and to stimulate smallholder agriculture and self-sufficiency, many developing countries sought to redistribute land from big landowners to poorer peasants and the landless. From the 1980s on, however, market-based approaches to land reform have been dominant. Proponents of land market reforms argue that formal titling and a lightly regulated market for land increases the efficiency of land distribution and boosts agrarian productivity. They argue that the recognition of property rights will reduce poverty and boost capital accumulation in developing countries. With formal titles in hand, the poor will be able to mortgage their property and thereby unlock their hidden capital assets.[1]

In recent years, land market reforms have been carried out in countries as diverse as Brazil, the Philippines, Syria, Côte d'Ivoire, Uganda, Malawi and Zambia. This chapter examines the implementation and impact of market-based land reforms in one of these countries: Zambia. In 1995 the Zambian government, requested by donors, implemented land reform legislation with the aim of stimulating investment and agricultural productivity. This chapter explores how these land market reforms have played out on the ground, particularly in relation to the ninety-four per cent of Zambian land that is held in 'customary' tenure. In particular, this study asks: How has market-based land reform fared in terms of its stated objectives of increasing tenure security for smallholders? Has the administration of land become more or less efficient and equitable following the implementation of the 1995 Land Act? Have pre-existing tensions between customary governance and formal state administration been reduced or exacerbated by the Land Act?

There is little reliable quantitative data on how land-ownership in Zambia has changed since land market reform was introduced. There are also few systematic assessments of the impact of the land reform at a local level.[2] To gain an understanding of land administration at the central level and to place the Land Act in its historical and political context, therefore, this study began in Lusaka with interviews of government officials, current and former politicians, academics, land lawyers, surveyors, members of the donor community and civil society activists. These interviews, along with primary and secondary sources such as contemporary and archival newspaper articles, case studies compiled by the Zambia Land Alliance and other civil society organisations, and published and unpublished field studies, highlighted a number of 'hot spots' where conflicts over the conversion of customary to leasehold tenure were particularly virulent. Field trips were made to seven of these 'hot spots' in Lusaka, Southern, Central and Northern Provinces to gather specific case studies and to gain an understanding of the specific social, political and economic context in which contestation over land was

---

1 The most prominent advocate of market-based land reform is Hernando de Soto, whose book, *The Mystery of Capital*, published in 2000, has had a significant influence in policy circles.

2 The Zambia Land Alliance has been instrumental in documenting the abuses and failures of the Land Act. The Catholic Commission for Justice and Peace has carried out a cursory, but insightful survey of the impact of the land reform on poor people's livelihoods (Muyakwa *et al.* 2003) while Oxfam has carried out a set of studies on land insecurity in the Copperbelt (Hansungule and Feeney 1998; Palmer 2001).

taking place. In each field site we[3] carried out structured and semi-structured interviews with district-level officials, chiefs, headmen, local and outside investors, those embroiled in land disputes, small holders of titled land and customary rights holders. These interviews were supported by direct observation and participatory research methods. Research was conducted during 2002 and 2003.

The chapter is broken into three sections. The first part outlines the administration of land in Zambia from the colonial regime through the market-based land reform of 1995. The second section explores the impact of land market reform on customary lands. It demonstrates that the conversion of customary to leasehold land tenure has led to social and economic exclusion, elite capture, displacement, intra-community conflict, and the enclosure of common pool resources. The third section explores the administrative weaknesses and political forces that have influenced the allocation of land in Zambia.

Land administration in Zambia

Land tenure in Zambia, as in much of Africa, is of two types: Communal and private titled. This distinction is not just tenurial, it is also social, political and economic. Titled land is owned, bought and sold by individuals who possess registered leasehold title. It is administered by the central government (the Ministry of Lands) using common law and is subject to taxation. Private tenure is concentrated in and near Zambia's cities, along the railway line between Livingstone and the Congo border, in the mining areas of the Copperbelt, and in certain productive farming areas. Customary lands, on the other hand, may be indirectly held, but the allocation and use of these lands (to a greater or lesser extent) are administered by chiefs and headmen on behalf of 'tribal communities'. On customary land, titles do not exist, land taxes are not paid, and transfer and use are governed by 'customary' law. The vast majority of land in Zambia (ninety-four per cent) is classified as customary (Roth 1995; Zulu 1993). The most valuable and productive land, however, is held as private tenure (see Figure 3.2).

---

[3] Bennett Siamwiza of the University of Zambia and Chris Singelelngele of Women for Change made significant fieldwork contributions to this study. Thanks is also owed to those who took the time to speak with me, especially officials within the Ministry of Lands; chiefs, headmen, and villagers in various field sites; and Henry Machina of the Zambian Land Alliance. Martin Adams, Craig Jeffery, Miles Lamar, Robin Palmer and Marja Spierenburg as well as the participants at conferences in Amsterdam and Durban provided insightful comments on earlier drafts.

This division between customary and private titled land has its origins in the colonial era and has been perpetuated by the post-colonial state. To understand the current system of land administration in general and the conflicts and inequalities arising from the 1995 Land Act in particular, it is crucial to explore the legacy of Zambia's colonial and post-colonial history.

Colonial land administration

In most of British Africa, colonial authorities drew a political and tenurial distinction between areas of white settlement and 'tribal' areas. In *Citizen and Subject*, Mahmood Mamdani (1996) focuses on this dichotomy. He argues that the colonial state was 'bifurcated' not only spatially but also politically. On the one hand rural African *subjects* were governed by chiefs and custom and lived on spatially distinct communal lands. On the other hand, *citizens* (whites and other urban dwellers) were governed by modern civil law and owned or rented private property.

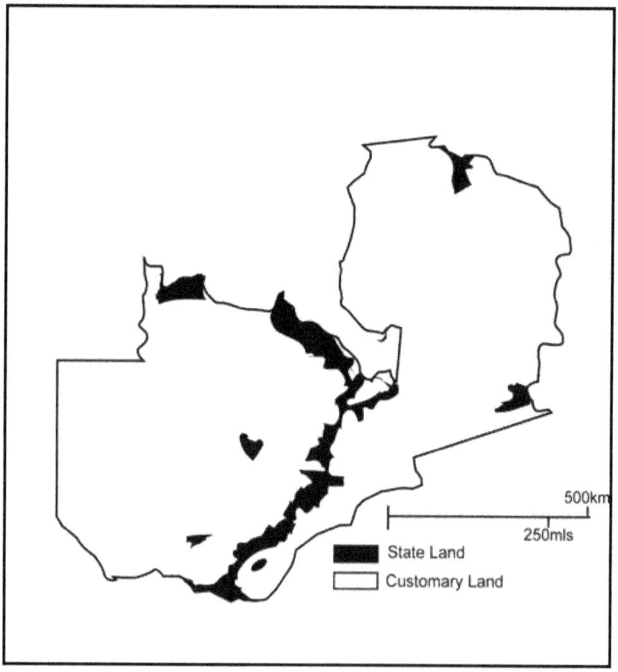

Figure 3.1 Distribution of customary and state lands in Zambia (adapted from Van Loenen 1999)

Mamdani's dichotomy aptly applies to the policy pursued in Northern Rhodesia (later Zambia). The colonial authorities demarcated as crown lands those areas most appropriate for European settlement and all land known to contain mineral resources. Land was held as freehold or leasehold and its use and conveyance was governed by common law. Settlers and resident Africans living in these areas were directly administered by the colonial governor and a legislative council under British law.

The colonial authorities divided the remainder of Northern Rhodesia into two other tenure categories: native reserves and trusts. Native reserves were carved out on the edges of white farming areas to provide a home for the sixty thousand indigenous people who had been displaced by the demarcation of crown lands and to provide a ready supply of labour (Roberts 1976: 183). In 1947, the colonial government established a new category of customary land: native trusts. Trusts were created from unutilised crown land and the large swathes of land that had been uncategorised by the demarcation of crown lands and reserves. These trusts, encompassing fifty-seven per cent of the colony, were set aside for 'the use or common benefit direct or indirect of the "natives"' (Government of Northern Rhodesia 1947). Restrictions were placed on alienating reserve and trust lands to Europeans or other non-indigenous people. In reserves, five-year renewable 'rights of occupancy' could be granted to 'non-natives' at the behest of the chief and the central government. In trusts, the governor could grant Europeans and other non-indigenous people 'rights of occupancy' for a period of ninety-nine years. These lands, however, could not be converted to crown land and remained under customary tenure.

A critical element of the British system of indirect rule was the recognition and codification of 'customary' communal land tenure within tribal areas. In drafting land policy, most administrators assumed that African land tenure systems were characterised by communal, not individual, rights to land. Colonial administrators tended to assume that vacant land was the communal property of tribes and that chiefs held administrative authority over these lands (Colson 1971; Ranger 1983; Chanock 1985). The colonial regime therefore granted chiefs a great deal of control over the use and allocation of land and natural resources in their domains, and treated customary land tenure and judicial processes as a fixed in precedent and practice.

Land tenure under the Kaunda regime

In the two and a half decades that followed independence in 1964, Zambian land tenure policy was characterised by economic socialism and nationalism. In the early years of the Kaunda regime, all crown lands were renamed state lands and vested in the President rather than the British sovereign. The Kaunda regime maintained the distinction between state lands and trust and reserve lands. In customary areas, the government maintained many aspects and of indirect rule and explicitly recognised the role of chiefs in allocating trust and reserve lands. The government, however, took a very direct role in the administration of state lands. In 1969, the Zambian constitution was amended to allow the acquisition of undeveloped and unutilised lands by the state, particularly those lands held by absentee landowners. In 1975, the state abolished freehold tenure and converted it to statutory leasehold (*The Land (Conversion of Titles) Act* 1975). Through this legislation, the state suppressed the market for land and instead sought to administer directly all leasehold land transfers. Land was deemed to have no intrinsic value and only improvements on land (such as buildings or agricultural infrastructure) could be bought and sold. In 1985, legislation was passed that restricted the alienation of land to foreigners, with the exception of presidentially certified investors and charitable organisations.

The 1995 Land Act

The current phase of land reforms in Zambia dates from the election of the Movement for Multiparty Democracy (MMD) government in 1991. The MMD sought to break with Kaunda's socialist policies and to instigate wide-ranging market reforms. A market-based land policy was deemed to be an essential component of these reforms, as the MMD's election manifesto highlights:

> The MMD shall institutionalise a modern, coherent, simplified and relevant land law code intended to ensure the fundamental right to private ownership of land (…). To this end, the MMD government will (…) bring a more efficient and equitable system of tenure conversion and land allocation in customary lands; land adjudication legislation will be enacted and coordinated in such a way that confidence shall be restored in land investors (…) the MMD shall attach economic value to undeveloped land [and] promote regular issuance of title deeds to productive land owners in both rural and urban areas (MMD 1991).

Land market reform was not only an electoral pledge, it was also one of the key conditionalities that the Zambian government was required to meet in order to restructure its international debt. As a result, donors played a significant role in ensuring that land administration in Zambia was liberalised. In mid 1993 at the behest of the World Bank and IMF and with funding from USAID, the MMD government convened a National Conference on Land Policy and Legal Reform. In 1995, the Land Act was passed by parliament following two years of ill-tempered and divisive national debate that pitted the newly established government against most Zambian civil society organisations, church groups and traditional leaders.[4]

---

[4] When the government first proposed the Land Act, it proved so contentious that consultative and promotional meetings had to be abandoned due to protest and, in several cases, violence. Lack of support for the Act extended to the National Assembly where the government, despite its clear majority in the house, was only able to secure passage of the bill by threatening to expel any rebel MPs from the MMD. The provisions of the Land Act and the un-democratic manner in which it was drafted and passed into law, have led to continued and wide-

What were the key provisions of the 1995 Land Act? First, the Act significantly strengthened the property rights of titleholders on state land. Although the Act did not reintroduce freehold tenure, it considerably bolstered leaseholders' rights. By repealing the 1975 *Land (Conversion of Titles) Act*, the 1995 Act made it possible for land *per se* – not just improvements on land – to be bought and sold. Land remained vested in the President, but the 1995 Act made it much more difficult for the state to repossess undeveloped land. Moreover, the bureaucratic hurdles to acquiring and transferring titles (such as presidential consent for all land transactions) were reduced to mere formalities.

A second aspect of the Land Act was that it eased restrictions on landownership by foreigners. The Act made it possible for approved foreign investors, foreigners who are Zambian residents or foreigners who have received personal presidential consent to acquire title to land.

Third, the 1995 Land Act created a Lands Tribunal to protect leaseholders and customary rights holders from abuse and to ease congestion within the High Court. The Tribunal's broad mandate is to 'inquire into and make awards and decisions relating to land' (GRZ 1995: Part IV, Section 22). The Tribunal was intended to be informal, low-cost and mobile so as to be accessible to rural and low income Zambians.

Fourth, the Act made both cosmetic and substantive changes to the administration of customary land tenure. The categories of reserve and trust lands were amalgamated into a new category: 'customary areas'. The Act explicitly recognised existing rights to land in customary areas. The Act, however, made it easier for both outside investors and indigenous Zambians living on customary lands to acquire private title to customary land.[5] Under the provisions of the Act, investors (whether foreign or domestic) can convert land in customary areas to leasehold if the investor's proposed use of the land is deemed to be of 'community' or national interest. The Land Act also made it easier for indigenous Zambian to acquire private title to their lands. The 1995 Act outlined the procedures through which 'any person who holds land under customary tenure' could convert their landholdings to leasehold tenure (GRZ 1995: Part II, Section 8). The justification for this provision, according to the government, is that customary land tenure is 'insecure' and

---

spread animosity to the Act by many civil society organisations, opposition politicians and many traditional leaders.

5 This is not to say that it was impossible to gain title to customary land during the Kaunda era. Throughout the 1970s and early 1980s, well-connected individuals were able to alienate trust and reserve lands. In 1985, partially to reassure chiefs about these conversions, procedures for alienating land were set out in a cabinet circular (Land Circular No. 1). According to this circular, individuals could only acquire title deeds to customary lands if they had permission of the local chief, the district council and the president. This circular also set an upper limit for these conversions of 250 hectares.

has 'severe limitations' compared to leasehold tenure (GRZ 2000: 1). By converting their customary holdings to leasehold, the government argues, villagers will be able to use their land as collateral to secure credit to invest in farms and businesses.

Although the 1995 Act ostensibly recognises and protects customary land rights, the Act is designed to permanently diminish the amount of land held under communal tenure and to open up more land for investment. Once a villager or investor is granted a leasehold title for a piece of land, it ceases to be customary land and becomes state, essentially private, land. Customary rights are extinguished and the land cannot be reconverted back to customary tenure.

The impact of land market reform at the village level

How has the 1995 Land Act played out on the ground? Who has the Act benefited and who has it marginalised? How has land market reform been shaped by local- and national-level political processes? To answer these questions, this section provides a picture of how land market reform has been implemented at the village level.

The extent of conversions

The Ministry of Lands has not maintained adequate records of the number of title conversions it has approved over the years. It is therefore difficult to assess accurately the number of conversions that have taken place since 1985 when procedures for title conversion were regularised and especially since the implementation of the Land Act in 1995. It is possible, however, to gauge the rough trend of conversions. According to officials at the Ministry of Lands, the number of conversions rose gradually in the late 1980s and early 1990s. Following the Land Act, conversions increased rapidly until they levelled off in the late 1990s at around two thousand per year – the maximum number that the limited capacity of the Ministry of Lands could process annually.

Lack of official data also makes it difficult to accurately assess the areal extent of title conversions. The official figures state that only six per cent of Zambia's land (4.5 million hectares) is held as state leasehold. This statistic, however, has not been updated since the early 1970s and therefore fails to account for any title conversions that have taken place since then. While officials within the Ministry of Lands still use the six per cent figure, they say privately that it is likely to be as high as 10 percent.

Conversion of customary land has taken place throughout Zambia. There are, however, several hot spots for privatisation. Title conversions have been concentrated in peri-urban areas and in those parts of Zambia where commercial agriculture and tourism have the most potential. In particular, the greatest number of titles has been issued in rural districts surrounding Lusaka and the cities of the Copperbelt and in the vicinity of prime tourist destinations (Livingstone and Victoria Falls, South Luangwa National Park and Lower Zambezi National Park). There are title conversions in other, less commercially vibrant, parts of the country, although in these cases, local or domestic elites rather than foreign investors usually acquire the land. Some parts of Zambia have been largely untouched by privatisation. For instance, according the officials at the Ministry of Lands, there have been few, if any, title conversions in Western Province in part due to the tight, hierarchical control over land and resource use that the Lozi Paramount Chief, the Litunga, exercises.

Conversions for elites

There are no countrywide statistics disaggregating by income those who have acquired a title. A look at the allocation of leases in several chieftaincies, however, provides a snapshot of the economically skewed character of titling in Zambia. Take the chieftaincies of Mwemba and Sinazongwe along Lake Kariba. According to district officials and local surveyors, there have been several dozens of title conversions in these areas during the past decade. Of the titles issued, eight have been acquired by outside (white and ethnic Indian) investors for commercial fishing, tourism, crocodile farming, or game ranching. Successful local shopkeepers, retired civil servants, district-level officials, and the chiefs' family members have acquired the remainder of the titles. No poor or even middling households have secured leasehold land. The converted plots range in size from 150 to several thousand hectares, but most are near the legal limit of 250 hectares.

The same pattern is revealed in other chieftaincies surveyed. In Chief Shakumbila's area to the west of Lusaka, around fifteen title deeds have been issued during the past five years. One of these leases was for a 10,000-hectare sugar cane plantation and refinery. The other leases have been for retired civil servants, investors from Lusaka and several successful local farmers. In Chief Mukonchi's area near Kapiri Mposhi, all but a few of the more than twenty title deeds issued in the past five years, have been granted to wealthy Lusaka and Copperbelt residents. The same skewed pattern of leasehold conversion is found in the chieftaincies near Lusaka, Lower Zambezi National Park (Chiawa) and Victoria Falls (Livingstone).[6]

One of the primary aims of the 1995 Land Act was to promote foreign investment, and the Act made it far easier for non-Zambians to acquire land

---

[6] There are strong incentives for wealthier (mostly urban) Zambians to invest in land and to seek the conversion of customary to state leasehold tenure. In an economy characterised by high inflation, fluctuating exchange rates and low interest rates, land is one of the only good investments that can be made.

than it had been under the Kaunda regime. In recent years, therefore, there has been a significant increase in the amount of land in Zambia owned by foreigners. Exact figures are difficult to acquire, but according to the Zambia Investment Centre, 240 investment certificates were issued to large-scale commercial farmers between 1995 and December 2002. Because many investors do not pass through the Investments Centre (they may go directly to State House or to chiefs) the actual number of foreign farmers is likely much higher. The Ministry of Agriculture for instance, reports that over the past several years, more than 130 Zimbabweans have purchased farms in Zambia. Although these figures are revealing of the overall number of foreign investors in the agricultural sector, they are not disaggregated according to whether these investors are farming converted or long-standing leasehold lands. What is apparent, however, is that most of the largest leasehold conversions in Zambia have been made to accommodate investors.

Why is it that only Zambian elites and foreign investors, and not small-scale commercial or subsistence farmers, have secured title to land? One obvious reason is that few rural villagers are aware of the Land Act and that conversion is a possibility. As will be described below, many chiefs and local government officials are only partially aware of the technicalities of land administration in Zambia. It is hardly surprising, therefore, that subsistence farmers would also be ill informed about land policy.

Even if villagers were fully informed of government procedures and wished to gain title to their lands, most could not afford to do so. The transaction costs of converting customary to leasehold title are too high for most villagers. To acquire an initial fourteen-year lease, applicants must not only secure the permission of the chief and district council, they must also hire a surveyor to draw a sketch map of the land and pay a lease charge – outlays which are at least 500,000 kwacha (about $100) and often amount to much more. In addition there are significant travel costs involved in securing a lease: A claimant must travel repeatedly to the district headquarters and the Ministry of Lands offices in Lusaka or Ndola. For someone living outside of Lusaka or the Copperbelt, these costs can quickly spiral into the millions of kwacha. These costs are even greater if the landowner wants to convert his or her fourteen-year provisional lease to a full ninety-nine-year lease. For this, a rigorous boundary survey is required – something that can cost millions of kwacha in fees and transportation depending on how far the survey team has to travel from Lusaka. Lastly, once the land is converted a lessee must pay an annual ground rent to the Ministry of Lands. While urban businessmen, civil servants, politicians, and foreign investors can afford these costs, they are far too high for most rural Zambians, whose annual income averages less than $300.

Most Zambians are also at a disadvantage when it comes to protecting their land rights. As was mentioned above, the Lands Tribunal was initially conceived of as an accessible, affordable and efficient way to resolve conflicts over land. One of the Tribunal's primary mandates was to provide poorer, non-titled individuals with a fair and accessible venue in which they could protect their customary rights to land. In practice, however, the Tribunal has been ineffective, inaccessible and costly. Few Zambians know that the Tribunal exists or what it does. Despite its mobile ambitions, the Tribunal seldom travels beyond Lusaka due to budgetary constraints and the preferences of its members. Those pursuing claims must therefore incur the costs of travelling to the capital city and supporting themselves while there. Since its inception, the Tribunal has also become increasingly formalised – so formal in fact that it is now difficult to distinguish its procedures from those of the high court (to which it was intended to provide a more approachable and efficient alternative).[7]

Due to its formality and costliness, the sorts of cases that the Tribunal entertains are much different than those it was originally designed to tackle. Rather than dealing with land disputes throughout Zambia, most of its cases are from Lusaka. Rather than resolving conflicts arising from the conversion of customary to state land, most of the Tribunal's time is consumed with inheritance disputes and appeals to decisions taken by the Commissioner of Lands. Furthermore, the Tribunal is currently over-burdened and under-funded: It has a backlog of cases of more than two years and is chronically understaffed.

Land speculation

The titling of customary lands has led to widespread land speculation. Investors pay nothing for the customary lands they convert – barring registration and survey costs and the 'facilitation payments' that are often given to chiefs. These costs, though often prohibitive for communal farmers, are only a small portion of the market value of the land. Some Zambians and foreigners have sought to profit from the discrepancy between the market value of titled land and the low cost of acquiring it. As middlemen they have been able to acquire land for next to nothing, then sell it on at significant profit. This speculation has occurred widely on agricultural land, but is perhaps most common in tourist areas. In Mfue next to South Luangwa National Park, there are several notorious cases in which South African investors have acquired land at no cost from Chief Nkanya only to sell it on to a safari operator for tens and in some cases hundreds of thousands of dollars. In one case, Chief Nkanya granted a long-resident safari guide ten

[7] Initially, it was envisioned that claimants would be able to pursue their cases though the Tribunal without any legal representation. The Land Act states: 'The Tribunal shall not be bound by the rules of evidence applied in civil matters' (GRZ 1995: Part IV, Section 23(5)). In practice, however, the Tribunal's chairman will not permit a case to be reviewed unless the affidavits and forms are professionally drafted.

hectares along the Luangwa River. Shortly afterwards the safari guide sold the land for $70,000. In another case, a South African investor was able to acquire even more land from the chief. Once he had the title, the investor returned to Johannesburg where he sold the title for $200,000. In both cases, the chief was led to believe that these particular individuals were investing for the long term and thought that he was granting them the use, but not the ownership, of these lands.

One product of land speculation is that, since the implementation of the Land Act, the amount of absentee land-ownership in rural Zambia has increased. Unlike previous Zambian land legislation, which required land-owners to begin developing their lands within eighteen months of acquisition, the 1995 Act does not penalise those who fail to develop their land. As a result there is an incentive for outsiders to acquire as much land as possible, but little incentive to encourage them to develop it. As one observer writes: 'Ironically, proponents of the Act argued that by giving land a value and opening an official (as opposed to unofficial) market in land, it would encourage greater security, greater investment in land and greater productivity. But in practice the Act is a charter for absentee landowners' (Palmer 2001: 9).

Displacement

Leasehold conversions have displaced many villagers. The 1995 Land Act offers some legal protection to sitting tenants on customary lands. The Act states that land should not be alienated 'without consulting any other person or body whose interest might be affected by the grant' (Part II section 4(c)). This proviso, however, is seldom adhered to, especially if the chief or district council is either unaware of the interests of existing inhabitants or is unwilling to protect these interests over those of investors. Once land has been converted, moreover, the Land Act strongly defends the exclusive property rights of title-holders. In particular, the Act criminalises the occupation of vacant titled land and threatens occupants with eviction, no matter how long they have been living on the land.[8] The Lands Tribunal, as was mentioned above, offers little practical recourse from such displacement.

Long-term occupants of converted land have been forced to resettle or have found themselves transformed into 'squatters' overnight. There are cases throughout Zambia in which chiefs and councils have granted approval for local and outside investors to acquire already-occupied land. In some cases this is an oversight: The chief has simply failed to consult on the ground before offering assent. In Chief Mwemba's area along Lake Kariba, for instance, four households have been served with eviction notices for

---

[8] '(1) Any person shall not without lawful authority occupy or continue to occupy vacant land'. And '(2) Any person who occupies land in contravention of subsection (1) is liable to be evicted' (GRZ 1995: Part II, Section 9).

lands that they have farmed for decades because the chief failed to check with his headmen to determine if the land was occupied before signing the conversion request.

In other cases, chiefs and government officials have allocated land knowing full well that it was already occupied. This is often the case with large-scale commercial investments in which it is believed the economic benefits will outweigh any human cost of relocation or when authorities have an economic or political stake in the project.

In Chief Mukonchi's area near Kapiri Mposhi, for instance, the chief, the district secretary, and the Office of the President have all given their assent to the demarcation of a large tobacco farm. This farm – a Zimbabwean and British joint venture, the Mulingushi Agricultural Development Corporation (or MADCO) – plans to invest 27 million dollars in the development of 33,000 hectares of land. In mid 2002, the chief met with representatives from MADCO to discuss their plans for the area. The chief approved the plan and endorsed the conversion of 26,000 hectares of customary land to leasehold title.

Nearly 2,000 people in five villages inhabit the land on which the farm is to be built. In February 2003, a group of district officials representing MADCO visited the potentially displaced villagers. The representatives told the villagers that the project had been given approval by their chief, the Ministry of Lands, the District and Provincial Administrators, and the President. They explained that those living on the MADCO land had two choices: They could remain in the area and be offered jobs on the farm or they could move and receive compensation for their dwellings.[9] Villagers were given three weeks to make their choice.

Enclosures

> When a place is for grazing cattle and used by all the villagers, how then can one person come and get title for it? Where will the other people take their animals to graze especially if rich green grass is available on only one location in the village? Maybe for people in town it is OK to have title to their land but in villages, because of communal ownership of some scarce resources it will be very difficult.[10]

Common pool resources contribute to the livelihoods of most rural Zambians. Villagers draw their water from rivers or village wells, graze their

---

9 Since customary land has no market value, the compensation offered was only for the value of the structures on the land. In most cases the amount of compensation was expected to be between 500,000 and 1,000,000 Kwacha ($100 to $200).

10 Elderly woman, Hamapande village, Monze District, Zambia (from Muyakawa *et al.* 2003: 4.2.2).

livestock on communal pastures, cut firewood and building materials from common forests and catch fish on shared rivers and lakes.[11] These common pool resources not only provide villagers with crucial livelihood inputs, they also provide them with a safety net in times of stress. During times of drought and crop failure, wild foods become a crucial component of household diets. Access to river water and riparian grazing is essential in dry times. For instance, in southern Zambia, where rains are often late and meagre, the Zambezi River and its banks provide villagers with their only reliable source of year-round water and grazing.

As land is converted from customary to state tenure, local rights to common pool resources are being eroded and commons are being enclosed. Nowhere is this more apparent than along Zambia's major rivers, where both commercial farmers and tour operators have been setting up operations in recent years. During the past decade, much of the agricultural investment in Zambia has flowed to riparian areas where farmers can more easily irrigate their crops. At the same time, a growing number of safari lodges have been built on the banks of the Zambezi and Luangwa Rivers. In 1996, for instance, there were only three investors with title to land in the Chiawa chieftaincy, on the outskirts of Lower Zambezi National Park. By 1999, nineteen more tour operators held title (Bond 1998: 148). These lodges, owned primarily by white Zambians or foreign investors, are built on riverside locations where scenery and wildlife viewing are at their best. Both farmers and lodge owners generally fence or patrol their land and seldom recognise previously held use rights.

Along the shores of Lake Kariba, near Victoria Falls (Livingstone) and next to South Luangwa and Lower Zambezi National Parks, villagers complain that they are losing access to riparian resources. The growth of tourism and the number of lodges in the Victoria Falls area, for instance, has led to the enclosure of more and more riverfront property in this particularly arid part of Zambia. As a result, some villagers now have a difficult time accessing the river to collect drinking water, to graze and water their animals, to fish or to gather thatching grass. As one villager reported to researchers from the Catholic Commission for Justice and Peace:

> We used to go to the river to pick reeds for mats and even fish but now we are not allowed to go there. Our children will be thieves because they will have no livelihood or skills to survive. Even though cattle are permitted to drink water at the river the Zambia Wildlife Authority ZAWA confiscates them because the guards are paid by these same investors who own lodges to beat and harass villagers. If they catch you with fish on the road they will beat you up. And yet

[11] This is not to say that these resources are efficiently or fairly managed; some are and some are not. They may be open access resources in the sense that there are no restrictions on who can utilise them, or they may be common property resources in that there is a delimited user group.

you are not even at the river but on the road. If it means paying we should also have the opportunity to pay for some rights (Muyakawa *et al.* 2003: 4.2.2).

Planning restrictions exist that ostensibly prevent title holders from owning the riverbank itself. These easements, however, are seldom enforced and lodge owners generally claim not only the riverbank but also much of the river. As a result, they prevent locals from using the riverbank for fishing, grazing or cutting reeds. Some lodge owners also prevent locals from fishing too close to the lodges for fear that they will 'spoil the guests' views'.

Conflict and resistance

Land conversions have spawned a great deal of intra-community conflict and resistance. The commodification of customary land is transforming social and political relations between chiefs and villagers, between villagers and one another and between locals and outsiders.

In most of the field sites we visited, villagers engaged in 'everyday forms of resistance' (Scott 1985) against those who have acquired private title to communal land. In particular, villagers have cut fences surrounding privatised lands, released livestock on enclosed fields, destroyed or sabotaged commercial farm machinery and irrigation systems, and bewitched private land owners.[12]

In recent years, there have been a number of prominent cases in which pro-development chiefs and their subjects have collided over the titling of land. In the Chiawa area described above, for instance, Chieftainess Chiawa has had a series of run-ins with her subjects about her pro-development stance. The Chieftainess has been an outspoken proponent of outside investment in her area. She even appeared in a television advertisement promoting the virtues of the 1995 Land Act, using tourist and agricultural developments in Chiawa as her backdrop (Bond 1998:147).[13] The number of leasehold conversions the Chieftainess has sanctioned has polarised her chieftaincy. The Chieftainess' 'positive attitude to private investors (particularly tour operators) and to wildlife conservation (...) has undermined her support locally', writes one observer. 'There are complicated accusations and counteraccusations surrounding her interest in promoting tourism. She is accused by some local people, including key personalities and leaders, of having hidden personal interests at heart and of failing to listen to the community's point of view' (Bond 1998: 143-4).

---

[12] See Brown and Siamwiza (2002) for a more detailed account of resistance to land conversion in Southern Province.

[13] The Chieftainess has since distanced herself from the advertisement and has more recently taken a more sceptical view of land market reform in Zambia (Bond 1998: 197).

A more volatile conflict between a chief and his subjects has developed in Mbeza along the Kafue River. Mbeza's chief, Bright Nalubamba, has been pushing for a section of the fertile floodplain, known as the Kafue flats, to be developed as an irrigated rice farm. With the backing of Italian investors, the chief hopes to transform the local economy from subsistence agro-pastoralism to one based on private commercial farming. The opposition to the Mbeza Integrated Project has, however, been impassioned and organised. Although no one will be displaced by the proposed project, opponents stress that their traditional pastoralist livelihoods and way of life will be disrupted. The Ila people of Mbeza are first and foremost pastoralists. The Kafue flats and the higher ground surrounding the flats, provide Ila herders with their best grazing in both the dry and wet seasons. To challenge the chief, opponents of the project formed a committee, the Indigenous People's Rights Committee (IPRC). The conflict between the chief and the IPRC has escalated over the past several years to the point of open confrontation. On 21 September 2002, a gathering of 700 local residents including thirty-six headmen gathered to protest the irrigation scheme and to call for the suspension of Chief Nalubamba. As a result of this opposition, the project has been put on hold. The antagonism between the chief and many of his subjects, however, remains. In November 2002, the chief obtained a court order blocking members of the IPRC from making statements to the effect that he had sold their land to foreign investors. In April 2003 the chief dismissed five headmen in retaliation for their continued vocal opposition to the project. As of mid-2003 the situation remained tense with several court cases pending and police posted in the area to prevent the two sides from fighting.

The (mal)administration of land

Any system in which a valuable and scarce good is administratively allocated for free is prone to corruption. This is the case in Zambia, where customary land does not have a market value until it is converted to leasehold. As gatekeepers to this valuable – yet virtually free – resource, chiefs, district-level officers, and bureaucrats at the Ministry of Lands are in a position to exploit their strategic position within a 'soft system'. Lack of complete information at each level of the system exacerbates the problem. At all levels of land administration, administrators can bend or ignore the rules governing the conversion of customary land to leasehold. This section briefly explores the three levels of land administration in Zambia – the chiefdom, the district, and the central government. It highlights the weaknesses in the system that creates opportunities for officials at each of these levels to use their position to their advantage.

Chiefs

The government of Zambia grants chiefs the legal authority to oversee customary lands and to protect their community's culture and general welfare. In practice, the *de facto* authority of Zambian chiefs over land varies greatly. In most parts of the country, however, chiefs (with the assistance of advisors and headmen) grant occupancy and use rights to customary land and oversee the transfer of it between subjects. They regulate common pool resources (for instance, the opening and closing of grazing areas or the cutting of thatching grass or trees) and adjudicate a range of land-related disputes. Chiefs are also often the only point of contact between state officials, donors and rural communities.

The 1995 Land Act simultaneously threatens chiefly authority and provides chiefs with economic and political opportunities. The Act gives chiefs the legal power to approve requests for tenure conversions, which sometimes enriches individual chiefs. It threatens chiefs in that the Land Act has the potential to promote conversions to the extent that chiefs lose their physical domain.

Most Zambian chiefs are not much wealthier than their subjects: Their income comes primarily from subsistence farming and a meagre government allowance. Their 'palaces' tend to be modest; rarely more than glorified huts. Chiefly authority over title conversions, however, is a potentially large source of revenue. When making any request to a chief, villagers and outsiders are expected to offer an honorarium – often a bag of sugar, maize meal, or a small amount of cash. In some cases involving requests for land conversions, however, this courtesy has mutated to the extent that recent 'facilitation' payments to secure a chief's letter of approval have included new palaces, vehicles, or cash. Several Southern Province chiefs, for instance, have acquired new four-wheel drive vehicles from investors in the past few years. In another example, the palace of one of the chieftainesses on the outskirts of Lusaka is currently being rebuilt; courtesy of one of the new investors in her area. In several other cases, chiefs have been able to play investors off of one another in order to maximise their personal gain. Several years ago, a chief in one of the more popular safari destinations in Zambia instigated a bidding war between two investors for a prime piece of riverfront property. By the end of the bidding, the chief had earned $30,000. In another case a chief assigned title deeds to the same land to two investors, and received payments of several thousand dollars from each.[14]

---

[14] Some chiefs have used title conversions for political as well as economic gain. In the case of the MADCO tobacco farm discussed above, one of the primary reasons that Chief Mukonchi has agreed to allocate land to the investors is to counter what he sees as a political challenge. Tonga people from Southern Province inhabit much of the land in the part of the chieftaincy for which MADCO seeks title. The chief sees these outsiders as a political threat. 'These

Despite the opportunity for personal gain, most Zambian chiefs worry that the Land Act is undermining their authority. Although the Act explicitly recognises customary tenure and the role of chiefs as administrators of this land, it also makes it easier for villagers to convert their customary holdings to leasehold (GRZ 1995: Part II, Sections 7 and 8). Once converted, customary rights are extinguished and these lands no longer remain under chiefly authority. Most chiefs therefore fear that gradually, over time, their authority will decline. As a chief from Northwestern Province complained to the Minister of Lands during a conference of traditional leaders in 2002:

> We appreciate your effort to make land available to investors, which is important for development and food security. But we have serious concerns. *Chiefs are not chiefs without land.* When we look at the Lands Act we feel that chiefs don't own the land anymore because all land is vested in the President and the chiefs have become only the agents who help to process the land for investors.

Chiefs are caught on the horns of a dilemma. They believe that they must attract investment to their areas if they are going to show leadership, improve the lives of their subjects, and 'develop' their areas. But to attract this investment, chiefs must grant investors title deeds, which, over time, will undercut their authority over land and their subjects.

Many chiefs feel betrayed by outsiders who acquire land title. Investors often promise that they will bring jobs, schools, clinics and other benefits to local communities if they are granted leases. In practice, however, investors seldom fulfil their promises once they are in possession of titles. As a chief from Northern Province stated at the same conference of traditional leaders mentioned above: 'They [investors] come softly when they want land. But once they have it, all respect [for the chief and for custom] is lost'.

District Councils

The 1985 Administrative Circular delegated to district councils the authority to administer land within each of Zambia's seventy-two districts. This authority was reiterated in the 1995 Land Act. Under these arrangements each council is responsible for processing applications for leases of state land and for evaluating requests for the conversion of customary to state land. To recommend conversion, the council must ensure that the chief has been consulted, that a layout plan has been properly drawn, and that the land has been physically inspected to 'confirm that settlement and other persons'

---

people [the Tongas]', he declared, 'are acquiring land and even becoming headmen themselves. They no longer respect me [the chief] (...) and are even trying to set up their own chieftaincy'. Chief Mukonchi is willing to alienate a substantial portion of his chieftaincy in order to counter this perceived political threat.

interests and rights have not been affected by the approval of the application' (GRZ 1985: Section 4.D).

On paper, these procedures seem to protect the interests of customary landholders and limit the possibilities for administrative abuse. In practice, however, some council secretaries and council members have used their positions of authority to allocate lands to themselves and to local elites or investors. The problem is so out of hand that the Commissioner of Lands complained to me that 'eighty per cent of the applications for land conversions are just council staff applying for land for themselves with which to speculate'. This is undoubtedly an overstatement, but it captures the degree of the problem.

The half-hearted and contradictory character of bureaucratic decentralisation in Zambia has created confusion, conflict, and corruption in the administration of land at the district level. District Councils have been delegated the authority to process applications for title, but there are no land offices in the intermediate provincial level and all substantive administrative functions remain centralised in Lusaka.[15] Moreover, the Ministry of Lands does not have the capacity to provide technical assistance or personnel to the districts. As a result, there is an unabridged gap between local and national administration of land. This creates an informational asymmetry in which, as the Commissioner of Lands declared, 'We [the Ministry of Lands] don't know what's going on the ground'. District officials have been able to use this informational asymmetry for their personal advantage.

In a rather extreme example of this, the council secretary and several of his colleagues on the Mumbwa District Council (200 kilometres west of Lusaka) conspired to carve up 56,000 hectares of customary land. The council secretary approached Chief Kaindu with a proposal to establish a game ranch on a portion of customary land adjoining Kafue National Park. The secretary told the elderly chief that the creation of a game ranch would bring development and prosperity to the local communities and that the council had the people's best interests at heart. The chief gave his assent to the plans and approved a sketch plan for the demarcation of the ranch. He was unaware, however, that by acquiescing to the plans he was agreeing to the conversion of the land from customary to state tenure. Once the council secretary had the chief's letter and the approval of the district council, he

[15] Since the mid-1980s there have been unfulfilled calls to decentralise the functions of the Ministry of Lands to the provincial level but thus far these calls have been unheeded and unfinanced. For instance, the 1985 Administrative Circular, Number 1 states: 'Necessary plans to further decentralise the various aspects of land administration and alienation to the Provincial Headquarters have been made. These plans will be operational as soon as funds are available' (GRZ 1985: section 6). Similar promises were made during the drafting of the 1995 Land Act.

travelled to the Ministry of Lands where the Commissioner of Lands certified the conversion and granted the District Council title to the land. Shortly after title was acquired, the Minister of Local Government vetoed the plans for the game ranch for being beyond the remit of a district council. Rather than return the land to its customary users, however, the council demarcated it into six farms ranging from 4,000 to 15,000 hectares. In the early 1990s, the council secretary set about selling the land to investors. Two Afrikaners (Botha and Swanepoel) formed a partnership and purchased most of the land, again with the intention of creating a game ranch. Swanepoel died in 2001 and Botha sold the land on to a consortium of Lebanese and Saudi Arabian investors who are seeking to create a hunting reserve.[16]

Ministry of Lands

The conversion of customary to leasehold tenure is intended to be a bottom-up process. The applicant should first acquire permission from the chief and district council then move on to the Ministry of Lands for final approval. In practice, however, this process is often reversed and applicants start at the top, not the bottom of the administrative hierarchy. 'There are many examples of money talking', one highly placed official within the Ministry of Lands confided. 'People go directly to the top [to the Ministry of Lands or to State House] to get permission rather than going through the proper channels – the balancing is done somewhere very high up'.

Chiefs complain that foreign investors and Zambian elites secure titles directly from the Ministry of Lands. 'Now when an investor wants land he starts in Lusaka and not here,' complained Southern Province's Chief Mweemba. 'They get the paper in Lusaka and then come and tell us what to do'. His neighbour, Chief Sinazongwe, reinforced this opinion: 'There is no respect for chiefs. When someone from outside wants land, they can bypass chiefs entirely and go to State House and get a title deed. They then show up with the deed in their hand and tell us what to do'.

There are also instances in which government officials have acquired title deeds to large areas of customary land and then subdivided it for personal gain.[17] In the mid-1990s, for instance, an official within the Ministry of Lands secured title to several thousand hectares of customary land in Chief

---

16 Several years ago, the current Chief Kaindu (the chief who approved the conversion died) travelled to the Ministry of Lands in Lusaka to complain about the land concession. He believed that he had a constructive conversation with the Commissioner of Lands, but when he returned to Lusaka later in the year to 'chase up' the case, the file on the case had mysteriously gone missing. 'I suspected something', the current chief explained, 'when something like that goes missing you suspect that it has been taken on purpose'.

17 This is a longstanding problem. A clause within the 1975 Land Act granted the state the powers to approve all land transfers resulted in an 'increased pool of resources available to those with access to public office' (Szeftel 1983: 17).

Mukonchi's area near Kapiri Mposhi. In the ensuing years, he has sold off this land to outsiders, including the sale of 347 hectares for five million kwacha and a vehicle in 2002.

What makes the Ministry of Land so 'soft' and prone to manipulation by elites and bureaucrats? The most obvious reason is that the Ministry's financial and human resources are inadequate. There are, for instance, only thirty chartered surveyors in Zambia, and the Ministry has only two global positioning systems (GPSs) – only one of which is currently working. As with other Zambian ministries, funding is inadequate and erratic. In 2002, for example, the Ministry of Finance allocated two hundred million kwacha (about $44,500) to the operating expenses of the Lands Tribunal. Of this, only seventy million kwacha (about $15,500) was dispersed.

This lack of capacity coupled with hierarchical decision-making (e.g. all leases must be approved by the Commissioner of Lands) has created bottlenecks and backlogs within the Ministry. In 1998, the backlog of land applications was estimated to be 30,000 (Subramanian 1998: 271) – a figure that Ministry officials concur has not declined in the years since. This backlog of applications has created a strong incentive for applicants to look for informal ways to expedite the registration process and jump the queue. In such circumstances, graft and corruption are all but inevitable.

The effective and fair administration of land in Zambia is further hampered by the failure of the government to draft the regulations required to properly implement the 1995 Land Act. The Land Act is an enabling law that provides a broad framework for the administration of land. Following the implementation of the Land Act, the government failed to pass any statutory instruments – the rules and procedures that govern the everyday administration of land. This lack of regulations has created confusion over due process among both local and central government officials. For strategically placed officials, however, such opacity can be an advantage. 'The absence of prescribed regulations' one observer writes, 'hands too much discretionary power to the Commissioner for Lands and generates work for well-informed attorneys' (Adams 2003: 94). In such circumstances, decisions over land claims are arbitrary and prone to manipulation. For those in gate keeping positions, opacity in the administration of land is a valuable resource.

Conclusion

At a time when market-based land reforms are underway throughout Southern Africa, and policy makers and donors (influenced by De Soto 2000) are promoting secure private tenure as a precondition to economic development, it is crucial to understand the social and political processes that shape land reform on the ground.[18] With this in mind, this chapter has explored the ways in which changes to Zambia's land tenure policy have filtered down to the local level.

The Land Act sought to promote both outside investment and local land-ownership. In practice, the Act led to some foreign investment in the Zambian agriculture and tourism sectors (though not nearly as much as anticipated). It also led to an increase in the number of conversions to leasehold. The study shows, however, that the Act is generating economic and social exclusion in part of the country. The benefits of market-based land reform have accrued to local elites and outside investors – not to poor and middling villagers. In areas where the issuance of titles is widespread, longstanding economic, social and political relations are being transformed. The transfer of customary land to leasehold has led to the enclosure of common pool resources. It has also, in some cases, generated significant intra-community strife as villagers, chiefs and outsiders have collided over title conversions.

The chapter also provides insights into the character of the Zambian state and its administration – particularly at a local level. The administration of land has proved to be highly malleable; it is subject to perversion by local elites, traditional rulers, outside investors and local and central government officials. *De jure* institutions such as the Lands Tribunal are intended to prevent such abuse. In practice, however, these institutions are easily co-opted or ignored. The study shows that this malleability stems partially from the state's limited human, financial and technological capacity. In addition, fair and effective land administration has also been hindered by the presence of parallel and competing authorities at a local level. Chiefs, headmen, district secretaries, district planning officers, district council members, MPs, district administrators and a range of provincial officials all have some (real, imagined or assumed) authority over the administration of land.

Are there lessons from the Zambian experience that might be relevant to other countries considering market based land reform? Three themes arising from this research are particularly pertinent. First, donors bear much of the responsibility for the inequitable, contentious and confused administration of land in Zambia. Tenure reform was a donor conditionality. Donors invested in sponsoring the conference and background research that led to the 1995 Land Act. Funding dried up, however, when it came to implementation, and there was little support for drafting the regulations necessary to improve the administration of land. Second, administrative capacity in most African countries is extremely weak. Policies that do not fully acknowledge and accommodate these limitations are bound to fail. Donors and government

---

[18] In a March 2004 land policy conference, the World Bank and IMF committed tens of millions of dollars to titling lands in Africa and throughout the developing world.

policy makers, in other words, should not assume that the existence of state administrative structures implies that these structures are functional or that they function uniformly across space. Third, the character of local politics and historical experience will have a profound influence on the outcomes of any policy, particularly a policy as contentious and as fundamental to development as land reform.

References

ADAMS, M. (2003) *Land tenure policy and practice in Zambia: Issues relating to the development of the agricultural sector*, Oxford: Makoro Consulting.

BOND, V. (1998) *Household capacity and 'coping up' in rural Zambia: Dealing with AIDS, other illness and adversity in Chiawa*, Ph.D. Thesis, University of Hull, U.K.

BROWN, T. and B. SIAMWIZA (2002) *Chiefs, commoners, and enclosures in the Gwembe Valley, Zambia*, Paper presented at the Ninth Conference of the International Association for the Study of Common Property, Victoria Falls, Zimbabwe, June 2002.

CHANOCK, M. (1985) *Law, custom and social order: The colonial experience in Malawi and Zambia*, Cambridge: Cambridge University Press.

COLSON, E. (1971) The impact of the colonial period on the definition of land rights, in: Turner, V. (ed.) *Colonialism in Africa 1870-1960*, Cambridge: Cambridge University Press, 3, pp. 193-215.

DE SOTO, H. (2000) *The mystery of capital: Why capitalism triumphs in the West and fails everywhere else*, New York: Basic Books.

GOVERNMENT OF NORTHERN RHODESIA (1947) *Native Trust Land Order-in-Council 1947*, Lusaka: Government of Northern Rhodesia.

GRZ (Government of the Republic of Zambia) (1975) *The Land (Conversion of Titles) Act*, Lusaka: Ministry of Lands, Republic of Zambia.

GRZ (1985a) *A report of the Commission of Inquiry into land matters in the Southern Province*, Lusaka: Government Printing House.

GRZ (1985b) *Land (Conversion of Titles) Amendment, no. 2, act no.15*, Lusaka: Ministry of Lands, Republic of Zambia.

GRZ (1995) *The Lands Act. Chapter 184 of the Laws of Zambia*, Lusaka, Republic of Zambia.

GRZ (2000) *Land Tenure Policy*, Lusaka, Ministry of Lands, Republic of Zambia.

HANSUNGULE, M. (2002) *The 1995 Land Act: An obstacle or instrument of development?*, Lusaka: National Land Alliance.

HANSUNGULE, M., P. FEENEY, *et al.* (1998) *Report on land tenure insecurity on the Zambian Copperbelt*, Oxford: Oxfam GB.

MAMDANI, M. (1996) *Citizen and subject. Contemporary Africa and the legacy of late colonialism*, Princeton: Princeton University Press.

MOVEMENT FOR MULTIPARTY DEMOCRACY (MMD) (1991) *MMD Election Manifesto*, Lusaka: MMD.

MUYAKWA, S., M. MUNALULA and F. MUNALULA (2003) *Research on the impact of the Land Act 1995 on the livelihoods of the poor and peasants in Zambia*, Lusaka: Catholic Commission for Justice and Peace.

PALMER, R. (2001) *Land tenure insecurity on the Zambian Copperbelt, 1998: Anyone going back to the land?*, Oxford (UK): Oxfam.

RANGER, T. (1983) The invention of tradition in colonial Africa, in: Hobsbawn, E. and Ranger, T. (Eds) *The invention of tradition*, Cambridge: Cambridge University Press.

ROBERTS, A. (1976) *A history of Zambia*, London: Heinemann.

ROTH, M. (1995) Land tenure, land markets, and institutional transformation in Zambia, in: Roth, M. and Smith, S.G. (Eds) *LTC Research Paper 124*, Madison: Land Tenure Center, University of Wisconsin.

SCOTT, J. (1985) *Weapons of the weak: Everyday forms of peasant resistance*, New Haven: Yale University Press.

SUBRAMANIAN, J. (1998) Zambia country profile, in: Bruce, J. (Ed.) *Country profiles of land tenure. Research Paper number 130*, Madison: Land Tenure Center, University of Wisconsin, pp. 270-5.

SZEFTEL, M. (1983) Political graft and the spoils system in Zambia – The state as a resource in itself, *Review of African Political Economy*, 24, pp. 4-21.

VAN LOENEN, B. (1999) *Land tenure in Zambia*, Orono: University of Maine, Department of Spatial Information.

ZULU, M.C. (1993) Land policy and administration including systems of land allocation in Zambia, in: Ng'andwe, A. (Ed.) *Report of the National Conference on Land Policy and Legal Reform in the Third Republic of Zambia*, Lusaka: Centre for Continuing Education, UNZA, 19-23 July 1993.

4

'We fought the war to return to the old ways.' Conflicts about land reforms in Dande, Northern Zimbabwe

Marja Spierenburg

Introduction

Zimbabwe has a long history of shifting authority over land in the Communal Areas, moving back and forth between 'traditional authorities', 'modern' bureaucratic structures and more or less representational local government institutions. These shifts seem to be related to two issues: 1) changing ideas concerning the viability and efficiency of communal tenure and 2) changing ideas about the degree of control over natural resources that should be devolved to the local level.

Between the late 1920s and the late 1950s, the problem of declining agricultural production in the Reserves or Tribal Trust Lands of what was then called Rhodesia, was explained by a narrative that redefined a political problem – that of limited access to land by the black population – as an environmental problem requiring technical solutions and the education of 'traditional', 'backward' farmers. This narrative (cf. Roe 1991; 1995) was used to justify attempts to abolish communal tenure in the Reserves – albeit without conferring private property rights to its inhabitants – and remove the authority to allocate land from chiefs and headmen. These attempts culminated in the introduction of the Native Land Husbandry Act of 1951. The implementation of this Act, however, led to such resentment and protest that it was abolished in 1963 (Drinkwater 1991).

Following the Unilateral Declaration of Independence in 1965, a 'community' approach to the development in the Tribal Trust Lands marked a return to the ideology of communal tenure. This approach relied heavily on the co-operation of the chiefs and headmen, who had their rights to allocate land restored (Thomas 1992; Government of Zimbabwe 1994). The underlying motive for this reversal of authority can be seen as an attempt to replace African nationalism with 'tribal government', which would be more controllable and act as a buffer to grass-roots opposition (Ranger 1985).

Those fighting for the Independence of Zimbabwe defined the problem of the Reserves as a political problem, namely, the unequal distribution of land between the European and African farming sectors. The new, post-Independence government promised to redistribute the land between those sectors. Yet, the dual property regime concerning land remained in place. The former European Areas were re-named Large-Scale Commercial Farming Areas where land was to be held under a private property regime. The former Reserves/Tribal Trust Lands became Communal Areas, with land vested in the president, managed by the communities.

The first post-Independence development plan presented envisaged the resettlement of 162,000 families onto former European Land before 1986. By 1991 about 48,000 families had been resettled (Palmer 1990; Blanckenburg 1994: 30). Though quite an achievement, this was far less than the target set. Despite positive experiences in the resettled areas in terms of production and economic growth (see Kinsey 1999), halfway through the 1980s the pace of land redistribution slackened. From the mid-1980s a shift in government policy, which now favoured internal land reforms within the Communal Areas, marked a return to the colonial logic of blaming communal farmers for the problems in their areas.

It was not until 2000, after the ruling party had lost a referendum concerning a new constitution, that the government returned its attention to the unequal distribution of land between black and white farmers and stimulated war veterans to invade white-owned farms. The ruling party claims that the invasions have resolved 'the land issue' and have democratised access to land. This, however, remains to be seen. Those now occupying the invaded farms and trying their hand at small-scale farming have received little to no assistance from the government in terms of farm inputs, technical assistance, or credits. They are still uncertain about their legal status of tenure or title (*ibid.*: 23) and numerous land invaders have been evicted from confiscated farms to make way for high-ranking ZANU(PF) party members or their allies (see for example, *Zimbabwe Independent*, 5 July, 2002). As a result there is serious doubt about whether the ruling party really wants to solve the land issue in favour of those who are suffering from land shortages in the Communal Areas. The internal land reforms in the Communal Areas have shown that during at least fifteen of the twenty-four years that ZANU has been in power, it has not considered the communal farmers fit to take over the Large Scale Commercial Farms.

One of the areas which was subjected to internal land reforms was Dande Communal Land, situated in the Zambezi Valley, Northern Zimbabwe.[1] Dande was not a typically congested Communal Area, quite the contrary, it still contained unclaimed and unreclaimed lands. Farmers from overpopulated Communal Areas on the Plateau of Zimbabwe and (ex-)farm labourers looking for a place of their own came to Dande in large numbers. The internal land reforms, introduced in 1987, were intended to control the influx of migrants, and reorganise 'haphazard' settlement patterns in such a way that more migrants could be accommodated.

The reforms were based on familiar biased preconceptions of how communal farmers use their lands, preconceptions that can be traced to colonial days and generated a simmering resentment. In this chapter I will describe how deeply ingrained was the bias that government officials implementing the programme fostered against communal farming. Furthermore, I will describe local reactions to the land reforms, which involved calls to revert control over land to local authorities. *Mhondoro* spirit mediums played an important role in expressing local grievances. In the struggle against the state's attempt to take control over land, they invoked images of wise traditional leaders well aware of the needs and capacities of their subjects in relation to land. Yet, pre-project land allocation to migrants shows that the rights of traditional leadership to allocate land were frequently challenged by local residents. Furthermore, an internal struggle took place over who should have rights to land should the land reforms continue. This struggle also showed the limitations of the possibilities for returning control over land to traditional leaders. These limitations are related to the heterogeneity of the populations in Communal Areas and the accountability of traditional leadership.

Authority over land in the Communal Areas

As mentioned above, after Independence the dual property structure concerning land remained intact. For the majority of black Zimbabweans access to land continued to be based on group membership and restricted to the

[1] The fieldwork on which this chapter is based was made possible by the support of the Netherlands Foundation for the Advancement of Tropical Research (WOTRO). I thank the Centre for Applied Social Sciences, University of Zimbabwe, for granting me the status of Research Associate during my stay in Zimbabwe.

former Tribal Trust Lands, now renamed Communal Areas.[2] Prior to the 2000 land invasions these made up forty-two per cent of all land in Zimbabwe and were home to fifty-seven per cent of Zimbabwe's population (Moyo *et al.* 1991: 58; Weiner *et al.* 1991: 147).

The Communal Lands Act of 1982 states that authority over land in Communal Areas is vested in the president who holds all Communal Lands in trust for the people. The Ministry of Local Government, Rural and Urban Development was made responsible for administering Communal Land through the District councils (Thomas 1992; Government of Zimbabwe 1994: 22). The act stated that Councils shall '(...) have regard to customary law relating to the use and allocation of land' (Government of Zimbabwe 1994: 23).

The installation of district councils in the Communal Lands so soon after independence and before a new administrative structure had been officially introduced had caused considerable resentment among local residents (Alexander 1995: 181). The establishment of district councils indicated an attempt to re-establish a powerful state bureaucracy in the rural areas, in which the main protagonists were the Ministry of Lands and the Ministry of Local Government. Decisions concerning development policy and land reform were taken at the national level, and the channelling of state resources to rural areas was controlled by the ministries, with little sensitivity to bottom-up demands, as noted by Alexander (*ibid.:* 183).

In 1984 the Prime minister issued a directive outlining the institutional framework for development in Zimbabwe. Democratically elected Village Development Committees (VIDCOs) were to be the basic planning unit in this new system of local government. Each VIDCO would represent about 100 households. The VIDCOs would fall under Ward Development Committees (WADCOs), which would represent about 600 households. The WADCO would co-ordinate the plans from all VIDCOs under its jurisdiction. Each WADCO would be chaired by a ward councillor, who would sit on the district council. The ward councillors would be assisted by a District Administrator (DA) – who also served as the chief executive officer[3] – appointed by the Ministry of Local Government, Rural and Urban Development.

The prime minister's directive officially constituted an attempt to decentralise government and promote community participation in developing development policies. In practice, however, district councils tended to be dominated by the government officials serving on them. Furthermore, all WADCO development plans had to be submitted to a District Development

---

[2] Hence, land became 'de-racialised', but not 'de-tribalised', as Mamdani (1996) would describe it.

[3] Though there are cases, for example in the Guruve District Council, in which the two functions are executed by two different people.

Committee which was comprised of the district heads of central government ministries and departments, together with representatives of the state security organisations, and chaired by the DA. The District Development Committee was therefore a central government committee (Murombedzi 1992; Thomas 1992). District councils were almost entirely dependent on grants and on resources and expertise provided by sectoral ministries (Alexander 1995: 183). Plans to train VIDCOs and WADCOs in administrative skills proved over-ambitious because of a lack of sufficient financial and human resources (Thomas 1992: 12). Where training was provided, the emphasis was on implementing central government policies rather than training VIDCOs and WADCOs to develop their own development policies.[4]

In 1988 the Rural District Councils (RDC) Act was adopted, though it was only implemented in 1993. In theory, this Act provided a deepening of the decentralisation process, but in practice it firmly established the state's authority at the local level (Hammar 1998: 25-6). The Act aimed at establishing a single type of rural local authority through amalgamating two previously separate types of councils; the district councils that served the Communal Lands, and the rural councils that served the Large Commercial Farming Areas. The RDCs were empowered to function as the land allocation and land conservation authority by the Act (*ibid.*; Roe 1992). The act supposed a considerable devolution of power and resources to elected local authorities. Nevertheless, as has been the case with the district councils, the RDCs were far from autonomous in relation to the centre – either in terms of resources or in terms of decision-making powers.

Meanwhile, significant changes in the position of 'traditional leadership' took place. Though the 1984 directive excluded chiefs and headmen from the new institutional framework and they were attacked as anachronisms who stood in the way of progress by technical planning ministries, there were also voices in the new government which defended them. Immediately after Independence, former employees of the Ministry of Internal Affairs lobbied for a perpetuation of the role of chiefs and headmen on the grounds that their exclusion from local government could lead to confusion, even anarchy, in the Communal Areas (Alexander 1995: 186). In many districts chiefs were soon to be invited as *ex-officio* members to the meetings of the District Council. As early as 1982 a Chiefs and Headmen Act was passed which recognised the institution of the Chief, stating their right to a government stipend well in excess of that of ward councillors (Alexander 1995: 182, 187). The act did not, however, recognise the institution of the headmen, nor did it provide for a restoration of the chiefs' power over land allocation or court matters (Zimbabwe Government 1994: 25). Since

---

4 A ward councillor in the area where I conducted my research showed me the training material he received and the notes he took during the training he was given in 1994.

Independence the courts presided over by chiefs and headmen had been transformed into community courts, operating under the Ministry of Justice. In 1992 civil jurisdiction was restored to chiefs on all matters except land issues (Zimbabwe Government 1994: 26).

Although 'communal tenure' had been maintained in the Communal Areas after Independence, at the same time this form of tenure was considered unproductive. As described above, plans to introduce land reforms in the Communal Areas (re-)surfaced in the mid-1980s. Many authors have pointed out the similarities between the land reforms and the Rhodesian Native Land Husbandry Act of 1951 (Drinkwater 1991; Alexander 1995; McGregor 1995; Keeley and Scoones 1999; 2000; Spierenburg 2003b).

The reforms were officially introduced in the first Five Year Development Plan of 1986, but in fact had already been prepared when the Communal Land Amendment Act was passed in 1985 (Thomas 1992: 15). In contrast to the prime minister's 1984 directive, which appeared to seek to promote 'grass-roots' development, the Communal Land Amendment Act authorised non-elected governmental officials of the District Development Committees to prepare and adopt development plans of their own volition[5] (Thomas 1992: 15). No mention was made of any consultation with local people, other than the fact that when a plan had been prepared and approved by the District Council, a copy should be sent to the chairman of every VIDCO of the Council affected by the plan (Section 4 (5), cited in: Thomas 1992:15), who was given thirty days to consult local inhabitants and report back any objections to the plan to council, together with *the identity of the objectors* (Section 4 (6), cited in: Thomas 1992: 15, emphasis added).

In the end, the Ministry of Local Government Rural and Urban Development took direct control over land allocation in those Communal Areas that were subjected to internal land reforms. In these areas land allocation was carried out by its Department for Rural Development, and not by the district councils (Government of Zimbabwe 1999).

Land reforms in practice: The Mid-Zambezi project

The Mid-Zambezi (Rural Development) Project in Dande, where I conducted my fieldwork, was one of the pilot projects of the land reforms the government wanted to introduce in the Communal Areas of Zimbabwe. It was officially introduced in 1987 covering virtually all of Dande Communal Land. Dande is situated in the north of the country, in the Zambezi Valley. Because of its inhospitable climate, with temperatures soaring to 45 degrees Celsius in summer and unreliable rainfall, the area had never been of any interest to white settlers. Land shortage therefore never was a problem there,

---

[5] Communal Land Amendment Act Section 4 (1), cited in Thomas 1992: 15.

but lack of services and infrastructure was. As already mentioned, despite these disadvantages, the area had attracted large numbers of migrants. The goal of the Mid-Zambezi Project was to control this spontaneous migration. A number of studies had drawn attention to the influx of migrants that was occurring in the whole of the Zambezi Valley. Gloomy pictures were painted of hordes of people moving into the valley with their cattle, causing wanton destruction of the environment (see for example, Reynolds 1984; Whitlow 1988). Calls for 'proper land-use planning' were made by several organisations. In response, the FAO developed the Mid-Zambezi Project in co-operation with the government of Zimbabwe and it was based on the already existing plans for land reforms in all Communal Areas of Zimbabwe (ADF 1986). The project was funded by the African Development Bank.

Though the aim of the project was to control migration, this did not mean that government wanted to stop the influx of new settlers. Quite the contrary, the area could serve as an 'overflow' for the crowded Communal Areas elsewhere in the country. The idea was that if local land-use practices could be 'rationalised' and rendered 'more efficient', the area could be home to 3,000 more families. These new settlers were to be placed in 130 newly created villages. On the basis of the 1982 national census, it was estimated that approximately 4,600 households were already living in the project area prior to implementation. These would have their villages reorganised and their arable fields re-distributed (ADF 1986).

The implementation of the project was the responsibility of the Department of Rural Development (DERUDE, a department of the Ministry of Local Government and Rural and Urban Development of the Government of Zimbabwe) and the agricultural extension service Agritex. The project team consisted of a project manager appointed by DERUDE, seven Resettlement Officers, and a special team from Agritex responsible for demarcation.

The land-reform exercise closely followed the guidelines of the old Native Land Husbandry Act of 1951. All arable land was to be (re-)distributed with households receiving twelve acres of arable land and a one-acre residential stand in a re-organised village. Agritex was responsible for demarcating the grazing areas, residential stands and fields and for developing cultivation plans for the twelve acre-units. The stands and fields were to be allocated to individual households by the Resettlement Officers. Scattered homesteads would have to be abandoned and people would have to move to new, centralised villages (ADF 1986).

The actual land-use planning exercise was conducted by the Agritex Planning Branch at the provincial level. I have not been able to interview any of the staff members involved, but I did have access to the plan drawn up for Matsiwo A Ward in 1993.

The report starts with a description of the current situation. Population figures are presented, based on data provided by VIDCO secretaries, but no mention is made of the fact that these clearly indicate that the population numbers mentioned in the overall project proposal (ADF 1986) – which are repeated in this document – could not have been accurate (see below). A striking passage is reminiscent of the debate about land-use planning to satisfy a need for order by planners (see Scott 1998):

> Settlement has not been planned, migrants have settled haphazardly. Fortunately enough for Matsiwo A, due to water shortages people have tended to settle in clusters along or close to the two perennial rivers, giving some degree of orderliness although there are always exceptions (Agritex 1993: 7).

Stereotypical ideas about communal farmers, and particularly those in Dande, recur frequently in the document. The authors state that cattle owners do not use manure to fertilise their fields (*ibid.*: 11). The authors are surprised that farmers leave crop residues in the fields to be grazed by cattle (*ibid.*: 13), and yet, according to Scoones (1986), this is a commonly applied method of both feeding cattle and applying manure to fields at the same time. The authors claim, however, that farmers do not remove residues because they think it is too much work (Agritex 1993: 12).

After the presentation of the agricultural production, the authors of the Agritex report move on to their vision for Matsiwo A Ward. Land Capability analyses are presented for each village, and the number of acres of arable and non-arable land are calculated. Non-arable land is defined as areas that are closely dissected by streams, areas of extensive gravel outcrops, and the verges of rivers and streams '…which are not recommended for cultivation for conservation purposes'. In the document it is stated that because of agricultural activities near the riverbanks and on the riverbeds a silting process has been inevitable (*ibid*.: 7), but how this has been determined is not explained. According to the overall project document (ADF 1986), in the whole of the project zone farmers were to move away from 'non-arable' land, that is, riverine fields.

State intervention in stream bank cultivation dates back to the colonial era. The Natural Resources Act of 1942 prohibits cultivation within 100 feet (nowadays often interpreted as 100m) of a stream bank. In the 1960s the ban was lifted for the European farming areas. Farmers in the Communal Areas, however, remained bound to the old act (see Murombedzi 1991).

The Land Capability analyses apparently were only used to determine arable and non-arable land, since the recommendations concerning allocation of land and cropping patterns are standard for all villages and conform to patterns endorsed for the other wards in Dande. In their review of local agricultural production, the authors conclude that the plot holdings in Matsiwo A Ward range in size from 0.5 hectares for small families with no draught power to 1.5-3 hectares for larger families or those with cattle. Nevertheless, they opt for a plot size of 4.5 hectares – equalling twelve acres – per household. The authors admit that if this allocation pattern is followed almost 300 households will not be able to receive a plot in those areas that they have classified as arable. 'The excess households will have to be settled elsewhere outside the ward (...)' (Agritex 1993: 19). No mention is made of the fact that other wards may suffer from the same problem and that there may be no other areas where 'excess households' can be settled.

The maps prepared by the Agritex District Planning Branch showed little overlap with existing settlement patterns. Once the maps were designed, teams of Agritex officials sent by the provincial office, assisted by local Agritex officers, moved into the project area and started demarcating fields and stands with metal pegs. The Resettlement Officers were charged with allocating the so-called 'arables' and 'residentials' to local farmers.

On the basis of the 1982 census, the Project Appraisal (ADF 1986) stated that approximately 19,000 people, equalling about 4,600 households, were already residing in the project area prior to the implementation of the Mid-Zambezi Project. For some reason, census data that were available in 1985 at the Guruve District Council, listing 24,000 people living in the project area (Derman 1995: 15), were ignored by the project planners. The Resettlement Officers soon discovered that far more people were already living in the project area than the plans catered for. Derman (1993) estimates that about a third of the population, that is, about 3,800 households, would have been rendered officially landless if the project ever had been completed. Where these new landless would have had to go to was absolutely unclear.

The goal of moving new settlers to the area was abandoned, but all those already present were supposed to conform to the new land-use patterns. The discovery of this major planning error did not lead to adaptations of the maps with new villages and fields, and the number of fields and residential plots to be allocated remained the same. The process of moving farmers to their new fields proved to be a tremendous task, especially since there was no budget for transportation. In some cases whole villages had to be moved according to the project plan.

Originally, the project was scheduled for completion in 1992. However, owing to technical and organisational problems, exacerbated by increasing resistance by the local population, the project remained far behind schedule. In 1992 project funding was extended for another three years.

When I first arrived in Dande in 1988, the Mid-Zambezi Project had been running for less than a year. In one ward, Matsiwo B Ward, most designated plots had been pegged and the Resettlement Officers and Agritex extension officers were selecting people who would receive a new plot. At that time, many project staff members were still enthusiastic about the project, really thinking they were doing something good for Dande, finally bringing development to those who in the past were always last in line to receive any positive attention from the government. They enthusiastically adopted the title of Chambers' famous book 'Rural Development: Putting the Last First' as slogan for the project. This slogan had been printed on T-shirts and in

1988 many project staff members could still be seen wearing these T-shirts. Most had not actually read Chamber's book, and thus did not know that the book is advocating a participatory approach to rural development, which the Mid-Zambezi Project clearly was not.

But even at this early stage some project personnel started to have doubts about the feasibility of the Mid-Zambezi Project. The Resettlement Officer, for instance, who was responsible for allocating the fields and stands in Matsiwo B Ward, already foresaw in 1988 that the project would never be completed in time:

> The [Mid-Zambezi Project] is the biggest project undertaken by the government. It is a rural reorganisation project, a (...) resettlement scheme but in a Communal Area. The main constraint with resettlement projects is that they are not properly planned, there is no organisation.
>
> The project should be finished by 1992. But the officers have to stay until all the people can fully utilise their 12-acre plots. I am convinced it will take a lot longer than 1992.

There were few doubts, however, that the project was needed. The idea that farmers in Dande were not good at farming was quite pervasive. When I asked the Project Manager why the Mid-Zambezi Project was introduced he said:

> To bring development, of course, to stop soil erosion. Many people are farming where they should not. The people here have been left to their own devices for a long time. Now we will educate them about where they can farm and where they cannot. That is why we are pegging the plots.

All staff members I spoke with spontaneously offered the phrase 'people are farming where they should not' as an explanation of why the Mid-Zambezi Project was introduced. The question of why local farmers had selected the areas where they were farming was not asked. The 'originals', as they were referred to by project staff in English, were considered uneducated and stubborn. Even the Resettlement Officer who was most sympathetic to the plight of the local farmers in the interviews I had with him commented:

> I have been here only one season, the rainfall was unusually high so the yields were also very high, but that is not standard. There is a serious problem with development here. People do not know how to organise themselves.

He did, however, seem to realise what the main problem with the Mid-Zambezi Project was: 'But still people feel powerless, it is imposed on them'.

When I returned to Dande in 1992 the Mid-Zambezi Project lagged seriously behind schedule. The project had just obtained extra funding to continue for another three years. Major problems were experienced in Matsiwo A Ward, and that is where I chose to settle for a two-year period.

The Project Manager was having a difficult time. The Provincial Governor and the Ministry were putting plenty of pressure on him to finalise the implementation, but this turned out to be very difficult. The people in Matsiwo A refused to take up their plots, and even in Matsiwo B, where implementation was nearly complete, people were complaining about the lack of plots. The Project Manager summarised the progress made with the Mid-Zambezi Project during my absence:

> Matsiwo B has been pegged. Most people have taken up their plots. There is still illegal farming, people extend their plots and farm beyond the boundaries. Perhaps there is a problem with the extended families, they do not have enough land. In Matsiwo A we have a lot of problems, especially with the spirit mediums.

The Project Manager acknowledged the fact that not enough plots were available was the main problem experienced with the Mid-Zambezi Project. He brought up the problem without me having mentioned it, and sometimes seemed sympathetic and understanding, then yet again taking a firm stand:

> In Matsiwo B there were too many people with small plots, that was no problem, but with the twelve acre plots there were too many people. There are problems with grown-up children who want land after the pegging, they cannot be accommodated in their old area. We cannot peg again. People will have to move but they want to stay in their old area. People will resist. They resist changes, development.

The problem of the shortage of plots featured regularly on the agenda of the Rural District Council meetings. The Project Manager was often invited to the meetings to respond to the requests from ward councillors for the pegging of more plots in their wards. These invitations angered one of the Resettlement Officers:

> The [Mid-Zambezi Project] cannot be expanded like a rubber band. We go by the advice of Agritex. But the problem will lead to illegal cultivation. The correct number of people and cattle has to be in place, otherwise the project makes no sense, then it will cause degradation. But the councillors and the people do not think so, the councillors are sympathetic to the people.

Local farmers often complained to me about the attitude of project staff:

> They are always shifting us around, telling us we are farming where we should not. But do they know this area? No they do not. Look at the plots they have pegged, some have big rocks in them, others get waterlogged when it rains. These people from up there (*Mugari wechikomo*) they do not know this area. The *sabhuku* [village headman] does.

According to many valley residents, the project staff's unfamiliarity with Dande not only resulted in waterlogged plots, it was also considered as the direct cause of the land shortage. As the person cited above argued:

> The *sabhuku* [village headman] (…) knows his people. Some people are strong, they can cultivate many acres, so they will be allocated many acres by the sabhuku. Other people can just cultivate one or two acres. It is not good to give people twelve acres and then tell them that if they cannot manage they will loose their fields. With our traditional system everybody can have a field, some small ones, some bigger ones.

Whether the Mid-Zambezi Project contributed to or even created land shortage in Dande was an issue that divided project staff and valley residents. Another contested issue was that of riverine cultivation. The Project Manager and the Resettlement Officers I spoke with all condemned the practice. They all claimed it was causing erosion and siltation. When they talked of people 'who were farming where they should not', they often meant people who were farming *mudimba.* When I asked them why they were so against riverine cultivation when the ban on the practice had been lifted for Commercial Farmers, they would either say that they followed the advice provided by Agritex, or refer to the lack of education among the 'originals' of Dande.

However, Agritex personnel were not so adamant in condemning the practice as the Resettlement Officers and Project Manager believed. When I interviewed the District Agritex Officer, and asked him about the ban on riverine cultivation, he hesitated:

> I think in the valley it is okay, the valley bottom is quite flat, the rivers do not run so fast. But I am afraid I cannot say that at the level of the Province. But do not worry, I think scientists will soon develop a model for streambank cultivation, then we can admit freely there is no problem.

Unfortunately, neither local people's knowledge concerning riverine cultivation nor the officer's own experiences with it were deemed valid enough to lift the ban, the waiting was for a scientist to prove what people in Dande have known for a long time.

The implementation of the Mid-Zambezi Project was a difficult task. The Project Manager had to oversee the different activities in a project area that covered an enormous geographical area where roads were few and often in bad condition. He had to co-ordinate with other ministerial departments for the execution of certain tasks. But the most difficult part of his and his staff's job was dealing with a large population that was not convinced of the goals of the project. Convincing people to move to their new plots when they did not want to, and no provisions were made for transport, proved to be much more of a problem than the FAO consultants who had written the project document had foreseen.

Project personnel were confronted with existing local government structures, both the structures set up by the government as well as 'traditional' structures. In the initial phase of the project, both sets of local government structures were completely ignored by the project team. Pressure on the part of the Chief Executive Officer of the District Council led to a limited role for VIDCOs and ward councillors, who were to list and select applicants for the twelve acre-plots following criteria laid down in the project document. Village headmen and chiefs were not assigned any role. This did not prevent many Resettlement Officers holding them accountable for the problem of continued in-migration.

After the extension of the project a change of strategy was decided upon. Especially in Matsiwo A Ward the implementation of the project had proved to be extremely difficult and the Project Manager decided to involve the Chief. His idea was that if the Chief and his headmen could be persuaded to accept the Mid-Zambezi Project, their subjects would follow. As will be shown below, this assumption turned out to be highly problematic. Even before the new strategy was tried out, some of the Resettlement Officers expressed doubts about the extent of the influence 'traditional' leaders held over their subjects. As one Resettlement Officer remarked: 'People go to the person who will do what they want. Sometimes they will ask the Chief, if he does not listen, they go to the councillor'.

This opinion voiced by one of his subordinates should have made the Project Manager think twice about embarking upon his new strategy.

Resistance to the land reforms: Reasserting 'traditional' authority over land

The people of Dande have struggled to get their objections to the project across to the project management. In the early days of the project, several protest marches were staged to the District Administration and Council offices. The District Administrator, however, turned a deaf ear to the protesters and reacted by enlisting the help of the provincial governor in calling in the army. The protest marches stopped, but this did not mean an end to the struggle for control over land in Dande. It continued, but no longer as openly as in the beginning.

In villages where resettlement has officially been completed, that is, where all arable plots and residential stands have been distributed and allocated, it is not uncommon to find many people living in the village who have not been allocated land there. In many cases, people who were rendered landless by the project obtained permission from village headmen to settle in the grazing areas. In other cases they 'borrow' land from people who had not (yet) cleared all of their twelve acres. People who had access to riverine fields prior to the implementation of the project often still cultivate their *mudimba*.

The continuation of pre- and post-Independence policies was not lost on the people subjected to the Mid-Zambezi Project. One of the teachers living in Mburuma kept referring to project staff as 'those people from the Native Land Husbandry Act'. A woman in Mahuwe village, who apparently associated me with the Mid-Zambezi Project, put it to me in the following way:

> You people think you can shift us to where ever it pleases you. First Smith [Ian Smith, the last prime minister of Rhodesia] told us to move and live along lines. Now you people come and tell us to do the same. This is not what we fought the war for, this is what we fought against.

In the face of the difficulties with implementing the project, the Project Manager decided to involve the hitherto ignored 'traditional' leadership, that is, village headmen and chiefs.

Early in 1992 Chief Matsiwo had been approached by a delegation of the project staff. He was asked to give permission for the implementation of the resettlement exercise in Matsiwo A Ward. The Chief, who may have felt caught between his subjects and his employer, the state, then referred the case to another 'traditional authority', the medium of a royal ancestral spirit, a *Mhondoro,* claiming that the *Mhondoro* are the 'real owners' of the land in Dande.

Mhondoro are the spirits of royal ancestors, the great rulers of the past. All present-day chiefs of Dande claim descent from one of the *Mhondoro.* The spirits are believed to continue looking after the territories they once ruled when they were still alive, by providing rain and ensuring soil fertility. In Dande, these areas have relatively clear-cut boundaries which are known by most inhabitants; they are termed 'spirit provinces' by Garbett (1969; 1977). The land and all other natural resources in a spirit province ultimately belong to the *Mhondoro* of that province. The *Mhondoro* are thought to communicate with the living through a medium (see also Lan 1985).

The spirit mediums of the *Mhondoro* can be consulted by individuals in cases of sickness and misfortune. More commonly, however, they are consulted by village elders in the event of droughts or other natural disasters. The explanation of climatological mishaps offers scope for *Mhondoro* mediums to voice social comment. Mediums and spirits are believed to be completely separate: A medium cannot be held responsible for what the spirit utters when taking possession of the medium's body. However, as I have argued elsewhere (Spierenburg 2000), there is room for adherents to influence the pronouncements of *Mhondoro* mediums. Mediums who do not take public opinion into account run the risk of being accused of speaking with their own voice instead of the spirit's, hence tantamount to being frauds (see also Bourdillon 1979).

The *Mhondoro* mediums of Dande had all blamed the severe 1991/2 drought on the introduction of the Mid-Zambezi Project and what they interpreted as the government's breach of the promises made during the struggle for Independence. Whereas project staff members presented the project as an attempt to help the population develop their area and combat soil degradation, the *Mhondoro* mediums expressed the population's interpretation of the project: It was designed to wrest local control over land away from them. The mediums challenged the government's authority over the land; only the *Mhondoro*, who control the rains and the fertility of the land, have this authority. In the past the chiefs – the great-grandchildren of the *Mhondoro* – and their village headmen had been administering the land on behalf of the *Mhondoro*. The way they administered the land was presented as much more efficient and fair, as some of the villagers quoted in the section above also remarked, taking into account differences in production capacities and ensuring that no household would be left without land. The 1991/2 drought was presented as a show of power on the part of the *Mhondoro*. Frequent references were made to the war for Independence. The freedom fighters had received assistance from spirit mediums in mobilising popular support for the war (see Lan 1985). At every national celebration of Independence, President Mugabe thanks God and the *Mhondoro* for their contribution to the struggle. A sense of betrayal can be detected in the remark made by one the *Mhondoro* mediums when I asked him – or rather, the spirit – what he thought of the Mid-Zambezi Project:

> We see it as war. A long time ago people were shifting from where their homes were because of termites eating their huts or they were able to change their fields because they were no longer good. So (…) when these people were fighting during the war [for Independence] they said they wanted to live in their traditional way. (…) the Mhondoro looked after the boys [guerrilla fighters] well because in the bush there were lions, snakes, elephants, buffaloes, and rhinos but none of them was injured because the Mhondoro were always taking care of them. After the war we were expecting to live in our own traditional way. Then after the war they came saying they wanted to peg plots. (...) All the spirits are saying the war is not yet over and when it is over we will start seeing people practising the life of the old days.

The Chief referred the Project Manager to the medium of a *Mhondoro* called Chidyamauyu, who was responsible for the spirit province in which the stubborn Matsiwo A Ward was situated. After mediation by the Chief, a meeting was organised with the medium of Chidyamauyu and the village headmen at Tsokoto, one of the most sacred places in Dande. About fifty villagers, young and old, were present as well. During the meeting the possessed medium asked the Chief why he had called Chidyamauyu. The Chief answered that the *Mhondoro* are the real owners of the land. When the Project Manager and the Resettlement Officer asked whether they could get permission to start the demarcation exercise, this is what the possessed medium said.[6]

> You people from DERUDE are just tempting the mediums and the *Mhondoro*, but you do not satisfy our needs. The first time DERUDE came to Dande, the *Mhondoro* were not consulted. Now that you are facing problems you consult the *Mhondoro*. I have already told you that Sapa stream is where you should stop demarcating. And still you come to ask me permission to continue. I cannot accept that. (…) In the areas that have been demarcated sacred areas of the *Mhondoro* have been allocated to people. I am not happy about that and the other *Mhondoro* are not happy about it either. DERUDE is using power so they can demarcate without my permission. I am refusing and if you want to put my medium in prison, that is fine, I dislike the demarcation. DERUDE will have to pay a fine for the areas it has already demarcated without my permission. (…) The *Mhondoro* of Zimbabwe caused last year's drought because Mugabe is not listening to them.

Upon this statement from the possessed medium, the Chief publicly remarked that he too opposed the project. The audience reacted enthusiastically, the men cheered and the women ululated. The Project Manager turned to the audience and asked them to say yes or no to the project. The medium answered instead: 'Tell your seniors that Chidyamauyu has refused (…) Matsiwo [the Chief], report to me any trouble you have with DERUDE'.

The medium of Chidyamauyu had joined the ZANLA guerrilla forces during the war for Independence. When the medium continued to reject the Mid-Zambezi Project, some government officials appeared on the scene and promised that the government would reward him handsomely for his assistance during the war. The medium did indeed receive quite a herd of cattle and Mid-Zambezi Project staff built a house for him. At a public meeting the Project Manager tried to make it look as if the medium had been bribed into accepting the project. Most people in the area then withdrew their support from the medium and rumours started to circulate that he had been abandoned by his spirit and was speaking with his own voice. These rumours continued until the medium publicly denounced the project again.

---

6 I am indebted to Bill Derman for providing me with the transcript of this meeting.

The old ward councillor had chosen the side of the opponents of the Mid-Zambezi Project and had publicly denounced the project. In 1994, when ward councillor elections took place, he lost his support from the ZANU(PF) district branch, which decided to put forward a candidate who was pro-Mid-Zambezi Project. The pro-Mid-Zambezi Project candidate won in election that was 'supervised' by officers from the Central Intelligence Office.

The new ward councillor tried to persuade the management of the Mid-Zambezi Project several times to continue with the implementation of the project, despite the directives of the spirit medium. The Project Manager promised the ward councillor that the land reforms would finally be implemented, but nothing happened. When I asked him why he did not go ahead with the project, the Project Manager told me:

> No one wants to take responsibility. The village headmen refer the problem to the Chief and the Chief refers the problem to the medium of Chidyamauyu. (…) Nobody dares to say yes to the project. They are afraid that if they do so, (…) they will have problems with rain later…

Apart from the organisational problems of moving large numbers of people, most of them against their will, fear on the part of the project personnel may have played a role. Quite a number of them were afraid that if they continued with their work, the *Mhondoro* would punish them with illnesses, accidents, and bad luck. During the final stages of the Mid-Zambezi Project I came across one of the Resettlement Officers, who without any encouragement on my part started to tell me a story he had heard:

> You know what, did you hear that story about the Agritex team working on the dam in Chitsungo? The spirit medium of that area told them to stop. But they went ahead anyway. Then one day they went to the pool to take some measurements. On their way to the pool they were followed by bataleur eagles [believed to be messengers from the spirits]. One of the Agritex people was so scared, he got out of the car and went into the bush. They have never seen him again. When the others returned to their camp they found that all the figures had disappeared from their notebooks. And last week there was a car from DERUDE involved in an accident, one person died. Did you hear that? You know, the people here are strong.

When I asked the Project Manager what he thought of the medium of Chidyamauyu he said:

> I don't understand why he keeps rejecting the project. Now that he is living in a house built by us, he should know better. (…) These people here, they have lived very isolated lives. They are traditional and stubborn. They do not want to change, even if things were to get better. Their traditions are very strong, and

> they have these (...) powers, well (...) you know what I mean, you have been here long enough.

Having got to know the hidden ways in which people refer to certain issues, I assumed he was referring to witchcraft. It seemed that the references to the *Mhondoro* did affect project staff, though they may have interpreted these in a different way, relating to witchcraft rather than the benign *Mhondoro* spirits.

In 1995 project staff was withdrawn from Dande without having been able to implement the land reforms in Matsiwo A Ward. This task was handed over to the District Development Fund. What would happen to the residents in other Wards who had not obtained an 'arable' and were now labelled 'squatters' was not clear. Upon their departure, project staff had referred the problem to the District Council, but neither the government officials or the ward councillors serving on the Council dared to deal with this problem.[7]

Problems with the proposed return of 'traditional authorities'

At the time of internal land reforms, Dande was not the only place in Zimbabwe where a call for a return of power to chiefs and headmen could be heard. In the early 1990s the government set up a Commission of Inquiry into Appropriate Agricultural Tenure Systems, under the chairmanship of Professor Mandivamba Rukuni, which visited several Communal Areas, where its members heard similar calls. In its final report (Government of Zimbabwe 1994: 24) the Commission concluded: 'Inhabitants of Communal Areas however, still refer most land matters and requests to traditional leaders'. In its recommendations to the government the Commission advised that the role and powers of both chiefs and headmen be restored in matters of land:

> While traditional leaders are clearly not mentioned in the land laws, the requirement in the law that land administration is done with regard to customary law in itself implies some role of traditional leaders, given their status as executors of customary law (*ibid.*: 24).

---

7 Now that the government has shifted its attention again to the unequal distribution of land between black and white farmers, it might be expected that the 'squatters' would be left alone. However, these days those 'squatters' who are suspected of supporting the opposition party, the Movement for Democratic Change, experience enormous pressure to move away from Dande. (Derman, personal communication)

Alexander (1995: 179) cites two reasons for the re-emergence of traditional leadership. Once the war ended '[b]acked by a strong pressure for a return to 'normality' after the trauma of war, traditional leaders – and male elders in general – reasserted their power'. Another factor constitutes what she refers to as the authoritarian and modernising ethic of the development bureaucracies. She argues that the land reforms in the Communal Areas have contributed to an increasing local respect for chiefs and headmen (*ibid.*: 187). In the light of the reforms and owing to the structures in which they operate, VIDCOs and WADCOs were perceived as instruments of local administration, essentially implementation units for plans that continue to be developed in a 'top-down' fashion (see also Thomas 1992: 12). Alexander argues that by formulating an agenda based on a popular revival of 'tradition', traditional leaders were able to draw on a constituency that found itself threatened by the new agricultural policies. They invoked a version of the past in a bid to challenge the authority of the state and local development bodies (Alexander 1995: 187).

This seemed to be the case in Dande as well. Apart from challenging the government's control over land by referring to the *Mhondoro*'s power over rain and the fertility of the soil, the *Mhondoro* mediums also portrayed the chiefs – the *Mhondoro*'s great-grandsons – as wise authorities who made sure that land was distributed and allocated fairly, taking into account the needs of all their subjects. However, just as the assumptions underlying the land reform were a simplification of the problems in the Communal Areas and communal farmer practices, the same could be said for the portrayal of the chiefs as the rightful and wise authorities over land. A study of land allocation to migrants in Dande – prior to the implementation of the Mid-Zambezi Project – revealed that allocation was more complicated than presented in the counter-narrative (Spierenburg 2003a). Migrants approached different authorities for permission to settle in Dande, depending on their personal circumstances and convictions. Some migrants had actually been recruited by village headmen. Others, for example, had learnt about the availability of land in Dande during the war of Independence when their unit had operated in Dande; these people approached one of the ward councillors who was an ex-combatant himself. Then there were migrants who had developed friendships with families from Dande at their – temporary – workplace in town or on commercial farms and had been invited by these friends to come and live in Dande. Whether these migrants approached the headmen or the VIDCO chairmen depended on the relations their local friends had with either set of authorities. In some villages migrants had come to outnumber 'autochthons' and had managed to obtain positions within the VIDCOs, acting as facilitators for other newcomers to settle in Dande. In 1988/9 I interviewed thirty migrants about how they had obtained land in Dande. Just over a third of them told me that the actual allocation of fields was done by the village headmen (thirty-seven per cent). Others (twenty-seven per cent) had received their fields from the VIDCO chairmen (twenty-seven per cent) or by both these local authorities working in co-operation (thirty-six per cent). Nobody mentioned having been allocated land by the Chief, though some – admittedly very few – had seen the Chief to ask permission to settle.

Before the staff of the Mid-Zambezi Project was withdrawn from Dande, the struggle for control over land took place at two different levels. On the one hand, there was the challenge to the government's authority by the *Mhondoro* mediums, a challenge that was supported by the majority of valley residents. The project, however, also sparked off conflicts within the communities of Dande over who would have the right to land under the project should implementation not be stopped. These conflicts often occurred between migrants and those who considered themselves autochthons. They were related to the fact that the land reforms did not follow local land-use patters. As the number of immigrants expanded, it became increasingly difficult for them to gain access to riverine fields other than by resorting to borrowing or renting. The fields allocated by chiefs and headmen to the more recent newcomers were therefore generally situated further away from the riverbanks. When existing villages were reorganised, immigrants stood a better chance obtaining fields since they were often already farming in the upland areas demarcated by Agritex. 'Autochthons' had most of their fields near the rivers which were deemed non-arable by the project staff and planners, and were told to abandon their fields often without having been offered a twelve-acre plot in exchange. Conflicts arose over the definition of 'migrants' and 'autochthons' and their respective rights to land.

Once Agritex had demarcated twelve-acre plots in a certain area, this was often followed by a scramble for the land within the new boundaries. Autochthons suddenly claimed large parts of the newly demarcated fields, stating that long ago the chiefs had allocated land to them for future use. They transferred all their labour to the new plots, clearing as many acres as possible in order to stand a better chance of obtaining the land from the Resettlement Officers. In those areas where migrants dominated, the tensions experienced by the VIDCOs between themselves and the headmen increased over the question which households should qualify for a plot.

Both traditional authorities and representatives of local government institutions have tried to retrieve a grip on the situation and redress some of the problems arising from the Mid-Zambezi Project in their own ways. When compiling lists of people requesting twelve-acre plots, the VIDCO secretaries did not always apply the official selection criteria, for example, by registering divorcees (who did not have the right to a plot according to project criteria) as widows. ward councillors frequently challenged project management during District Council meetings, demanding that more twelve acre-plots be demarcated. Village headmen have – illegally – allocated land to those who did not obtain land through the Mid-Zambezi Project and were left landless. Farming 'outside the project' became an important strategy for dealing with the consequences of the Mid-Zambezi Project. People who had access to riverine fields prior to the implementation of the project have often still cultivated their *mudimba*. This, however, is increasingly causing conflicts with farmers who own cattle but no stream-bank fields, and want to graze their livestock in those riverine areas now designated as communal grazing areas.

In short, the reason for establishing the Commission of Inquiry into Appropriate Agricultural Tenure Systems, namely '[t]his profusion of overlapping and incongruent local organisational structures (...)' (Government of Zimbabwe 1994: 26), was very much present in Dande, both before as well as after the implementation of the Mid-Zambezi Project. Though in their opposition to the Mid-Zambezi Project *Mhondoro* mediums – and many of their followers as well – suggested that a desire for a return to 'traditional' government existed in Dande, not everybody may feel that local chiefs and headmen represent their interests. Perhaps the fact that the Chief 'backed out' of the conflict by referring it to the *Mhondoro* mediums, leaving them to tell the story of the chiefs' and headmen's benevolent reign, was already a telling sign.

Concluding remarks

In this chapter I have described the biases against communal farmers that have informed the internal land reforms in Dande Communal Area. These biases stem from the colonial era when the declining productivity in the increasingly congested areas reserved for black farmers were explained by accusing black farmers of damaging land-use practices. After the Independence of Zimbabwe there was a brief shift to a political definition of the problems in the former Reserves, the new Communal Areas. However, in the mid-1980s the post-Independence government changed its policy from redistribution of land between black and white farmers to plans to introduce land reforms within the Communal Areas. Dande, though it was one of the few Communal Areas that did not experience a shortage of land, was subjected to a pilot project for the reforms. The project documents show a clear bias against communal farmers' land-use practices, indicating that the government did not consider communal farmers fit to take over white-owned farms. Project staff adopted the same negative attitude towards farmers in Dande. despite this, there was some understanding for the feelings of resentment against the project, and some staff members came to doubt the validity of the ban on riverine cultivation.

The case of the Mid-Zambezi Project shows at once the consequences of a far-reaching re-centralisation policy, as well as the difficulties of enforcing such a policy. Because of the complicated logistics inherent in the project, it could not be implemented without the help of local government structures. Yet, it also became clear how difficult it was to obtain this cooperation in the face of resistance by a major part of the population. Even the strategy of enlisting the help of traditional authorities did not help. Relations between chiefs and their subjects were misunderstood, the 'conversion' of a chief is not automatically followed by that of his subjects. Caught between his subjects and the state the Chief referred the case of the project to a *Mhondoro* spirit medium as the representative of the real owners of the land. Spirit mediums are not included in any legislation pertaining to local government or traditional authorities, their rights and duties are laid down in the Traditional Medical Practitioners Act of 1981, which attempts to assign them a medical role rather than a political one. Yet, they turned out to be very powerful actors in the conflict about the land reforms in Dande, and their involvement had unforeseen consequences for the project.

The *Mhondoro* mediums put forward a narrative which stressed the ancestral bonds with the land, and assigned ownership and authority over land to those who provide rain and fertility, and denied the authority of the state over land. This authority was to be transferred to the great-grandchildren of the *Mhondoro*, the chiefs and their headmen, who were said to have administered the land wisely and fairly before the introduction of the Mid-Zambezi Project. The references to the ancestral spirits did affect some staff members, and it seems that part of the reluctance by the Project Manager to continue to enforce the project on the people of Dande could be attributed to fear of supernatural consequences. Project staff continued to defend the Mid-Zambezi Project, but no longer dared to implement it.

However, the story told my the *Mhondoro* mediums provided a simplified version of pre-Mid-Zambezi Project land management, as data on access to land by migrants shows. The swings between a recourse to traditional authorities and attempts to establish a modern local government structure, which have taken place since the Rhodesian period, has resulted in complications and confusion about who is responsible for the allocation of land and other resources. A simple return of authority over land to traditional leaders is no longer an option. Undoubtedly some groups may not feel they are represented by these local government structures. Over time they have built their own 'constituencies'. I agree with Alexander (1995) that most problems with local government structures stem from a lack of true decentralisation. If cries for a return to 'tradition' could be heard, these should be interpreted as serious demands for local control over land and other natural resources.

References

ADF (African Development Fund) (1986) *Appraisal Report for the Mid Zambezi Valley Rural Development Project*, Agricultural and Rural Development Department.

AGRITEX (1993) *Land Use Plan for Matsiwo A Ward, Dande Communal Area*, Mashonaland Central, Harare: Agritex.

ALEXANDER, J. (1995) Things fall apart, the centre can hold: Processes of post-war political change in Zimbabwe's rural areas, in: Bhebe, N. and Ranger, T. (Eds) *Society in Zimbabwe's Liberation War: Volume Two*, Harare: University of Zimbabwe Publications, London: James Currey, Portsmouth: Heinemann, pp.175-91.

BLANCKENBURG, P. VON (1994) *Large-scale commercial farmers and land reform in Africa. The case of Zimbabwe*, Aldershot (etc.): Avebury.

BOURDILLON, M.F.C. (1979) Religion and authority in a Korekore community, *Africa*, 49: 172-81.

CHAMBERS, R. (1983) *Rural development: Putting the last first*, Horlow: Longman.

DERMAN, W. (1993) *Recreating common property management: Government projects and land use policy in the Mid-Zambezi Valley, Zimbabwe*. Harare: Centre for Applied Social Sciences, unpublished paper.

DERMAN, W. (1995) *Changing land-use in the Eastern Zambezi Valley: Socio-economic considerations*, report submitted to World Wide Fund for Nature-Zimbabwe and the Centre for Applied Social Sciences, University of Zimbabwe.

DRINKWATER, M. (1991) *The state and agrarian change in Zimbabwe's Communal Areas*, Basingstoke/London: MacMillan.

GARBETT, K. (1969) Spirit mediums as mediators in Valley Korekore Society, in: Beattie, J. and Middleton, J. (Eds) *Spirit mediumship and society in Africa*, London: Routledge and Kegan Paul, pp. 104-27.

GARBETT, K. (1977) Disparate regional cults and a unitary field in Zimbabwe, in: Werbner, R. (Ed.) *Regional cults*, London: Academic Press, pp. 55-92.

GOVERNMENT OF ZIMBABWE (1984) *Structure of village development committees, ward development committees and extension services*, Harare: Government Printer.

GOVERNMENT OF ZIMBABWE, MINISTRY OF LAND, RESETTLEMENT AND RURAL DEVELOPMENT (1985) *Communal Lands Development Plan. A 15 year development strategy. First draft*, Harare: Government Printer.

GOVERNMENT OF ZIMBABWE (1994) *Commission of Inquiry into appropriate agricultural tenure systems, under the chairmanship of Professor Mandivamba Rukuni*, Volume One: Main Report, Harare: Government Printer.

HAMMAR, A. (1998) *Speaking with space: Displacements and claims in the politics of land in Zimbabwe*, paper presented at CODESRIA General Assembly, Dakar (Senegal), 14-18 December.

KEELEY, J. and I. SCOONES (1999) *Understanding environmental policy processes: A review,* IDS Working Paper, no. 89, Brighton: Institute of Development Studies.

KEELEY, J. and I. SCOONES (2000) *Environmental policymaking in Zimbabwe: Discourses, science and politics*, Brighton: Institute of Development Studies.

KINSEY, B. (1999) Land reform, growth and equity: Emerging evidence from Zimbabwe's resettlement programme, *Journal of Southern African Studies*, 25: 173-96.

LAN, D. (1985) *Guns and rain. Guerrillas and spirit mediums in Zimbabwe*, Harare: Zimbabwe Publishing House.

MAMDANI, M. (1996) *Citizen and subject. Contemporary Africa and the legacy of late colonialism*, London: James Currey.

MCGREGOR, J.A. (1995) Conservation, control and ecological change: The politics and ecology of colonial conservation in Shurugwi, Zimbabwe, *Environment and History*, 1: 257-79.

MOYO, S., P. ROBINSON, Y. KATERERE, S. STEVENSON. and D. GUMBO (1991) *Zimbabwe's environmental dilemma, balancing resource inequities*, Harare: ZERO.

MOYO, S. (1995) *The land question in Zimbabwe*, Harare: SAPES Books

MUROMBEDZI, J. (1991) *Wetlands conservation under common property management regimes in Zimbabwe*, Harare: Centre for Applied Social Sciences (University of Zimbabwe), NRM Occasional Papers.

MUROMBEDZI, J. (1992) *Decentralization or recentralization? Implementing CAMPFIRE in the Omay Communal Lands of the Nyaminyami District*, Harare: Centre for Applied Social Sciences (University of Zimbabwe).

PALMER, R. (1990) Land Reform in Zimbabwe, 1980-1990, *African Affairs*, 89: 163-81.

RANGER, T.O. (1985) *Peasant consciousness and guerrilla war in Zimbabwe*, Harare, Zimbabwe Publishing House.

REYNOLDS, N. (1984) *Land tenure and agricultural productivity in a developing country – Economic aspects and models*, Harare: Institute for Agricultural Extension Zimbabwe Symposium, Monograph 3.

ROE, E. (1991) Development narratives, or making the best of blueprint development, *World Development*, 19: 229-32.

ROE, E. (1995) Except-Africa: Postscript to a special section on development narratives, *World Development*, 23(6): 1065-69.

SCOTT, J. (1998) *Seeing like a state. How certain schemes to improve the human condition have failed*, New Haven: Yale University Press.

SPIERENBURG, M. (2000) Social commentaries and the influence of adherents: The role of the *Mhondoro* cult in the struggle over land in Dande (northern Zimbabwe), in: Van Dijk, R., Reis, R. and Spierenburg, M. (Eds) *The quest for fruition through Ngoma. Political aspects of healing in Southern Africa*, Oxford, James Currey, pp. 76-98.

SPIERENBURG, M. (2003a) *Strangers, spirits and land reforms. Conflicts about land in Dande, northern Zimbabwe*, Ph.D. Thesis, University of Amsterdam.

SPIERENBURG, M. (2003b) Natural resource management in the Communal Areas: From centralisation to de-centralisation and back again, in: Darnolf, S. and Laakso, L. (Eds) *Zimbabwe, twenty years of independence. From liberation to authoritarianism*, Basingstoke/New York: Palgrave (MacMillan), pp. 78-103.

THOMAS, S.J. (1992) *The legacy of dualism and decision-making: The prospects for local institutional development in CAMPFIRE*, Harare: Centre for Applied Social Sciences/Branch of Terrestrial Ecology, Department of National Parks and Wildlife.

WEINER, D., S. MOYO, B. MUNSLOW AND P. O'KEEFE (1991) Land use and agricultural productivity in Zimbabwe, in: Mutizwa-Mangiza, N.D. and Helmsing, A.H.J. (Eds) *Rural development and planning in Zimbabwe*, Aldershot: Avebury.

ZIMBABWE INDEPENDENT (2002), *War veterans refuse to act*, 5 July.

5

Fractionating local leadership: Created authority and management of state land in Zimbabwe

Bill H. Kinsey

Introduction

The cyclical waves of enthusiasm and disenchantment that characterise the development industry have, for the present, marginalised centre-led approaches to development and promoted instead the virtues of 'indigenous knowledge' and local leadership. One does not have to search very far in contemporary development planning literature to find *local leadership* functionally linked with proposed outcomes such as, for example, enhanced AIDS awareness, empowerment of women, better education, improved food security and nutrition, and conservation of natural resources.[1]

The efforts of Zimbabwe's ruling party – ZANU-PF – to extend its hegemony more completely into rural areas have been accompanied by both the state-mandated creation of new forms of authority and the resurrection of older, 'traditional' forms of leadership.[2] The outcome has been widespread confusion linked to an unsurprising process of functional fission on the one hand and a much less predictable pattern of splitting of communities on the

1 See, for example, Cornwall and Gaventa 2000; Cuddeford 2002; Mutangadura 2000; Phiri, Nzima and Foster 2000; World Bank 2000 and ZINISA 2003.

2 The most thorough treatment of the 'quest for hegemony' theme in rural areas is Munro (1998), but see also Spierenburg (2003 and this volume) and Hammar (2001) for detailed treatments of recent cases.

other. These patterns are perhaps most pronounced in the resettlement areas (RAs) established on state land in the early 1980s.

In the RAs established soon after independence, villages were managed for more than twenty years by democratically elected chairmen. This sort of elected leadership was a new experience for rural communities. Indeed, for those resident in RAs, the election of their village leadership constituted the full extent of their voting rights for a number of years. Their partial disenfranchisement resulted from the creation of RAs on state land outside the jurisdiction of both district and rural councils. Recently, however, efforts were made to compel these villages to revert to traditionally hierarchical, quasi-hereditary forms of local leadership.[3] The Traditional Leaders Act (TLA) sought to turn back the hands of time for those in RAs. The responses of communities to imposed patterns of leadership have been divergent.

The motives behind the new legislation are complex. At one level, the legislation appears to be a response to the call of the 1994 report of the Land Tenure Commission (Zimbabwe 1994) to restore control of land and resource management to traditional authorities. Thus, the legislation seems to repudiate the state's mistrust of a system of local leadership that had served the colonial government.[4] Pertinently, recent events suggest that the government has decided it can go further and use the same instruments to extend its hegemony in rural areas that were used by the colonial government. As Rugege (2001: 22) notes in examining the TLA, 'It is (…) evident that a chief, and headman under him, is an agent of the central state with no autonomy in terms of service delivery or other local government functions'. In addition, deliberate use of a traditional leadership structure may in part be a strategy both to conceal and to counterbalance the weakened presence of civil servants – such as resettlement officers – in rural areas.

The chapter explores the introduction of the Traditional Leaders Act as observed in culturally heterogeneous resettlement areas in four different areas of the country. The primary focus is the transition from elected village chairs to village heads selected in various ways. The chapter documents the perceptions by villagers of the strengths and weaknesses of both traditional

---

3 I am grateful to David Hughes for reminding me of the flexibility and contestation among lineage-based leaders regarding relative status, final authority, and jurisdictional boundaries. The state's recognition of some, but not all, of these leaders has compounded ambiguity even more, and, to make matters more confusing still, leaders often have to defend themselves from cousins and brothers who claim the title. Succession disputes can simmer for years, and subjects use them as means of putting pressure on and ultimately replacing leaders. Comments of Medicine Masiiwa on an earlier version are also gratefully acknowledged.

4 On the other hand, one-third of the commissioners on the 1994 Land Tenure Commission were chiefs, the only clearly identifiable voting bloc among its membership, so perhaps this change of direction is not so surprising.

village heads and modern village chairmen. The theme of the chapter then is a treatment of the 'desirable' balance between the perceived virtues of the old and the new systems of leadership in dealing with ordinary problems of the commons in resettlement areas in a culturally sensitive way. These problems include: Land allocation; village planning and layout; destruction of reserved grazing areas; inheritance of land rights; and intrusions of 'resource-poachers' from other tenure domains.

Methodology and data

The data on which the analysis here is based come from fieldwork carried out by the author and three research assistants in four resettlement areas in northern and eastern Zimbabwe over the period 1999 to late 2003.[5] During this period, nearly 100 past or current village chairmen and village heads were interviewed. Besides this, interviews were conducted in small, informal focus-group settings within villages and with elected councillors and non-elected administrative staff serving the areas in which the villages lie.

The resettlement areas in which the research was conducted are Mupfurudzi, Mutanda, Sengesi, and Mayo. All four were established in the early 1980s but, that fact aside, they are remarkably heterogeneous. Resettlement began in Mupfurudzi in 1980 and in the other three in 1981. Sengesi, with only 289 households in eight villages on 8.4 km^2 of land, is among the smallest schemes in the country, while Mayo, with an initial 1,279 households in sixty-seven villages on 738 km^2 of land, is among the largest. Little is known of the household histories of settlers in Mayo, but those in Mupfurudzi tend to have come from the 'protected villages' established during the war; those in Mutanda were 'self-selected' settlers who left Buhera to squat on abandoned commercial farmland; and those in Sengesi were often 'involuntary' settlers, who had previously been evicted from the communal areas for various reasons by their former neighbours. In terms of political allegiances, because it lies in a traditional ZANU-PF stronghold – Mashonaland Central Province – it would be expected that Mupfurudzi would be most strongly and overtly pro-ZANU-PF, while the other three, all to the east of Harare, would be considerably less so.[6]

---

5 I would like to express my gratitude to Nyaradzo Dzobo, Michael Shambare, and Blessing Karumbidza not only for their assistance but also for their invaluable insights into the concealed layers of rural social and political dynamics.

6 Unquestioning allegiance to ZANU-PF tends to weaken the farther east from Harare a rural area lies. In addition, Hwedza District, where Sengesi is situated, was a power base for Bishop Muzorerwa in the late 1980s and early 1990s, and Robert Mugabe's party still receives mainly lip service in some areas of the District.

Interviews were conducted in nine villages in Mupfurudzi (fifty per cent of the total), six in Sengesi (seventy-five per cent), seven in Mutanda (twenty-four per cent), and eight in Mayo (twelve per cent). Interviewing became progressively more complicated as time went on, largely because of the factors described below. By late 2003, in order to get a reasonably comprehensive picture of 'village leadership', it was necessary to interview not only groups of village members but also in some cases three different individuals – each of whom claimed some segment of the leadership role.

The setting

The populating of Zimbabwe's first post-Independence resettlement scheme, beginning in October 1980, marked the beginning of a profound transformation of almost every dimension of the rural landscape. First, resettlement involved a change in the tenure classification of the land itself. The large-scale commercial farms acquired for resettlement were held predominantly as freehold, albeit often heavily indebted (although a small number of the farms acquired were occupied under lease). When acquired for resettlement, the deeds to freehold land were cancelled and the farms became state land. This transformation brought in tow a parallel change in administrative structures. No longer freehold farmland, the resettlement areas (RAs) now fell outside the jurisdiction of the rural councils; and, having left the Communal Areas (CAs), the new settlers were no longer under the authority of the district councils.[7] Those in RAs were, in effect and in actual practice, direct wards of the responsible minister and had no elected representation outside their immediate village locale. They were governed not so much by the laws passed by parliament as by a set of rules and regulations specific to the RAs. These regulations sharply curtailed what they could and could not do and were enforced by the local representative of the minister – the resident resettlement officer.

Second, those opting to be resettled submitted themselves to very new patterns of living. For one thing, the spatial configurations differed from what they had known previously. Instead of spreading themselves across the landscape and residing in the midst of their fields, at a distance from their neighbours, the settlers found themselves 'crowded' into villages in an 'untraditional' fashion on tightly clustered residential plots of just over 4,000 square metres each.[8] Moreover, their fields were often at a considerable

---

7 For an account of some of the key changes in approaches to local governance since independence, see Mutizwa-Mangiza 1991, and, especially for more recent practice, Hammar 2003.

8 For those who were landless or who resettled from urban areas, as some did, this space may have seemed luxurious, but many of those who came from the Com-

distance from their homesteads – in many cases a walk of more than an hour in each direction.

Social configurations also differed significantly. Selection of beneficiaries for the resettlement programme was based largely on criteria related to 'need' and the willingness of families to be relocated. This meant that individual families were selected rather than groups or entire communities. Those selected found themselves living in new communities with drastically reduced networks of kinship – whether of blood or marriage – and other forms of 'social capital'. In the sense that the RAs were largely 'a land of strangers', the villages therein were anything but 'traditional' Zimbabwean rural communities.[9]

The early resettlement experience was stressful. Not only was there the distancing from old social networks, but also the early years were badly affected by repeated drought, crop failures, and food shortages and characterised as well by enormous demands for labour for building houses and other structures, clearing and planting land, and constructing community facilities such as teachers' houses and cattle dips. Despite investing heavily in new social relationships over the years after resettling, resettled households differ from CA households in their response to shocks and stresses by being more individualistic and relying more upon their own assets and less upon assistance from neighbours. Each new village appears to have developed its own risk-sharing culture, shaped in part by the social and ethnic composition of the village and in part by a shared past (Dekker 2004a).

In the setting described here, those in resettled villages elected from among themselves a village chairman to represent them in transactions with the resettlement officer and to serve as the point of contact with other government officers, in dealings with other villages, and with the 'outside world' at large. These chairmen were of two clearly differentiated types and elected in two distinct ways: There were those elected from the full adult population of the village by the full adult population, and those nominated and 'elected' only by ZANU-PF members resident in the village. In the latter cases, the main role of the chairmen was perceived as party-political in nature and not as broadly representative (see the boxed text near the end of

---

munal Areas complained bitterly to the author in the early 1980s that living in such close proximity was 'unnatural'. In addition to considering the arrangement a departure from tradition, the reasons for their distaste included the medical – 'it is unhealthy to live so close together' – to the social – 'it is not good to be so close that neighbours can hear the sounds of enthusiastic nocturnal sex'.

9 For path-breaking work on social trajectories in RAs and the way in which these communities have evolved new networks for mutual assistance and risk-sharing, see Barr 2000a; 2000b; 2000c; 2001; 2002a; 2002b; 2003a; 2003b; 2004; forthcoming; and Dekker 2002; 2004a; 2004b).

the chapter).[10] Although it is impossible to know with certainty why particular individuals were elected to the post of village chair, the main attributes emphasised by villagers in informal discussion were the ability of the leader to attract development, to accept free expression of dissenting views, and to resolve issues in a non-partisan manner. While seldom overtly declared, there was a growing competition for authenticity in RA villages, one that tested who were the real men of the people in terms of their ability to deliver 'development'. Under the early resettlement programme, 'development' had been a commodity exclusively claimed by ZANU-PF. The striking decline in deliveries of new resettlement land and reversals of development in existing RAs in the 1990s, however, left local ruling party officials with little to do but squabble with donors over who would get credit for food relief supplies.[11]

Resettled villagers continued to elect village chairmen in this way for two decades. In addition, later during the 1980s, they were enfranchised to vote for representatives to various bodies in the new local government hierarchy that extended from village to ward to district to province (Mutizwa-Mangiza 1991). The most significant of these bodies, in terms of proximity to the villages, were the village and ward development committees, but villagers were also able to vote for a councillor to represent them in the rural district councils. However, as part of what Hammar (2003) refers to as a continuing 'political reworking of traditional authority',[12] in 1998 government passed the Traditional Leaders Act (TLA) (Zimbabwe 1998).

In a deteriorating economic environment and with weakening capacity on the part of the state to implement programmes, the provisions of the TLA were introduced in piecemeal fashion. In resettlement areas, a triggering mechanism appears to have been the dismissal, at the end of 1999, of all the scheme-resident resettlement officers in response to severe budgetary pressures. One resettlement officer, based without transportation at district headquarters, was now supposed to serve the local needs of all schemes

---

10 A personal impression is that the authority villagers willingly cede to local party chairmen has steadily waned since the early 1980s, when it was virtually impossible to visit resettled villages without the knowledge and approval of the resident party representative.

11 ZANU-PF has always sought to identify itself as the provider of food aid, but such attempts became even more histrionic following the disruptions to the food supply caused by the farm invasions. For just one example of traditional leadership's role in this farce, see *The Zimbabwe Standard* (November 27, 2002).

12 It is impossible to detail the many changes made in the decades following 1980 and the motives for them. ZANU-PF responded to perceived political vulnerabilities and sought to strengthen the party's position by regularly tinkering with local governance policy and practices – but the changes, as Hammar (2003) notes, often served only to deepen the ambiguities in localised authority.

across an entire district.[13] In the absence of a direct representative of the local government ministry in RAs, implementation of the TLA suddenly assumed greater priority. ZANU-PF's first electoral defeat in the constitutional referendum of February 2000 can only have accentuated concern to have a cadre of party loyalists throughout the rural areas.

Key provisions of the TLA

In its ten sections, the TLA spells out how chiefs, headmen and village heads are to be appointed, the duties they are to perform, and the actions to be taken against them in cases of misconduct in office. The Act also defines, often in reference to the Rural District Councils Act, the functions of village, ward and provincial assemblies and the Council of Chiefs. The critical provision here, however, is that the TLA assigns communities on resettlement land to the authority of the chief for the area concerned, yet it does so while preserving the status of resettlement land as a category distinct from communal land.

What is important is that the TLA sweeps away, on paper anyway, elected village government. Chiefs, the leading members of royal lineages, are appointed by the president, albeit often not without protracted delays and a great deal of prior disputation within the chiefly clan. Chiefs, in turn, nominate headmen – *sabhuku* – normally of the same lineage, who are subsequently appointed by the relevant minister. In the CAs, headmanship is customarily granted by the chief to the head of the family that is believed to have founded a village (Spierenburg 2003); however, such a system is not possible within the RAs. Not only are CA villages larger and more dispersed – creating large areas to be governed – but also the smaller, consolidated RA villages bear no relationship to villages that may have existed seventy or more years ago. Thus, the concept of 'village' in an RA is very different from that in the CAS; and under the TLA, a *sabhuku* will typically be responsible for three to five RA villages.

In contrast to the previous system, where village chairmen were elected by the villagers, headmen then nominate candidates for the posts of village head – the lowest step in the hierarchy, who must reside in the village, and these individuals are appointed by the permanent secretary of the relevant ministry.[14] Importantly, chiefs and headmen are paid salaries and allowances

---

13 More than four years after these changes were made, some RAs have yet to receive their first visit from the district resettlement officer.

14 It is remarkable that the reinvention of the 'traditional' in the TLA should preserve the term *sabhuku*, a Shona derivation from the English colonial term 'the keeper of the book', that is, the village register. Similarly, another 'traditional'

from central government, while village heads are entitled to allowances from the rural district council – but as prescribed by the minister.

The village assembly retains its composition – defined as all village residents aged over eighteen, but it is now chaired by an appointed village head rather than an elected village chairman. While the assembly elects the village development committee – VIDCO (also chaired by the head) – its primary responsibilities are to 'consider', 'review' and 'make representations'. The assembly is also 'to consider and resolve all issues relating to land, water and other natural resources within the area (…)' (Article 15c).

The TLA spells out the official duties of village heads under sixteen different headings, the most relevant of which are (Zimbabwe 1998, Article 12):

> a) to assist the chief and headman in the performance of their duties; and
> b) to carry out all lawful and reasonable orders of the chief or headman; and
> c) to lead his [*sic*] village in all traditional, customary and cultural matters; and
> d) to, subject to the Communal Land Act, consider, in accordance with the customs and traditions of his community, requests for settlement by new settlers into the village and, in consultation with the village assembly, to make recommendations on the matter to the ward assembly; and
> e) (…) to settle disputes involving customary law and traditions, including matters relating to residential, grazing and agricultural land boundaries and, where necessary, to refer these matters for settlement by the headman; and
> f) to preside over the village assembly; and
> g) to ensure that all land in his [*sic*] area is utilized in accordance with any enactment in force for the use and occupation of communal or resettlement land; and
> j) to collect levies, taxes and other charges (…); and
> m) to promote sound morals and good social conduct among members of his [*sic*] village; and
> n) to maintain an up-to-date register of names of the inhabitants of his [*sic*] village, and their settlement permits.

The roles of the various tiers of traditional leadership have been periodically reinforced since 2000. In one instance, speaking at the installation ceremony of a newly appointed chief in Gutu district, Zimbabwe's former vice-president, Simon Muzenda, quoted almost *verbatim* the full list of duties enumerated above. He emphasized that traditional leaders at all levels should play 'an active role in the distribution of land', although he was careful to point out that traditional leaders were not empowered to allocate land under the TLA (*Sunday Mail* 2001). Instead, village headmen and ward assemblies 'were expected to work closely with rural district

---

common usage for village head is *kraalhead,* which is half Portuguese, via Afrikaans, and half English.

councils in the approval of new settlements' so as to safeguard the environment.

Interestingly, Muzenda also warned headmen about the disciplinary procedures for corruption contained in Article 10 of the Act, and is said to have declared (*Sunday Mail* 2001):

> Representations have been lodged with my office of headmen who demand cattle or money before they forward names of their friends for appointment as village heads (…). This outright bribery cannot be tolerated (…).

The vice-president was not quoted, however, as cautioning traditional leaders about engaging in political activities, which are prohibited under Article 45 of the TLA:

> No chief, headman or village head shall canvass, (…) for any candidate, or nominate any candidate for election as State President, member of Parliament or councillor in any local authority.

Campaigning in one form or another had already been a major endeavour for traditional leaders leading up to the parliamentary elections in 2000 and was to become even more important in ensuing elections, including the presidential election of 2002. As recently as early 2004, traditional leaders were charged in the press with intimidating voters and were credited with capturing a by-election for ZANU-PF (*Daily News* 2004, *Sunday Mirror* 2004, *Zimbabwe Independent* 2004).[15]

Implementation of the TLA in resettlement areas

As noted earlier, the TLA was implemented in a piecemeal and highly variable fashion, at least in the resettlement areas studied. The research team first began to observe implementation activities in Mupfurudzi in 2000, although it was a year, or even two years, later that similar activities began in the other areas. This section treats these activities as though they were contemporaneous across time and space, although in reality they were not.

---

[15] In RAs, ward chairmen were said to have been mandated with the duty of ensuring that ZANU-PF won the Gutu by-election. *Zimbabwe Independent* (6 February 2004) quoted one resettled farmer's explanation of how this was done: 'Before the election days, each chairman was asked to circulate a form to the electorate demanding their names and political affiliation. The forms were later submitted to the ruling party. Over and above that, the chairman had to bring his people to the polling station on election days'.

Selection as village head and training for the position
Of the forty current village heads interviewed in the course of this study, a minority – forty-five per cent – had stood for election to the office in 2000, 2001 or 2002. The balance of village heads had all been appointed by the chief for the area.[16] All candidates who stood were opposed by at least one other candidate for the post of headship. Asked why they thought the villagers had elected them, the winners of the elections put forward several explanations. Personal qualities were clearly important, but an established record of capable, non-partisan leadership in the village was the most common response – mentioned by fifty-five per cent of those elected. Personal frankness and encouraging others to speak freely were mentioned by just over a quarter of respondents, while a background in party positions was important to less than a fifth of those elected.

There were significant regional differences in the procedures followed to select village heads. In Mupfurudzi, the idea to appoint 'traditional' heads was said to have come from the council and not to be a popular choice. The council spelled out criteria for eligibility: Those aged thirty-five or above, plot-holders, and males with an education above grade five. To these the chief added that a candidate must have no criminal record. Council officials also held sessions to educate people on the 'positive aspects' of the new system of leadership. 'Election' was then usually done by show of hands at a public meeting of the village. In Mutanda, the DA announced the government's intention to install village heads via the area councillor. The councillor's version of the criteria for choosing a village head was that anyone who had previously been elected as village chairman would automatically become the village head. The choice of chairmen was then confirmed through a show of hands at a meeting. Presiding over the procedures were outside officials like extension staff, politicians, and councillors. The chief endorsed those chosen as chairmen on party lines as 'village heads-in-waiting', and all seven village heads interviewed in Mutanda reported that they were 'appointed' by the chief rather than standing for election. Some village chairman observed that there was nothing to indicate that inheritance rules would apply as in CAs. In Sengesi, all the heads stood for election and none was appointed; rather they were 'recommended' after being chosen by the villagers. In Mayo and Mupfurudzi, on average three-quarters of village heads were nominated directly by chiefs.

All serving village heads are supposed to have received training in the duties and responsibilities of their position, however just over thirty-seven per cent of heads interviewed declared they had received no training since assuming the headship. Of these, over seventy-one per cent stated that they

---

[16] In some cases, there were two or three individuals in a village claiming to be its head: the nominated head under the TLA; an elected head-chairman; and a ZANU-PF party chairman. See further discussion below.

would find training useful. The single most important type of training desired by those who had received none was in methods of dealing with resolution of conflicts and disputes in the village; however a second strong theme was how to lobby successfully for development projects and resources.

Those who had received training received it from a number of sources. Most commonly, it was a chief or sub-chief who trained the new village heads; however district administrators were also widely involved. Often the two trained together. Headmen acted as trainers in about a fifth of the cases, and party officials, members of parliament and civil servants provided inputs in occasional instances.

Those trained indicated that a wide range of subject matter was covered. The single most important theme – twenty-four per cent of responses – was conservation of natural resources, followed closely by material related to general leadership and ensuring village welfare (twenty-one per cent) and observing traditional customs and *chisi*[17] (nineteen per cent). About twelve per cent of training was reported to deal with general rules and regulations, and the same figure was given for dealing with rules of evidence in resolving disputes.[18] In less than five per cent of cases was party loyalty and discipline mentioned as a subject of training, suggesting that ZANU-PF's hegemonic agenda was either covert at this stage or taken for granted.

Perceptions of the powers village heads can exercise

Much of the fieldwork upon which this chapter is based was devoted to an exploration of the powers, perceived and real, that village heads possess. Before attention is directed specifically to the issue of powers used to manage the village's resource base, however, it will be useful to have some idea of village heads' concepts of the generic powers they possess as office-holders.

Table 5.1 ranks current village head's responses to a question asking them to enumerate their most important powers as head of their village. The wide range of responses received shows there was clearly some confusion

---

[17] *Chisi* is a day considered to be set aside by the ancestral spirits of an area when they move about observing what their 'children' are doing. While its importance and practice vary considerably across Zimbabwe, *chisi* is normally reserved for social and community activities; it is usually considered very bad form to work for individual profit on this day. Villagers note that party-elected chairmen cannot enforce observance of chisi, while a village head has traditional backing to do so. Christians are said to have been 'a particular problem' with respect to *Chisi* observance.

[18] An almost universal need expressed by village heads was to have documentation of the various legal codes, instruments, rules and regulations they were supposed to implement or enforce in conjunction with those identified who fell outside the realm of their authority.

between the concept of power and the notion of responsibility, but the listing is not a bad representation of the duties of village heads as set out in the TLA.[19] It is striking that enforcement of rules relating to the conservation of natural resources is the second most important power listed. The remainder of the chapter addresses this theme in greater detail.

Table 5.1
Domains of perceived authority I

Village heads' perceptions as to their most important powers	Percentage of responses (n=117)
Solve conflicts/mediate disputes/adjudicate	15.5
Ensure conservation of natural resources	11.8
Discipline/control/punish/expel/fine rule- and lawbreakers	10.9
Deal with welfare-related problems in village	10.0
Allocate land/advise/enforce compliance/collaborate with headman	8.2
Collect and forward taxes to the authorities	8.2
Maintain peace/order/harmony in the community	7.3
Initiate/oversee development projects	5.5
Represent/speak for village people/liaise with agencies	5.5
Call and chair meetings	4.5
Ensure observance of customary practices and rituals	4.5
Overall jurisdiction of village/power to appoint new committee	3.6
Serve as a conduit for all information about the village	1.8
Look after any visitors	1.8
Make sure that all the people support ZANU-PF	0.9

Source: Responses of forty village heads in four resettlement areas across three provinces.

Before continuing, however, brief attention needs to be drawn to the mechanisms village heads have at their disposal for exercising their powers. Table 5.2 sets out the responses to a question exploring how village heads seek consensus and enforce judgments. Surprisingly, as a village assembly is mandated in the TLA for all villages, one-quarter of village heads reported that no assembly has been established. Over eighty per cent of responses, however, show that there is a village court, which is not called for in the TLA. Although caution must be applied in interpreting the answer, a remarkable degree of consensus is reported by village heads for villagers' agreement with the regulations enforced within the village.

---

[19] It is noteworthy that only one response was received that pointed to the interests of ZANU-PF as paramount.

Table 5.2
Existence of administrative and enforcement mechanisms

	Positive responses (per cent)
Is there a village court in the village?	8.1
Is there a village assembly in the village?	7.4
Are village 'laws'/regulations agreed by the villagers themselves?	7.4

Source: Responses of thirty-eight village heads in four resettlement areas across three provinces.

Managing the commons in resettlement areas

The tenurial changes that accompanied creation of the resettlement programme mean that RAs face particular problems in managing their commons. Principal among them is the challenge of creating a sense of stewardship among tenants on state land. In addition, however, there are a host of other issues (for example, land allocation, cultural heterogeneity, village planning and layout, inheritance of land rights, and intrusions of resource users from other tenure domains) that bedevil conservation efforts in RAs. Moreover, the success of many RAs in permitting their occupants to acquire very substantial cattle herds threatens reserved grazing areas, even were outsiders to cease encroaching in these areas. This section addresses selected themes relating to identity and resource use in the commons of RAs and the way in which village heads attempt to be active in ensuring sustainable resource-use patterns.

The physical layout of RAs with centralised villages and large expanses of uninhabited land surrounding villages both fosters relatively strong senses of village identity and renders difficult the monitoring of resource use across a wide landscape. Even though villagers lack a sense of ownership of the land (but see further discussion on this point below), over the years they tend to have developed a strong sense of who has use rights for what they identify as their village's resources. Indeed, in Mutanda there have been pitched battles (resulting in at least one death) as a consequence of those with no recognised rights beginning to cultivate in defined grazing areas. By way of illustrating the relationship between social identity and use rights, Table 5.3 reports perceptions about the utilisation of the resource base in various ways by those identified as 'outsiders' in terms of villagers' own social identity.

Table 5.3
Social identities and access to common pool resources I

	Positive responses (per cent)
Does the village have its own woodland/grazing area distinct from those of other villages?	97.4
Do 'outsiders' cut trees without permission?	87.2
Do 'outsiders' graze livestock in the grazing area without permission?	79.5
Do 'outsiders' cultivate in the grazing area without permission?	20.5
Do 'outsiders' from other areas ever seek permission to cut trees or graze cattle?	18.9

Source: Responses of forty village heads in four resettlement areas across three provinces.

Only one village head reported that his village had no areas villagers identified as distinctively reserved for their own use for grazing or sourcing wood for building or fuel. Otherwise, all villages were said to possess such areas reserved for common use by the villagers. It is clear that people from outside the villages commonly make use of both woodland and grazing areas. Although permission is sought for such use at times, by far most of this resource use is done, blatantly or surreptitiously, without permission from the village. The practice of cultivating in the grazing area is a problem in only one area, Mutanda, where a particular chief has been sending his people from the communal area into the RA to settle 'illegally' for years.

Conflicts over use of common pool resources are not, of course, limited solely to those between insiders and outsiders. Those entitled to utilise the resources are just as capable of damaging the environment as are those without recognised rights. In principle, the regulations governing the resettlement programme impose limits on the number of cattle a household can keep in an RA; however, in practice these regulations have never been enforced.[20] Village heads are somewhat ambivalent about cattle numbers in their areas. Something over half of them believe that villagers should be able to keep as many cattle as they wish in the village grazing area, whether these cattle belong to villagers or come from outside the scheme (see Table 5.4). Those who responded negatively to this question were almost certainly well aware of the environmental consequences of overstocking, while those who responded positively no doubt viewed with distaste the prospect that they might be assigned some official role in what would be a very unpopular de-stocking exercise.

There was a stronger consensus in response to the questions about entitlements to use trees and their products. It is surprising, however, that the

---

[20] For an indication of the way in which cattle numbers have grown since resettlement began, see Kinsey, Burger and Gunning 1998.

proportion of positive responses is so high for trees growing in arable lands and that it is not higher for trees growing on the homestead, where one would have expected exclusive use-rights for the homesteader. While trees that have been planted are usually regarded as private property, trees growing naturally in fields have almost always been associated with semi-communal use-rights.

Table 5.4
Social identities and access to common pool resources II

	Positive responses (per cent)
Should people be allowed to keep as many of their own cattle as they wish in the village's grazing area?	57.9
Should people be allowed to keep as many cattle belonging to people from outside the village as they wish in the village's grazing area?	57.9
Does the household head have sole control of all the trees growing on his arable lands?	68.4
Does the household head have sole control of all the trees growing on his residential stand?	77.8

Source: Responses of forty village heads in four resettlement areas across three provinces.

Table 5.5
Autonomy and control of resources

Where do those 'outsiders' who cut wood, graze livestock and cultivate land come from?	Percentage of responses (n=74)
From communal area villages	44.6
Both communal and resettlement areas	21.6
This resettlement area, another village	16.2
Another resettlement area	5.4
Illegal settlers from communal areas	5.4
Gold panners [area of origin unknown or not disclosed]	2.7
Other	2.7
Purchase areas	1.4

Source: Responses of forty village heads in four resettlement areas across three provinces

The majority of the 'outsiders' who encroach on the village resource base come from nearby communal areas and may well be former neighbours of those who now reside in the RAs (Table 5.5). At least a fifth of the outsiders accessing resources from within the village's domain are identified as coming from a resettlement area, either the RA where the respondent lives, or another one. This fact is one indication that the RAs are not uniformly endowed with the full set of resources necessary to support a completely rural livelihood.

When encroachment and resource misappropriation take place on a village's land, under the TLA it is the responsibility of the village assembly rather than the village head to deal with the matter. Nevertheless, it is the head to whom most resource abuse is reported (see Table 5.6). Two resource 'abuses' are not consistently reported. One of these is when people expand the arable land originally allocated to them by clearing additional land. This practice is symptomatic of one or both of two things. First, highly successful farmers have learned to cope with more land than they were originally given. Such success is highly admirable; many will wish to emulate it, and so they will not report those who do it – who may now be relatively rich and powerful in any event. Second, families have grown over the two-plus decades they have been in the RAs. The problem of having adult sons who need land to farm is commonplace, and increasingly clearing additional land is the way land is provided.[21] Subdivision of a person's original arable land has always been forbidden, but it is not clear which is the more risky route to providing land to male children: Clearing or sub-division. From an environmental perspective, both practices are likely to be equally unsustainable.

Table 5.6
Domains of perceived authority II

Events reported to me, the village head, as the appropriate authority	Positive responses (per cent)
When outsiders are cutting trees in the woodlands/grazing area	80.0
When someone is cultivating in the grazing area	82.4
When people from the village are extending their fields	57.1
When people do things that cause erosion	77.8
When people are working for profit on *chisi* day	52.8

Source: Responses of forty village heads in four resettlement areas across three provinces.

Despite the fact that responsibility for overseeing resource use is not explicitly assigned to village heads by the TLA, they do nevertheless address violations in certain limited ways. Table 5.7 indicates the actions taken in response to violations of resource-use regulations. The most common response is a vague one that involves some unspecified action on the part of the village head and then reporting the wrongdoer to an appropriate official. In just under half the cases, the village head reportedly deals with the

21 There is no empirical evidence of which I am aware that indicates whether or not the fast-track resettlement that began in 2000 has helped to meet the demand for land by sons of the first generation of post-independence settlers.

offence by publicly shaming the guilty party.[22] In under one-fifth of cases is a fine imposed. Slightly less than two-thirds of the village heads interviewed reported that the villagers normally support their decisions or actions in dealing with violations involving natural resources.

Table 5.7
Village heads' declared methods of dealing with violations involving natural resources

Action applied by the village head to the guilty party/parties	Percentage of responses
Impose a fine	17.1
Shame the wrongdoer in public	45.7
Take my own individual action and then report them to an official	76.5

Source: Responses of thirty-eight village heads in four resettlement areas across three provinces.

The TLA assigns to village heads the duties of dealing with boundary disputes for grazing and agricultural land (Article 12e) and ensuring that land is utilised in accordance with resolutions in force for the use and occupation of resettlement land (Article 12g). This latter duty compels the village head to enforce the conditions of use stipulated in the system of permits adopted in the early 1980s (and still in force) that governs land use in Ras.[23] The concluding part of this section looks at how well these assigned responsibilities are recognised and understood by the village heads.

Three sets of normative questions were asked of village heads relating to who decides who can use the village woodlands or grazing areas, who can allow a villager to extend his or her arable land, and who can make the decision to allow a villager to rent part of his or her arable land for cash. The responses of the village heads are arrayed in Tables 5.8 to 5.10.

Considering that nearly two-thirds of the village heads interviewed had recently been trained in the duties of their new posts, the range of responses to the questions posed was enormously wide. In Table 5.8, for example, fourteen distinct responses were received to the question about where the authority lies to grant use-rights to woodlands and grazing areas. The most common response makes it a collective responsibility, either for the village head and assembly or village development committee. Just under a fifth felt

---

[22] This response is puzzling. Public shaming is a treatment likely to be truly effective only when the miscreant comes from within the community, suggesting that a high proportion of offenders are not 'outsiders'.

[23] This is despite the fact that the Government Printer ran out of stock of the permits in the early 1990s, and they ceased to be issued for years. It is not known whether they are currently being issued.

it was the duty of the village head acting alone. A surprising number of answers invoked the authority of one or other officials, mostly various civil servants, a set of answers that may be a carry-over from the way RAs were managed before the TLA came into force.

Table 5.8
Decision-making powers I

Who should decide who may or may not use the village woodlands or grazing areas?	Percentage of responses (n=37)
The village head and the villagers/VIDCO/village assembly	26.3
The village head	18.4
The villagers/VIDCO	18.4
The chief	5.3
Village head and committee members	5.3
Village heads and village chairpersons	5.3
Ministry of Lands through a local official	2.6
Officials from the Ministries of Agriculture and Local Government	2.6
Resettlement officials	2.6
The village assembly	2.6
VIDCO and officials from the Ministry of Agriculture	2.6
Village head, chief and councilor	2.6
Village head, chief, DA, and officials from Ministry of Agriculture	2.6
Villagers after consultation with the Ministry	2.6

Source: Interviews with forty village heads in four resettlement areas across three provinces.

The second question addressed not so much use-rights as such as the manner in which a particular resource – in this case arable land – may be used (Table 5.9). The pressure on resettled farmers to extend their arable land has been noted above. Nevertheless, for years such extensions were deemed ‘illegal’, and extending one’s fields was even supposed to be grounds for eviction from the resettlement scheme. Certainly, the practice was commonly reported to the Natural Resources Board during the 1980s, although no instances are known where the reports resulted in eviction or, indeed, in any other response at all.[24]

The most common response – village head, chief and extension officer – reflects an interesting marriage of the old and the new systems. The need for a technocratic input from the agriculture ministry is recognised, as is that for local knowledge – the village head. Invoking the authority of the chief recognises that chiefs now again have responsibility for the areas they lost as long ago as the 1930s. Further, it acknowledges that under the TLA chiefs

[24] Agricultural extension staff in Mupfurudzi, Mutanda, and Sengesi gave up reporting violations to the NRB as required because in not a single case was there ever any follow-up by the Board.

are charged with preventing unauthorized uses of land (Article 5h) and controlling over-cultivation (Article 5i). In practice, however, chiefs preside over areas far too large for them ever to be able to participate directly in a decision of this nature, and they delegate it to the headman or the village head.

The equal second most common responses are completely divergent. The one views the decision entirely as that of the village head, and the other sees it purely as a technocratic decision to be made by staff of the ministry dealing with agriculture. The remaining answers to this question are scattered so widely as to defy coherent analysis.[25]

Table 5.9
Decision-making powers II

Who should decide about allowing a villager to extend his/her arable land?	Percentage of responses (n=38)
Village head, chief and extension officer	34.2
The village head	10.5
Ministry of Lands and Agriculture/the extension officer	10.5
No permission is given for extending lands, N/A	5.3
The councilor	5.3
Village head and committee members	5.3
VIDCO and the councilor	2.6
Village head, chief, councillor and extension officer	2.6
The chief	2.6
Chief and village council of elders	2.6
Chief and village head	2.6
Resettlement officials	2.6
Resettlement officials or extension officer	2.6
The DA	2.6
The DA and the extension officer	2.6
The DA and the village head	2.6
The village assembly	2.6

Source: Interviews with forty village heads in four resettlement areas across three provinces.

Finally, and potentially most contentious, is the question about renting part of one's arable fields in the RA for a cash return. Yet it is precisely here that the strongest consensus emerges (Table 5.10). Nearly sixty per cent of village heads' responses indicate that such decisions are for the plot-holder alone to make. What is more, this proportion rises above two-thirds if account is taken of the responses that state the plot-holder can decide so long as he/she advises others of his/her decision. This pattern offers clear support

[25] Nevertheless, the invention of a new body, the 'village council of elders' reported in Table 5.9, is a remarkable innovation for the RAs.

for the idea that rights to use farmland in resettlement areas are both individual and non-transitory in nature, something contrary to the message preached by resettlement officers for two decades. The response that renting land is not allowed is an interesting surviving artefact from that earlier period.

Table 5.10
Decision-making powers III

Who should decide about allowing a villager to rent part of his/her arable land for cash?	Percentage of responses (n=39)
The individual plot-holder alone	57.9
The village head	13.2
The individual plot-holder after notifying/consulting with the village head	10.5
Renting out land is not allowed here	5.3
The chief	2.6
The individual plot-holder after letting others know	2.6
The individual plot-holder with ministry permission	2.6
The individual plot-holder, who should inform the village head and the chief	2.6
The village head, who in turn reports to the chief	2.6

Source: Interviews with forty village heads in four resettlement areas across three provinces.

This section has examined the implementation of the TLA in resettlement areas. It has done so by describing, first, how the new village heads were selected and variations in the selection procedures used in different parts of the country. It then looked briefly at the training given – or not – to the new village heads. Noting that village heads perceive management of natural resources to be among their most important responsibilities, attention then turned to a set of issues relating to common pool resources in RAs. The focus here, however, has been almost entirely on the perceptions of village heads. The concluding section will widen this perspective by incorporating other viewpoints.

Early outcomes from implementing the Traditional Leaders Act

The primary source of empirical data heretofore has been a set of interviews with forty village leaders in RAs in different parts of the country. This section looks more broadly at the social context in which the TLA has been introduced by drawing on the views of those who live in the RA villages where the TLA has sought to change the leadership.

Although this chapter addresses only the implementation of the TLA in resettlement areas, where it is particularly contentious for reasons already noted, the Act has been controversial for broader reasons. Some of the controversy arises from questions about the true motives behind the Act. Recent press reports, for example, have chastised chiefs, headmen and village heads for not remaining strictly apolitical and suggested that, since they have played no meaningful role in governance since the advent of colonialism, it is time for them to go.[26] Other press reports nevertheless make it very clear just how far ZANU-PF is prepared to go to ensure that chiefs do not remain apolitical (*The Herald* 2004; Kwinika 2004; Mugari 2004; Sibanda 2004).

There are those who argue nevertheless that the TLA may mark a positive end to a long historical cycle of empowering and disempowering traditional leadership. Campbell, Mukamuri, and Sithole (1998), among many others, have noted that the post-independence imposition of new local bodies, such as VIDCOs, created institutional conflicts while replacing many of the roles of traditional leadership with structures that had little real ability to maintain control over resource use. Consequently, local 'traditional' rules were weakened and the resource base collapsed. The basic argument here is that the imposed institutions lost control of the land and resources because they lost the people. Campbell, Mukamuri, and Sithole see the measures in the TLA as potentially a genuine marriage of the best in both traditional and modern systems.

Mandondo (2001) has also argued that widespread lack of respect for imposed by-laws, as well as poor enforcement and high default rates in the payment of fines, point to 'long established traditional jurisdictions' as potentially appropriate units for resource management. He observes the close correspondence between the Traditional Leaders Act and the conclusion of the Land Tenure Commission (Zimbabwe 1994) that traditional villages, under village heads, are the legitimate and appropriate units for natural resource management below the district level. He expresses caution however that:

> (…) [T]he call for new approaches to governance appears based on the unstated assumption that old is undesirable 'because we have seen it not working' and that new will work better 'because we have not seen it failing anywhere'. Thus, placing governance powers closer to citizens should not automatically imply that new arrangements will be more egalitarian and work better. Neither should it be seen as a call for a total return to community because communities, councils and the state have become intricately interwoven (Mandondo 2001).

---

26 See, for example, *Zimbabwe Independent* March 7, 2003 and Musa (2003).

The TLA is also controversial in the resettlement communities being examined here. Discussions in these communities generated a wide set of viewpoints as to the merits and demerits of the alternative ways of selecting village leadership – by open and democratic elections or through appointment via a hierarchical traditional system. The main points emerging from these discussions are summarised in the text box below.[27]

Villagers clearly liked the democratic aspects of electing village chairmen and preferred a system where anyone could stand; and they could select whomsoever they liked. They also cited neutrality and impartiality as inherent in this system and felt the elected chairman was a unifying force for the village. Proponents of the traditional system, in contrast, slated elections for creating chaos and causing 'instability' in leadership. Curiously, given colonial history and more recent events, they also tended to see a more traditional system as insurance against excessive politicisation and hence inherently more representative. And they liked the fact that the new leaders were being trained.

The lack of training was an acknowledged shortcoming of the village chairman system,[28] but most of the negatives put forward about village chairmen relate to their perceived lack of competence in dealing with matters relating to traditional rituals and customs. The major category of shortcomings of the traditional system on the other hand relate to the fact that leadership comes from a particular lineage, leading to a rigid, exclusive, and undemocratic pattern of leadership. Concerns were also expressed indicating that people had doubts about how well the system would work in resettlement areas with their very different histories and physical layout.

Following the implementation of the Traditional Leaders Act, over a number of years it has been made possible to observe not only some of the processes involved but also a number of outcomes. Among the most surprising of the latter has been the way the Act has resulted in substantial fission among communities in RAs. It would appear that yet one more

---

27 It must be noted that discussants not infrequently failed to distinguish between party political chairmen in villages and apolitical village chairmen. In some instances, of course, these posts were held by the same individual, but normally this was not the case. The confusion may then arise because of doubt as to who is the village's 'true' representative.

28 The absence of training for village leadership was one of many oversights in the resettlement programme. As noted by Chidhakwa (2001), the transition from state to local control and management has remained so purely rhetorical because, in practice, the control and command approach is what is primarily discernible on the ground. He observes that terms like *community participation*, *local empowerment*, and *decentralisation* are loosely used (in the face of reduced budgets for state institutions) but in reality have never been translated into practice.

Perceived pros and cons of alternative village leadership models

Elected chairmen/women

Pros:

- Much development took place during the era of the chairmen
- Flexible and modern in their approach – unresolved issues were taken to neutral civil servants, the resettlement officers
- Inherently democratic – anyone can be elected, younger men and 'even women'
- Impartial and deal fairly with everyone – don't favour relatives and friends
- Act as a unifying force in the village

Cons:

- Chairmen were never trained in leadership and did as they pleased
- 'Strangers' are not the best people to oversee the affairs of a community having a traditional claim to a particular area of land
- Incompetent to deal with traditional issues and rituals, e.g. rain-making
- Cannot enforce observance of traditional customs (e.g., *chisi*)
- Dominated by ZANU-PF. Confusion between the roles of village chairmen and village party chairmen – party-imposed chairmen's decisions are not respected
- Older people not 'at ease' listening to young party people
- Valued customs were being lost

'Traditional' village heads

Pros:

- New village heads are being trained, unlike their predecessors
- Promotes stability since village heads cannot be removed 'willy nilly'. Permanence enhances stability
- Will eliminate disorderly settlement by squatters
- Village heads can raise taxes and impose levies
- 'There is no reason a woman cannot serve'
- The village head will represent everyone unlike a chairman elected on a 'party ticket'

Cons:

- Exclusion of Christians
- Exclusion of those not of the same totem as the village head
- Rivalry over who should be village head will generate long-term inter-kin-group frictions
- Inheritance of headship is inherently undemocratic and 'frightening'
- Creates an inflexible hierarchy of authority, with the chief's ruling final
- Haphazard allocation of residential stands
- Destruction of reserved grazing areas
- Favouritism resulting from extra powers vested in the village heads (e.g., composition of village courts)
- Younger men cannot serve as village heads since they do not have land

Note: The points in the text box above are either direct quotations or close paraphrases of statements made in informal group discussion meetings or by village leadership respondents in discussion surrounding their formal interviews.

upheaval in rural institutional structures has been more than many in RAs could tolerate.

In essence, what has happened is that, instead of unifying village leadership, the TLA has divided it up into factions – in some cases functional, in others disputatious. Villages therefore have so far been unable to reconcile some of the more powerful divergent perspectives hinted at above. Many resettled villagers express a compelling preference to continue to deal with the established chairman: He was elected and 'he has been there a long time'.[29] In contrast, not only is the village head new, but he was also imposed by the chief; and many people in RAs feel no obligation to the traditional authority.[30] A further point expressed by many is that, in cases where the village chairman is also a party official, the party linkages provide more benefits that do traditional institutions. It appears then that villagers' perceptions of benefits are shaping their choice of leadership model; multiple models are currently at work simultaneously, each perhaps being consciously weighed against the others to see which generates the most benefit.

The manifestation of this process is that many 'villages' now have two leaders, and in some cases three. First, the previously democratically elected village chairman has taken over as village head. Second, the 'old chairman-new head' co-exists with the new, imposed traditional village head. And, finally, the elected party chairman, who is perceived as the village chair in charge of party issues acts in cases as village leader. Villages that have multiple leaderships have in some instances physically split into factions – and 'sub-villages' – along leadership lines. Each of these separate 'sub-villages' claims to have its own independent leadership and, in some cases, each also now claims to be under a different chief.

In some cases, the imposed village head, the party chair, and the old village chairman tend to work together as a sort of *ad hoc* village management committee; in others, they do not cooperate at all. Some sort of functional specialisation appears to be emerging, with villagers calling on different leadership fractions for different purposes, although this is only a tentative and incomplete trend. People in RAs are still more comfortable with the elected heads, so they tend to avoid the imposed traditional head, even in matters that normally require the authority and powers of a traditional head. It is then said to be up to the elected head to consult with the imposed one to ensure that activities requiring a customary interpretation are given the appropriate attention.

---

[29] This may be one representation of dissent about proposals 'from above', as suggested by Ranger (1993).

[30] In one village in Mayo, the people refused to support the candidates who were put up for election, and the village chair had to become the village head.

Conclusion

The Traditional Leaders Act attempts to (re)create authority to manage Zimbabwe's rural areas. Will the Act live up to its imagined potential? While the Act is politically suspect to some and a potential blessing for resource conservation to others, the early experience with its implementation in the older established resettlement areas has been marked by confusion and resentment. Early outcomes are indicative of the unacceptability of imposed forms of leadership in areas where a full generation has experienced democratically elected local leadership. In these areas, there is peasant resistance not only to the more obvious forms of statist imposition but also to the entire apparatus of 'bogus traditionalism' (Ranger 1993: 382). Resolution of the kinds of intra-village tensions that have emerged in RAs over the last several years is clearly necessary, especially if villages are to exercise effective control over their own resources. Nevertheless, it should not be forgotten that what to some observers appears to be chaos is also the way in which civil society in resettlement areas is sending a message about the kind of leadership it wants.

References

BARR, A. (2000a) *An experimental approach to the analysis of informal institutions*, paper presented at the Conference on Institutional Reform and the Informal Sector, University of Maryland (February 2000).

BARR, A. (2000b) *Familiarity and trust: An experimental investigation*, paper presented at the Conference on Opportunities in Africa: Micro-evidence on Firms and Households, 9-10 April 2000, Centre for the Study of African Economies, St. Catherine's College, University of Oxford.

BARR, A. (2000c) *Trust, reciprocity, and land reform: An experimental investigation*, paper presented at St. Johns College, University of Cambridge (May 2000). [Available from: http://csae.ox.ac.uk].

BARR, A. (2001) *Social dilemmas and shame-based sanctions: Experimental results from rural Zimbabwe*, Working Paper Series No. 2001-11, Oxford: Centre for the Study of African Economies, University of Oxford.

BARR, A. (2002a) *From strangers to neighbours: Identifying the preconditions for social capital development*, Research Report ESCOR R7650, Oxford: Centre for the Study of African Economies, University of Oxford.

BARR, A. (2002b) *Risk pooling and the depth of poverty in resettlement areas of Zimbabwe*, Paper presented at the conference on Understanding Poverty and Growth in Sub-Saharan Africa, Oxford: Centre for the Study of African Economies, Oxford University, March 18-19 2002. [Available at: http://csae.ox.ac.uk].

BARR, A. (2003a) Trust and expected trustworthiness: Experimental evidence from Zimbabwean villages, *The Economic Journal*, 113(489): 614-30.

BARR, A. (2003b) *Risk pooling, commitment and information: An experimental test of two fundamental assumptions*, Working Paper Series 2003-05, Oxford: Centre for the Study of African Economies, University of Oxford.

BARR, A. (2004) Forging effective new communities: The evolution of civil society in Zimbabwean resettled villages, *World Development*, 32(10): 1753-66.

BARR, A. (forthcoming) Kinship, familiarity and trust: An experimental investigation, forthcoming in: Henrich, J. *et al.* (Eds) *Foundations of human sociality: Experiments in 15 small-scale societies* (compiled under the McArthur Foundation's project on Cross-Cultural Experimental Economics).

BRAND, C. (1991) Will decentralization enhance local participation?, in: Helmsing, A.H. *et al.*, *Limits to decentralization in Zimbabwe: Essays on the decentralization of government and planning in the 1980s*, The Hague: Institute of Social Studies, pp. 79-96.

CAMPBELL, B.M., B.B. MUKAMURI and B. SITHOLE (1998) *Managing sacred woodlands in Zimbabwe, The World Bank/World Bank Institute's community based Natural Resource Management Initiative*, [http://srdis.ciesin.columbia.edu/cases/zimbabwe-010.html], Last accessed: January 2004.

CHIDHAKWA, Z. (2001) *Continuity and change: The role and dynamics of traditional institutions in the management of the Haroni and Rusitu forests in Chimanimani, Zimbabwe*, paper presented at the CASS/PLAAS CBNRM 3rd Regional Workshop, October 8-9, 2001, Maputo, Mozambique.

CORNWALL, A., and J. GAVENTA (2000) From users and choosers to makers and shapers: Repositioning participation in social policy, *IDS Bulletin*, 31(4): 50-61.

CUDDEFORD, V. (2002) *Communities revive a traditional method of storing grain in times of need*, Package 62, no. 7, January 2002, Ontario: Developing Countries Farm Radio Network [www.farmradio.org/english/scripts/62-7.php].

DAILY NEWS [Zimbabwe] (2004) Chiefs intimidate voters, 3 February 2004.

DEKKER, M. (2002) *On bridewealth and household security in rural Zimbabwe*, paper presented at the conference: Understanding Poverty and Growth in Sub-Saharan Africa, Centre for the Study of African Economies, Oxford University, March 18-19 2002 [Available at: http://csae.ox.ac.uk].

DEKKER, M. (2004a) *Risk, resettlement and relations: Social security in rural Zimbabwe*, Tinbergen Institute Research Series No. 331, Amsterdam: The Tinbergen Institute and the Free University Amsterdam.

DEKKER, M. (2004b) Sustainability and resourcefulness: Social support networks during periods of stress, *World Development*, 32(10): 1735-51.

FINANCIAL GAZETTE [Zimbabwe] (2003) Chiefs demand long-awaited service vehicles, 8 May 2003.

GOVERNMENT OF ZIMBABWE (1994) *Report of the Commission of Inquiry into appropriate agricultural land tenure systems*, Harare: Government Printer.

GOVERNMENT OF ZIMBABWE (1998) *Traditional Leaders Act* [Chapter 29: 17] No. 25/98,Harare: Government Printer.

HAMMAR, A. (2001) Speaking with space: Displacement and claims in the politics of land in Zimbabwe, in: Webster, N. and Engbeg-Pedersen, L. (Eds) *In the name of the poor. Contesting political space for poverty reduction*, London and New York: Zed Books, pp. 129-56.

HAMMAR, A. (2003) The making and unma(s)king of local government in Zimbabwe, in: Hammar, A., Raftopoulos, B. and Jensen, S. (Eds) *Zimbabwe's unfinished business: Rethinking land, state and nation in the context of crisis*, Harare: Weaver Press, pp. 119-54.

THE HERALD [Zimbabwe] (2004) Chiefs get hefty allowances, 20 April.

KINSEY, B., K. BURGER. AND J.W. GUNNING (1998) Coping with drought in Zimbabwe: Survey evidence on responses of rural households to risk, *World Development*, 26(1): 89-110.

KWINIKA, S. (2004) Zanu PF targets chiefs in Lupane campaign, *Zimbabwe Standard*, 29 February.

MANDONDO, A. (2001) Allocation of governmental authority and responsibility in tiered governance regimes: The case of the Chivi Rural District Council land use planning and conservation by-laws, *African Studies Quarterly*, 5(3) [http://web.africa.ufl.edu/asq/v5/ v5i3a3.htm]. Last accessed: February 2004.

MUGARI, S. (2004) Chiefs' benefits to gobble up $27,5b, *Zimbabwe Independent*, 15 May.

MUKARO, A. (2004) Traditional leaders win Zanu PF Gutu North, *Zimbabwe Independent,* 6 February.

MUNRO, W.A. (1998) *The moral economy of the state: Conservation, community development and state making in Zimbabwe*, Athens, Ohio: Ohio Center for International Studies, Ohio University.

MUSA, V. (2003) Time to do away with traditional leaders, *Daily News* [Zimbabwe], 28 April.

MUTANGADURA, G. (2000) The smallholder agricultural sector's response to HIV/AIDS, *Sexual Health Exchange*: 3.

MUTIZWA-MANGIZA, N. (1991) Decentralisation and local government administration: An analysis of structural and planning problems at the rural district level, in: Helmsing, A.H. *et al.* (Eds) *Limits to decentralization in Zimbabwe: Essays on the decentralization of government and planning in the 1980s*, The Hague: Institute of Social Studies, pp. 51-78.

PHIRI, S.N., M. NZIMA and G. FOSTER (2000) *Expanding and strengthening community action: A study to explore ways to scale up effective, sustainable community mobilization interventions to mitigate the impact of HIV/AIDS on children and families*, Harare: Unesco [http://www.harare.unesco.org/hivaids/webfiles/Electronicper cent 20Versions/ Expandingper cent 20andper cent 20Strengtheningper cent 20Communityper cent 20Action.doc], last accessed: February 2004.

RANGER, T. (1993) The communal areas of Zimbabwe, in: Bassett, T.J. and Crummey, D.E. (Eds) *Land in African agrarian systems*, Madison, Wisconsin: University of Wisconsin Press, pp. 354-85.

RUGEGE, S. (2001) *The institution of traditional leadership and its relation with elected local government*, paper presented at the Colloquium Constitution and Law IV, 26 October 2001, Potchefstroom University, Faculty of Law, Johannesburg: Konrad-Adenauer-Stiftung, pp. 3-26, [www.kas.org.za/Publications/SeminarReports/Constitutionper cent 20andper cent 20Lawper cent 20iv/rugege.pdf].

SIBANDA, D. (2004) Concept of chieftainship restored, *Chronicle*, 23 April.

SPIERENBURG, M. (2003) *Strangers, spirits and land reforms: Conflicts about land in Dande, Northern Zimbabwe*, Amsterdam: Amsterdamse School voor Sociaal Wetenschappelijk Onderzoek, University of Amsterdam.

SUNDAY MAIL [Zimbabwe] (2001) Chiefs have a role in land distribution, 22 April.

SUNDAY MIRROR [Zimbabwe] (2003) Smallholder farmers switch to drought resistant crops, 5 October.

SUNDAY MIRROR [Zimbabwe] (2004) Zanu PF accused of dirty tactics in Gutu North, 25 January.

WORLD BANK (2000) *Dynamic risk management and the poor: Developing a social protection strategy for Africa* (draft), Human Development Group, Africa Region, Washington, D.C.: The World Bank.

ZIMBABWE INDEPENDENT (2003) Traditional chiefs or Zanu PF agents?, 7 March.

ZIMBABWE INDEPENDENT (2004) Traditional leaders win Zanu PF Gutu North, 6 February.

ZIMBABWE STANDARD (2002) Leave with your food, chief tells donors, 27 November.

ZINISA (2003) Save the Children revives zunde ramambo in the valley, *Emergency Preparedness Bulletin*, no. 16, Harare: Zimbabwe Network for Informal Settlement Action (ZINISA).

6

First-comers and late-comers: The role of narratives in land claims

Carola Lentz

Introduction

Rights to land are intimately tied to membership of specific communities, be this the nuclear or extended family, the larger descent group (clan), the ethnic group, or, as is the case in modern property regimes, the nation-state. Membership in these groups, however, is not a 'given', irrefutable fact, but contested and negotiable. Land rights are therefore intimately linked to struggles associated with power, history, and social boundaries, as a number of recent studies have shown (cf. Berry 2001; Chauveau 2000; Juul and Lund 2002; Lentz 2003a). Claiming membership of the group of first-comers to an area is the most widespread strategy to legitimate land rights in West Africa, much as it is in the rest of the continent (Kopytoff 1989), since first-comers are believed to have established a special relationship with the spirits of the land. These pioneers and their descendants often allocate land to later immigrants, grant the right to build houses and bury their dead, and mediate in conflicts over territorial boundaries and land use. In many cases, they consider themselves to be the allodial owners of the land, or, to be more precise, custodians for the ultimate owners, namely the ancestors and spirits of the land (cf. Schoffeleers 1979; Spierenburg 2001; Zwernemann 1968). However, first-comer claims are far from unambiguous. What is considered to be the 'pivotal event' (Murphy and Bledsoe 1989: 124-5) that determines who is recognised as a first-comer is open to debate. Furthermore, delineating the territorial and social reach of the group to claim first-comer status entails further room for manoeuvre.

In all of this, narratives, which relate the migration of one's ancestors into the area, explain the establishment of the new settlement and track subsequent property transactions, play a decisive role. In conflicts over land or political allegiance connected with land ownership, contestants inevitably present different versions of the settlement history to buttress their respective interests. Even under modern property regimes, narratives, like those presented in court cases, are crucial to legitimating one's claims. Although, coercion and physical violence certainly played, and in some areas continue to play, an important role in gaining access to land, as did (and do) 'extra-legal' mechanisms like trickery and material wealth (Ribot and Peluso 2003), the ritual appropriation of new territories – and, along with them, property rights – such as that effected through the transfer of earth shrines or rain cults from the earlier inhabitants to the newcomers, was of equal importance. Such transfers were necessarily accompanied by the narration of 'good stories' (Jacob 2002; 2003). Because long-term uninterrupted use of landed resources cannot rely on violence and coercion alone, the situation requires strengthening one's claims to access by building consensus and gaining recognition – that is, by establishing property (Lund 2002: 12-13). Moreover, law and property are in themselves important sources of power and can establish power differentials.

It is important, then, to look at property as a 'bundle of powers', as Katherine Verdery (1998: 161) proposes. But we should also explore the ways in which images of community and legitimate ownership provide 'a vocabulary of legitimation for requests to be made and pressure to be exerted' (Li 1996: 509). More generally, property rights reflect power relations, but also need to be strengthened by 'persuasion', as the historian of law Carol Rose (1994) has succinctly argued. It is exactly because property narratives help to persuade and to build consensus that they are important. Yet narratives are also crucial to articulating challenges to existing property rights and in helping to 'define alternatives' (Fortmann 1995: 1054).

Drawing on material from my own research on mobility, property rights, and the politics of belonging in North-western Ghana and South-Western Burkina Faso, the chapter will explore the role of narratives in stating, defending, and contesting land claims. I will begin with a brief outline of some of the ambiguities that are typical of 'traditional' land tenure in Africa, that is, land rights in a dominantly oral context, without cadastres, land surveys and written titles. It is these ambiguities that make narratives so indispensable: They specify particular claims and convince others of one's claim to specific property rights. After some remarks regarding the empirical basis of my argument and the presentation of an example of how property narratives are brought to bear on current land conflicts, I will analyse the repertoire of admissible arguments and images as well as the criteria that define a 'good' story. Finally, I will look at the institutional settings in which property narratives are validated and discuss how social networks and political interests influence the competition between different property narratives and the settlement of land claims. In this chapter, then, I aim to combine a political-economy approach, which takes into consideration power relations in a broader context, with symbolic anthropology, which pays particular attention to the poetics of the narratives and the more subtle power exerted by metaphor and ritual.

The dynamics of African land tenure

Despite all the emphasis on the resilience of legal pluralism in land matters, 'customary' land tenure itself and, more specifically, the pre-colonial dynamics of property regimes have received relatively little attention in the recent literature on African land rights. Some policy-oriented studies still seem to share, albeit perhaps mainly for strategic reasons (Li 1996), the rather romanticist view of pre-colonial land tenure that early colonial officials developed in co-operation with African chiefs.[1] This perspective on indigenous land tenure was guided by the axioms that Africans associate land with deep religious meaning, that land is held for them in trust by the chiefs, and that land is ultimately inalienable. These rather 'naive' (though certainly not innocent) early conceptions of African land tenure, however, were soon revised and refined. By the mid-1940s, C.K. Meek (1946: 11-31), drawing on anthropological expertise, was able to present quite a nuanced picture of the complex web of interlocking communal and individual rights to land and customary practices of pledging, if not the outright 'selling' of land. Whether the insights of Meek and others actually changed colonial land policies premised on the axiom of inalienable 'communal tenure' is another matter,[2] but what interests me here is that even Meek, and the anthropologists of his time, continued to think of traditional land tenure in terms of a coherent, homogenous, and stable system of rules and beliefs. Legal pluralism (although this term was not yet used) was regarded as a result of the incorporation of traditional African societies into modern market economies and the colonial political order. The idea that Africans could have debated, and held conflicting views about property rights even before the advent of colonial rule, did not enter the minds of colonial officials and early scholars.

---

1 For a recent example of a rather simplistic view of 'customary' tenure, see Ensminger 1997: 168-70.

2 On the history of British land policies in West Africa, see Phillips 1989, ch. 4 and 6.

One of the first substantial criticism of European views of African land tenure was advanced by Paul Bohannan (1963) who argued that indigenous systems were the products not of Western grid-type maps made up of bounded pieces of land, but of a 'folk geography' based on a rather flexible, elastic map of social relations, characterised by 'short term farm tenure', a system that differed radically from Western notions of property. In Bohannan's view, the axiom of the communal ownership of village territory was an erroneous colonial translation of complex indigenous systems, but at least one that allowed local communities to continue their traditional practices of farm tenure. Elizabeth Colson took a less benign view of the colonial 'invention' of communal tenure, which was ultimately vested in the chiefs, and emphasised the problematic consequences of the transformation of land that was previously merely a community's 'territory or domain' into an 'economic holding', and of 'the confusion of sovereignty with proprietary ownership' (1971: 197-8). Later writers have taken Colson's criticism of colonial customary law further, arguing that the 'invention' of communal ownership of land was a product of collaboration between chiefs and colonial administrators that boosted the former's power and revenues while also serving European interests in land (cf. Coquery-Vidrovitch 1982; Chanock 1985; 1991). However, as Sara Berry (1992) has convincingly shown, the colonial codification of 'customary law' did not end the debates and conflicts, but rather institutionalised unceasing negotiations of and competition over chiefly hierarchies and the boundaries of property-holding communities.

Both images of the pre-colonial past – the colonial idea of inalienable, uncontested communal property held in trust by chiefs or earth priests, as well as Bohannan's and Colson's concept of ritual territories with flexible farm tenure without actual property rights (and hence similarly inalienable) – seem to be misleading, or, at the very least, grossly simplified. A number of studies have shown that at least since the early nineteenth century, land in agricultural frontier zones with emerging cash-crop economies increased enormously in value, and that land markets developed here (even Colson observed this much) (cf. Benjaminsen and Lund 2003; Ensminger 1997: 170-5; Lavigne Delville 1998: 119-22; Platteau 1996). Pre-colonial land transactions in 'backwater' savannah regions have, so far, received much less attention. The sources, of course, pose a problem, because there are virtually no written documents going back to that time. However, oral traditions, such as those from the Black Volta region of North-Western Ghana and South-Western Burkina Faso, do indeed testify to the importance pioneers attached to the material and ritual control of the new territories into which they moved, and relate a long history of contestation over whether earth shrines, which invest allodial property rights, can be transferred to newcomers or are always to remain the inalienable property of first-comers (cf. Kuba, Lentz and Werthmann 2001; Kuba and Lentz 2002).

More generally, the dominant paradigm that land in Africa was a free and plentiful good, that political control tended to be over people rather than over land and that Africans were indifferent to being rooted in physical space[3] needs to be reassessed. Competition over resources such as land, water, pasture, and trees, between 'first-comers' and 'late-comers' and between agriculturalists and pastoralists, sometimes articulated in the idiom of ethnic difference, seems to be a phenomenon of *longue durée.* It is, therefore, necessary to apply the concept of 'legal pluralism', of ambiguity, negotiability and the political embeddedness of land rights to the pre-colonial past as well.

Three basic features of indigenous tenure regimes allow for a variety of local interpretations and contestation, which are usually couched in the idiom of historical narrative. The first concerns the boundaries of the property-holding group, or the composition of the 'bundle of owners', as Geisler and Daneker (2000: xiii) aptly put it. Access to land was, and still is, mediated by membership in specific communities or groups, which is based on descent, shared histories of migration or flight, physical proximity, and political allegiance. The boundaries of these groups, however, were and continue to be notoriously fuzzy, meaning that membership needs to be negotiated. Membership in property-holding groups is usually acquired through descent, and sometimes also through marriage. This gives membership the appearance of naturalness. Yet in many cases the members of a given group do not all have the same rights to property. Moreover, since these communities reproduce themselves over time – growing, declining sometimes even ceasing to exist entirely – membership is subject to interpretation and negotiation and far from automatic.

The second feature of indigenous tenure regimes concerns the fuzzy geographical boundaries of the territories that property-holding groups claim to own. The kind of boundaries Africans traditionally set, be they linear or otherwise, has been subject to debate among scholars (cf. Tonkin 1994), but there is consensus that linear boundaries between fields and construction lots – owned by different lineages and within the lineages by different individuals – were indeed usually marked off by ditches, paths, hedges of shrubs, or marks on trees. By contrast, the nature of the 'borders' of earth-shrine areas or lands controlled by chiefs was, and often still is, more difficult to define. When land was plentiful, earth-shrine areas, and similarly the lands of a given chiefdom, were probably perceived not as flat homogenous territories, but as fields of ritual or political power with a well-defined centre (the shrine or the stool) situated in the inhabited and regularly cultivated space which was surrounded by concentric circles of influence, thinning out towards the uncultivated bush or forest beyond which neigh-

---

3 See Goody 1971: 29-30 and Kopytoff 1989: 22, 41, for classical formulations of these conventional assumptions.

bouring settlements lay. The 'territories' controlled by first-comers were not necessarily contiguous either, but consisted of various stretches of land, interspersed with areas 'owned' by neighbouring communities. The bush or forest, in any case, was a zone of contact rather than separation. Furthermore, where first-comers engaged in hunting, they were interested in controlling rather vast areas and were little concerned with fixing boundaries (Ingold 1986: 222-42; Barnard and Woodburn 1997; Jacob 2002). As more and more bush was cultivated, the boundaries between neighbouring territories needed to be defined more precisely. In border zones, the allegiance of houses and fields was usually defined according to which earth priest or chief had originally given the permission to cultivate or build. This process of boundary making continues, and, under the increasing population pressure, potentially results in conflicts, in which competing interpretations of past land grants and oral agreements are brought into play (cf. Berry 2001; Lentz 2000; 2003b).

Finally, the third feature concerns the multiple layers of rights to natural resources, or the characteristic 'bundle of rights', as Meek (1946: 1) put it. These layers have a socio-spatial dimension, that is, several different persons or groups hold some kind of interest in any given piece of land. They also have a temporal dimension, namely that these rights may have different 'expiry dates', so to speak, or that some resources are used by different right-holders at different times. In the savannah area, for instance, earth priests claim allodial rights to all resources, including farmland, water, and uncultivated bush as well as gold or other minerals, lost objects, or stray cattle. They assign usufruct rights to villagers and 'strangers', which often vary depending on the resources in question. It is thus possible to allow someone to grow annual crops on a field, while at the same time reserving the right to harvest any trees that may be found on that land. Pertinently, earth priests often retain certain rights over bodies of water, even though they may have given perennial rights to farm and build on the land around that water. Even in an urban setting, with surveyed and registered building lots, an earth priest may still claim to be ritually responsible for cleansing the earth after a suicide. Again, these bundles of rights are complex and negotiable, containing numerous opportunities for competition and conflict.

One may ask whether these bundles of rights are adequately described in terms of 'property'. Bell (1998) has recently proposed that the concept of 'property' be reserved for things that can be alienated and acquired in a market situation. While this may help to gauge the historical transformation of property rights towards capitalist forms of private, individualised ownership more carefully, it does so at the expense of unnecessarily 'othering' non-capitalist societies. A wider concept of property, which emphasises the social and political embeddedness of ownership and allows for a continuum of rights (ranging from mere access to complete alienation) as well as right holders (from individuals to extended families and larger communities), seems more useful (cf. Hann 1998; Lund 2002; Benda-Beckmann 1999). Hobhouse's early elucidation of the minimal conditions under which control over an object, in our case land, may be understood as property, provides a useful point of departure: This control 'must in some sort be recognised, in some sort independent of immediate physical enjoyment, and at some point exclusive of control of other persons' (1915: 7, quoted in Ingold 1986: 229). To put it in other words: Property implies social recognition, long-term control, and some kind of exclusivity.

The ambiguities of indigenous property rights are intrinsically related to the socio-historical context of mobility that has been, and still is, characteristic of much of Africa (De Bruijn *et al.* 2001). Establishing control over immobile resources, such as land, in regions where people, including agriculturalists, have been continually on the move, constitutes a particular challenge. The possibility to redefine first-comer status provided the flexibility needed to adapt the landscape of property rights continually to accommodate new arrivals (and departures) while preserving the repertoire of legitimate arguments and property-constituting rituals. As mentioned above, these ambiguities are also closely related to the characteristics of an oral culture, which lacks maps, written titles, and cadastres, and in which the 'bundles of owners', 'bundles of rights' and territorial boundaries have to be constantly interpreted and reaffirmed through narratives and rituals. Narratives in particular are needed in order to delineate the contested boundaries of property-holding groups and of the resource in question, to explain the history of mobility and to order the bundle of rights according to some hierarchy of priority. The various claims must then also be legitimated, or least made plausible – and this is normally achieved by embedding them in narratives of migration-and-settlement, that is, in histories of the appropriation and, sometimes, the subsequent transfer of the resource.

How narratives matter: An example from Burkina Faso

Before discussing the poetics and politics of property narratives more generally, I wish to briefly elucidate the empirical basis of my argument. Furthermore, an example of a recent land conflict in Ouessa District, Burkina Faso, should demonstrate the importance of migration-and-settlement histories for current property claims and illustrate how, and why, different parties make strategic references to different versions of local history.

The research

My study of mobility and land tenure among Dagara- and Sisala-speaking groups in North-Western Ghana and South-Western Burkina Faso developed in the context of a larger research project on the settlement history, the appropriation of land, and the development of ethnic relations in the Black Volta region.[4] Because written sources predating the arrival of the French and the British in 1897 are entirely absent, oral traditions were our most important sources in reconstructing the regional history. Over the years, our team of researchers collected over 500 stories of 'migration-and-settlement' in more than 150 villages, covering settlements of all relevant ethnic groups in an area of about 3,500 square kilometres. The interpretation of these oral traditions, however, involved thorny methodological questions. One stumbling block is that these traditions rarely go back further than four or five generations. Furthermore, in this area there are no indigenous professional 'historians', like the *griots*, and no official 'village histories', so that we were confronted with numerous and contradictory accounts related by different patrilineages. Finally and most importantly these competing traditions play an important role in supporting claims to land and positions of authority and so can obviously not be taken at face value.

In order to understand the micro-politics of oral traditions, therefore, we complemented the survey-type interviews in a large number of villages with in-depth case studies in selected localities (*cf.* Kuba, Lentz and Werthmann 2001; Lentz 2001). At the same time, the collection of a substantial corpus of stories from a wider area allowed us to identify both the poetic repertoire typically employed in settlement narratives, as well as the stories and episodes which deviate from regionally dominant *topoi* that often provide particularly valuable information about historical events. There are, for instance, typical differences between the Dagara's narratives of the founding of settlements and their neighbours' accounts. As Sisala-, Phuie-, Dyan-, and Nuni-speaking groups were often displaced from their former settlement areas by incoming Dagara groups, there are also 'winner's' and 'loser's' versions of accounts relating struggles over land rights. Convergence and disagreement between these versions and the different ways in which they draw on a limited pool of *topoi* can provide insights into how these struggles evolved and were resolved. More generally, comparing oral traditions over a wider area is an important step towards reconstructing the locally and regionally differentiated process of settlement and the establishment of property rights.

However, the overwhelming number of migration-and-settlement narratives that our local interview partners volunteered raised questions beyond our initial interest in the reconstruction of the regional history of mobility,

---

4 The project was part of the interdisciplinary Special Research Project 268 (*Sonderforschungsbereich*) on the West African savannah, at the University of Frankfurt/Main. Fieldwork was carried out mostly between 1997 and 2002, with the financial support of the *Deutsche Forschungsgemeinschaft*. For some results of our project, see Kuba 2003; Kuba, Lentz and Werthmann 2001; Kuba and Lentz 2003; Werthmann 1999; 2000.

property rights, and ethnic relations. Outside the interview situation in which we explicitly asked for oral traditions concerning settlement, we began to ask ourselves who narrated such stories, why, and when, and to which audiences? What were these stories supposed to achieve, who listened and who judged, and according to which criteria? It is in the wake of such questions that I began to understand these migration-and-settlement accounts as 'property narratives', as eloquent and often elaborate attempts to state, defend, or contest claims to land. Although it is difficult to reconstruct the context in which such settlement narratives were 'performed' in the past, it is possible to observe how such narratives are being used in current conflicts – and it is to one such conflict that I will now turn.

The Kierim-Kolinka conflict

A few years ago, the elders of Nuuzuo-yir (Nuuzuo's house) in Kolinka, a Dagara village in Ouessa District in South-Western Burkina Faso, were alerted by their neighbours to the fact that a Mossi farmer had begun planting neat rows of cashew seedlings on a field that they had left fallow for some time. Across the entire region planting trees is regarded as a serious matter. It signals long-term interests in land, and, in principle, only the landowner is allowed to do so. Conversely, whoever plants trees without being challenged, may interpret this as tacit acknowledgement of his claims to ownership. The Mossi man, who some years earlier had come from central Burkina Faso to Hamile, a small, but thriving town on the Ghanaian border only a few kilometres away from Kolinka, was planting these lucrative cashew trees in an attempt to diversify his activities as a trader and farmer even more. When the Nuuzuo elders confronted him, he explained that a man from Kierim, a Sisala village situated between Hamile and Kolinka, had shown him the field and given him the go-ahead to plant the trees. The Nuuzuo elders insisted that the land on which he was preparing to establish his plantation was part of Kolinka, not Kierim, territory. This land had been given to their grandfather by the earth priest of Ouessa, the oldest Dagara village in the area, and was lying fallow only because they had reserved it for the younger generation. They told the Mossi in no uncertain terms to stop planting trees, and informed the Ouessa earth priest of the incident. The Mossi, for his part, turned to his landlord in Kierim, who, in turn, consulted the Kierim Kuoro, chief and member of the earth-priestly family of Kierim, and complained to the *préfet*, the district head, about the defiant attitude of the Dagara of Kolinka.

The *préfet* convened a meeting at his office in Ouessa, inviting the forestry agent, the Sisala landlord, the Kierim Kuoro, the Nuuzuo elders from Kolinka, and the Ouessa earth priest.[5] In order to support Kierim's claim to the disputed land, the Kierim Kuoro went far back, narrating how his ancestors had arrived in the area a long time ago (much earlier, in any case, than the Dagara of Ouessa); that the latter had actually received their land, together with an earth-shrine stone, from the Sisala of Kierim; and that they still had to consult the earth priests of Kierim in serious matters (such as suicide). As tangible proof of Kierim's allodial rights over Ouessa territory the Kierim Kuoro cited the problems into which the Dagara had run at the Ouessa pond when they had fished there without consulting their ritual overlords, causing the pond to 'rebel' by allowing some of the young Dagara men to be bitten by snakes. Since Kolinka was a satellite settlement on land protected by the Ouessa earth shrine, it also ultimately fell under Kierim's ritual overlordship. However, the Kierim Kuoro insisted categorically that the contested cashew plantation-to-be was not even part of the original land grant to Ouessa, but belonged to the Kierim land reserve, and the Nuuzuo family had no right whatsoever to interfere with any uses to which the Sisala decided to put it. This was not the first time, he complained, that the Dagara, whom the Sisala had once invited to settle alongside them out of friendship, had 'misbehaved' and surreptitiously extended their territory beyond what they had been allotted.

Hien Daniel, the Ouessa earth priest, was furious at having to listen to all these 'outrageous lies' and countered in his own narration that his ancestor, Kontchire, who then still lived on the western banks of the Black Volta, had, on one of his hunting expeditions, discovered the territory that was later to become Ouessa. Since game was plentiful, he repeatedly hunted in the area, but soon realised that it was not empty, as he had hoped, but inhabited by Yeri or Phuo iron-smelters to whose activities ancient slag heaps still bear witness. As Kontchire wanted to settle on the newly discovered territory, he invited some of his nephews of the Kusiele patriclan, who had a reputation as strong warriors, to help him kill or at least drive away the Yeri-Phuo inhabitants.[6] Eventually, only the wife of the Phuo earth priest survived and, pleading for her life, promised to introduce Kontchire to the secrets of the earth shrine. Kontchire accepted her offer and even took her into his house. The Sisala of Kierim played no role in any of this, Hien Daniel asserted; on

---

5 I was not present at the meeting, and could not obtain the minutes (if there were any) but rely on the information the litigants presented to me shortly afterwards; interviews with the Kierim Kuoro Bombieh Naagyie *et al.*, 19 December 1997, the Ouessa earth priest Hien Daniel, 8 January 1998, and with Hien Delle, Somda Yelezaar *et al.* from Nuuzuo-yir, Kolinka, 10 January 1998 and 23 November 2001.

6 In many Dagara and Sisala narratives, the terms Yeri and Phuo, popularly often called Pougouli, are used synonymously; research among these groups, however, suggests differences in origin, migration routes, and often language; see Kuba 2003.

the contrary, the Kusiele warriors eventually took to raiding nearby Sisala settlements, capturing slaves and selling them to the regional slave markets, meaning that no Sisala would have dared to come near Ouessa, let alone offer them an earth-shrine stone. Hien Daniel also insisted that the Kierim Kuoro's claims regarding the pond were a blatant lie: The earth priests of Ouessa were the legitimate owners of the land and the pond, but had some time back invited ritual specialists from Kierim who knew how to prevent the fish from 'escaping' into the Volta river. The pond had indeed 'rebelled' lately, but not because of any disrespect towards its alleged Kierim owners, but because the Dagara themselves had failed to perform the necessary sacrifices.[7] As for Nuuzuo and other houses of Kolinka, Hien Daniel concluded, it was the Ouessa earth priest who once gave them their lands, including the contested field, and the Sisala had no right to use, let alone 'sell' this land to strangers.

Somewhat overwhelmed by these contradictory stories, the *préfet* allegedly told the litigants that, being a stranger to the area and a relatively young man, he could not possibly judge a case of disagreement among 'his parents' – thus referring politely to the age of the litigants. They should go back to their respective villages and continue to consult the elders. When I asked the different parties about the further course of events, the Kierim Kuoro insisted that the Dagara indeed accepted his assertion that Kierim had originally given them the land and that therefore no 'boundary' existed between Ouessa, Kolinka, and Kierim. To cool matters down, however, he asked the Mossi to leave the disputed land and offered him a different plot. Some of my Dagara informants narrated that the retreat of the Mossi farmer was rather due to the fact that Hien Daniel planted some 'medicine' on the land, which the Sisala of Kierim dared not remove, lest the earth god were to punish them with misfortune and illness, because they were not the true owners. The Nuuzuo-yir elders related that the trees which the Mossi had planted miraculously fell victim to some bush fire, and that their sons now once again farmed the land, not least because this was the best way to nip future false claims in the bud. When I asked for their comment on the Kierim Kuoro's statement that there was no 'boundary' between Kierim and Kolinka, they explained that in fact, when the Ouessa earth priest had given their grandfather land, he had not demarcated a linear boundary, but indicated a suitable location for the house and shown the direction into

---

7 Hien Daniel's version of the foundation of Ouessa and its earth shrine is by no means the only one that the Dagara elders of Ouessa narrate. However, I refer to it here at some length, because it was the one put forward in the land conflict. Over the years, I have collected three different, and indeed incompatible, accounts in Hien Daniel's family alone, and another five versions among the members of other patriclans; see Lentz 2001b for a more extensive discussion of the politics of memory in Ouessa.

which they should farm. Since the Dagara were more numerous than the Sisala and had more hands to clear the bush, they soon extended their farms quite a distance in the direction of Kierim. They related that when the Kolinka farmers 'met' the Sisala from Kierim, who also pushed their farms towards Kolinka, a boundary was pragmatically agreed upon.

In this wise, both sides saw their claims validated. The Kierim Kuoro could not prevent the Dagara from reworking the disputed land, but insisted that they did so only because he permitted it and that they actually recognised his property claims. The Dagara from Kolinka interpreted the outcome of the dispute rather differently, namely as an assertion of their ownership. The case never reached final settlement and may even be reopened in the future, if the balance of power changes. During the initial confrontation, for instance, a relative of the Nuuzuo-yir was Member of Parliament, a fact that possibly contributed to the reluctance of the *préfet* to take a more decisive stance. Political fortunes may shift, however, and a better-connected Kierim Kuoro, or a less belligerent Ouessa earth priest, may turn the tables. But regardless of the direction of such political shifts, historical narratives will play a prominent role in the legitimation of claims and counter-claims.

Narrative strategies

Many aspects of the Kolinka-Kierim case, and particularly the way in which historical narratives were used to specify vague territorial and social boundaries and to defend contested claims, are typical of land conflicts among Dagara and Sisala as well as many other West African societies. By invoking the history of first possession and the establishment of an earth shrine, and tracing the variegated history of subsequent transfers of some, or all, rights over the land, the litigants situated themselves, and their claims, in larger communities. They connected the biography of their piece of land with the regional history of migration and settlement. This is why, in the Kierim-Kolinka case, the conflict quickly acquired ethnic overtones, and was cited by many in the area as another incident in a long history of competition between 'the Sisala first-comers' and 'the Dagara late-comers'.

The Kolinka-Kierim conflict illustrates how narratives (those told to one's relatives or allies as well as those presented to adversaries and before the state authority) and practical action (pushing frontiers through cultivation, 'burning' trees and the like) together can either facilitate or hinder access to land and can legitimate property claims. It also provides a glimpse of the variety of institutional contexts in which property narratives are told: In ritualised settings of sacrifice (at the pond, for instance); in public confrontation between the earth priests, both in and outside the district head's office; in the more informal inter-ethnic public sphere of the market place (rumours and off-stage comments); and in the context of customary host-stranger or landlord-immigrant relations (as between the Mossi and the

Kierim Kuoro). Audience and institutional context have, of course, an impact on the narrative strategies deployed, as I will show below. In this section, however, I will concentrate on the narratives themselves and have a look at the elements – metaphors, images, episodes, and lines of argument – out of which they are created.

To begin with, all narratives are constructed from culturally specific and circumscribed repertoires of arguments and images. How convincing and practically effective a particular migration-and-settlement account or a story of property transfer may become depends not so much on 'historical truth' as such, but on its plausibility in the eyes of the audience. Different versions may compete, but all have to present their claims within a limited range of images and arguments, if these are to be considered credible. There are, then, regionally dominant *topoi* and hence limits to invention and variation.

As mentioned above, claiming to be the first-comers to an area is the most common and important narrative strategy to legitimate property rights in much of Africa. In the Black Volta region, too, first-comer narratives constitute a widespread social and cultural 'grammar', which all groups share transcending cultural and linguistic differences. They provided the framework in which mobility and contact, competition and cooperation, assimilation and segregation could be negotiated. As the Ouessa earth priest's story demonstrates quite clearly, the first-comer argument is so powerful that even notorious 'late-comers', such as the Dagara, present their claims in this idiom. Hien Daniel narrated that his ancestor, Kontchire, 'discovered' an apparently empty territory and only later perceived that there were traces of previous inhabitants. The Sisala of Kierim, on the other hand, insisted on having been the true first-comers to the area that later welcomed and settled the Dagara immigrants. Informants in neighbouring Sisala villages, however, and even the Kierim Kuoro himself, in the interview he gave me, offered alternative versions of Kierim's history, namely that the founders of Kierim on its present site were refugees from an older village whose inhabitants had been displaced by Dagara warriors. The Kierim Kuoro also conceded that although Kierim's actual territory was indeed 'empty' when the refugees arrived, it had been previously owned by another Sisala group, which lacked descendants. More generally, the founding of villages and the opening of 'virgin' bush was usually a collective enterprise, and quite often expanding groups preferred to settle where others had already gone before them. Even so, virtually all Sisala and many Dagara village histories claim that the founding ancestor arrived at the new abode as a lonely hunter, deciding subsequently to bring his relatives since the site seemed attractive for a new village.

The Kierim-Kolinka case is also an example of the two possible 'openings' in first-comer narratives, mentioned in the introduction, which allow competing claimants to advance incompatible claims by drawing on the same first-comer argument. The first concerns what is considered to be the 'pivotal event' that determines who is recognised as first-comer – was it the discovery of the site of the new village on a hunting expedition, or the actual clearing of the bush and the construction of solid houses? While the Kierim Kuoro relied on the 'lonely hunter' motif, the Ouessa earth priest added to this motif notions of 'conquest' and the superiority of Dagara hunters and peasants over Phuo blacksmiths. The Kolinka elders, in turn, referred to property rights arising from the effective appropriation of the land through active cultivation.

The second opening to provide room to manoeuvre is the delineation of the territorial and social reach of the group that claims first-comer status. A group may insist on being the first-comers and founders of the village, including the various sections and satellite settlements established subsequently. However, the founders of these sections and satellite settlements may in turn claim to be first-comers in their own right, for instance towards late-comers in their own sections. This is precisely what the Kierim Kuoro and Ouessa earth priest attempted to do. While the former declared that Ouessa was actually founded on Kierim hunting territory with Kierim's consent, Hien Daniel denied that the latter ever extended as far as the Black Volta, not least, because there was no visible sign of effective occupation. He insisted that what later became Ouessa territory was partly empty and partly used by Phuo ironworkers. The Kolinka elders, for their part, strengthened the Ouessa earth priest's claim to allodial title over the entire territory of Ouessa, including Kolinka, by asking Hien Daniel to support their rights against those of Kierim. They would perhaps have been more reluctant to do so had the Ouessa earth priest invoked this title in order to claim a share in the revenues they received from leasing parts of their lineage land to strangers. In the event of conflict, they could attempt to transform the minor earth shrine, which the Ouessa earth priest had once established in Kolinka, into an independent major one, as has happened in other villages. Such a transformation would, however, have to be supported by narratives which accuse the Ouessa earth priest of neglecting his spiritual duties and which boost the power of the minor shrine (cf. Goody 1957) – narratives that aim at convincing, first and foremost, the inhabitants of Kolinka, the convincing of the former ritual superiors in Ouessa being of only secondary importance. More generally, narratives can play off hierarchies between senior and junior earth shrines against each other, and can manipulate the relative chronology of settlement foundation in multiple ways. In addition, first-comer claims are sometimes extended from a single lineage to the lineage's entire ethnic group, thus conferring first-comer status on all members of that ethnic group, even if some are actually latecomers, as is, for instance, the case with some of the Kierim Sisala families.

While some narrative strategies – images, episodes, arguments – are employed by all groups in the region, others are culturally quite specific. For instance, Sisala, Phuo, and Nuni settlement accounts often refer to conflicts between brothers, such as one over the sharing of (or rather the failure to share) the spoils of a joint hunting expedition, cited as the reason for migration. Other accounts invoke the 'pregnant-woman-slit-open' motif, that is, a dispute about the sex of an unborn child, which resulted in the death of the woman (and the embryo), because one party 'operated' on her (and subsequently had to migrate) in order to determine who was right (cf. Schott 1990). Significantly, and in keeping with their particular ethos of mobility, Dagara narratives never resort to these motifs in order to explain migration. Similarly, Sisala and Phuo narratives sometimes refer to a contest between two hunters who both claim to be first-comers; the narrative then describes how their claims were put to a test, namely by examining the whereabouts of the object which both claim to have thrown into the pond near the new settlement. Usually, one hunter has used a mud brick, the other a stone or an iron object, and, of course, the brick has dissolved in the meantime. Therefore the test does not necessarily privilege the true first-comer, but the more intelligent or wilier pioneer. Interestingly, this type of episode is never narrated in Dagara stories, which present their first-coming-hunter claims much more plainly. This is because for a Dagara audience, such a test to determine the identity of the real first-comer would sound implausible, or at least would not enhance the general credibility of the story.

More generally, in stories told by the Dagara and their neighbours, we find two basic lines of argument to legitimate property. The first is similar to the *res nullium* argument that also helped legitimate European expansion in North America (Pagden 1995: Ch. 3) and according to which the 'new' territory is defined as empty, the possible traces of earlier inhabitation generally being ignored, so that the 'discoverers' become the legitimate owners. This is the argument that the Sisala and Phuo usually present. It is even quite possible that historically their ancestors, while on hunting expeditions, were indeed the 'first' to discover many of the areas that are now claimed by Dagara villages. Hunting rights were originally oriented towards securing fairly large territories for communal hunting expeditions, defining spheres of interest or zones beyond which wounded game would no longer be pursued. Such zones did not have linear and exclusive boundaries, but vague and open ones, usually indicated by ritually charged landmarks such as rocks, rivers, or unusually large trees. However, it is from these older rights over hunting lands that Sisala and Phuo now derive property rights over agricultural land: In their eyes the ultimate spiritual and administrative control over the whole area has always rested with them. This is why they usually claim that the Dagara immigrants asked them for permission to settle and cultivate the land, an act that acknowledges their property rights. These arguments, then, resemble in some ways a combination of the *res nullium* and consensus theories of property, introduced into European thinking by Hugo Grotius (cf. Schlatter 1951: Chs. 5, 6; Tully 1980: 69 ff; Rose 1994: 11-23).

The second line of argument is very much reminiscent of John Locke's labour theory of property or the Common Law idea of ownership derived from continued possession (cf. Locke 2002 [1690]: Ch. 5; Tully 1980; Reeve 1986: Ch. 5). This is basically the argument used by the Dagara in Ouessa, Kolinka and many other settlements, and it is an argument typically invoked by 'late-comers'. The group that actually takes possession of a territory, by cutting down the bush, fighting wild animals, building houses, and cultivating the earth, and finally also establishing an earth shrine, becomes by these very acts its legitimate owner. In practice, however, the two argumentative strategies – possession through discovery and possession through labour – often intertwine.

As is to be expected, first-comers and late-comers also hold different ideas about legitimate forms of the transfer of landed property. Most importantly, they do not agree on whether allodial property can be transferred at all. Some believe that only more or less comprehensive rights to use land can be ceded, but not full property rights, which would include the right to spiritual control and the allocation of land to third parties. In the eyes of the Kierim earth priests, for instance, the Sisala have always retained ultimate control over Ouessa land, even though they granted very extensive rights to the Dagara by giving them an earth-shrine stone.

The Dagara in Ouessa and many other villages admit that they are in fact late-comers and that the Sisala, Phuo, or Nuni settled there earlier. But then they go on to insist that their ancestors had actually 'bought' an earth shrine (using the word *da*, which is also applied to market transactions) and all its secrets from the previous inhabitants and that they thereby acquired all allodial rights over the land, with no further obligations towards the original owners. The Sisala deny that this is even possible and claim that an earth shrine, and hence the land, is in principle inalienable. If they do concede that a transfer of an earth-shrine stone has taken place, they compare it to a marriage, employing the metaphor of land as a woman for whom one can receive a dowry, but who always remains a member of her original family to which she can return at any time.

In practice, however, people are pragmatic and forward arguments from the entire regional repertoire of legitimations of property rights and property transfers, not least because first-comer and late-comer positions are always relative and context-dependent. If the Kolinka elders, for instance, were to attempt to become ritually and economically fully independent of Ouessa, the Ouessa earth priest would certainly not hesitate to declare that the Ouessa shrine could not be further alienated or subdivided into independent entities. More generally, property narratives manipulate, to use Fortmann's (1995) terms, 'the voice of the teller' (who are the relevant actors and the 'we' of the story), 'the time frame' (how far back does the story reach), 'the framing of the issue' (is it, for instance, use rights or rights to allocate land, economic or ritual control, which the story defines as the centre of the dispute) and, as I would add, the spatial frame (to which territories do the narrated events relate). Within the range of accessible *topoi* and arguments, these narrative devices are employed according to the aims of the narrator and the institutional context in which the stories are related, and it is this context to which I will now turn.

The institutional context: Validating property narratives

It is not sufficient to narrate 'good stories', they also must be authorised and validated. The validation of competing narratives depends ultimately on the social networks which the competing parties can rally in order to support their claims – and it is at this point where politics and questions of power play a decisive role. Depending on who the parties to a conflict are and what is at stake, these networks may consist mainly of the locally relevant authorities of elders, earth priests, and chiefs, or they may also embrace lawyers and politicians at the regional and national levels, as well as urban allies such as educated migrants or hometown associations. Furthermore, questions of demographic power and economic clout may also influence the likelihood that particular versions successfully convince and become effective.

In the Kierim-Kolinka case, as in many segmentary societies that traditionally did not have chiefs, the first authority invoked to decide between competing claims is that of the lineage elders. In many cases, however, these elders will eventually bring the earth priest, as the holder of the allodial title, and other knowledgeable local figures into play, particularly if the conflict is not within a lineage, but between different kin groups or between local landowners and a 'stranger'. Calling on the earth priest usually shifts the issue from the contents of a particular decision (in the Kierim-Kolinka case: The allocation of land to a stranger for planting trees) to the question of who has a right to decide (the Kierim Kuoro, the Kolinka elders, or the Ouessa earth priest). It is this shift that broadens the spatial and, more importantly, the temporal frame in which the conflict is interpreted and ultimately linked to the history of 'first possession'. However, there are no neutral witnesses who could decide between competing versions if the contestants themselves cannot agree on what constitutes a 'good story' (Jacob 2002). For instance, they may invite the spirits of the land to judge the case through the acceptance or refusal of a sacrifice (demonstrated by the way in which the sacrificial chicken dies, on its back or otherwise) or through an oath, accompanied by swallowing crumbs of the soil, thereby invoking the wrath of the earth god in the case of a lie. However, the gods' decision, which is conveyed by death, illness, or misfortune visited on the trespassers, is as contingent on human interpretation as is the question of which version of the settlement history is valid, and, unsurprisingly, not all parties agree on how to interpret the signs of such tests. Hence, here again, ultimately all depends on the networks each party can enlist to support his version and claims.

In addition, although earth-priestly authority is generally imagined to be related to a specific territory, an aggrieved party can make use of the complicated (and contested) hierarchy of senior and junior earth shrines in order to invite a different earth priest to settle the matter. In short he can turn to a strategy of 'forum shopping', to use Von Benda-Beckmann's (1981) term. If, for instance, the earth priest of one village sets an ebony stick in the disputed land, the affected party may reactivate some historical link to the neighbouring earth priest who is invited to pull the ebony stick out, thereby enabling his new client to continue using the land. There is, then, no supreme authority that decides between competing claims, and there are always ways to overturn or circumvent a verdict. In any case, the 'losers' at any given moment will preserve their version of the story until a new opportunity to right past wrongs arises. In the Kierim-Kolinka case, for instance, the temporary 'success' of the Dagara's property claims is partly attributable to the latter's demographic supremacy: They outnumber the Sisala by far, and more of them are educated migrants living in the cities who can come to the aid of those in the village in all legal matters, when the need arises. However, the economically as well as, at the national level, politically powerful Mossi generally feel that their personal interests in secure access to land for commercial purposes is better served by close ties with the Sisala who control much more land in total than the Dagara. Mossi support may eventually tip the balance in favour of Sisala stories claiming allodial ownership.

These processes of mediation and decision-making (or, just as often, of keeping matters pending) are not terribly different in societies with traditional chieftaincy, although there procedures may be somewhat more streamlined and standardised. But even in societies with a tradition of chieftaincy, the enforcement of one version and one claim over another is ultimately a question of social networks and political power, as Sara Berry (2001) has convincingly shown in her study of land conflicts among the Asante in Ghana.

Conflicts, then, are often merely suspended. While pragmatic solutions, informed by the current configuration of power and influence, regulate the immediate use of the land, competing claims concerning more comprehensive rights remain unresolved. Litigants may resort to the local administration or the courts and enlist the support of their educated relatives to frame their claims in ways that make them more successful in state-controlled arenas. As in the Kierim-Kolinka dispute, local administrators do not always, leave matters in the hands of 'the elders' either, but sometimes actively 'shop' for conflicts in search of opportunities to increase their revenues and authority through land litigation. However, even if state institutions intervene and reach a decision, the defeated party may still cling to its version of the case and merely await a new opportunity to pursue its claims once again.

Local property narratives can be informed not only by indigenous theories of legitimate ownership, but also by existing land legislation and wider political interests. However, this influence seems to be stronger in southern Africa (cf. Cousins 2002; Peters 1994), with its rather different trajectory of European intromission in local tenure regimes, than in many areas of West Africa, where the colonial and post-colonial legislation pertaining to land ownership has in general not radically challenged the dominant ideology of first-comer claims. In Northern Ghana, for instance, the colonial and post-colonial state held land in trust for the local population, but with the Constitution of 1979, the allodial title officially reverted to its 'original owners', that is, the earth priests and chiefs. As a result, when the Lands Commission or courts intervene in land conflicts, they must establish evidence in keeping with local property narratives (Kunbuor 2003). By comparison, in many Francophone West African countries, land continues to be defined as 'national estate', vested in the government. However, the states lack the legitimacy and administrative infrastructure to implement national land laws systematically down to the grassroots level, so that the mundane day-to-day administration of land often remains in the hands of local elders and 'customary' authorities (Toulmin *et al.* 2002). But even when courts and local government institutions are involved in the mediation of land conflicts, they have rarely been able or willing to depart radically from local patterns of argumentation that link property rights closely to settlement history (Hagberg 1998; Lund 1998; 1999).

Yet even when the context of these conflicts changes from that of an oral culture to that of the modern bureaucratic nation-state with its apparatus of land legislation and courts, the written evidence provided by cadastres and land markers on surveyed plots must be accompanied by narratives. However, when these narratives are introduced as evidence in higher-level courts or other institutions in the national arena, the local migration-and-settlement stories undergo significant changes. In conflicts over administrative boundaries or political rights at the local level, or, more generally, when it is important to justify politico-territorial claims within the modern state, contestants generally no longer argue only with individual first-coming ancestors, but supplement, or even substitute, these lineage narratives with accounts relating the migration of entire tribes (cf. Lentz 1994). In some cases, the new 'tribal' histories which are invoked to support property claims in the context of larger political projects have also been informed by the international discourse on the rights of 'indigenous peoples' (or, as they are sometimes called, 'first peoples').[8] Thus, depending on the actors involved and the issues at stake, property narratives may have to satisfy local criteria of legitimacy as well as the expectations of modern land legislation and NGO-mediated international audiences. Some local narratives may have a greater potential of discursive connectivity than others and may be more suitable for presentation in supra-local settings.

However, a more detailed analysis of the influence of multi-facetted audiences on these narratives strategies goes beyond the scope of the present chapter, the primary aim of which was to argue that narratives play an important, even indispensable, role in supporting property claims. Narratives connect the history of particular plots, fields, and territories to a broader regional history of migration and settlement; they specify the multiple 'openings' of indigenous tenure regimes in a predominantly oral environment; and they seek to persuade others of the legitimacy of property claims by drawing on a repertoire of locally or regionally accepted arguments, images, and episodes. The power of persuasion – and hence the security of property claims – however, cannot rely on 'good stories' alone, but also depends on the effective manipulation of social networks and political power.

References

BARNARD, A. and J. WOODBURN (1991) Property, power and ideology in hunter-gatherer societies: An introduction, in: Ingold, T., Riches, D. and Woodburn, J. (Eds) *Hunters and Gatherers*, Oxford: Berg, Vol. 2, pp. 4-31.

BELL, D. (1998) The social relations of property and efficiency, in: Hunt, R.C. and Gilman, A. (Eds) *Property in economic context*, Lanham: University Press of America, pp. 29-45.

BENDA-BECKMANN, K. VON (1981) Forum shopping and shopping forums: Dispute processing in a Minang Kaban village in West Sumatra, *Journal of Legal Pluralism*, 19: 117-59.

BENDA-BECKMANN, F. VON and K. VON BENDA-BECKMANN (1999) A functional analysis of property rights with special reference to Indonesia, in: Van Meijl, T. and Benda-Beckmann, F. von (Eds), *Property rights and economic development: Land and natural resources in Southeast Asia and Oceania*, London: Kegan Paul, pp. 15-56.

BENJAMINSEN, T.A. and C. LUND (Eds) (2003) *Securing land rights in Africa*, London: Frank Cass.

[8] A case in point is Cameroon, where the inalienable rights of 'minorities' have been introduced into the national constitution and autochthony discourses are instrumentalised in the political arena as well as in land conflicts; on this, see Geschiere and Nyamnjoh 2000; Konings 2001.

BERRY, S. (1992) Hegemony on a shoestring: Indirected rule and access to agricultural land, *Africa*, 62(3): 327-55.

BERRY, S. (2001) *Chiefs know their boundaries: Essays on property, power and the past in Asante, 1896-1996*, Oxford: James Currey.

BOHANNAN, P. (1963) 'Land', 'tenure' and land-tenure, in: Biebuyck, D. (Ed.) *African agrarian systems*, London: Oxford University Press, pp. 101-15.

CHANOCK, M. (1985) *Law, custom and social order: The colonial experience in Malawi and Zambia*, Cambridge: Cambridge University Press.

CHANOCK, M. (1991) Paradigms, policies and property: A review of the customary law of land tenure, in: Mann, K. and Roberts, R. (Eds), *Law in Colonial Africa*, Portsmouth: Heinemann, pp. 61-84.

CHAUVEAU, J.-P. (2000) Question foncière et construction national en Côte d'Ivoire, *Politique Africaine*, 78: 94-125.

COLSON, E. (1971) The impact of the colonial period on the definition of land rights, in: Turner, V. (Ed.) *Colonialism in Africa, 1870-1960, vol. 3: Profiles of change: African society and colonial rule*, Cambridge: CUP, pp. 193-215.

COQUÉRY-VIDROVITCH, C. (1982) Le régime foncier rural en Afrique noire, in: Le Bris, E. *et al.* (Eds) *Enjeux fonciers en Afrique noire*, Paris: Karthala, pp. 65-84.

COUSINS, B. (2002) Legislating negotiability: Tenure reform in post-apartheid South Africa, in: Juul, K. and Lund, C. (Eds) *Negotiating property in Africa*, Portsmouth: Heinemann, pp. 67-106.

DE BRUIJN, M., R. VAN DIJK and D. FOEKEN (Eds) (2001) *Mobile Africa: Changing patterns of movement in Africa and beyond*, Leiden: Brill.

ENSMINGER, J. (1997) Changing property rights: Reconciling formal and informal rights to land in Africa, in: Drobak, J.N. and Nye, J.V.C. (Eds) *The frontiers of the new institutional economics*, New York: Academic Press, pp. 165-96.

FORTMANN, L. (1995) Talking claims: Discursive strategies in contesting property, *World Development*, 23: 1053-63.

GEISLER, C. and G. DANEKER (Eds) (2000) *Property and values: Alternatives to public and private ownership*, Washington: Island Press.

GESCHIERE, P. and F. NYAMNJOH (2000) Capitalism and autochthony: The seesaw of mobility and belonging, *Public Culture*, 12: 423-52.

GOODY, J. (1957) Fields of social control among the LoDagaba, *Journal of the Royal Anthropological Institute of Great Britain and Ireland*, 87: 75-104.

GOODY, J. (1971) *Technology, tradition and the state in Africa*, London: Oxford University Press.

HAGBERG, S. (1998) *Between peace and justice: Dispute settlement between Karaboro agriculturalists and Fulbe agro-pastoralists in Burkina Faso*, Uppsala: Acta Universitatis Upsaliensis.

HANN, C.M. (1998) Introduction: The embeddedness of property, in: Hann, C.M. (Ed.) *Property relations: Renewing the anthropological tradition*, Cambridge: CUP, pp. 1-47.

INGOLD, T. (1986) *The appropriation of nature: Essays on human ecology and social relations*, Manchester: Manchester University Press.

JACOB, J.-P. (2002) *La tradition du pluralisme institutionnel dans les conflits fonciers entre autochtones. Le cas du Gwendégué (Centre Burkina Faso)*, Document de travail de l'Unité de Recherche 095 Nr. 3, Montpellier: IRD/GRET.

JACOB, J.-P. (2003) Imposer son tutorat foncier. Usages autochtones de l'immigration et tradition pluraliste dans le Gwendégué (centre-ouest Burkina Faso), in: Kuba, R., Lentz, C. and Somda, C.N. (Eds) *Histoire du peuplement et relations interethniques au Burkina Faso*, Paris: Karthala, pp. 75-96.

JUUL, K. and C. LUND (Eds) (2002) *Negotiating property in Africa*, Portsmouth: Heinemann.

KONINGS, P. (2001) Mobility and exclusion: Conflicts between autochthons and allochthons during political liberalization in Cameroon, in: De Bruijn, M., van Dijk, R. and Foeken, D. (Eds) *Mobile Africa: Changing patterns of movement in Africa and beyond*, Leiden: Brill, pp. 169-94.

KOPYTOFF, I. (1989) The internal African frontier: The making of African political culture, in: Kopytoff, I. (Ed.) *The African frontier. The reproduction of traditional African societies*, Bloomington: Indiana University Press, pp. 3-84.

KUBA, R. (2003) Comment devenir Phuo? Stratégies d'inclusion au sud-ouest du Burkina Faso, in: Kuba, R., Lentz, C. and Somda, C.N. (Eds) *Histoire du peuplement et relations interethniques au Burkina Faso*, Paris: Karthala, pp. 135-65.

KUBA, R. and C. LENTZ (2002) Arrows and earth shrines: Towards a history of Dagara expansion in southern Burkina Faso, *Journal of African History*, 43: 377-406.

KUBA, R., C. LENTZ. and K. WERTHMANN (Eds) (2001) *Les Dagara et leurs voisins. Histoire de peuplement et relations interethniques au sud-ouest du Burkina Faso*, Frankfurt: Sonderforschungsbereich 268.

KUNBUOR, B. (2003) Multiple layers of land rights and multiple owners: The case of land disputes in the Upper West Region of Ghana, in: Kröger, F. and Meier, B. (Eds) *Ghana's north: Research on culture, religion and politics in Northern Ghanaian societies*, Frankfurt: Peter Lang, pp. 101-28.

LAVIGNE DELVILLE, P. (Ed.) (1998) *Quelles politiques foncières en Afrique? Réconcilies pratiques, légitimité et légalité*, Paris: Karthala.

LENTZ, C. (1994) A Dagara rebellion against Dagomba rule? Contested stories of origin in north-western Ghana, *Journal of African History*, 35: 457-92.

LENTZ, C. (2000) Of hunters, goats and earth-shrines: Settlement histories and the politics of oral tradition in northern Ghana, *History in Africa*, 27: 193-214.

LENTZ, C. (2001) Ouessa. Débats sur l'histoire du peuplement, in: Kuba, R., Lentz, C. and Werthmann, K. (Eds) *Les Dagara et leurs voisins. Histoire de peuplement et relations interethniques au sud-ouest du Burkina Faso*, Frankfurt/M: Sonderforschungsbereich 268, pp. 29-61.

LENTZ, C. (2003a) 'Premiers arrivés' et 'nouveaux-venus'. Discours sur l'autochtonie dans la savane ouest-africaine, in: Kuba, R., Lentz, C. and Somda, B.N. (Eds) *Histoire du peuplement et relations interethniques au Burkina Faso*, Paris: Karthala, pp. 113-34.

LENTZ, C. (2003b) This is Ghanaian territory: Land conflicts on a West African border, *American Ethnologist*, 30: 273-89.

LI, T.M. (1996) Images of community: Discourse and strategy in property relations, *Development and Change*, 27: 501-27.

LOCKE, J. (2002) [1690] *The second treatise of government and a letter concerning toleration*, Mineola: Dover Publications.

LUND, C. (1998) Struggles for land and political power: On the politicization of land tenure and dispute in Niger, *Journal of Legal Pluralism*, 40: 1-22.

LUND, C. (1999) A question of honour: Property disputes and brokerage in Burkina Faso, *Africa*, 69: 575-94.

LUND, C. (2002) Negotiating property institutions on the symbiosis of property and authority in Africa, in: Juul, K. and Lund, C. (Eds) *Negotiating property in Africa*, Portsmouth: Heinemann, pp. 11-43.

MEEK, C.K. (1946) *Land, law and custom in the colonies*, Oxford: Oxford University Press.

MURPHY, W.P. and C.H. BLEDSOE (1987) Kinship and territory in the history of a Kpelle Chiefdom (Liberia), in: Kopytoff, I. (Ed.) *The African frontier. The reproduction of traditional African societies*, Bloomington: Indiana University Press, pp. 121-47.

PAGDEN, A. (1995) *Lords of all the world: Ideologies of empire in Spain, Britain and France, c. 1500 – c. 1800*, New Haven: Yale University Press.

PETERS, P. (1994) *Dividing the commons: Politics, policy, and culture in Botswana.* Charlottesville: University Press of Virginia.

PHILLIPS, A. (1989) *The enigma of colonialism: British policy in West Africa*, London: James Currey.

PLATTEAU, J.-P. (1996) The evolutionary theory of land rights as applied to sub-Saharan Africa: A critical assessment, *Development and Change*, 27: 29-86.

REEVE, A. (1986) *Property*, Atlantic Highlands, N.J.: Humanities Press International.

RIBOT, J. and PELUSO, N.L. (2003) A theory of access, *Rural Sociology*, 68: 153-81.

ROSE, C.M. (1994) *Property and persuasion: Essays on the history, theory and rhetoric of ownership*, Boulder: Westview Press.

SCHLATTER, R. (1951) *Private property: The history of an idea*, New Brunswick: Rutgers University Press.

SCHOFFELEERS, J.M. (Ed.) (1979) *Guardians of the land: Essays on Central African territorial cults*, Gwelo: Mambo Press.

SCHOTT, R. (1990) 'La femme enceinte éventrée'. Variabilité et contexte socio-culturel d'un type de conte ouest-africain, in: Görög-Karady, V. (Ed.) *D'un conte à l'autre. La variabilité dans la littérature orale*, Paris: Éditions CNRS, pp. 327-39.

SHIPTON, P. and M. GOHEEN. (1992) Understanding African land-holding: Power, wealth and meaning, *Africa*, 62(3): 307-25.

SPIERENBURG, M. (2001) Moving into another spirit province: Immigrants and the Mhondoro cult in northern Zimbabwe, in: De Bruijn, M., van Dijk, R. and Foeken, D. (Eds) *Mobile Africa: Changing patterns of movement in Africa and beyond*, Leiden: Brill, pp. 47-62.

TONKIN, E. (1994) Borderline questions: People and space in West Africa, in: Hastings, D. and Wilson, T.M. (Eds) *Border approaches: Anthropological perspectives in frontiers*, New York: University Press of America, pp. 15-30.

TOULMIN, C., P. LAVIGNE DELVILLE and S. TRAONE (Eds) (2002) *The dynamics of resource tenure in West Africa*, Oxford: James Currey.

TULLY, J. (1980) *A discource on property: John Locke and his adversaries*, Cambridge: Cambridge University Press.

VERDERY, K. (1998) Property and power in Transalvania's decollectivization, in: Hann, C.M. (Ed.) *Property relations: Renewing the anthropological tradition*, Cambridge: Cambridge University Press, pp. 160-80.

WERTHMANN, K. (1999) 'Ihr habt keine Erde hierhergebracht!' Landrechtskonflikte in einem Umsiedlungsprojekt im Südwesten Burkina Fasos, in: Hahn, H.-P. and Spittler, G. (Eds) *Afrika und die Globalisierung*, Hamburg: Lit, pp. 503-12.

WERTHMANN, K. (2000) Gold rush in West Africa. The appropriation of 'natural' resources: Non-industrial gold mining in South-Western Burkina Faso, *Sociologus*, 50: 90-104.

ZWERNEMANN, J. (1968) *Die Erde in Vorstellungswelt und Kulturpraktiken der sudanischen Völker*, Berlin: Reimer.

7

State formation, access to the commons and autochthony among the Berbers of the Middle Atlas, Morocco

Bernhard Venema

Introduction

In the past, many scholars assumed that the new states in Africa and elsewhere in the world would become the foci of their inhabitant's loyalties. Nowadays, however, scholars agree that current events attest that nation-states seem to be almost non-existent. Within any state there are several collective identities – for example, ethnic, religious or residential communities – with which people seem to identify more than they do with the state. In this contribution the central theme is the competing claims to land among the Berbers of the Middle Atlas, and whether or not this leads to conflict. The purpose is to contribute to a better understanding of the obsession with autochthony and ethnicity in Africa. Both concepts relate to the us-them opposition, but while ethnicity suggests the existence of a more or less clearly defined group, autochthony is less specific and more elusive: It creates a sense of belonging, yet goes beyond ethnicity's specificity. Following Geschiere and Nyamnjoh (2000: 424), in this chapter autochthony refers to a sense of belonging, defined against outsiders and the affirmation of the roots of home and origin. These are based on ideas and emotions regarding the defense of ancestral land.

It will be argued that there are five elements which help to clarify the issue of competing land claims and autochthony in the Middle Atlas, namely:

1 Competing claims to land between early settlers and newcomers, with autochthony assuming importance because it marks membership and access to land. Most of the early settlers are Tamazigh-speaking Berbers who call themselves *imazighen* ('original and independent people'), and claim that the territory is their ancestral land.
2 The policy during the first years of the French Protectorate to maintain customary law and local political institutions in the countryside. This very important policy was an expression of the larger French politics of divide and rule between the urban population – mostly of Arab background and accepting the Sharia (Islamic law) as the basis of their legislation – and the rural Berber population, which was severed from Sharia by the French administration and placed under customary law. As a result of the role of customary law and the maintenance of customs, tribes and ancestral land became even more essential characteristics than they were before the arrival of the French.
3 The growth of capitalism brought the development of a land and labour market in the Middle Atlas as elsewhere in Morocco. After the arrival of the colonial state, French *colons,* Moroccan city-dwellers and local tribal leaders had bought land and a demand for labour grew from the colonial administration and on the farms of the newcomers (*colons*) and those of the well-to-do Moroccans. The development of private property and forced access to the commons destroyed the role of customary law and traditional management institutions. This resulted in feelings of frustration among the local population, which, after independence, led to a restoration process.
4 After independence, there was increasing government pressure to accept official law (for example, to allow strangers to access land). However, this barely got off the ground. Between 1956 and 1970, the Berber tribal leaders and councils resisted the new legislation and succeeded in denying strangers access to the commons; this meant that the restoration process was put into effect.
5 Since 1970, the state has been more successful in replacing local Berber leaders and local institutions with governmental agencies and government officials. In other words, there has been a gradual shift from custom and community towards official law and the state.

The aim of this contribution, however, is to show that even in a strong state such as Morocco, legal pluralism continues to have a palpable impact, with the autochthonous community remaining a strong point of identification and determining access to land to a large degree.

This contribution is based on research carried out during the period 1986-1994 and 2000 to 2003, with a total of twelve months fieldwork. Different research methods were employed. During the fieldwork period, the main research method was interviewing respondents, from simple farmers to the provincial governor, in Souk el Had, Toufestelt, Ain Leuh, Azrou and Ifrane.

In all more than hundred interviews were conducted with about fifty respondents, but not all interviews were used for this chapter. In addition information is based on personal observation at ceremonies with and visits to government authorities, council members, local tribal officials and farmers. Besides interviewing and observation I made an extensive study of the existing literature of different sources in order to acquire a well-balanced view of recent historical developments. Lastly a nine days archive research was carried out at the *Archives d'Outre Mer* in Nantes in 1992.

Ancestral land and political institutions in the period of autonomy

At the end of the seventeenth century, Sultan Moulay Ismael (1672-1727) built garrisons in the Middle Atlas (for example, at Azrou and Ain Leuh) in order to stop the migration of Berbers from the south. However, after his reign, Morocco collapsed into disorder. The Berbers seized the opportunity to start a long-term migration movement to the fertile lands of the Middle Atlas. They arrived there at the beginning of the nineteenth century, drove off the Beni Mtir tribe, took over the cleared land and the pasture areas, and settled down (Beaudet 1969: 8).

Among these settlers were the Beni Mguild Berbers, who occupied the central-northern part of the Middle Atlas. Their political organisation was a loosely organised confederation of tribes grouped together in their efforts to conquer new areas and defend their patrimony. The confederation was composed of four tribes,[1] each of which was divided into clans and lineages. The maintenance of tribal structure has been attributed to opposition between its minor segments: It was a system of segmental opposition in which tribal groups could cooperate when confronted by outside enemies (Gellner 1969: 64-9; Waterbury 1970: 61-9). Each level had a council (*jemaa*) and these councils elected some of their members to be representatives the higher level. At the level of the tribe and confederation, councils operated only when necessary, most conspicuously in matters of warfare; the councils at the clan and lineage level dealt with the day-to-day affairs, such as the redistribution of pastureland, regulating access to water and handling local social and religious matters. Tribes and tribal segments were groups of people defending their access to land, water, and pasturage, and sharing local governing agencies. Although tribal groups were a social reality, they became more in the wake of the intervention of the French administration, when tribal groupings were confined to administrative districts.

---

[1] These tribes are the Ait Abdi, Irklaouan, Ait Arfa du Guigou, and Ait Sgougou.

The Middle Atlas is an area of mountains and vast highlands (altitude 1500-2200 m), where water never ceases to flow. Snow falls in December, January, and February, and in the summer it is cooler and wetter than on the lower plains. This mountainous land is called *jbel*. The fertile lowlands (*azarghar*) of the central plateau (altitude 700-1100 m) enjoy ample rains in the spring and autumn, but they have hot, dry summers.

The economy of the Beni Mguild is based on sheep breeding. The tribes used to move camp between the highland summer pastures and the lowland winter pastures, which may have been dozens of kilometres apart. In the highlands, food for livestock could be found until autumn. In wintertime the flocks were kept in the lowlands, and it was only in April that the sheep farmers gradually started moving back towards the highlands. The social unit that moved together was traditionally the tent encampment (*tigemmi*), generally comprising ten to twenty tents.

The pastures were collectively owned by the tribes and were sub-divided among the clans and lineages by the tribal council. Collective management of common property was used as the pastoral strategy to spread the risks inherent in the unstable and variable environment. Care was taken to make sure that outsiders respected the boundaries of the collective pastures. The lineage council (*ighsen*) ensured that a watchman (*naib*) was recruited to supervise access to and the use of the collective pastures; the watchman was usually appointed for life and was always a person of influence in the lineage. His main task was to deny the herds of others access to the collective pastures and to ensure that the spring resting period for the grassland was respected.[2] If the lineage watchman could not find a solution to a conflict, the matter was handled at the higher, tribal level.

Access to the commons remained flexible, however. Different tribes made different arrangements to have access to pastures elsewhere in order to avert the effect of an early spell in winter or drought in summer. There were internal and external arrangements. For example, within the Ait Abdi tribe there was an internal agreement between the Mhammed ou Lahcen tribal group – which possessed only a small winter pasture – and the Ait Meroual sub-tribe, which had large winter pastures: Each winter the latter group allowed the Ait Mhammed ou Lahcen to pitch at least a hundred tents on its pastures. As regards external movements, the Ait Arfa du Guigou tribe had no winter pastures and sent its livestock to the commons of the Irklaouan tribe, which in turn sent its livestock to the Beni Mtir and Guerouane tribes (Beaudet 1969: 19). There were no rigid boundaries because of the necessity of seasonal migration because of the ecological imperative of transhumation.

Although the main economic activity was sheep raising, the Beni Mguild also grew crops in the summer and winter pastures. The councils divided up

---

[2] In addition, the village council often appoints an irrigation watchman (*amghar n'wamane* or *amghar taroua*), who is paid by the village.

parcels of land among the individual families to allow the cultivation of irrigated or rain-fed crops, such as wheat, barley, and maize. The families had only usufruct rights, but as the plots were inherited by the sons, in practice the families had a permanent usufruct title. If there were no heirs, however, the land was taken over by the lineage council. In addition, the stubble fields had to be open up for common use. There was private property (*milk*) only around the towns where people lived under the Sharia.

From 1930, the sheep farmers began to undergo a process of sedentarisation. Today they have all settled, mostly in the lowlands because of the better climatological conditions there. Only thc large herd owners still practise semi-nomadic sheep raising: They contract shepherds to herd the flocks on the summer pastures. The tent encampment, as a grouping, has completely disintegrated and no longer has any political function. However, the larger social unit – the lineage – still operates as a political unit. Sedentarisation has generally taken the form of people settling in villages or rural market centres. Village populations belong to one or more lineages claiming common descent, while in the market centres newcomers now live alongside the lineages of the settler population. The village council is made up of the married men of the village or centre who are wealthy enough to lodge guests and pay for travel expenses; one or two influential tribal notables usually dominate the council, however (see also Beaudet 1969: 22). Although in small villages the council may in fact be a lineage council, in larger settlements the members generally belong to several lineages. The council decides on local religious and social matters, such as theft, family disputes, the maintenance of the mosque and the like. In matters to do with land, it decides on the date of the opening and the closing of pastures, and the date of sowing and harvesting, and it appoints the watchman, who controls access to the pastures and use of the water (Venema 2002: 107-11). As we shall see, newcomer families have only a minor say in the village council.

Inclusion of strangers during the autonomous period

Until 1912 the inhabitants mostly lived autonomous of the sultanate, with the tribes even dominating the urban centres as elsewhere in the Middle East and North Africa (Gellner 1969), although there have been intermittent periods when the sultan controlled the towns, for example, during the reign of Moulay Ismael, mentioned earlier. It was only during the reign of Sultan Moulay Hassan (1873-1894) that the sultanate again tried to establish some authority over the Beni Mguild: Just before the end of his reign, Moulay Hassan installed a 500-man garrison in Azrou, and built barracks and a prison in the Quesla quarter. He also built a wall around the Kissaria quarter, where traders from the south had established themselves because they were often harassed by the Beni Mguild (Ihraï-Aouchar 1989: 176).

In 1912, Sultan Moulay Hafid signed a treaty in Fez with the French authorities, under which Morocco became a French Protectorate. In an attempt to preserve their autonomy the Berber tribes of the Middle Atlas, including the Beni Mguild, reacted by besieging Fez. However, the French army 'liberated' the town, marking the start of the military campaign in Morocco under the leadership of Resident-General Lyautey. It took the army until 1934 to defeat all the tribes. Lyautey aimed not to undermine the tribes that had not submitted, but took his time and encouraged them to surrender; his instructions to his generals were very clear on this point (Bidwell 1973: 13).

Until the beginning of the colonial period, strangers were allowed to settle among the Berbers, but only by being included in the tribe. Conquerors settled down to practise agriculture and they controlled access to the commons in order to secure sheep rearing. The defeated tribes were chased away, but young men – and even adult men and families – could stay or move in to work for the new settlers, if they could find a protector. The stranger would sacrifice one or more sheep at the door of his intended protector as an entreaty; this ceremony was called *tamghrouste*. If the man so entreated accepted the offering, he became the patron of the stranger. It was thus impossible to settle independently. Traders, too, had to find a protector. For itinerant traders, there was generally a lodge (*fondouk*) in the larger settlements where a room could be rented. Temporary sojourn among the Beni Mguild entailed no specific obligations. However, traders who wished to establish themselves permanently had to obtain the protection of tribal notables. This was a necessity for the traders living in Azrou, Ain Leuh and Mrirt. Woodcutters, such as those living in a ward of Ain Leuh (Bernard 1917), also had to have a protector. In other words, tribes are not homogeneous descent groups.

A man could become a full member of the Beni Mguild by marrying a local woman – but only under certain conditions: He had to undergo what is called 'temporary marriage'. A stranger could be invited to work for the family head. The man was called *amhars,* meaning 'a person riding on the back of the owner'. All his produce was for the head of the family, but the stranger slept with a daughter or a sister of the head and later received part of the revenues. It was a formal contract because the lineage council decided on amount of the goods he should receive in order to establish himself, the share of the revenues at the end of the contract, and the length of time he had to work for the family head. If the woman agreed to marry him, the case was decided by the tribal council. If the council agreed, he became a full member of the Berber community.

Thereafter he had access to land – on which to farm and build a house – and to the common pastures, so he could start sheep-rearing independently (see also Bruno 1917: 135, 186). Succinctly, a stranger gained access to land only by being included in the community. He could now participate in the village meetings. Becoming a member of a Beni Mguild community, however, brought with it several new responsibilities: He had to participate in warfare and in collective work (for example, repairing local irrigation channels and roads), and to contribute to the village funds to pay for the maintenance of the mosque, the salary of the Koran expert, and blood money (Bendaoud 1917: 290, 291, 299; Bruno 1917: 192; 1918: 302, 303).

The first period of colonial administration: Preservation

At the inception of the Protectorate, Resident-General Lyautey (1912-1925) did much to ensure that colonisation was in harmony with the development of the local population rather than in conflict with it. He wanted a Berber policy based on their customs, traditions, social organization, and language, and dealing with the Berbers' aversion to anything to do with the government, which they have always regarded as an oppressive power (Julien 1978: 100). Having learned the high cost of direct occupation from their experience in Algeria and realising that administration by French civil officials required more human and financial resources than they had at their disposal, he found it more sensible and economical to rule through the existing tribal institutions. He was surrounded by administrators who had served in other colonies, especially in Algeria and Tunisia. On the basis of their experience, these administrators believed in the value of indirect rule and the maintenance of the traditional authority system as the only feasible form of administration in tribal territory. Therefore Lyautey developed a style of ruling through traditional institutions. In September 1914, legislation was passed granting Berber tribes the right to continue to govern themselves according to their own laws and customs under the supervision of the authorities (Bidwell 1973: 208-12).

More precisely this meant that the French administration anchored the semi-nomadic tribes to the present confines of their territory by establishing administrative districts along the boundaries of the *territoire du tribu*, the latter often named after the dominant tribal group within the area. At the beginning, the French military district officers (*Officiers des Affaires Indigènes*) did their best to make *trance-humance* arrangements but later on this became more difficult (Bidwell 1973: 183, 184; Beaudet 1969: 31-3). Secondly, the application of indirect rule meant that the tribal leaders were mandated to rule their areas in the name of the French colonial state: They became the *caids* (local government representatives) within the colonial system. If a tribal leader was strong enough to exert influence, the French tried to gain his allegiance rather than oppose him. If there was no tribal leader, the French consulted the local tribal council to assist in selecting a *caid*. This often worked out well for the French administration. For example, this method produced such chiefs as *caid* Amkor of the Ait Abdi tribe, who was to rule for thirty years and become a personal friend of Marshal Juin and a holder of the Grand Cross of the Legion of Honour.

Thirdly, the French authorities ensured that local land tenure was left much as it was, thus leaving the traditional management of common land untouched. Lyautey prevented the large-scale arrival of colons during his thirteen-year reign. Whole rural districts – especially those in the mountainous areas – were closed to colons, with the help of French military district officers. Common land tenure was maintained because the Protectorate authorities were afraid that the rural population would sell their land to the French colons and to Moroccan citizens (Bidwell 1973: 209). The records of the *Cercle* of the Beni Mguild contain numerous letters from officers to would-be settlers warning them not to come. After the decree of August 1913, the registering of common land was commenced at the *Conservateur Foncier*, assisted by the French military officers and the *caids*, while the decree of July 1914 made tribal land inalienable. Later on, lists were drawn up at the *Service des Collectivités* showing which lineages had right of access to the commons. The tribal councils were charged with managing these common pastures, and they could continue to manage the grassland and water sources and to distribute land for cultivation.

In this area, the Berbers allowed newcomers to settle only if they were placed under protection as cited above. In addition, independent settlement was impossible because there was no concept of private property in the rural areas. The Berber tribes in the rural areas did not recognise private property, only permanent usufruct right (*bien milk d'usage*). This could not be sold, only passed on within the tribe. However, a decade later this changed. After Lyautey, there had been what Berque called 'the golden times for the broker and lawyer' when Berbers were swindled out of their land by 'scandalous examples' of land grabbing (Berque 1955: 43).

The second period: Capitalist development and independent settlement

It was soon apparent that native customs and laws were being preserved only if they did not conflict with European interests. Shortly after the establishment of French rule, many newcomers arrived in the Middle Atlas, and elsewhere in Morocco. The colonial administration had to face the arrival of many *colons*. Some years after the establishment of the Protectorate, during training courses Captain Bondis was teaching the French military officers that one of their principal duties was to persuade the local people that it was in their own interest to sell their land to the *colons*. This followed the demand made by the Chambers of Agriculture in 1920:

> Generally speaking we ask the administration to give orders to the French military district officers so as to inform them that they are first and foremost responsible for leaning towards the development of a French predominance in this country and as a result they have to help and aid the French settlers (Bidwell 1973: 181) (author's translation).

The collaboration Lyautey sought with the Moroccan population became a process of segregation between the European and Moroccan communities, which intensified over time (Julien 1978: 107).

This led to the fact that in the 1920s foreign entrepreneurs began a capitalist expansion into agriculture and forest exploitation. These people could settle autonomously because of the size of their numbers and the fact that the French administration would protect them. At the start of the Protectorate era, the rural centre of Azrou became the capital of Azrou province; it grew considerably as the French established administrative facilities and increasing numbers of foreigners (most of whom were French) arrived there to try their luck. As early as 1914 foreigners tried to open a sawmill in Azrou; however, Commandant Colombat refused them permission, as he was afraid of the French monopolising the sector. In July 1917, Captain Maitrat allowed them to set up shop in Azrou, but not to buy any property. Six months later, Captain Lefèvre told his chiefs in Meknes that so many Europeans had arrived in Azrou that a surveyor was needed to design a proper European village (Bidwell 1973: 43). As a result of the expansion of agriculture, trade, forest exploitation and construction activities, newcomers (including French, Greeks and Arabs from Fez and Meknes) established themselves in Azrou, which expanded steadily: Its population grew from a few hundred at the turn of the twentieth century, to 1593 in 1926 and 8494 in 1953 (Beaudet 1969: 71, Venema 1993: 168, 169).

Smaller settlements like Ain Leuh, which at the beginning of the Protectorate had only about a hundred inhabitants, also expanded. With the introduction of electricity in 1924, forest exploitation grew apace and there was a substantial influx of newcomers: Up to about 400 forest labourers settled in and around Ain Leuh each year. The ranks were swelled even more by the influx of Arabs from Fez and Meknes; between 1926 and 1947, the population of Ain Leuh grew from 1593 to 7983 (Venema 1993: 168, 169).

The buying and selling of land started in 1920, first around Mrirt, and then around Azrou (Beaudet 1969: 24). The French authorities bought land from the Beni Mguild; in the 1930s they had acquired about 1,000 ha and by the early 1950s some 3,500 ha. These *lots de colonisation* were sold to *colons*. The *colons* themselves made private deals with the Berber population. In the early 1950s they had acquired an additional 3400 ha in this manner (Beaudet 1969: 21, 24, 57). In total, the *colons* acquired about twenty-five per cent of the land under cultivation. Whether through public or private deals, in both cases colonisation meant that land had been acquired without the due intervention of the tribal councils.

Local notables – such as the *caids* and their assistants, *shaykhs* – expanded their holdings by acquiring land in the winter pastures before registration was introduced.[3] Because some of their own leaders had sold land to foreigners without consulting the lineage council and had illegally acquired land illegally, individual farmers followed suit. In a nutshell, colonisation involved land being acquired or sold without the lineage council being properly informed. Ina further break with tradition, the *colons* and tribal chiefs did not place themselves under the protection of a Berber tribesman but acted independently.

As a consequence, Arab newcomers began to settle independently too. Those who could afford it bought parcels of land. There are no figures concerning the amount of land bought by Moroccan citizens, however, and informants in the research area have quite different opinions. What is certain is that those who bought did not place themselves under patronage. Even the poorer newcomers seeking to work as a labourer for a Berber farmer no longer sacrificed a sheep (*tamghrouste*) and became simple workers. Similarly, the Berber farmers no longer informed the tribal councils about the arrival of newcomers. According to informants, the *tamghrouste* ceremony had become obsolete by the end of the 1930s (cf. Dabancens 1951: 102). The process of incorporating strangers into the Berber communities had ended halfway through the Protectorate.[4]

Independence: The institution of official law

Immediately after independence in 1956, the national movement – which had formed the new government – abolished customary law among the Berber tribes and proclaimed a uniform, nationwide legislation. This was possible because the national movement, under the banner of the Istiqlal political party, was based on the Arab urban bourgeoisie and leaders of the commercial and religious establishment. These men had an aversion to customary law because, according to them, it was based on pre-Islamic barbarian customs, the period of *jahiliyy* (ignorance). They thought that the whole country should be governed by the national law, which should end the existence of *tribus de coutûmes berbères*. According to the leader of the national movement, Allal al-Fassi, customary law was a primitive institution incapable of progressing with the times, an instrument of the colonial power against the Sharia and Islam, and an attack on the national unity (al-Fassi 1977, quoted in Bouderbala 2000: 110). As a result, a national law – inspired by the Sharia (which in practice is mainly in the domain of family law) – was introduced.

---

3 Examples are *caid* Said ould Haddou ou Akka of the Irklaouan and Ait Arfa tribes; *caid* Amkor of the Ait Abdi tribe; *caid* Ben Youssef of the Air Arfa de Guigou tribe; *khalifa* Oubajja of Timahdite; and the *shaykhs* of Ait Alla and Ait Faska (sections of the Irklaouan tribe).

4 Member of the rural council of Ain Leuh, 15 September 1990.

The government decreed that justice in rural areas would no longer be administered by tribal chiefs and tribal councils, but by appointed junior judges under Istiqlal control who would supervise the application of official law. Strengthening state control, officials of the Ministry of the Interior were now appointed the guardians of the villages and their land. The provincial governor's official task was transformed into the supervision of the local populations (*tutelle sur les collectivités locales)* and in his jurisdiction he was therefore responsible for law and order. In order to exercise his power, the *caids* of the rural districts provided him with the necessary information; in this, the *caids* were aided by their assistants, *shayk*s and *muqaddams*.

The official law acknowledged that everybody had the right to settle wherever they wanted, because now everybody was Moroccan and was therefore free to settle anywhere in order to make a living. People were to have the right of settlement (*droit de cité*), provided they were able to provide their own accommodation. The only responsibility of the local government officials was to ensure that new settlers were properly registered. As one informant reported: 'After 1956 there was freedom to settle wherever you wanted. People therefore looked for a fertile location to earn a living; that was the only important thing'.[5] From now on nobody could be prevented from settling, because they would say: 'I'm a Moroccan. I now have the same rights as you'. Our informants made the point that they had fought for Moroccan independence so that everybody could live and go where they chose.[6]

Where it concerns tribal common land, which had been preserved in the colonial period, it persisted under the national law but was now managed by the Ministry of the Interior. The government decided that access to tribal lands was no longer to be a matter for the lineage council and traditional watchmen, but for the government. In fact, the Ministry of the Interior – in particular the Directorate of Rural Affairs – decreed itself the sole representative of the rural population's interests and the sole institution with authority with respect to access to common land (Basri 1988: 113).

Opposition and countervailing processes

However, the application of the official law met with much opposition, because after the departure of the French the local Berber population expressed their resentment about the arrival of so many newcomers who now obtained legal protection from the national law and the official authorities.

In addition, new officials were appointed, mostly Arab-speaking Istiqlal party men who started to manage tribal affairs without involving the tribal

---

5 Secondary-school teacher at Azrou, 11 September 1990.

6 The same happened in the High Atlas. As an Ait Morghad pastoralist contended: 'We armed ourselves, went hungry, left our homes and sacrificed all we had so we could become independent, roam freely, and cast off the oppressive chains of the Christians and their friends' (Ilahiane 1999: 39).

notables and councils. From the summer of 1956, dissatisfaction in the Moroccan interior began to manifest itself. In the Middle Atlas, two Berber leaders – Lahcen Lyoussy, a former *caid* of Immouzzer, and Mahjoubi Aherdane, a former *caid* of Oulmes – took advantage of the growing resentment. In the years leading up to independence, they had not collaborated with the French administration but had been active in the independence movement and had thus acquired considerable prestige. In August 1956, Lahcen Lyoussi convened a tribal gathering of several hundred Berber leaders and their followers in order to show their opposition to the new policies. In January 1957, the governor of Tafilalt, Addi ou Bihi, closed down the Istiqlal headquarters in Midelt and threw all the offending persons in gaol (including the police chief and judge), because he wanted to appoint the *caids* and their assistants instead of having to put up with the Istiqlal party men appointed by the government. Lyoussi and Addi ou Bihi summoned Berber tribes, including the Beni Mguild, and incited them to launch an armed revolt. They did so, but the uprising was soon put down by the army (led by the then Prince Hassan II) and the Beni Mguild, like other tribes, were quick to regain their homelands. This, however, did not put an end to the discontent among the rural population of the Middle Atlas (Ashford 1961: 194-203, 319-26; Bendourou 1986: 66-7).

In 1958, the same tribal leaders who earlier had expressed their resentment so forcefully decided to go into politics in order to maintain traditional governance. Lyoussi and Aherdane founded the *Mouvement Populaire* political party (the 'Berber party', as is it known locally), which they used as a vehicle to advance their political goals, including the key issue of giving the indigenous population greater influence over their own affairs. These party leaders were opposed to the excessive power of the Ministry of the Interior, and advocated the delegation of power to the local population and local functionaries. They preferred to invest tribal leaders in the administrative positions, whether or not these leaders had acquired land illegitimately during the Protectorate (Leveau 1976: 237, 240, 241).

Although it was not official policy, the leaders of the Berber party declared that access to collective land should continue to be decided by the lineage council and the *naib*s. The upshot was that newcomers who had settled under the new right of free settlement were only to be granted access to collective pastures if they had lived in the village for at least fifty years (cf. Ashford, 1961: 321).[7]

Afraid of a Berber-Arab divide, King Mohammed V pressured the tribal leaders to stop the rallies. However, the monarchy, not wanting to lose the support of the rural elite, encouraged the establishment of the *Mouvement Populaire* and tacitly supported its policies. Under the king's plan, the Berber party was to be the backbone of a traditionalist party that would cooperate

---

7 Chairman of the rural council in Timahdite, 29 October 1989; member of Ain Leuh council, 15 September 1990.

with the Ministry of the Interior to maintain traditional social and political structures and prevent to introduction of social change promoted under the banner of the urban bourgeoisie (Leveau 1976: 51, 242; Ben Kaddour 1972: 263). As a consequence of the monarch's support, this party dominated the Berber countryside. In the 1960 and 1964 local elections, the *Mouvement Populaire* gained strong support in the area (Leveau 1976: 88, 152).

After independence, the Middle Atlas was governed by officials from other regions. In Meknes province the newly appointed heads of the regional offices as well as the provincial governor (*gouverneur*) were Arabic-speaking. At the district level, however, *caids* were recruited from the local population; these were men who had not opposed King Mohammed V in his support for independence (Ashford 1961: 134-145, Venema 2002: 106).

The tribal leaders resumed full control of their former positions, which had been weakened in the colonial period. The first *caid* of the Ait Ichou Ouali from the Ait Abdi tribe evicted all the newcomers' herds from the collective pastures. Another influential Berber who acted likewise was one of the notables from Ait Amy Driss. He was an *ancien combattant* who had trained at the Dar el Beïda military academy and served as an officer in the Moroccan army from 1956 to 1974. Between 1956 and 1970 he too drove independent Arab and Saharaoui settlers off the commons and forced them to sell any land owned as private property.

The conduct of these and other local notables set an example to the common Berber farmers: They too started to oppose any members of the population who had settled without performing the *tamghrouste* ceremony. As one informant said: 'The strangers wanted to strangle us on our own land and break the bond with our forefathers who shed their blood in battles over borders'.[8] The line taken by most lineage councils and watchmen was that those who had not been traditionally adopted and had not performed *tamghrouste*, as well as their descendants, were not deemed to be part of the indigenous population. As such, they were barred from membership of the lineage council and from grazing their cattle on the commons. Free, unsubordinated settlement therefore came to mean exclusion from the Berber community and hence from the associated equal rights.

Under these circumstances, there was a revitalisation of traditional institutions and customary law. The village council now functioned again as the trustee of the lineage estates, land, and springs belonging to the ancestral heritage. It was at the village level that decisions were made regarding access to and the use of land not cleared or in use as collective pastures (Venema 2002: 109-11).

[8] Farmer in Ait Hamza, 23 November 1988.

The state and official law gain in strength

For some decades now, the district officers have been contributing to the growing influence of the newcomers in this area. Since the 1970s these officials have generally been recruited from the *Ecôle de Perfectionnement de Cadre* at Kenitra rather than from the tribal notables. In general, the district officers comply with government decrees regarding access to collective pastures (see also El Khyari 1987: 254). The rule they apply is that outsiders wishing to settle in the village are forbidden to rear sheep as an occupation, and they and their assistants enforce this rule. A *caid* generally grants newcomers access to the collective pastures if they have lived in the area for one generation or longer and have agriculture as their main occupation. Those born in the area have automatic access. As the district officer of Timahdite said: 'Not allowing newcomers into the lineage heritage causes problems, obliging them to return to their home areas, which will create even more problems'.[9] So the district officers do not support the autochthonous population only.

Therefore, there are now two authorities that impose rules concerning access to lineage estates, and this results in frequent and severe conflicts. If the provincial governor and the *caid* are unable to resolve such conflicts, the matter is taken to the Ministry of the Interior in Rabat – which means that it takes a considerable time before a decision is made, if at all. Many Arab families have lived in the area for more than a generation but still have difficulty accessing the commons and need assistance from the state officials. An example is the Ait Khaoua lineage. They are originally from Missour, but have lived with the Ait Abdi since the 1920s. There used to be fourteen families immediately after their arrival and they earned their living as shepherds for the Ait Abdi. Now they are forty-five families and they have their own flocks, comprising a total of 6500 head of sheep. There are regular mêlées between the Ait Abdi and the Ait Khaoua, and the *caid* has to intervene to protect the latter.

This has made the *caid* an influential person. If a village council is unable to arrive at a common position, the parties may turn to the *caid.* Some village councils are paralysed by internal conflict as a result of long-standing disputes over land, pastures and/or water points. Under such conditions the *caid* is able to exert his influence. It also has to be said that not everybody accepts the authority of the village council just like that. The 'intelligentsia' (that is, those with a modern education) regularly criticise the village council; they do not always attend the meetings and prefer to go directly to the *caid.* In their view, the council members are old-fashioned and have no knowledge of today's world. Some of them hold that the council has no special authority, because it is not referred to in the Koran. They therefore deny that the council is a sacred institution. They do not accept the council's decisions out of hand but judge them critically. In the event of a dispute with the village council, they prefer to address the *caid* or the court rather than to pursue a local settlement (Venema

9 Interview, 7 February 1991.

2002: 108-9). On market days the *caid*'s office is full of people seeking pronouncements on a variety of issues.

Nowadays, those appointed as the watchmen of the collective pastures have seen their influence weakened by the new authority system. All watchmen are now registered at the *caid*'s office. This they do not appreciate this because it means they often have to visit his office to discuss disputes. The result is that although the *caid* or the court will make the ultimate decision, it is the watchman who has to confront the people with a negative decision. The people report that it is now very difficult to find people willing to be elected to the post of watchman, and that not every lineage has its own watchman (Venema 1992: 311-2).

Inclusion and exclusion of strangers today: Competing jurisdictions

Land is the basis of tribal identity, and newcomers are not allowed to enter the commons. However, as shown above, newcomers may take their case to the *caid.* Now it is possible that newcomers, assisted by the *caid*, can manage to take matters to the court if the local population does not comply with the orders of the local officials in matters of government legislation. The following two case studies illustrate this situation.

Mohammed Ali

Mohammed Ali is a sheep farmer who is originally from Missour. In 1937 he bought land from the Ait Mouli, a grouping within the Ait Abdi tribe, and started rearing sheep. He and his son were not allowed to herd their animals on the collective pastures. The son brought this problem repeatedly before the *caid*, but because the *caid*s were recruited from the Ait Abdi population until the 1970s, no action was taken. Only when an (Arabic-speaking) outsider was appointed *caid* in Ain Leuh was his case brought before the provincial governor and later the *Direction des Affaires Rurales* of the Ministry of the Interior. Following a successful lawsuit in 1982, he was granted access rights (because he had lived in the area for so long) and the *caid* ordered the Ait Abdi to leave him undisturbed. However, the Ait Mouli continue to work against him, especially because they cannot stand the fact that he has become a wealthy man (he owns 1,600 sheep and two lorries). They have therefore decided that he is not allowed to water his flock at the Akadous water point just a short distance from his farm. Now his son must fetch water by lorry from another source, nine kilometres away. This is a government-built water point and the Ait Abdi were not entitled to deny him access (Venema 2002: 110).

Son of a watchman
In early 2001, the son of a watchman from Toufestalt found an Arabic Ait Khaoua shepherd with his flock on the Narten collective pasture. He told him to move on because he had no right to graze his sheep there. The shepherd reportedly answered: 'Long live democracy! We also have a right to this land. We've been living in the midst of the *jemaa* of Ait Mouli for a long time, so what can you do to me?' In reply, the son attacked him with a sickle, wounding him on his back, head, and knees and leaving him unconscious. Other Ait Khaoua men came to the shepherd's rescue and took him to the hospital at Ain Leuh, where first aid was given before he was transferred to the larger hospital at Azrou. Many Ait Khaoua men accompanied him and surrounded the hospital, shouting that they would take revenge. The police went looking for the son of the watchman. He was brought before the local court and sentenced to two months' imprisonment and a fine of 6,000 dirhams. The Ait Khaoua were not satisfied with this and attacked the watchman's second son, who also had to be hospitalised. They then took the case to the higher court in Meknes. A year later, no legal decision had been taken (personal observation, Mguild, 10 May 2001).

These two cases are unequivocal examples of the official assistance given to newcomers who claim access to land. Both cases also demonstrate that the local population finds ways to resist these claims, despite official assistance and legislation: The autochthonous community evoking a strong sense of identification.

Crossing the boundary between settlers and strangers
The influx of migrants has evoked the feeling of outside domination, for which the embracing of autochthony is almost the inevitable outcome. In the everyday language of the Middle Atlas, stereotypes about Berbers, Arabs and other ethnic groups are common. The Berbers say that they hate newcomers. With reference to Arabs, one informant stated: 'They are the evil eye: Avoid looking at them, because they may bring bad luck'.[10] Bad feelings are particularly common if newcomers are successful in their trade or occupation. One Berber informant who was complaining about this point ended by saying: 'Strangers come today, and tomorrow they have a large family; but they will never be allowed to take advantage of us'. In a dispute between a Berber and an Arab, I heard the former shout *Raa arabic!* ('Go back to your Arab countrymen!').

Arabs also regularly have recourse to stereotypes. One informant said: 'They live as savages in tents near caves and forests. They're nomads who use boots and plastic for clothing. They don't speak or read Arabic and don't know the Koran'.[11] Another informant said: 'They don't think about the

10 Farmer in Toufestalt, 24 October 1989.
11 Shopkeeper in Ain Leuh, 24 September 1987.

Hereafter. They live like barbarians: They don't have a family life and their daughters are prostitutes'.[12] I heard many similar statements.

However, there is no complete social separation between the Berbers and the newcomers. The newcomers are not always seen in relation to the group to which they belong and are not attributed stereotypical characteristics. The boundaries between the early settlers and the newcomers have not closed completely. Wealthy and influential newcomers who adapt to village customs are allowed access to the commons. The other side of the coin is that poor Berber settlers help strangers gain access to the commons by deceitful means.

Outstanding newcomers might be invited to attend the meeting of the village council as are particularly pious men such as those organising the ritual sacrifices (*sadakas*) on the holy days. More broadly, the only ones who are eligible are those who have behaved appropriately towards the 'original imazighen' by helping to solve conflicts, contributing to the village fund and – if rich – helping the needy by providing them with loans. As one informant said: 'In every village newcomers from elsewhere may take part in the lineage meetings if they help pay the salary of the *fqih* [Koran expert] and organise *sadakas*. They can have access to our pastures if they are well-mannered. If not, they are excluded'.[13]

As members of the lineage councils, these newcomers help decide on a variety of community issues, including rural council candidacy, the salary of the Koran teacher, and access to the common pastureland. They themselves have often obtained access to the pastures, as the following examples show (these examples concern men claiming to be of religious descent (*shorfa*)); this has an impact on the Berbers because they are afraid of them. A well-informed farmer told me:

> We Berbers of the region very much believe in the *shorfa* because of the belief that somebody who has displayed anger towards a *cheriff* will be punished by becoming gravely ill or by losing his cattle: There will be a catastrophe either at home or with the herd.

Here follow two examples of strangers who have broke through the boundary between early settlers and newcomers.

Haj Moulay Brahim

Haj Moulay Brahim is a descendant of a *shorfa* family from Tindjad. His father settled in Souk el Had without performing the *tamghrouste* ceremony. He became a seasonal labourer in France, where he worked for many years. He was able to buy a sizeable tract of land, and his sons intensified farm

---

12 Teacher in Sidi Addi, 24 September 1990.

13 Farmer in Timahdite, 22 November 1988.

operations by buying a tractor and starting arboriculture. The family are well-off: They own a Peugeot 405 and several houses, which they rent out. The cattle are allowed to graze the commons. Haj Moulay Brahim has travelled to Mecca, and hence bears the title El Haj. Whenever he returns, he says his prayers in the mosque and organises *sadaka* on the holy days to honour the forefathers. He tries to settle conflicts by applying Koranic law, and even mediates in conflicts between settlers and newcomers over access to the commons.

Moulay Mohammed

Moulay Mohammed too is a descendent of a *shorfa* family from Tafilalt whose father also settled in the area without performing *tamghrouste*. Moulay Mohammed now lives among the Ait Boubker, near the hamlet of Faliba. He is a rich farmer, and has a tractor with which he ploughs the fields of other farmers. He has access to the collective pastures and has even built stables there. He is a religious man, attending all the prayer services, and is much respected for his pious scholarliness. He is a member of the lineage council of Faliba and helps decide on community affairs and resolve conflicts among families.

The dealings of poor Berber herders with newcomers also contribute to the weakening of traditional management of the commons. Several Berbers themselves now enter into secret and informal contractual relationships with newcomers, especially those who have sunk into poverty. These poor Berbers rent their right of access to newcomers, especially as they have no herd themselves. This is profitable to both parties: newcomers gain access to the pastures and the Berber farmer, by providing shepherding services, receives a quarter of the wool and a quarter of the new lambs. Among the Ait Arfa Berber, 19.1 per cent of the Ait Arfa pastoralists engage in herding in association with outsiders, while 24.1 per cent of the total sheep population is under the annual tenure system. (Bencherifa and Johnson 1991: 411; Hanafi 1984: 273). Because local management is gradually being transformed into state management, the collective pastures are increasingly becoming open-access commons because the rules of access have become unclear.

Conclusion

In this chapter I argued that autochthony and the inclusion and exclusion of outsiders is based on disputes about access to land and other resources. The competition gives rise to a sense of belonging and first settlement remaining a strong point of identification in relation to newcomers. The process of state formation heavily impacted on autochthony.

Until the beginning of last century, when the Berbers were still fairly independent of the authority of the sultanate, newcomers were integrated into

Berber society by adoption and thus became full members of the community and gained access to land. The distinction autochthonous/allochthonous did not exist. At first, colonial policy did not affect the inclusion or exclusion of newcomers because customary law and tribal governance was maintained. In the 1920s, however, a land and labour market developed in the Middle Atlas: newcomers could buy land and could settle without informing the tribal councils and without being placed under protection. As a result, the traditional tribal institutions were undermined. Under the impact of the new state of affairs, Berber society disintegrated and newcomers were able to settle independently.

After independence (1956), the government attempted to monopolise decisions regarding land issues and settlement. However, the Berber *Mouvement Populaire* party and the monarchy were intent on encouraging a kind of neo-traditionalism and an obsession with ancestral land. As a result, local tribal leadership was maintained and tribal notables became district officers. As a consequence, the newcomers who had settled independently were barred from both the commons and official positions. Inevitably, land claims are embedded in the issue of belonging and autochthony.

However, since about 1970 official law and courts have become reality. Since then, *caid*s and provincial governors are no longer recruited from among the local population and no longer collaborate to deny outsiders access to lineage land. Gaining access to land along ethnic lines is consequently more difficult. There is growing government influence in the Middle Atlas, with the provincial governor and the *caid* now providing an additional avenue for resolving disputes. This has weakened the position of the village council. This leads to disputes within the council, with the result that the regional state officials sometimes succeed in taking matters into their own hands.

Indubitably, the local Berbers have great respect for well-educated Arabs, such as teachers, men of religious descent, and Koran experts. These and other newcomers who serve the community by means of their religious knowledge, by helping with conflict resolution and by contributing amply to village funds enjoy the same rights as the original settlers. This offers newcomers another way to become accepted into the community and to gain access to the commons. Besides, the Berber population has a variety of interests of its own and acts accordingly. Some members of the original settler population rent their grazing rights to outsiders.

Although there have been several cases of violence, many newcomers consider that they now have more room to manoeuvre as the state allows them legal procedures to access land. As this chapter shows, however, there are also local processes at work demonstrating that although newcomers may have legal rights they still might be excluded from land having to bow to the claim of autochthony by the first-comers. Whether or not one belongs to the autochthonous population, it is argued in this chapter, is not fixed but influenced by the process of state formation.

References

ASHFORD, D.E. (1961) *Political change in Morocco*, Princeton: Princeton University Press.

BASRI, D. (1988) *L'administration territoriale. L'expérience Marocaine*, Paris: Bordas.

BEAUDET, G. (1969) Les Beni M'Guild du Nord. Etude Géographique de l'Evolution Récente d'une Confèderation Semi-nomade, *Géographie du Maroc*, 15, Rabat: Faculté des Lettres.

BENCHERIFA, A. and D.L. JOHNSON (1991) Changing resource management strategies and their environmental impacts in the Middle Atlas Mountains of Morocco, *Mountain Research and Development*, 3: 183-94.

BEN KADDOUR, A. (1972) The Neo Makhzan and the Berbers, in: Gellner, E. and Micaud, C. (Eds) *Arabs and Berbers. From tribe to nation in North Africa*, London: Duckworth, pp. 259-67.

BENDAOUD (1917) Notes sur le Pays Zaian, *Achives Berbères*, 2(3): 276-306.

BENDOUROU, O. (1986) *Le pouvoir exécutif au Maroc depuis l'indépendance*, Publisud.

BERNARD, A. (1917) Les forêts de cèdres de l'Atlas Marocain, *France-Maroc*, 12.

BERQUE, J. (1955) Les Mezûda Style historique d'une tribu marocaine, *Revue Historique*, CCXIV.

BIDWELL, R. (1973) *Morocco under colonial rule. French administration of tribal areas, 1912-1956*, London: Frank Cass.

BOUDERBALA, N. (2000) La Loi Nationale entre ciel et terre, *Etudes Rurales*, 155-156: 107-16.

BRUNO, H. (1915-1918) Notes sur le statut coutumier des Berbères Marocains (Iguerouan du sud, Ait Ndir, Ait Mguild), *Achives Berbères* 1(3); 2(3); 2(4).

DABANCENS, J. (1951) Les Ait Abdi du Moyen Atlas, et leurs réactions au contact des étrangers, *Les cahiers d'Outre-Mer*, 4: 101-18.

EL KHYARI, T. (1987) *Agriculture au Maroc*, Editions OKAD.

GELLNER, E. (1969) *Saints of the Atlas*, London: Weidenfeld and Nicolson.

GESCHIERE, P. and T. NYAMNJOH (2000) Capitalism and autochthony: The seesaw of mobility and belonging, *Public Culture* 12(2): 423-52.

HANAFI, A. (1984) *La mutation économico-sociale de la tribu semi-nomade Irklaouan (Moyen Atlas)*, thèse 3eme cycle, Toulouse: Université de Toulouse-Le Mirail, U.E.R de Géographie.

IHRAÏ-AOUCHAR, A. (1989) Les communautés rurales de la Haute Moulouya du 17e siècle à nos jours, *Hespéris-Tamuda*, 26; 27.

ILAHIANE, H. (1999) The Berber agdal institutions: Indigenous range management in the Atlas Mountains, *Ethnology*, 38(1): 21-46.

JULIEN, C-A. (1978) *Le Maroc face aux impérialismes 1415-1956*, Paris: Editions J.A.

LEVEAU, R. (1976) *Le Fellah Marocain, défenseur du trône*, Paris: Presses de la Fondation Nationale des Sciences Politiques.

VENEMA, L.B. (1992) Ecological crisis and local power constellations: The case of the Middle Atlas, in: *La recherche scientifique au service du développement*, Colloques et Seminaires, no. 22, Rabat: Université Mohammed V, Faculté des Lettres et des Sciences Humaines.

VENEMA, L.B. (1993) Stagnatie en groei van een plattelandskern in de Midden Atlas van Marokko: Een macro-perspectief, *Afrika Focus*, 9(3/4).

VENEMA, L.B. (2002) The vitality of local political institutions in the Middle Atlas, Morocco, *Ethnology*, 42(2): 103-18.

WATERBURY, J. (1979) *The commander of the faithful: The Moroccan political elite – A study of segmental politics*, London: Weidenfeld and Nicolson

8

Land and the politics of identity. The case of Anywaa-Nuer relations in the Gambella region

Dereje Feyissa

Introducing the study area and its people[1]

The Gambella region is located in western Ethiopia about 780 kilometres from the national capital, Addis Ababa. Its current land size covers 25,274 square kilometres, consisting of nine *wereda*s (hereafter districts). Gambella is a border region, covering one of Ethiopia's largest international boundaries with the Sudan. This physical setting partly explains its socio-economic marginality and strategic (political) sensitivity.

According to the 1994 census, the population size of the Gambella region is 200,000. There are five ethno-linguistic groups living in the region: The Anywaa (twenty-seven per cent), the Nuer (forty per cent), the Majangir (six per cent), the Opo and the Komo (three per cent). These groups of people are defined by the current Ethiopian government as the indigenous people of the Gambella region. Although the indigenous people are linguistically inter-related and engage in various forms of social and economic exchanges, they

[1] The data used in this paper is extracted from the fieldwork I carried out in the Gambella region for my doctoral study.

nevertheless form distinct ethnic communities. Even in a situation where there are inter-ethnic marriages, the ethnic boundary is reproduced through the effect of assimilation. The ethnic boundary is also marked by difference in livelihood strategies. The Anywaa and the Opo are predominantly cultivators, the Nuer practise transhumant pastoralism (steadily changing into agro-pastoralism), while the Majangir combine hunting and gathering with shifting cultivation (Stauder 1971).

Gambella is also home for immigrant people who have come to Gambella from different parts of the country at various times and for different reasons. They are known by the generic name *degegna* (highlanders).[2] The term highlander is as much a geographic description as it is a metaphor for power, for ever since the incorporation of the Gambella region into the Ethiopian empire at the turn of the 20th century the Ethiopian state has been introduced through, identified with and is represented by the highlanders.[3] Despite their diverse ethnic background, the highlanders speak Amharic (the national language) in everyday communication, whereas the 'indigenous' groups use their respective languages, although many of them are bilingual and Amharic is the administrative language of the Gambella regional state. There is also a 'physical' boundary between the highlanders and the 'indigenous' groups, marked by a very strong discourse on colour: The 'black indigenous' are contrasted with the 'red highlanders' (lighter in their skin colour). The social relevance of the physical boundary has kept intermarriages between them to the minimum.

The demographic imbalance does not match the settlement pattern. The Gambella region consists of nine districts, out of which the Anywaa live in eight of the nine, constituting the majority in five of the districts. The total land area that is settled and claimed by the Anywaa makes up about seventy per cent of the region's landmass. The majority of the Nuer, on the other hand, live in two districts covering only twenty-four per cent of the land size of the region. The majority of the highlanders live in the regional capital, where they make a living as traders and civil servants. Many of the highlanders had prior experience in business in the regions of their origin, and have a wider social network, whereas only a few of the 'indigenous' groups extract wealth from commerce. Their coming from a relatively more developed region of the country and their competence in the national culture have also enabled the highlanders to dominate the civil service. A small number of highlanders also live in the rural areas as cultivators.[4]

---

2 Gambella is a lowland region (500 m above sea level), whereas the neighbouring highland regions rise as high as 2800m.

3 Both the Anywaa and the Nuer use the same word to refer to the highlanders as a group of people and the Ethiopian state.

4 These are remnants of the 1980s resettlement program. More than 60,000 famine-stricken highland farmers were brought to the Gambella region by the

Prior to 1991 Gambella was peripheral to national politics and the highlanders dominated the local administration. Economically it was one of the most backward regions and lacked basic social services. The 1990s brought tremendous political changes to the Gambella region. In 1991 the socialist regime (1974-1991) was overthrown by the EPRDF (Ethiopian People's Revolutionary Democratic Front) and a new federal government was established, consisting of nine ethno-regional states. Accordingly, Gambella was reorganised from a district to a regional state, the Gambella People's National Regional State (hereafter the GPNRS). The EPRDF has adopted ethnicity as the official state ideology and this is institutionalised by the 1994 constitution. According to this constitution, every ethnic group (nation and nationality in the Ethiopian parlance) is accorded the right to self-determination up to secession and develops its own culture and language.

Institutionalised ethnicity is, therefore, one of the new political contexts within which the social struggle between the Anywaa and the Nuer is situated. The Anywaa and the Nuer constitute the two largest ethnic groups and are politically dominant in the GPNRS whose combined population make up more than sixty-five per cent of the region's population. In the new political dispensation, the highlanders emerge as a residual category because as recent immigrants they now belong by definition to one or other of the new ethno-regional states. Thus, they do not form a political constituency and are not represented in the regional council. They nevertheless continue to be economically dominant and to identify with the federal government. In fact, the new representatives of the federal government who wield substantial vis-a-vis the regional authorities are categorised as highlanders. Having a stake to mind (economic security) and with their association with the Ethiopian state, the highlanders are one of the main collective actors and have become 'the significant others' in the contestation between the Anywaa and the Nuer for power and resources.

Contrasting ethnic identity formation and differing discourses on land

The field of ethnicity exhibits one of the highest polemical densities that have produced what Jenkins sarcastically described as more heat than light (2001: 4826). Drawing on an ideal type definition, existing anthropological theories define ethnicity either as a type of solidarity group formed on the basis of the 'givens of social existence' that centre on ideas of a common

socialist state (1974-1991). They were resettled in traditionally Anywaa territories.

origin and a shared culture with which people make sense of their existence (Geertz 1973), or else ethnic group is defined as a solidarity group which is subjectively constructed in the pursuit of perceived interests. Thus the cultural differential that constitutes a given ethnic group is variable, situational and is subject to manipulation (Barth 1969). The first approach is known in the literature as primordialism, principally concerned with the meaning dimension of ethnicity. The second approach is variously known as instrumentalism or constructivism, principally concerned with the interest dimension of ethnicity. This scholarship overlooks how primordialist and constructivist approaches/ideologies could be used themselves as languages of identity construction.

One way of avoiding definitional hurdles is to adopt a formal and flexible definition of an ethnic group. This is possible through a conceptual shift from an ideal type to a family resemblance. Following scholars of a similar persuasion (Horowitz 1985; Eriksen 1991), I draw on Wittgenstein's concept of family resemblance in my understanding of an ethnic group. This allows the possibility for discovering *kinds* of ethnicities without destroying their structural comparability: They are similar enough to be compared, but could exhibit variation in their central features (ideas of common origin, boundary formation and degree of shared sociality), as in a continuum. In such a conceptualisation ethnic groups are 'families' of 'resemblances', not necessarily identical in the degree to which they involve the defining features. On this conceptual basis and judged against the people's own ideas of relatedness and the nature of their ethnic boundaries, I argue that the Anywaa and the Nuer represent two *kinds* of ethnicities, echoing the primordialist and the constructivist approaches respectively. With a stronger idea of origin (an apical ancestor), a land-based identity discourse (territoriality), an ideology of ethnic endogamy and an internal mode of imagining the relevant other (the symbolic contrast between God and humanity), the Anywaa represent an emic primordialist conception of ethnicity. With a weaker descent ideology, open ethnic membership criteria and assimilationist practices, the Nuer represent an emic constructivist conception of an ethnic group. Thus, the content of Anywaa ethnicity predominantly emphasises the meaning dimension of ethnic identity (with a stronger accent on social order and the symbolic dimension of the land), while the content of Nuer ethnicity focuses more on the interest dimension (with a stronger accent on pragmatism).

Viewed from a diachronic perspective, the Anywaa identity discourse has moved from an assimilationist to a primordial mode of ethnic recruitment, while the Nuer have gone through the opposite transformation process, from an original ideology of ethnic purity to an elaborate assimilationism. The conditions under which the transformation of the identity discourses has occurred are specifiable in terms of differing interactional settings. The Anywaa ethno-genesis seems to have occurred in the context of relative isolation and/or weaker neighbours, while Nuer ethno-genesis seems to have occurred in a higher density of social interaction of a competitive type with their neighbours. Specific factors are also involved in the evolution of Anywaa primordialism. These are: (1) Changes in material existence (that is, from a pastoral to an agrarian mode of subsistence and the resultant strong attachment to the land) (2) A belief system that engenders territoriality (that is, a punitive God that is contrasted with the mother Earth) (3) A reproductive regime that is based on the economy of scarcity (that is, a bride wealth system based on scarce beads), and (4) A mode of governance that ties the people to specific territories.[5] These factors seem to have generated the Anywaa particularistic identity discourse, an internal dynamic that has been reinforced by the quality of the interactional setting (that is, territorial and cultural encroachments by their pastoral neighbours). The Nuer ethnic identity formation, on the other hand, has been shaped by a competitive inter-ethnic interactional setting, largely in the context of pastoral raiding and counter-raiding with their Dinka neighbours in southern Sudan. This seems to have generated an interest in demographic power, which in turn necessitates flexibility in ethnic recruitment (cultural definition of ethnic membership) and mobility, rather than a historical sense of rootedness to a place. As two kinds of ethnic groups, the Anywaa and the Nuer somehow echo the two theoretical approaches in the field of identity study. With a stronger idea of origin, an ideology of ethnic endogamy and an internal imagining of the relevant (spiritual) other, the Anywaa represent an emic primordialist conception of ethnicity, whereas with a weaker version of descent ideology, open membership criteria and an assimilationist ideology, the Nuer represent an emic constructivist conception of ethnicity. To the extent that they differ in the criteria of membership in their respective ethnicities, therefore, the Anywaa and the Nuer play, to borrow the Wittgenstein concept, a different 'language game' in their conceptualisation of what an ethnic group is. When they use the term ethnic group, they refer to different ideas of collectivities.

One domain of relevance where the difference in modes of ethnic identity formation between the Anywaa and the Nuer becomes clear is in the conflicting discourses it has produced on the land issue. As a landed-identity discourse, territoriality features strongly among the Anywaa. Anywaa territoriality is amply evidenced in the two mutually constituted concepts of *jobur* (people of the settlement) and *welo* (guests). In traditional Anywaa society, the dominant sub-clan of a village (*tung*) comprises the *jobur* and

---

[5] The Anywaa traditional political system is organised along village lines. Each Anywaa village was ruled by either headmen (*kwaro*) or nobles (*nyiyie*). There were more than a hundred such Anywaa village 'states' in the Gambella region before they were forcibly abolished during the socialist period. For a fuller account of the traditional Anywaa political system, see Evans-Pritchard (1940) and Lienhardt (1957).

the *welo*, people who have arrived later. Guests of a temporary or permanent nature are highly respected, but not really fully integrated as *jobur*. The *welo* might contribute to the economic or military strength of the village, but they can also leave at any time. Within the *jobur* there are earth priests called *wat-ngomi*. As described by Perner (1994), the Anywaa have two terms for earth: *ngomi* is the element, the material earth, while *piny* means earth in a moral spatial sense (land). The spiritual dimension of the earth is expressed in everyday forms of greetings. While enquiring about personal well-being an Anywaa asks, *piny bede nidi* (how is the earth?) to mean how are you? One replies *piny ber jak* (the earth is fine) or *piny rac* (the earth is bad) to mean everything is well or things are bad, respectively. In Anywaa spiritual imagination the relationship between earth and the people living on it is a very intimate one and this is mediated through the *wat-ngomi*, who is entitled to allow or refuse human intervention in nature. In addition to ensuring fertility (human and agricultural) and maintaining the dignity of the earth, the *wat-ngomi* also ensures the separation between the human and animal (wild) territories. At times when a wild animal encroaches on a human territory the *wat-ngomi* performs a ritual that 'reminds' the encroaching animal to leave the 'foreign' territory. The theme of territoriality is further instanced in a ritual of befriending the earth during the time of migration or changing one's residence by carrying the ancestral soil to the new sites. Accordingly, during the first days in the new country the person mixes the soil of the old site with the soil of the new site and dilutes it with water, and then drinks it until he feels accustomed to the new earth. Earlier scholars have also noted Anywaa territoriality. Evans-Prichard described it as follows: 'the Anywaa are strongly attached to the sites where their ancestors lived and often tenaciously occupied them in face of extermination' (Evans-Pritchard 1940b: 37). In a later work he further noted: 'however long strangers and their descendants live in a village and however much they intermarry with the dominant lineage or *jobur* they can never become members of it but remain *welo*, strangers' (Evans-Pritchard 1947: 93).

Anywaa territoriality sharply contrasts with the Nuer who have a more integrative concept of localisation, which they use as an argument for entitlement over Anywaa areas and inclusion into wider political communities. As compared with the Anywaa, the Nuer recognise a very loose sense of territoriality expressed in terms of three flexible concepts: *Diel*, *rul* and *jang*. A *diel* is a first-comer among the Nuer. As Evans-Pritchard (1940a) noted, a Nuer is *diel* only in a tribe where his clan has superior status. If he goes to other areas where his clan is not *diel* he is considered *rul*, stranger. The general trend is that a *rul* attaches himself to a *diel* by marrying into the *diel* family and over generations his descendants will fully localise in the new place. The background of a *rul* matters only for marriage purposes, for a *rul* is 'up for grabs' because the *diel* are exogamous. A third category of persons is called *jang*, designating the non-Nuer who are either captives or join the *diel* of their own accord. In a sense the integration of the *jang* into the *diel* is more effective than the *rul,* as they are cut off from their homeland ties. This partly explains why the Nuer are more interested in outsiders than fellow Nuer whose loyalty to a local community is precarious, as they could drop out and rejoin their natal community. In both cases, however, newcomers are encouraged to join the *diel*, eventually the ideology creating real social and economic ties. Unlike the Anywaa *jobur*, therefore, the Nuer *diel* is an inclusionary framework.

Such a difference in modes of identification is reflected in notions of belonging as well as in different notions of property. An Anywaa village comprises not only the actual settlement often scattered along the banks of a river, but also the adjacent territory which is not necessarily economically exploited but nevertheless is a constitutive part of the local community. The Anywaa notion of ownership does not entail effective occupation. It is enough to lay a claim on once occupied territory because it is *piny kwara* (land of the ancestors). The Nuer, on the other hand, recognise continued possession that accrues use-right. Accordingly, if one does not use the land (in economic terms), one does not own it. Implicit in this discourse is the assumption that the ultimate owner of natural resources is *kwoth*, God.

The initial encounter between the Nuer and the Anywaa resulted in the Nuer conquest of a large area of Anywaa territories. The Anywaa made attempts to regain lost territories. Although they were not successful in their irredentist project, their resistance had the effect of re-orienting Nuer strategies of access to resources from violent to peaceful means, paralleling the symbiotic exchanges between herders and farmers elsewhere in the world (Dafinger and Pelican 2002). These exchanges, however, involve a certain asymmetry that favours the Nuer. Flexibility in ethnic recruitment, economic clout (cattle wealth) and numerical preponderance have enabled the Nuer to expand continually into Anywaa territories. This expansion has largely occurred through micro-demographic processes: Instrumentalisation of inter-ethnic marriages and friendship networks. Typically, a Nuer man marries an Anywaa woman. This is initially beneficial to both partners. For the Nuer it is cheaper to marry an Anywaa whose bride wealth payment is lower,[6] and for the agrarian Anywaa, the marriage ensures the flow of cattle wealth. The Nuer anticipate additional gains from such exchanges: Marriage ties are then used as a legitimising discourse in establishing settlements in Anywaa territories. In virtually all the cases, children of the inter-ethnic marriages identify with the Nuer because the Anywaa ideology of ethnic purity makes it difficult for them to safely claim Anywaa ethnic identity. Unlike the emergence of a hybrid identity that often follows inter-group marriages, inter-

---

[6] Contemporary Anywaa bride wealth amounts to an equivalent of the value of three cows, whereas the average bride wealth payment among the Nuer is twenty-five cows.

ethnic marriages between the Anywaa and the Nuer have thus resulted in the expansion of an ethnic boundary. Moreover, the Nuer families which are tied with the Anywaa through marriage relationships gradually come to serve as a nucleus for more immigrants, and in due course the immigrants outnumber the Anywaa, who are then left with the option of either joining the Nuer kinship and political structures, or leaving their villages in order to maintain their cultural identity.

Here we find contrasting definitions of being a host and a guest that are premised on different conceptions of relatedness. For the Anywaa, being a guest (*welo*) is a permanent status, a concept that is also used in inter-group (inter-village) relations within Anywaa society. It is contrasted with the term *jobur*, first settlers of a village. For the Nuer, being a guest is a temporary status, a phase in the localisation process, a concept that is also applied intra-ethnically. The notion of a first-comer among the Nuer (*diel*) is a framework of inclusion for new comers (other Nuer and non-Nuer alike), within which localisation occurs through adopting the lineage name of the *diel*. For the Anywaa, the Nuer immigrants to their villages, now related through affinal ties, are defined as *welo,* no matter how long they stay. On a long-term basis, however, the Nuer have largely managed to establish their definition of being a host/guest through economic incentives, demographic power and manipulation of kinship ties. This instrumentalisation of inter-ethnic exchanges, coupled with flexible ethnic recruitment and elaborate assimilation ideology, has resulted in a one-way process of ethnic conversion and the expansion of Nuer cultural space, a process which has created different categories of Anywaa with different concerns. For some, ethnic conversion is regarded as a new life-chance which adoption of the pastoral economy promises. This is encouraged by the success of the Nuer integrationist system, which actively supports the process of becoming Nuer (which after all requires only cultural competence). With a memory of past territorial losses, combined with the significance of the land in Anywaa identity discourse, those Anywaa who are still outside the Nuer cultural orbit experience the imposition of the Nuer way as a form of symbolic violence to their scheme of things (a different mode of constructing ethnic identity), a cultural hegemony which has caused anxiety and produced a strong discourse of ethnic equality. Trapped by pragmatism, those Anywaa who still enter into exchanges with the Nuer while keeping their identity have engaged in subtle forms of resistance.

The strategic dilemma and the nature of the struggle for cultural identity are best illustrated by a local political practice called *chirawia,* meaning in the Anywaa language 'lifting up the hands'. C*hirawia* is a code word used by the Anywaa to denote their attempt to tap the Nuer resources (cattle) while discouraging the growth of Nuer settlements and the eventual takeover of their lands through underground violence. Accordingly, an Anywaa who has affinal ties with a Nuer withdraws his protection as a host and allows other non-related Anywaa (anonymous) to kill his Nuer 'guest'. Over a period of time, such practices have caused a growing irritation on the Nuer side. The Nuer interpret *chirawia* as 'cold-blooded', 'indiscriminate' killings by the Anywaa, as evidence for their morally corrupt nature. They call them '*luuch naath*', murderous people. *Chirawia* is compared with the Nuer 'minority policy' and the more 'humane' notion of a guest, *neekä* ('my people'). Among the Nuer, a guest is categorised under minority groups and the host has a strong moral obligation to protect his *neekä,* including people from other ethnic groups. The mutual anger between Anywaa and Nuer thus has induced a moral contestation over definitions of personhood and has the effect of a new 'primordial game' in inter-ethnic relations. For by fixing a 'substance' on the Anywaa nature, the Nuer are buying into the Anywaa conception of an ethnic group and compromising their own assimilation ideology, which is after all based on the assumption of a certain degree of sameness. Here we find the Anywaa and the Nuer starting to play the same language game. The conflict situation is, therefore, having the effect of defining them – yet another example of the production of similarity through opposition.

The Nuer pressure on the Anywaa riverine lands has been growing in recent times as a result of new economic processes related to a change in the pastoral economy (a shift towards agro-pastoralism). This is in turn related to limited pastoral mobility due to insecurity and cattle predation by armed political groups along the Ethio-Sudanese border, a spill-over effect from the civil war in southern Sudan. As a result, both spontaneous and organised Nuer migrations have occurred from southern Sudan into the relatively peaceful Gambella region; with these, new groups of local actors have entered into the regional identity politics, augmenting the demographic anxiety of the Anywaa. With a low level of production technology,[7] only 2.4 per cent of the arable land is cultivated.[8] Furthermore, the land type for which there is competition is the fertile alluvial riverine land, suitable for moisture cultivation during the dry season. This land type covers only 0.5 per cent of the total land area of the region (Ellman 1972). Most of this land type falls within Anywaa territories.

Confronting the Anywaa exclusionary practices the Nuer at first looked inward to make sense of the new situation they found themselves in. When the Anywaa say 'the land is ours' the Nuer reply 'there is enough land for us all', a discourse that at face value resonates with the colonial discourse of 'waste land'. The Nuer claim is, however, embedded in their notion of property. True the Nuer, too, have a sense of private and group property but

---

[7] Gambella is one of the few regions in Ethiopia where plough farming is not practised.

[8] Situational analysis for the Gambella People's National regional State, Bureau of Planning and Economic Development, 2000.

property right is tightly defined. One needs to possess it to put a claim on land or other forms of property. It connotes possession. Ownership of anything that is not possessed pertains either to *kwoth* or is up for grabs. Here is a potential for conflict. For the Anywaa the land is as much an economic resource as it is a basis of identity. For the Nuer, areas that are not actually settled by the Anywaa are considered as part of the economy of the commons. Moreover, the Anywaa settlements concentrate along the banks of the river and this is largely respected by the Nuer. In most cases the Nuer use peaceful strategies to have access to the Anywaa's riverine lands. As the Anywaa have become more assertive on land rights in post-1991 ethno-politics, however, the Nuer contest their exclusionary practices by invoking a different scheme of interpretation as the following excerpt from a Nuer elder demonstrates:

> The Anywaa do not like other people and they say all the land of Gambella is ours. This Baro River, is it the Anywaa who dug it all? Is it not from *kwoth*? Who owns water? Humans can drink, cattle can drink, and animals can drink water from Baro because *kwoth* gave us all these things. If somebody says do not go to the river, is that person a *kwoth*? You came from Gambella town. Have you seen many people living in all the areas [between Gambella and Itang]? The Anywaa live only along the banks of the river. Where does Ethiopia start? You cannot finish the land. It is the land that finishes the people (Tap Manytap, a Nuer elder from Makot village, Itang district).

The Anywaa respond to such claims as yet another piece of evidence for the territorial aggrandisement of the Nuer that ultimately threatens the survival of the Anywaa as a distinct ethnic group:

> In the years to come there would be no Anywaa left in the Gambella region. Nasir [Sudan] was ours; the Nuer took it. Jikaw and Akobo were ours; the Nuer took them. Wherever we go, they would follow us. They take our land, they take our rivers, they take our people. The Nuer behave like that because they think that they are many and it is their nature to be aggressive (an educated Anywaa from Gambella town).

The aforementioned definition of the situation expresses the fear of extinction, which is aptly described by Horowitz in his analysis of ethnic groups and conflict (Horowitz 1985), a fear, which has become greater in the context of ethno-politics and been manipulated by the elites in the competition for power.

Land as political capital

By promoting Gambella into a regional state, ethnic federalism has suddenly turned a peripheral region into a new political centre. The Anywaa were initially promoted by the new ruling party (the EPRDF) on the basis of their contribution to the regime change, whereas the Nuer were associated with the defunct regime, a political event which has created new forms of administrative power which the Anywaa have sought to use to renegotiate the unequal local power relations.[9] Furthermore, in ethnic federalism the Anywaa saw a new political possibility in their project of containing the Nuer. This has involved exclusionary political practices, principally using the 'citizenship card' in the distribution of new rewards (that is, administrative posts, modern goods and services). Despite differences in settlement history – some groups of Nuer already arrived in the Gambella region at the end of the 19th century – the Anywaa elites have defined all the Nuer as Sudanese, thus foreigners, creating a new homogenising element in the consolidation of Nuer ethnicity. The Anywaa have found evidence for their definition not so much from history books as from the Nuer practice of alternative citizenship: Switching between Ethiopian and Sudanese national identities. This was particularly true in the 1980s, when being a refugee was more rewarding than being a citizen in the context of an aid regime that catered for the needs of the southern Sudanese refugee population in the Gambella region (that is, provision of relief, physical security and access to social services).[10] At that time, the Ethiopian Nuer could pass as southern Sudanese more easily than the Ethiopian Anywaa, for more Nuer than Anywaa live in southern Sudan. On that basis, the aid agencies accepted the Ethiopian Nuer as refugees prima facie, while the Anywaa had to go through tight screening procedures. Nearly all of the current Nuer civil servants and politicians in the Gambella region were educated in the refugee camps under the auspices of the aid agencies. This has created a certain sense of envy on the Anywaa side, while it has made the Nuer vulnerable to the politics of exclusion in post-1991 Gambella, when ethno-politics has been framed in national terms according to which the Nuer are categorically defined by the Anywaa as Sudanese, thus non-citizens.

---

9 At the height of its projects of control in the 1980s the socialist regime alienated the Anywaa by abolishing their traditional political system and cultural practices. Anywaa discontent crystallised with the establishment of a liberation movement called the GPLM (Gambella People's Liberation Movement). The GPLM was allied to the EPRDF in the struggle to overthrow the socialist regime. The Nuer elites, on the other hand, were promoted to higher offices by the socialist regime.

10 By the mid 1980s there were more than 300,000 Sudanese refugees living in three camps. The majority of these refugees were Dinka and Nuer. All the camps were/are located in Anywaa territories.

The 1990s brought new structures of rewards to the Gambella region. The relief regime declined and the establishment of the Gambella regional state promised new avenues of social mobility and individual advancement for those who could claim Ethiopian citizenship. On their part, the Anywaa politicians have adopted a landed-strategy of political entitlement. They claim ownership rights over the Gambella region on the basis of settlement history. The exact time when the Anywaa settled in present-day areas is not yet well established. Nor do we know who the pre-Anywaa inhabitants of the Gambella region were. On the basis of genealogical reckoning and history of the Lwoo migration, scholars suggested the 15th century as the probable time for the ethno-genesis of the Anywaa, and the 17th century for the emergence of the Anywaa kingdom in present-day southern Sudan from where they gradually moved to the Gambella region (Perner 1994: 17), whereas the first groups of Nuer entered the Gambella region towards the end of the 19th century (Jal 1987: 14). The actual settlements of the Anywaa concentrate along the major rivers, but the whole area of land in and around the rivers forms wider units of identification that make up the eleven regions of Anywaaland.

The constituent parts of the new regional states are the *weredas* (districts). The GPNRS initially consisted of six districts: Gambella, Itang, Jikaw, Akobo, Abobo, Gog-jor and Godere. The Anywaa claimed ownership rights over all of these districts except for Godere, which is recognised as

Table 8.1
Land, population and political claims in the GPNRS

Wereda	*Land size*	*Population size*	*Ethnic groups living in the district*	*Claimant*
Itang	1,837	21,634	Anywaa Nuer Opo	Anywaa
Gambella	2,859	33,217	Anywaa Highlanders Nuer Komo Majangir	Anywaa
Abobo	3,515	16,064	Anywaa Highlanders Majangir	Anywaa
Gog	7,139	17,448	Anywaa	Anywaa
Jor	2,488	8,035	Anywaa	Anywaa
Akobo	3,830	28,712	Nuer Anywaa	Nuer
Jikow	2,193	48,785	Nuer Anywaa	Nuer

Source: The figures are adopted from the 1994 housing and population census; the population distribution and the claimants are identified from field notes.

Majangir's. The claim over Gambella, Abobo, Itang and Gognajor is on the basis of settlement pattern where the majority of the inhabitants are the Anywaa. Anywaa's claim over Akobo and some parts of Jikaw districts is historical, part of their irredentist project. There are still pockets of Anywaa settlements in Jikaw and Akobo districts, but these districts have already become home for the majority of the Ethiopian Nuer. Anywaa's claim over Itang district is as much on the basis of current settlement as it is a historical argument. Otherwise, nearly half of the population of Itang district is already Nuer. The political significance of who owns how many *weredas* is directly reflected in the system of political representation in the regional council and budget allocation. Each *wereda* is allocated five seats. This has automatically made the Anywaa a political majority, because they claimed at least four of the seven *weredas*. In addition, in 1992 the Gog-jor *wereda* was split into two, further adding Anywaa seats in the regional council. In 1996 the Anywaa managed to annex a new *wereda* from the neighbouring Southern Regional state, making the number of *weredas* claimed by the Anywaa six out of nine. Similar attempts by the Nuer to create new *weredas* were frustrated by the Anywaa.

On the basis of land-based political representation, the Anywaa have dominated the regional council in the three rounds of elections as the following table reveals:

Table 8.2
Political representation in the GPNRS council

Groups	1992	1995	2000
Anywaa	19	25	29
Nuer	12	10	19
Majangir	5	5	4
Opo	1	1	1
Komo	1	1	1
Highlanders	-	-	1
Total	38	42	55

Source: Commuted from field notes

Domination of the regional council has introduced new forms of power in Anywaa-Nuer relations. The new Anywaa administrative power has symbolic and material dimensions. Anywaa political domination is above all expressed in the form of the allocation of the office of the regional presidency, which is received by them as a symbolic representation of their ownership rights over the Gambella region. Here we find the value of power not only for material rewards but also as a means of renegotiating group status. As Horowitz noted, 'groups whose present worth has been cast in doubt will be most vigorous in seeking authoritative reassurance' (1985:

287). In material terms, the political representation in the council has determined access to new objects of the struggle: Employment opportunities in the budding bureaucracy (hitherto dominated by the highlanders) and access to modern goods and social services delivered by the distributive state. As the following table demonstrates, this has created imbalance in the distribution of posts in the regional ministries:

Table 8.3
Allocation of Managerial Posts in the GPNRS

Year	Regional Ministries	Anywaa	Nuer	Majangir	Opo	Komo	High-landers
1992	20	15	3	1	-	1	-
1995	19	14	4	-	-	1	-
2000	19	13	5	-	-	1	-
2002	18	11	6	-	-	1	-

Source: Commuted from field notes

Table 8.4
The Ethnic profile of the civil servants in the GPNRS

Ethnic group	Male	Female	Total
Anywaa	1053	344	1397
Nuer	205	38	243
Majangir	29	5	34
Opo	7	3	10
Komo	1	-	1
Highlanders	1476	684	2160
Total	2,771	1074	3,845

Source: Bureau of Civil Service, GPNRS

According to Table 8.4 the highlanders constitute 56.17 per cent, and the Anywaa 36.3 per cent, while the Nuer make up 6.3 per cent of the civil servants in the GPNRS. The imbalance in the distribution of offices is partly because of the differential start the Anywaa had in the modern sector, but access to government offices has been increasingly dictated by ethno-politics and the position of the various groups in the decision-making power. As in other areas of the modern sector, what matters here is also the perception, not the reality. Anywaa political dominance has been bitterly resisted by the Nuer, as it has meant differential access to the rewards of office, preferential treatment in the job market and access to administrative justice. The pattern of allocation of political offices has also inserted a symbolic politics of recognition and has fuelled issues of ownership. Reserving the upper echelons of power to the Anywaa has dramatised the subordinate political status of the Nuer in the regional politics.

Marginalised by the Anywaa from the distribution of these new rewards, the Nuer have engaged in the politics of inclusion on the basis of relative deprivation. This is further exacerbated by the fact that the 'reference group' (the Anywaa) is a one-time political minor in the traditional rules of the game where local forms of power (that is, numerical size, warriorhood, economic clout, and an inclusive identity discourse) determine the terms of exchange in interethnic relations. In the new political game, in which administrative power matters most, a reactive Nuer ethnicity has emerged, contesting Anywaa political domination through counter claims and creative strategies of entitlement, in particular through appropriation of state discourses.

Aware of the Anywaa's landed-political strategy of ethnic entitlement, the Nuer have fought to increase the number of their *weredas*, thus their political constituency. Out of the nine districts only two are recognised as Nuer. They proposed the creation of two additional *weredas*. Neither the regional nor the Federal governments heeded their plea. Instead they resorted to alternative bases for empowerment. Above all, the 1994 census has produced a new political fact: The Nuer were turned overnight from a largely 'foreign' group into an ethnic majority:

Table 8.5
Demographic composition of the GPNRS

Group	Urban	Percent	Rural	Percent	Total	Percent
'Indigenous' people						
Anywaa	9831	36%	34750	26%	44581	27%
Nuer	3014	11%	61459	45%	64473	40%
Majangir	64	0%	9286	7%	9350	6%
Opo and Komo	1067	4%	3735	3%	4802	3%
People from various highland areas of Ethiopia						
Amharas	4639	17%	7927	6%	12566	8%
SNNPR	1334	5%	12170	9%	13504	8%
Oromos	5890	22%	4635	3%	10525	6%
Tigrayans	1341	5%	1255	1%	2596	2%
Total	27180	100%	135217	100%	162397	100%

Source: Housing and Population Census, 1994

The objective of the census was stated as being to generate data 'for designing and preparation of development plan and for monitoring and evaluation of the impact of the implementation of the development plans'.[11]

[11] The 1994 population and housing census of Ethiopia, Central Statistical Authority, 1995.

Accordingly, the population size of the Gambella region was estimated at 181,862, of which the Nuer comprise forty per cent and the Anywaa twenty-seven per cent, whereas the highlanders comprise twenty-four per cent of the population. A seemingly denotative description has, therefore, an immediate performative effect. Ever since the results of the census were announced it has offered a new political capital for Nuer politicians in their politics of inclusion on the basis of a new ideology of entitlement: Majoritarianism. Using the national democratic rhetoric, the Nuer have challenged what now appears to be not only exclusion but also domination by a 'minority':

> A glance at the 1994 national census reveals that there is a direct imbalance in resource allocation throughout the country. It was only in 1995 that the Nuer got the position of vice-president in the Gambella regional state. This arrangement did not take into account the numerical size of the ethnic groups, for had that been the case, the Nuer would have been given the top position in the region because they are numerically the majority in the region ... The situation in Gambella is not different from that of Rwanda and Burundi where the Tutsi minority dominated the Hutu majority in all political spheres, and we are all aware of the consequences of that policy. (Nyang Baitiok, excerpt from a discussion with a Nuer student in Ethiopian Civil Service College, Addis Ababa, 6 September, 2001).

The Anywaa seriously dispute the census results on several grounds. For one, they perceive that the census has grossly undercounted the Anywaa areas, for most of the areas which were not counted fall within traditional Anywaa territories. More importantly, the Anywaa consider that the Nuer population size is inflated by the influx of refugees from southern Sudan:

> The increase in Nuer population includes political turmoil across the international border, producing a non-stop influx of refugees to neighbouring territories in the Horn of Africa. Since the birth of civil conflict in southern Sudan, Gambella has been hosting hundreds of thousands of refugees from across war-torn southern Sudan, the majority of whom are ethnic Nuer. This makes it more difficult for authorities in Gambella to differentiate who is Ethiopian or not in the struggle for power and resources. Prior to the mid 1980s only a few Nuer lived in the Gambella region. (Oman Gilo, an excerpt from a discussion with an educated Anywaa, Gambella town, 14 October, 2000).

Post-1994 politics in Gambella, therefore, has been fought through two competing political strategies of ethnic entitlement. The Nuer have pursued majoritarianism as a counter strategy to the land-based political strategy of the Anywaa. The two competing political strategies are mutually constituted: The more the Nuer insist on majoritarianism, the more the Anywaa cling to the land question as a strategy of ethnic entitlement and political capital for their project of containment – conflicting political strategies which are intimately connected with the conflict situation in the Gambella region.

Patterns of alliance with the national state: Discursive (dis)connectivity

Whose political strategy is winning and when is directly related to the pattern of alliances between the ethnic groups and the national state. In the on-going struggle, the Anywaa were initially better connected with the current Ethiopian government, largely because of their contribution to regime change. Settlement pattern has also enabled the Anywaa to pick the citizenship card in the political debate and social struggle, for although the census produced a new political fact by turning the Nuer into a majority, the majority of the Anywaa live in Ethiopia and only a tiny section live in southern Sudan. The population distribution is different among the Nuer. Although they are the majority in the Gambella region, the overwhelming majority of the Nuer live in southern Sudan. The settlement pattern and the Anywaa claim for better competence on the national culture (in particular better fluency in the national language) have substantiated the Anywaa landed-political strategy of entitlement. Playing the citizenship card has above all enabled the Anywaa to project their own concern onto the national level in the context of an uncertain political future southern Sudan.

Anywaa territoriality, however, is destined to disconnect with the state's own claim over the land. The Ethiopian state, across regimes, has always claimed land as the ultimate owner. After all, state ownership of the land is an instrument of control and means of legitimacy. Although the constitution 'generously' acknowledges self-determination, ultimate ownership of the land is bestowed on the federal state:

> The right to ownership of rural and urban land, as well as of all natural resources, is exclusively vested in the state and in the people. Land is a common property of the Nations, Nationalities and Peoples of Ethiopia and shall not be subject to sale or to other means of exchange. (Article 40: 3)

The state's right over the land includes large areas designated as national parks, the right to periodic redistribution of land to the farmers, and appropriation of land for re-settlement sites and for 'investment' zones. In fact, most of the rangeland in the Gambella region is designated as parkland, which has further compounded the issue of entitlement as the following picture on the next page illustrates.

The settlement is a Nuer village, the land is traditionally an Anywaa territory and the poles represent state ownership, one of the two designated parklands in the Gambella region. In the context of the ubiquity of state claims on the land, the Nuer resort to rhetorically empowering the state over the land, as this entails only a switch of reference from *kwoth* (God) to *kume* (government):

> As you know, land is owned by the *kume*. *Kume* is the father of all people. If there is no *kume*, those who do not like Nuer say the land is ours. Everything is from *kume*. If there is hunger, if there is no rain this year, the food comes from other places. You tell *kume* and it brings you food. *Kume* is like *kwoth*. Everything belongs to *kume*. Land is for *kume*. The people are for *kume*. That is why it asks for people when there is war. Even this tree belongs to *kume*. There is nothing which *kume* can't do. Nobody can take away the land of *kum*. (Kong Diu, Addis Ababa, 17 November, 2000)

Who owns the land?

Source: Feyissa 2003: 404.

Such discursive empowerment of the state is neither a commitment to the state nor an assertion of national identity. Instead, it is a local statement used as exit strategy to counter exclusionary discourses. Nevertheless, it has the effect of reproducing state ideologies at the local level, an aspect of 'everyday forms of state formation' (Nugent 1997). The Nuer term *kume* stands not only for the state as a set of institutions and administrative organ, but also as represented by the category of the highlanders who appear to benefit from such an inclusive discourse, while the Anywaa territoriality tends to threaten their economic security. In fact, the Nuer often make an explicit statement that the riverine land (the alluvial soil) after all comes from the highlands:

> Even all the Gaajak Nuer can't finish this soil. Anywaa and Gaajak together cannot finish this soil. After all, this river comes from the Buny area. *Pine* (alluvial soil) is from Buny. When it rains in the highlands, the rivers bring all the soil to us. It is red there, but when it reaches us it becomes black. This soil is

important for us all. *Pine* is for all, Anywaa, Nuer, Buny. It is food. If we don't work on it, we would be all hungry. If we sit idle [like we do now], we will all be hungry. You can't stop a hungry man. (Kong Diu, an elder from Makot village)

Outlook

This study has shown the problematic nature of settling competing land claims in the context of identity politics. Under the specificities of the study area collective actors and the national state represent these competing claims. The actors in the contestation construct different property narratives and invoke a wide array of ideologies of entitlement. As it stands, the national state represents the Meta power in determining whose narratives are validated when and why. This seeming state omnipotence, however, contains within itself openings for local actors to project their own sectional interest onto the national state, an interplay that has injected elements of indeterminacy into the contestation.

References

BAHRU, Z. (1991) *A history of modern Ethiopia 1855-1991*, Addis Ababa: Addis Ababa University Press.

BARTH, F. (1969) Introduction, in: Barth, F. (Ed.) *Ethnic groups and boundaries: The social organization of difference*, Boston: Little Brown and Company.

DAFINGER, A. and M. PELICAN (2002) *Land rights and the politics of integration pastoralists' strategies in a comparative view*, Max Planck Institute for Social Anthropology Working Papers, no. 48.

ELLMAN, A. (1972) *An agricultural and socio-economic survey of South Sudan refugee settlements and surrounding areas in Gambella Awraja*, Ethiopia: UNHCR Research report, Addis Ababa.

ERIKSEN, T.H. (1991) The cultural contexts of ethnic differences, *Man* (N.S), 26: 127-44.

EVANS-PRITCHARD, E. (1940a) *The Nuer: A description of the modes of livelihood and political institutions of a Nilotic people*, Oxford: Oxford University Press.

EVANS-PRITCHARD, E. (1940b) *The political system of the Anuak of the Anglo-Egyptian Sudan*, New York: AMS Press.

EVANS-PRITCHARD, E. (1947) Further observations on the political system of the Anuak, *Sudan Notes and Records*, 28: 62-97.

EVANS-PRITCHARD, E. (1956) *Nuer religion*, Oxford: Clarendon Press.

FEYISSA, D. (2003) *Ethnic groups and conflict: The case of Anywaa-Nuer relations in the Gambella Region, Ethiopia*, dissertation submitted to Martin Luther University.

GAMBELLA BUREAU OF PLANNING AND ECONOMIC DEVELOPMENT (2000) *Situational analysis for Gambella People's National Regional State*, research report, Gambella.

GEERTZ, C. (1973) *The interpretation of cultures*, New York: Basic Books.
HOROWITZ, D. (1985) *Ethnic groups in conflict*, Berkeley: University of California Press.
HUTCHINSON, S. (1996) *Nuer dilemma*, California: University of California Press.
JAL, G. (1987) *The history of the Jikany Nuer before 1920*, Ph.D. dissertation, History Department, School of Oriental and African Studies, University of London.
JENKINS, R. (2001) Ethnicity: Anthropological approaches, in: Smelser, N. and Baltes, P. *International Encyclopaedia of the Social and Behavioural Sciences*, Elsevier Science Ltd, pp. 4810-33.
KELLY, R. (1985) *The Nuer conquest: The structure and development of an expansionist system*, Ann Arbor: University of Michigan Press.
LIENHARDT, G. (1957) Anyuak village headmen I, *Africa*, 27: 341-55.
PERNER, C. (1994) *The Anyuak – living on earth in the sky, vol. II*, The Human Territory: Helbing and Lichtenhahn.
SAHLINS, M. (1961) The segmentary lineage: An organisation of predatory expansion, *American Anthropologist*, 63: 322-45.
SOUTHALL, A. (1976) Nuer and Dinka are people: Ecology, ethnicity and logical possibility, *Man (NS)*, 11(4): 463-91.
STAUDER, J. (1971) *The Majangir: Ecology and society of a Southwest Ethiopian People*, Cambridge: Cambridge University Press.
THE 1994 POPULATION AND HOUSING CENSUS OF ETHIOPIA (1995) *Results for Gambella region*, Addis Ababa: Central Statistics Authority.
THE CONSTITUTION OF THE FEDERAL DEMOCRATIC REPUBLIC OF ETHIOPIA (1994).
WITTGENSTEIN, L. (1983 [1953]) *Philosophical investigations*, (translation G.E.M. Anscombe), Oxford: Basil Blackwell.

9

Trumping the ancestors: The challenges of implementing a land registration system in Madagascar

Sandra Evers

Introduction

For the inhabitants of the extreme Southern Highlands of Madagascar, land plays a vital role in social relations. It is the main source of subsistence. It serves as a sign of visible wealth, and as an instrument of exclusion. In a country where poverty is widespread and where outlying regions are little influenced by the hand of central government, land is the principal avenue to power. And, finally, because you must have land to possess a tomb and ancestors, it is the *sine qua non* of a successful passage into the Hereafter.

The *tompon-tany* ('master(s) of the land')[1] control access and management of land in rural Madagascar. They generally do not register their land claims. Tombs are deemed to constitute sufficient evidence of ownership, since the Malagasy believe tombs are geographical markers of family origin

---

1 The concept of *tompon-tany* is known everywhere in Madagascar. I translate *tompon-tany* as 'master(s) of the land' and not 'owner(s) of the land' because, despite the fact that their claim to land is considered legitimate by all villagers, they do not have registered title to the land (cf. Constitution of the Republic of Madagascar: 8 April 1998 and *infra*).

in a particular region. Furthermore, the *tompon-tany*, who technically could register their land in the *cadastre*, rarely exercise this option because of the fear of possible tax consequences. This naturally raises the potential for disputes between claims based on local tenure practices and paper title that relies on a national land title system. Consequently, Madagascar still does not have an effective, and enforceable land registry system.

The current Ravalomanana government is in the early stages of introducing a new system of land registration, a key part of its strategy to battle poverty in the country. This policy, however, promises to bring the State into an area that is deemed to be the exclusive realm of the ancestors, who are widely believed to be the ultimate owners of the land. In practical terms, the *tompon-tany* act as guardians and interpreters of the ancestors' wishes, a status that makes them the effective power brokers at the local level. Throughout Madagascar, these *tompon-tany* resist any interference in their affairs by the central government, as they not only see themselves as the masters over land, but also over people. Naturally, any national land registry system which purports to offer land title to tenant farmers will be perceived as a direct onslaught on the rights of the *tompon-tany*.

In an article published in the Malagasy newspaper *Tribune* (30 July 2003), Prime Minister Jacques Sylla discussed the looming problem of competing jurisdictions between the central government and the local *tompon-tany*. Prime Minister Sylla has been touring the country as part of a series of public hearings, organised to bring local communities into the process of implementing a national land registration system. The Prime Minister stressed that local consultations on land management and registration were necessary in order to:

> *(...) approfondir ce sujet complexe mettant aux prises le droit positif, signe de notre ouverture au monde et le droit coutumier, attestant le profond enracinement de notre culture.*[2]

The reference to 'our culture' relates to the issue of local land management structures rooted in ancestral heritage, but administered by the *tompon-tany*. However, resolving the conflict between formal legislation and customary law by a pro-forma set of public 'consultations' sidesteps the more difficult question of whether the government dares taking a stand against the *tompon-tany* and thereby, in the latter's view, against the ancestors.

---

2 '(…) properly address the complexities of this issue, which attempts to reconcile positive law – the mirror of our joining the international community – and customary law – which reflects our historical attachment to our culture' (author's translation).

In order to understand the complexity of land registration issues in Madagascar, I will discuss a case in the extreme Southern Highlands of Madagascar. But, before I do, I propose a brief overview of the poverty situation in Madagascar at the time of my research, since the government has taken the position that the widespread poverty is the direct result of current land management structures and policies in the country.

Poverty

The extreme Southern Highlands are to this day relatively unfettered by state regulation. The downward political and economic spiral of Madagascar, especially during the 1980s, left its inhabitants to fend for themselves. Madagascar ranks among the countries with the lowest GDP *per capita* in the world (US$255.2 in 1999). The total population of Madagascar in 1999 was 14.6 million. The annual population growth rate was 3.0 per cent. At that rate, Madagascar's population would again double in twenty-five years. The International Monetary Fund estimates that three-quarters of Madagascar's total population lives under the poverty threshold (data from IMF report in August 2000).

At the local level, the generalised, pervasive poverty conditioned every aspect of day-to-day existence. Nobody was immune to its effects, regardless of their position in the socio-economic hierarchy. With this in mind, it cannot be over-emphasised that even the dominant *tompon-tany* group of the extreme Southern Highlands would be considered as very poor by any modern standards.

Poverty operates not just as a condition born of demographics, but as a trap, one which has proven an ironically fertile ground for the breeding of other phenomena: Localised forms of justice and retribution, radical expressions of inequality, and perhaps even an anchoring of the belief that people live in a stable and timeless universe, where things have never changed, and where the 'Malagasy customs' have pre-determined people's fates from cradle to tomb (cf. Evers 2002).

Current *tompon-tany* practices for the attribution of land in the extreme Southern Highlands

Over a ten-year period (1989-1999),[3] I conducted research, lived and participated in day-to-day life of the Betsileo people dwelling in the extreme Southern Highlands of Madagascar. Topographically, the region is a hilly transition between the Highlands (centre of the country) and the arid semi-desert flatlands of the South. This former no-man's-land between Ambalavao and Ankaramena has a colourful reputation, being notorious for outlawry, cow thefts, and supernatural phenomena. The Malagasy consider it to be a place for people who have depleted all their options elsewhere.

The extreme Southern Highlands are not densely populated. Until the latter half of the 1960s, settlement and acquisition of land was still relatively easy. The mere occupation of land gave settlers the opportunity to accede to the status of *tompon-tany*. For both the Merina and Betsileo, living respectively in the Northern and Southern Highlands, possession of land and a family tomb are markers of family origin in a particular region (cf. Bloch 1971: 106-8).[4] So, this initial wave of migrants (which commenced following the abolition of slavery by the French colonial government in 1896) 'became' *tompon-tany* simply by building a family tomb on their own land, thereby conferring upon it the status of ancestral land.[5] These settlers currently form the established group dwelling in the zone between Ambalavao

3 For both chronological and methodological reasons, my research falls into two periods, the first from 1989 until 1992 and the second from 1996-1999. These two periods cover six field trips, including 2.5 years spent in the extreme Southern Highlands. Throughout the initial phase ending in 1992, I adhered to a principally socio-economic approach, while relying on the life history method, the interactional perspective and network analysis. Upon my return to the region in 1996, after a four year absence, villagers thought that I was sufficiently 'behaving Betsileo' (*mitondra tena Betsileo ianao*) to be allowed participation in events having a cultural import. Most relevant in this respect were the funerals and their accompanying rituals (see *infra*).

4 Kinship groups are organised around the tomb. Communal rituals related to the ancestors perpetually strengthen their family bonds.

5 In reality, this land only became 'ancestral land' (*tanin-drazana*) by virtue of a *razana* being placed in the tomb. *Razana* means both 'ancestor' and 'dead person' or 'corpse' (Bloch 1971: 112). Those calling themselves *tompon-tany* say that they never replaced an ancestor from elsewhere in order to make their land ancestral, but simply waited until somebody in their family died. This is noteworthy, as it does not comply with the common practice in the Highlands of transferring at least one corpse from the old to the new tomb whenever a new tomb is erected. This also is consistent with the hypothesis that those who currently claim the status of *tompon-tany* actually are of slave descent and did not have tombs (see *infra*).

and Ankaramena. They claim either commoner (*olompotsy*) or even noble (*hova* or *andriana*) origins. Based on reports of slave settlement in the *Archives d'Outre Mer*, however, it appears more likely that this migrant group is of slave descent. But through their tombs they created ancestors who in their turn legitimised their status as free descent *tompon-tany*.

The *tompon-tany* consolidated their position as landowners by the creation of a land monopoly. In 1967, the *tompon-tany* held a meeting in the village of Marovato.[6] At this gathering, all unclaimed land was divided between them, and the *tompon-tany* concluded a pact pursuant to which land could henceforth only be leased and not sold. This amounted to nothing less than a *de facto* exclusion of later migrants (*mpiavy*) from *tompon-tany* ranks.

Settlement and land-lease policies of the villages in the extreme Southern Highlands are administered by the *tompon-tany* village councils. In order to provide some insight into the practice and consequences of this process of selection and socio-economic classification, I will take the village of Marovato as an example.[7]

In principle, the *tompon-tany* do not allow non-Betsileo to live in their villages and even Betsileo migrants are only admitted after rigorous scrutiny. Every Betsileo migrant[8] who wishes to live in Marovato must first report to the members of the *tompon-tany* village council.[9] This council unites the heads of the five largest *tompon-tany* families of Marovato. They always demand to know where the applicants' ancestral land and family tomb are located. Their aim is to gain an understanding of the origins of the newcomer. Any migrant who is vague about his descent is presumed by the

---

6 To protect the privacy of the villagers, place names and names of individuals are pseudonyms.

7 Marovato is a migrant village. 36.2 per cent of its population (458 individuals in 1992) has settled since 1970. They are called *mpiavy* ('migrants') because they do not have family tombs in the region. Later in my fieldwork, I discovered six more migrant villages in the Marovato region. The Marovato region includes these and other villages located within a fifteen-kilometre radius of Marovato. Villagers practise both agriculture (rice, manioc, maize) and cattle breeding.

8 These migrants' claim to be Betsileo is accepted by the *tompon-tany* at face value, whereas their social origin within the Betsileo group is subject to a further inquiry into whether the ancestral land and family tomb of these migrants really are in the Southern Highlands.

9 The *tompon-tany* village council functions alongside the formal *fokon-tany* council. Marovato has one representative in this assembly, who with four members from two neighbouring villages constitutes the council. The Marovato representative is appointed by the *tompon-tany* council. Generally, *tompon-tany* choose one of their relatives. The *fokon-tany* delegates represent the national government at the local level. They do not interfere with the *tompon-tany* settlement policy. In practice, I found *fokon-tany* councils to be passive entities. Their members only held meetings a few times per year.

tompon-tany to be of slave origin (*andevo*),[10] since all freeborn persons in the Highlands have ancestral land and a family tomb in their native region.[11] *Tompon-tany* refer to Betsileo who cannot name their ancestral homeland as people who do *tsy misy tantara* ('not have a history') or have *very tantara* ('lost their history'). This amounts to an automatic reason for marginalisation, as their past has given them no status or claim to recognition.[12]

Over the last few decades, the *tompon-tany* have only allowed migrants presumed to be of slave origin to settle in Marovato if they agree to live in the Western periphery. Migrants of free origin may locate themselves in the Eastern part of the village.[13] Dwelling in Western Marovato automatically entails being deemed by other villagers to be a member of an inferior group. Generally, Betsileo ideology considers the west to be the least favourable ritual location (*cf.* Kottak 1980: 137-41). In Marovato, land in the Western quarter is openly seen as impure. No Betsileo of free descent would consider living in the western periphery. Those who dwell in western Marovato are referred to as *andevo.*[14] People of free descent designate them as *olona maloto* ('impure' or 'dirty people'), whereas they call themselves *olona madio* ('pure' or 'clean people').

It is noteworthy that the *andevo* label is imposed upon the newcomers by the *tompon-tany*. The fact that migrants are unable to prove their free descent by means of a family tomb does not necessarily mean that they are of actual slave descent. Sometimes their place of origin and family tomb are too far away for the *tompon-tany* to conduct an in-depth inquiry. In such cases, the *tompon-tany* leave the newcomers with two options – departure or settlement in the Western part.

After numerous futile attempts to verify claims of *tompon-tany* origin personally, I knew that any similar research into the origin of migrants in West Marovato would serve no useful purpose. The important and central reality appeared to be that *tompon-tany* shaped the destinies of newcomers

---

10 Labels such as *tompon-tany* or *andevo* do not necessarily refer to historical realities. 'Free descent' is legitimised through acquisition of a tomb, however recent. In the same manner, one is '*andevo*' by virtue of being tombless. Nothing distinguishes the *andevo* physically from the free descent groups.

11 Most slaves lost their tombs upon enslavement. Slaves were prohibited to have permanent tombs throughout the period of slavery. They were forced to bury their dead in perishable tombs (Bloch 1971: 136). Because of their lack of permanent tombs, slaves were considered to be people without ancestors.

12 Bloch (1980: 120) writes on this issue: 'Without an ancestral homeland one was a non-person'.

13 This would appear to be a general phenomenon in the extreme Southern Highlands. I personally observed six Betsileo villages other than Marovato with similar east-west configurations. Kottak (1980: 137-8) also refers to this practice in his study on Betsileo villages around Ambalavao.

14 Fifty-seven people in Marovato are called *andevo*.

by ascribing their social identities according to their own criteria. These identities have become part of the world with which migrants have to deal, and even part of their own conceptual scheme.

Social exclusion of the *olona maloto* is articulated through the fear villagers of free descent have of being polluted by the *andevo*. Not only do they feel superior to 'impure' people, they also keep a great physical distance from the inhabitants of the western periphery. Villagers who come into contact with *olona maloto* immediately become themselves 'impure'. This pollution can only be eradicated by a ritual cleansing carried out by the oldest member of the former royal family in Anjoma (this is approximately twenty kilometres to the northeast of Marovato). However, there can be no doubt that the principle of keeping at a 'safe' distance from *olona maloto* is sometimes best honoured in the breach, as demonstrated by the seven mixed marriages in Marovato.[15]

Anyone entering into marriage with an *andevo* is, and remains, polluted until the marriage is dissolved. Children born of these marriages are also considered 'impure'. This form of pollution cannot be cleansed, as the villagers view it is an impurity of the blood (*ra*). For the parent of free descent, this already is sufficient reason to end the marriage, although a more fatal consequence decides the issue. Upon their death, the 'impure' children and *andevo* wife/husband cannot be placed in the tomb of the free descent parent. Therefore, when a man is of free descent, his *andevo* wife and children may not be buried in his family tomb. Informants told me that this means that they cannot be together as a family in the Hereafter. This form of exclusion constitutes a highly effective tool used by people of free descent to ward off 'impure people' from their families (see also *infra*).

Internalisation of the *andevo* label is a significant component of social relations in Marovato. It is most poignantly demonstrated by the *andevo* bowing to passing *tompon-tany* nobility, and in their self-imposed adherence to rules of avoidance determined by 'pure people'. According to the *tompon-tany*, the *andevo* deviate from the norms of Betsileo culture, which they say only serves to confirm their inferior status.

In fact, the *andevo* display a number of different behaviour traits from other villagers. For example, contrary to other villagers, none of them ever shook hands when greeting me. They also seemed to suffer from 'amnesia' when I inquired about their place of origin. Another distinguishing facet of life in West Marovato is that every household acts as a different socio-economic unit, hardly interacting with other villagers. This is a distinct departure from the usual practice in the rest of the village, where both women and men undertake their daily activities on a communal basis.

---

[15] In the majority of these marriages, slave descent of one of the marriage partners was only established after the union and the birth of children.

Tompon-tany social domination is coupled with economic control over migrants of Betsileo villages in the extreme Southern Highlands. This subordinate link is created through the dependence of newcomers upon *tompon-tany* families for land.[16] All migrants entered into a land-lease contract with the *tompon-tany* upon arrival. This ensures that the *tompon-tany* monopolise not only superior social status but also the basic means of subsistence. The inhabitants of Marovato practise both agriculture and cattle breeding. Although cows are important as status symbols, economic life in the village revolves principally around the cultivation of rice, manioc, maize and vegetables. The *tompon-tany* only cultivate one-third of their land. The rest lies fallow. They say that this land may be used in the future to replace the land that is now in use. Each year, just before the rainy season starts, villagers burn their land, a practice they refer to as *tavy*. They do this to prepare the new agricultural season, to set aside fallow land for a period of years or as a means of asserting uninterrupted 'ownership'.

A brief comparative overview of 1992 and 1996

In 1992, the *tompon-tany* employed no labour from outside the village. They cultivated their land themselves with the help of the migrants residing in the village. Upon arrival in the village all newcomers entered into a land contract with a *tompon-tany*, who retained control of the land and held certain rights over the newcomer. The *tompon-tany* could, for example, demand their labour during harvest time. The marginalisation of the *andevo*, provided *andriana* (*tompon-tany* claiming noble descent) with a permanent supply of workers throughout the year because *andriana* could demand the labour of *andevo* at any time. Generally, *andevo* performed the more demeaning and dirty tasks, such as mucking out cattle corrals and digging holes for foundations of *tompon-tany* houses. In the matter of living conditions in the *andevo* quarter, West Marovato was materially impoverished. The huts were all of poor quality and, contrary to *tompon-tany* families, the *andevo* possessed little or no cattle or farming equipment. All of these external signs pointed to the exclusion of the *andevo* from community life, while they remained a vital part of its socio-economic dynamics.

In 1996, upon my return after a four-year absence, I learned of the arrival of landless *mpikarama* ('labourers') and the corresponding decline of the *andevo* as an economic grouping. The *tompon-tany* had repossessed their

---

[16] Once again, although the *tompon-tany* claim of land is considered legitimate by the villagers, they rarely officially register their land. When asked why this is not the case, *tompon-tany* respond that there is no need for it. Their tomb is deemed to be sufficient evidence that they are actually the 'masters of the land'. To my knowledge, none of the migrants challenged this principle.

leased land from the *andevo* during the same period.[17] I also observed open acceptance by most *andevo* of their ascribed status. Furthermore, based on my numerous conversations with *andevo* and other villagers, I concluded that they retained their importance as a cultural category. Firstly, as a tombless and 'impure' people. Secondly, as a negative reference group for *tompon-tany* cultural values. These values take on particular importance with respect to funerals, tombs and perceptions of the Hereafter.

The location and architecture of *tompon-tany* tombs

For the Betsileo, tombs represent family unity and the entrance to the Hereafter (cf. Rajaonarimanana 1979: 182). In daily life, Marovato villagers often referred to tombs in order to demonstrate their social status. At the same time, it is strictly taboo (*fady*) to actually point out the exact location of the tomb. When I sought specific information in this regard, villagers generally responded by indicating its general direction, for example, by stating that the tomb was located to the northeast or north. When I discovered tombs near the village of Marovato, and asked villagers to whom they belonged, I met with evasiveness, usually justified by the explanation that revealing the names would bring bad luck. While participating in funerals, I gradually determined the location and ownership of Marovato tombs with greater precision.

Most tombs of the Marovato *tompon-tany* are located in the northeastern Ifaha mountains, approximately one kilometre to the north of the village. These *tompon-tany* tombs are generally constructed on the upper portions of their land, which coincides with the foothills of the Ifaha mountains. Their land extends downwards from the tombs in the direction of the Zomandao River.

The architecture of the tombs is uniform. The materials used in the cube-shaped, top portion of the tombs, visible from above-ground, are stones which are hauled from rock quarries and dressed sufficiently flat and small for the walls of the structure. A larger square slab of stone, supported by four columns, serves as the roof. Horns of zebus sacrificed to the ancestors during the funerals are placed on top of the tombs. The portals of the tombs are usually constructed of hardwood (often from merana or nato trees). Some tombs use the more traditional *rafeta*, a massive flat stone, as the entrance door. The tombs measure approximately two and a half metres wide, four in length, and two metres high. The tombs are generally divided into three

[17] In 1996, Marovato had 631 inhabitants. 314 of them were classified as *tompon-tany* ('masters of the land'), 151 as migrants (of whom thirty-one were referred to as *andevo*) and 166 as *mpikarama* (for a discussion of the *mpikarama* and the reasons underlying their entry into the region see Evers 2002).

parts: A *vazohon-kady* (small entrance and gallery) which leads inside the tomb, the underground *hady* (burial vault where the corpses are placed), and the *aloalo*, or upper cube-shaped construction.[18]

Tombs, ancestors and the perpetuation of inequality in the Hereafter

One does not become an ancestor simply by dying. The entrance to the hereafter is the funeral and its accompanying rituals, which can be divided into three phases, each of which plays a role in the process of 'ancestralisation':[19] (1) the funeral itself (*fandevenana*), where the *ambiroa*[20] of the deceased should enter the tomb; (2) the ritual of separation (*toets'ambiroa*), through which villagers lead the *ambiroa* further on its way to the ancestors; (3) the ritual *fiefana*, feast at the end of the mourning period, which marks the final integration of the *ambiroa* of the deceased into the general category of the ancestors (*razana*).

Funerals are the most crucial phase of the 'ancestralisation' process. Two types of funerals are common to people who claim free descent. Firstly, the more elaborate *tompon-tany* ceremony and secondly, the simpler ritual practised by migrants who have their tombs elsewhere.[21] Funerals in *tompon-tany* families can last as long as four days. Despite their efforts to display outward joy, funerals trigger ambivalent emotions among villagers. Their expressions and gestures during rites often betray nervousness, something subsequently explained to me as their fear of doing something wrong and displeasing the ancestors.

---

[18] For more detailed information on the physical construction of Betsileo tombs, see Rajaonarimanana (1979: 181-93) and Dubois (1938: 666-79).

[19] The process of 'ancestralisation' refers to the rituals required to ensure a deceased becomes an ancestor.

[20] The concept of *ambiroa* has received relatively little attention from Madagascar specialists. Abinal (1885: 211-20) and Dubois (1938: 729) trace the etymology of the word *ambiroa* to meanings such as 'being two', 'the body double', and 'the surplus of two'. The *ambiroa* leaves the body upon death.

[21] The funeral rituals of these migrants focus on directing the *ambiroa* of the deceased to the family tomb on their ancestral land. They bury their deceased in the migrant graveyard especially reserved for migrants who have their tombs elsewhere pending eventual transport of the body back home. Because of the costs involved, they rarely do so in practice. For comparative material on Highland funerals cf.: Bloch 1999: 211-31; Decary 1962; Dubois 1938; Edholm 1971; Kottak 1980; Rahamefy 1997; Rajaonarimanana 1979: 181-93; Razafintsalama 1983: 193-209.

This fear can best be understood in terms of the concepts of *hasina* and *hery*. Most authors studying Madagascar refer to *hasina*.[22] The concept has been dealt with in some detail with respect to the Merina and Betsileo (a.o. Bloch 1989: 46-88; Delivré 1967; Dubois 1938; Edholm 1971). Delivré (1967: 167-84) describes *hasina* as an energy that is innate to life. It is a supernatural essence that can be beneficial, but which also contains destructive properties (cf. Kottak 1980: 69, 212). My informants believe that the converse of *hasina*, vital energy, is *hery*, destructive energy. They assert that *hasina* can be transformed by ancestors and individuals into *hery* if they wish to express their discontent. Fertility, good harvests, health are all ascribed to *hasina*, whereas *hery* is said to cause infertility, illness and death.[23] *Hasina* is present in all living entities, but it may also be contained in inanimate things.[24]

Marovato villagers relate the concept of *hasina* directly to the position that people occupy in the current social configuration. *Hasina* resides with the ancestors. Its vehicle of transmission is the socio-political order. The *tompon-tany* family leaders and the *ombiasy* ('traditional healers'), as the most powerful members of the Marovato region, are said to possess the most *hasina*.[25] They are considered to be closest to the ancestors. Their roles

---

22 Southall (1986: 414) translates *hasina* as 'sacred ritual potency'. He considers it to be a central tenet held by all groups in Madagascar: 'Here is one of those pervasive themes which justify emphasis on the essential unity of all Malagasy culture, despite its apparent regional contrasts'. Bloch (1989: 65) also writes that the notion of *hasina* is the 'kernel of Malagasy thought'. For eschatological aspects and the ontology of the Malagasy cf.: Bloch 1971; Cole 2001; Dubois 1978; Heurtebize 1997; Lambek 1993; Mangalaza 1998; Molet 1979; Ottino 1998; Rahamefy 1997; Rainihifina 1958-1961; Rakotomalala 2001; Thomas 1996; 1997.

23 The concept of *hery* is highly ambiguous for the Malagasy. *Hery* commonly means strength and it is neither positive nor negative, it is morally neutral or amoral. It is a good thing only if you can control it (cf. Bloch 1989: 65). Delivré (1967: 188), however, describes *hery* in more negative terms, as do my informants. Delivré writes: '*La signification du hasina dépend donc essentiellement de l'utilisation qu'on en fait: cette puissance n'est bénéfique que lorsque les rapports hiérarchiques entre certains être (...) sont soigneusement sauvegardés. Mais si ces rapports sont inversés et que le hasina est détourné de sa fin propre, il devient accidentellement une force du mal, et on emploie de préférence le terme 'hery' pour le qualifier*'.

24 The concept of *hasina* parallels the notion of *mana*, the Melanesian term for an impersonal power or energy ascribed to people, animals, and plants but also to objects (see also Bloch: 1989: 66 and Kottak 1980: 72).

25 The *ombiasy* and their working methods are worthy of a separate study and beyond the scope of this chapter. It is nevertheless significant that the *tompon-tany* depend so heavily upon their *ombiasy*, who they believe have superior *hasina* to all other living beings. The *ombiasy* also interpret the wishes of the

during rituals are a reflection of this proximity. *Tompon-tany* claiming noble descent have more *hasina* than villagers of commoner descent. The *andevo*, who occupy the lowest position in the local hierarchy, possess the least *hasina*. This, combined with their presumed impurity, is the *tompon-tany* justification for excluding the *andevo* from rituals of free descent people.[26] *Tompon-tany* say the mere presence of the *andevo* will upset the ancestors and bring misfortune.

Bloch also discusses *hasina* as a source of legitimate or traditional authority. He postulates (1989: 64-5) that each *deme* (local kin group) of Merina society possesses *hasina*, which corresponds to its rank in the socio-political hierarchy. Bloch makes a division between what he calls *hasina* mark I and mark II. With *hasina* mark I, he refers to the supernatural virtue that is possessed in differing degrees by all living beings and whose 'innate religious superiority' was concentrated in the Merina king. The *hasina* and authority of the king was presumably unchallenged, bestowed, and sacred. *Hasina* mark II refers to the recognition of that *hasina*, that is, the practice of inferiors rendering homage to superiors.[27] Several authors have drawn parallels between the political component of *hasina* and the concept of 'honour' in English. Superiors might possess honour but only provided they continue to be honoured by inferiors (for instance, Bloch 1989: 66; Kottak 1980: 70).

Historically, the Merina king infused his subjects with *hasina* through the ritual of the royal bath (see Bloch 1986: 43-7). In turn, his subjects rendered homage to the king by giving him the symbolic gift of an uncut silver coin, also called *hasina* (cf. Callet 1908: 663-5; Delivré 1967: 186; Molet 1956). The replication of this interaction between king and subjects was performed within each kin group through the ritual of *tsodrano*. This means the 'blow-

---

ancestors and ensure that rituals are executed according to 'Malagasy customs'. They act as intermediaries between the living and the dead. *Ombiasy* have the knowledge to manipulate *hasina* and *hery* to perform sorcery (called 'Malagasy medicine(s)', *fanafody gasy*). 'Malagasy medicines' are usually amulets (*ody*) composed of herbs, roots, grains, and leaves which are infused with ancestral *hery* by the *ombiasy*. *Tompon-tany* rely on their *ombiasy* to use sorcery as an instrument of power or to avenge wrongs.

26 Rasolomanana (1997: 333), working on the Northern Betsileo, also observes that *andevo* are not allowed to participate in funerals of free-descent people. He writes: '*(...) une femme 'tsy madio' (ayant du sang andevo) qui voulait à tout prix s'intégrer dans le groupe des descendants s'acheminant vers le tombeau ancestral, a été enlevée par un tourbillon subit, pour ne plus être retrouvée!*' Unfortunately, he provides no further details on this issue (cf. Rasoamampionona 2000: 369-75).

27 *Hasina* mark I is a supernatural essence, an innate religious *state* of superiority, which flows in the form of fertility from the superior to the inferiors, whereas *hasina* mark II is a natural *action,* manifested by the giving of gifts, respect and honour, flowing upwards (Bloch 1989: 67-8).

ing of the water'.[28] As a father's *hasina* exceeded that of his sons, the rite was performed by elders for their juniors as a form of blessing for fertility and success. The juniors in turn respected and honoured the elders in order not to be deprived of *hasina*.

The fact that kinship groups possess differing degrees of *hasina* '... is not the result of their achievement but is given in their nature. The concern of the *hasina* holders should be to preserve it; creating *hasina* is out of the question' (Bloch 1989: 66). People try to achieve the preservation of their *hasina* through *deme* endogamy, which raises the question of the correlation between possessing *hasina* and belonging to the different status groups in Marovato. This is particularly evident in the link villagers make between the concepts of *hasina* and *hery* and the *olona madio* ('pure' or 'clean people') – *olona maloto* ('impure' or 'dirty people') dichotomy.

The relevance of the concepts of *hasina* and *hery* in the context of funerals is related to the concept of *ambiroa*. *Ambiroa* is the *trano*, 'house' or 'box', which envelops *hasina*. In their view, the *hasina* of the deceased can be transformed into *hery* when the funeral rites are not performed properly because of which the *ambiroa* fails to enter the tomb. This is disastrous as this means that the *ambiroa* will get 'lost' (*very*) and cannot join the ancestors. Villagers claim that it will then become frustrated and take revenge on his family members through the conversion of its *hasina* into *hery*. This in turn inevitably will lead to infertility, illness, and death within the family.

Becoming 'lost' is the inevitable fate of *andevo* deceased as they do not possess land or have tombs, when they die, they are believed to cause their descendants perpetual problems because of the *hery* being wreaked upon them by frustrated deceased who are seemingly forever barred from the Hereafter. As a consequence, the *andevo* funeral is primarily characterised by its lack of identifiable features. The negative attributes popularly associated with the *andevo* are also reflected in the funeral itself. No rituals. No publicity. No celebration. And most disturbingly, no signs of the intricate process of 'ancestralisation', which is meant to ensure the *ambiroa* may successfully leave the mortal plane and join the ancestors.

Andevo strongly believe that their deceased sow illness, misfortune, and death in their families. There is no empirical evidence that *andevo* actually have more problems with infertility, miscarriages, and infant mortality, or that they fall ill more often than free-descent villagers, or that they die sooner.[29] They nevertheless cling as steadfastly to this credo as the *tompontany*. The *andevo* themselves are convinced that these things occur because

[28] In the *tsodrano* ritual, the elder sprays junior family members with water from a saucer he holds before his lips (Bloch 1989: 68). In the Marovato region, this practice is still engaged in by free-descent fathers for their children.

[29] This kind of statistical data is virtually impossible to gather, because of the *andevo* reluctance to even be identified as a group.

they lack tombs. People of free descent often claimed that it is because the *andevo*, or to be more precise, the *hery* (contained in the *ambiroa*) of their deceased, that things go awry in the village. Although they stated that these deceased generally take revenge on their own descendants, *hery* is also believed to lie at the origin of more general problems that have afflicted Marovato over the previous decades, such as drought and low rice production.

Free-descent people rarely let an occasion slip to remind me that because *andevo* had no tombs, they could not become ancestors. They referred to them as *olona very*, 'lost people'. Even the *andevo* themselves remarked 'I think I will die', when sensing their own imminent demise. A free descent person would say: 'I think I will join the ancestors'.

Having no ancestors means that the *andevo* do not benefit from ancestral *hasina*, vital energy, acquired in the interactive ritual exchange between the ancestors and the living, or at another level between seniors and juniors within free descent families. On the one hand, the downward flow of *hasina* from the ancestors to senior family members and then junior members, what Bloch calls *hasina* mark I, does not take place in *andevo* families. Thus, *andevo* fathers do not perform the *tsodrano* ritual, 'blowing of the water' (*cf. supra*), to bless their descendants. On the other hand, the upward flow of inferiors rendering homage to elders and the ancestors, Bloch's *hasina* mark II, manifested by the giving of gifts, respect, and honour, also has no ritual relevance for the *andevo*.[30] They therefore do not perform *saotra* ('blessing', 'thanks') to express their gratitude towards the ancestors, a ritual that is omnipresent in free-descent ceremonies, especially during the process of 'ancestralisation'.

This absence of the flow of ancestral *hasina* was, after the negative influence of *hery* on their life, the second reason to which the *andevo* attributed their misfortune and health problems. *Andevo* defined themselves as human beings with very little *hasina* that they could never develop unless they created tombs and ancestors. The absence of ancestors and consequent deficiency in *hasina*, according to the *andevo*, was the principal reason why they were so 'different'. Free-descent people preferred to express this in terms of inferiority.

---

[30] In free-descent families, juniors generally treated seniors with great respect. This was not the case in *andevo* households. *Andevo* children rarely used the prefix '*Ra*' as a sign of respect when referring to their parents. They openly criticised their parents if they did not agree with them. The failure of *andevo* fathers to find husbands for their daughters was a common topic of discussion between the girls and me. They openly criticised their father as being too lazy ('*kamo izy*'). This comment would be inconceivable for free-descent youngsters, either publicly or privately.

Whether one refers to *hery*, or deficiency in *hasina*, or simply being 'different', the overriding feeling of the *andevo* is one of shame, which permeates *andevo* existence. This is reflected in their discourse concerning funerals. *Andevo* often told me that they were very sad and ashamed that they could not give their beloved a funeral in the same manner as free-descent people conducted theirs. As Ratsimbazafy, an *andevo,* said:

> We are overcome by shame (*henatra*). We try to bury dead people as soon as we can. We hope that nobody will see where we take them. We are not allowed to bury our dead people in the graveyard of the other migrants. They are the *olona madio* ('pure people'). They are afraid that we will pollute the graveyard and that their ancestors will get upset about that. So, we have to find burial spots ourselves. I do not know where other people like us bury their dead. We never speak about it. That is how ashamed we are.

Realising that both people of free descent and *andevo* believe that the *ambiroa* of *andevo* might cause harm for the whole village, one wonders why *tompon-tany* continue to deprive the *andevo* of land and tombs. The *tompon-tany*, without exception, refused to address this issue, asserting vehemently that the question indicated that 'I was behaving as a foreigner'. They added that their ancestors wanted things this way. Were they not to follow their ancestors, revenge would be wreaked upon them in a form of *hery* even more powerful and harmful then the *hery* of deceased *andevo.*[31]

The odds of any *andevo* actually acquiring a tomb would appear to be slim indeed in a society that has taken such harsh measures to exclude them from any type of meaningful role in day-to-day Marovato society.[32] However, under the new land registry system proposed by the government they might be able to acquire land ownership and erect tombs. This would be a dream come true for the *andevo*. They often make allusion to this by saying that their lives would change drastically if they were to possess land and tombs. Would the *tompon-tany* allow it though?

---

[31] Even *hasina* of the ancestors can transform into *hery*. This allegedly occurs when people of free descent violate *fomba gasy* ('Malagasy customs'), for example, by disrespecting the ancestors.

[32] In search for land ownership and therewith tombs, many *andevo* ended up in the socialist co-operative of Sahanala-Zomandao (cf. Evers 1997), located approximately twenty kilometres to the southwest of Marovato. In 1975, the Ratsiraka government granted 300 hectares of land to migrants who entered the cooperative. The local Bara *tompon-tany*, who claim that this is their ancestral land, are entangled in a bitter dispute over the land with the migrants. This often leads to cow thefts. And as soon as the *andevo* erected tombs, the Bara tore them down. The land disputes are rarely, if ever, settled inside the courtroom.

Conclusion

This case[33] is an illustration of the extent to which land is one of the central tenets of *tompon-tany* ontology. If, in fact, current *tompon-tany* are slave descendants, as my hypothesis suggests, they have legitimised their current status as the village elites through their land and tombs. Economic and social relations in the villages are conditioned by the total *tompon-tany* control over land access in the villages. It is a hard-won status, and one they are not likely to compromise easily, conditioned as it is by its very recent acquisition. This is also revealed by the way they treat the *andevo*.

The *tompon-tany* need to accentuate and perpetuate the attributed features of the *andevo* appears to be born of the precariousness of their own past, but also is an indicator of just how crucial land is in the equation of Maravato life. The *andevo*, the *alter ego* and negative mirror of the *tompon-tany*, are prohibited from establishing tombs, effectively excluding them from Marovato society. Because the *andevo* are prohibited from having tombs by express policy of the *tompon-tany*, they are denied access to the Hereafter. By necessary implication, they can neither create ancestors nor extended kinship groups. *Andevo* are said to be deficient in *hasina*, and unable to control the malignant forces of *hery*. Excluded from the process of 'ancestralisation', the *andevo* are *olona very*, 'lost people'. The *tompon-tany* fear nothing more than being 'lost' people. So, whatever the legal or macro-political finesses of land title, this is the reality which any land title system must face: A people who have constructed their identity by creating a land monopoly.

The very definition of *tompon-tany* is 'masters of the land', the privileged ones who have the *hasina* of the ancestors. Surrendering their position as exclusive landowners is simply inconceivable. For the *tompon-tany*, creating the monopoly was a technique for survival. Because its source of legitimacy is the ancestors, it has always been portrayed as a stable and timeless system, when, in reality, it only was established after the abolition of slavery. Even the labels *andevo* and *andriana*[34] were recently resurrected by the *tompon-tany* to reinforce the immanent nature of the system, and to perpetuate the inferior status of the *andevo*.

The *tompon-tany* succeeded in imposing their system of tombs, ancestors, and the concepts of *hery* and *hasina*, because their beliefs were shared by migrants (including the *andevo*). Nor is this a set of beliefs limited to the countryside. Even at the national level, ministers subscribe to the power of the ancestors, and their necessary backing in the form of *hasina* for a suc-

---

33 This case of social inequality in the extreme Southern Highlands is not representative of the rest of Madagascar but the concept of *tompon-tany* exists throughout the country.

34 *Andriana* ('noble descent') seems to be borrowed from the Merina.

cessful (political) fate. This belief is far more anchored than any recently imported political ideologies.

With the case above, I hope to shed some light on the issues that the Malagasy government must address in implementing a land registration system to permit land ownership to current tenant farmers. Taking exclusive land ownership principles out of the domain of the ancestors, and therewith out of the hands of the *tompon-tany*, will be a revolutionary card to play.

References

ABINAL, A. (1885) *Vingt ans à Madagascar*, Paris.

ARCHIVES D'OUTRE MER (Aix-en-Provence) Madagascar series 1Z: General material on Madagascar.

BLOCH, M. (1971) *Placing the dead: Tombs, ancestral villages, and kinship organisation in Madagascar*, London: Seminar Press.

BLOCH, M. (1980) Modes of production and slavery in Madagascar: Two case studies, in: Watson, J.L. (Ed.) *Asian and African systems of slavery*, Oxford: Basil Blackwell, pp. 100-34.

BLOCH, M. (1986) *From blessing to violence: History and ideology in the circumcision ritual of the Merina of Madagascar*, Cambridge: Cambridge University Press.

BLOCH, M. (1989) The disconnection between power and rank as a process: An outline of the development of kingdoms in Central Madagascar, in: Bloch, M. *Ritual, history and power*, Selected Papers in Anthropology by Maurice Bloch, London: The Athlone Press, pp. 46-88.

BLOCH, M. (1989) The ritual of the royal bath in Madagascar: The dissolution of death, birth and fertility into authority, in: Bloch, M. *Ritual, history and power*, Selected Papers in Anthropology by Maurice Bloch, London: The Athlone Press, pp. 187-212.

BLOCH, M. (1999) Death, women and power, in: Bloch, M. and Parry, J. (Eds) *Death and the regeneration of life*, Cambridge: Cambridge University Press, pp. 211-31.

CALLET, R.P. (1908) *Tantaran' ny Andriana eto Madagascar*, 2nd edition, Tananarive: Académie Malgache.

CALLET, R.P. (1974) *Histoire des Rois (Tantaran' ny andriana)*, translation by G. Chapus and E. Ratsimba, Antananarivo: Editions de la Librairie de Madagascar.

COLE, J. (2001) *Forget colonialism? Sacrifice and the art of memory in Madagascar*, Berkeley: University of California Press.

DECARY, R. (1962) *La mort et les coutumes funéraires à Madagascar*, Paris: Maisonneuve et Larose.

DELIVRÉ, A. (1967) *Interprétation d'une tradition orale. L'Histoire des Rois d'Imerina*, unpublished thesis, Paris. Published in 1974 under the same title, Paris: Klincksieck.

DUBOIS, H.M. (1938) *Monographie des Betsileo*, Paris: Institut d'Ethnologie.

DUBOIS, R. (1978) *Olombelona: Essai sur l'existence personelle et collective à Madagascar*, Paris.

EDHOLM, F. (1971) *Royal funerary rituals among the Betsileo of Madagascar*, Ph.D. thesis, London School of Economics.

EVERS, S.J.T.M. (1997) Solidarity and antagonism in migrant societies in the Southern Highlands, in: Ignace, R. (Ed.), *L'esclavage à Madagascar: Aspects historiques et résurgences contemporaines*, Antananarivo: Institut de Civilisations-Musée d'Art et d'Archéologie, pp. 339-47.

EVERS, S.J.T.M. (2002) *Constructing history, culture and inequality: The Betsileo in the extreme southern highlands of Madagascar*, Leiden: Brill.

HEURTEBIZE, G. (1997) *Mariage et deuil dans l'extrême-sud de Madagascar*, Paris: L'Harmattan.

INTERNATIONAL MONETARY FUND (IMF) (2000) *IMF Staff Country Report. Madagascar: Recent economic development and selected issues*, Washington: IMF.

KOTTAK, C.P. (1980) *The past in the present: History, ecology and cultural variation in Madagascar*, Ann Arbor: University of Michigan Press.

LAMBEK, M. (1993) *Knowledge and practice in Mayotte: Local discourses of Islam, sorcery, and spirit possession*, University of Toronto Press.

MANGALAZA, E. (1998) *Vie et mort chez les Betsimisaraka de Madagascar. Essai d'anthropologie philosophique*, Paris: L'Harmattan.

MOLET, L. (1956) *Le bain royale à Madagascar*, Antananarivo: Les Presses de l'imprimerie Luthérienne.

MOLET, L. (1979) *La conception malgache du monde, du surnaturel et de l'homme en Imerina*, Paris: L'Harmattan.

OTTINO, P. (1998) *Les champs de l'ancestralité à Madagascar: Parenté, alliance et patrimoine*, Paris: Karthala/Orstom.

RAHAMEFY, A. (1997) *Le roi ne meurt pas. Rites funéraires princiers du Betsileo, Madagascar*, Paris: L'Harmattan.

RAINIHIFINA, J. (1958-1961) *Lovantsaina betsileo*, 3 vol. (I. *Histoire,* II. *Coutumes betsileo*, III. *Littérature betsileo.*), Librairie Ambozontany re-edited the books in French (1975), Fianarantsoa: Ambozontany.

RAJAONARIMANANA, N. (1979) Achèvement des funérailles et offrande de linceuls. Rites funéraires et commémoratifs des Betsileo du Manandriana, in: Guiart, J. (Ed.) *Les hommes et la mort: Rites funéraires à travers le monde*, Paris: Le Sycomore – Objets et Mondes (Muséum national d'histoire naturelle), pp. 181-93.

RAKOTOMALALA, M., S. BLANCHY, and F. RAISON-JOURDE (2001) *Madagascar: Les ancêtres au quotidien. Usages sociaux du religieux sur les Hautes-Terres Malgaches*, Paris: L'Harmattan.

RASOAMAMPIONONA, C. (2000) La survivance d'inégalités dans les castes betsileo, in: Allibert, C. and Rajaonarimanana, N. (Eds) *L'extraordinaire et le quotidien: Variations anthropologiques. Hommage au professeur Pierre Vérin*, Paris: Karthala, pp. 369-75.

RAZAFINTSALAMA, A. (1983) Les funérailles royales en Isandra, d'après les sources du XIXe siècle, in: Raison-Jourde (Ed.) *Les souverains de Madagascar. L'histoire royale et ses résurgences contemporaines*, Paris: Karthala, pp. 193-209.

SOUTHALL, A. (1986) Common themes in Malagasy culture, in: Kottak, C.P., Rakotoarisoa, J.-A., Southall, A., Vérin, P. (Eds) *Madagascar society and history*, Durham: Carolina Academic Press, pp. 411-26.

THOMAS, P. (1996) *Place, person, and ancestry among the Tenambondro of Southeast Madagascar*, Ph.D. thesis, London School of Economics and Political Science.

THOMAS, P. (1997) The water that blesses, the river that flows: Place and the ritual imagination among the Tamambondro of Southeast Madagascar, in: Fox, J. (Ed.) *The poetic power of place: Comparative perspectives on Austronesian ideas of locality*, Comparative Austronesian Project Publication Series. Canberra: Research School of Pacific Studies, Australian National University, pp. 22-41.

TRIBUNE (Malagasy Newspaper) (2003) *Rencontre entre agriculteurs et institutions sur l'accès à la propriété et la sécurité cadastrale à Madagascar*, 30 july 2003.

Glossary

ambiroa	body double
andevo	slave(s) or being of slave descent
andriana	being of claimed noble descent. In Betsileo society: Those who reincarnate into crocodiles
fady	forbidden, taboo
fanafody gasy	Malagasy medicine(s), an euphemism for sorcery
fandevenana	funeral
fasana	tomb
fiefana	completion of the funeral. Ritual to mark the end of the mourning period
fomba gasy	Malagasy customs
hasina	vital energy innate to life
henatra	shame
hery	power or energy. Often seen as destructive.
hova	being of claimed noble descent in Betsileo society. Betsileo *hova* do not reincarnate into crocodiles. Commoner descent in Merina society
madio	clean or pure
maloto	dirty or impure
mpiavy	migrant(s)
mpikarama	labourer(s)
ody	amulet(s)
olompotsy	being of claimed commoner descent
olona madio	clean or pure person or people. Designation in Betsileo society for people who have 'proven' their free descent by pointing out their family tomb. They are considered to be of free descent
olona maloto	dirty or impure person or people. Designation in Betsileo society for people who cannot demonstrate their free descent by means of a family tomb. They are considered to be of slave descent

ombiasy	traditional healer
rafeta	flat stone blocking the entrance of the tomb
razana	ancestor(s), dead person or corpse
saotsa	blessing, thanks. Expression of gratitude to the ancestors
tanin-drazana	ancestral land
tantara	a history, a tale, a legend, a fabulous narration
tavy	slash-and-burn agriculture
toets'ambiroa	ritual of separation
tompon-tany	master(s) of the land
trano	house or box
tsodrano	blowing of the water
tsy madio	impure, not clean
very	lost

10

The struggle for land rights in the context of multiple normative orders in Tanzania

Rie Odgaard

Introduction

Discussions about land and development policies in Tanzania often leave the impression that there are huge uninhabited areas in the country, and that everybody who so wishes can get enough land to sustain their livelihood: Land is available if you are willing to use it and to work.

However, as early as in the 1920s pressure on land was reported in some of the most fertile areas of Tanzania, notably parts of the South-Western Highlands and in areas around Mount Kilimanjaro and Mount Meru in the North.[1]

Land scarcity in these and gradually also in other areas has over time implied that huge numbers of people have migrated in search of arable land and pastures elsewhere. Areas that are marginal with regard to fertility and situated in semi-arid parts of the country with erratic rainfall are now increasingly being used for cultivation, and access to grazing areas is consequently diminishing.

An increasing number of land conflicts are now occurring between different interest groups and between various types of land use. This chapter focuses on two specific types of struggle for land rights in Iringa District,

---

1 See for example Gulliver 1958; Gulliver 1961; Hall 1945.

South-Western Tanzania. The first concerns women's rights to land vis-à-vis those of men among the Hehe, for whom Iringa District is considered as home. The dispute illustrates that not only gender but also generation is relevant when analysing women's access to land. The example also shows that different interest groups among the Hehe have different interpretations of rules and norms related to land rights, depending on situational circumstances, raising the issue of balance between exercising rights and fulfilling obligations.

The second dispute is between Maasai pastoral immigrants and local cultivators, mainly the Hehe, and reflects some of the problems related to the issue of first-comers and late-comers, as well as competition between different land use systems: The pastoral system in which land is used mainly as a common property resource, and cultivation based on more long-term use of specific pieces of land.

While illustrating a dynamic interplay between different normative orders in Tanzania, the conflicts also reflect changing perceptions about land in relation to property, e.g. does land constitute property, and if so what is the nature of such property?

This chapter draws on fieldwork material from Iringa District.[2] Although local specific conditions and historical developments in the area have influenced the way these disputes are articulated, it is fair to say that similar disputes are found in many other parts of Tanzania and other African countries.[3]

---

2 The major part of the information presented here has been obtained during my involvement in Subproject 3 under the research programme Sustainable Agriculture in Semi-Arid Africa (SASA) from 1995-2000, financed by the Danish Council for Development Research. This fieldwork was carried out in Ismani and Mazombe Divisions, Iringa Rural District, in close collaboration with Jannik Boesen and Faustin P. Maganga. Other fieldwork periods in Iringa Rural District were part of my involvement in two studies carried out for the Danish International Development Agency (DANIDA) (1992) together with Hildegard Kiwasila, and for the World Bank (1994) together with Faustin P. Maganga. See Kiwasila and Odgaard (1992), and Odgaard and Maganga (1994). A variety of data collection methods were adopted: a) participant observation; b) structured interviews with selected key informants – among villagers: both men and women from a wide range of age groups and different socio-economic backgrounds representing locals as well as immigrants, and village leaders – both government employees and so-called traditional leaders; c) observations during village meetings; d) group discussions; e) informal talks with villagers when met accidentally; f) archival research and study of local court case material.

3 See for example Aarhem 1986; Odgaard and Maganga 1994; Cleaver 2003; Odgaard and Weis Bentzon 2003; Manji 2000; Lane 1993; Mwaikyusa 1993; Mustafa 1993; Meinzen-Dick *et al.* 1997; Rocheleau and Edmunds 1997; Lastarria-Cornhiel 1997; Muteshi 1997; Mackenzie 1989; IIED 1999; Woodhouse *et al.* 2000; Broch-Due 2000a; Broch-Due 2000b; to mention but a few.

Setting

Iringa District is the home area of the Hehe. The area was previously rather sparsely populated, but has during the past five to six decades received huge numbers of immigrants looking for pastures and land for cultivation from various parts of Tanzania, and a number of other ethnic groups are now living in Iringa.

The Hehe are parties in both examples analysed below. They have previously based their main livelihood on livestock keeping with agriculture only as a complementary activity, mainly carried out by the women. But this has changed dramatically during and after the colonial era, and agriculture is today by far the most important basis for the livelihood of the Hehe.

Maize is the most important food crop, usually inter-planted with various leguminous plants. Other crops are sunflower, sorghum, millet and, in places where irrigation is possible, different types of vegetables. Over the past twenty-thirty years, tomatoes have become an increasingly important cash crop, especially in villages most accessible from the main road, and land for that purpose is in very high demand.

The Maasai, who form the other party in example II, started migrating to Iringa District from the mid 1950s. The majority are from the Dodoma and Arusha Regions and base their livelihood mainly on livestock keeping. I shall therefore refer to them as pastoralists. Very few, if any at all, of the pastoral peoples in Tanzania today derive their entire livelihood from livestock keeping. Some element of cultivation has for a long time, and now increasingly, is forming part of the pastoral economy. However, the Maasai in question identify themselves mainly with livestock keeping and their seasonal mobility and migration strategies are governed mainly by the needs of the livestock and not their cultivation activities. This affects the type of land rights they are able to enjoy.

The concepts of ethnic group and tribe have been subject to heated debates in literature about Africa.[4] Without entering into that debate I want to emphasise that when I refer to the Hehe and the Maasai I am not talking about tribes in the colonial sense of the word, but about people who identify themselves, and who are identified by others, as belonging to these specific groups. As part of their self-identification they refer to specific norm sets and customary rules as forming part of their culture.

---

4 For example Iliffe 1979; Redmayne 1968; Mamdani 1996.

Rights to land in Tanzania: A conceptual framework

Sara Berry (1993; 1997), Sally Falk Moore (1999) and others look at land rights conceptually from the perspective of social relationships and see them as outcomes of processes of negotiation. Land rights are not just understood in terms of the rules and laws specifying them, but from the perspective of movement and interaction (Berry 1997). People's land rights depend very much on relations to an ethnic group, to family/clan, marriage relations, friendship, patron-client relations, relations to authorities at various levels of the society and so on. (Moore 1999). As will become clear, this perspective has much to offer in the analysis of land rights in the situation of legal pluralism existing in Tanzania, as in most other African countries.[5]

As defined by Woodman (1997), legal pluralism is: '(…) the condition in which the population observes more than one body of law'. The bodies of law related to land rights observed in Tanzania are unwritten customary laws[6] on the one hand, and on the other hand 'modern' laws and policies, namely state laws written down in law books, and government policies as they appear in written instructions, the press and so on. Legal pluralism implies that when these bodies of law are applied legally, for example in resolving cases of land disputes, the normative orders (e.g. local rules, norms and codes of conduct) observed by people in the empirical context where the dispute has occurred have to be taken into consideration and be used as sources of law. As expressed by Benda-Beckmann (2001: iii), 'The merit of the legal pluralism approach is (…) that it forces us to concentrate on the empirical reality behind the slogans about "the rule of law"; we should always ask, what is the actual effect of a particular normative order – whether state or non-state, public or private – on people's rights over essential resources and their "access to justice" in the true sense'.

This implies that even though women's land rights among the Hehe and Maasai land rights may not be dealt with specifically in state legislation, or may be completely overlooked in policies and written instructions, the legal plural situation implies that whatever rights these groups are entitled to in

---

5 For a detailed account of the legal system in Tanzania, see for example James and Fimbo 1973; URT 1983; Fimbo 1992; URT 1994; and the two new land acts in Tanzania (URT 1999a and b).

6 In Tanzania, with 120 different ethnic groups, customary laws are influenced by many meanings and also refer to customary law 'in court' – that is customary law as it is being interpreted in courts based on actual court cases. Customary law as a concept is dealt with in detail in Armstrong (1992). When used uncritically the term customary law as shown in, for example, Chanock (1998) and Mamdani (1996) can be very confusing and problematic. Here customary laws are seen as dynamic and as representing the traditions, rules and norms of local African communities and changes in them over time.

accordance with locally accepted rules and norms and/or are enjoying in practice have to be taken into consideration when resolving dispute cases. This plural legal situation is clearly reflected in the new Land Policy and the two New Land Acts in Tanzania, passed by Parliament in May 1999 and enacted by President Mkapa in May 2001.[7]

Looking at land rights as embedded in social relations and seeing them from the perspective of movement and interaction implies that the normative orders dealing with them cannot be studied independently from each other, as boundaries between them are negotiable and never fixed. The orders impinge upon each other, and have done so throughout history. In order to understand analytically the interplay between the different normative orders in the contexts where the disputes dealt with below take place, I have found the concept of semi-autonomous social field developed by Sally F. Moore[8] a very useful tool. According to Moore, a semi-autonomous social field is defined by the fact that it has '(…) rule making capacities, and the means to induce or coerce compliance; but it is simultaneously set in a larger social matrix which can, and does, affect and invade it, sometimes at the invitation of persons inside it, sometimes at its own instance' (Falk Moore 1978: 55).

An arena where groups such as fathers, daughters and sons among the Hehe, or groups of Maasai versus groups of the Hehe, for example, deal with each other as parties in disputes, may in accordance with Moore's definition be viewed as a semi-autonomous social field. But each of these groups may also by themselves constitute a semi-autonomous social field, depending on their respective capacities for generating and enforcing rules. The important point here is that a social field is semi-autonomous, not only because it can be affected by the direction of outside forces impinging on it, but because persons inside the social field can mobilise those outside forces, or threaten to do so, in their bargaining with one another (Falk Moore 1978: 64). The parties in the examples below are all, as will be seen, engaged in a process in which each of them strives to become both rules/norms generating and enforcing in relation to land rights.

---

7 For further elaboration see below and The Land Act and The Village Land Act (URT 1999a and b).

8 For an in-depth discussion of this concept, see Falk Moore 1978.

Regulation of land rights in practice in the Iringa District[9]

Over the years the context for land negotiation processes in the Iringa District has been ever changing. A number of internal as well as external factors have influenced the nature of these changes. There has been a great increase in population, a large part of which, as mentioned, is composed of immigrants from other parts of Tanzania with different customary rules and norms from those of the Hehe. Customary rules and norms have also been very much influenced by policies and legislation introduced during colonial and post-colonial times, and by Tanzania's position in the international community; new forms that may be seen as reflecting local law,[10] or institutional bricolage, as I think some scholars (Cleaver 2003) have called it, have emerged.

The majority of rural people in Iringa District hold land rights which are based on unwritten 'customary' rules and norms, but land endowments differ for different groups and individuals, not only in accordance with age, status and gender, but also depending on whether you belong to *wawenyeji* (Swahili word for 'indigenous'[11]) or *wageni* (guests/immigrants) – 'first-comers' or 'late-comers'.

For example, Hehe men and women, *wawenyeji* in the Iringa District, have two types of land endowments in principle: Indigenous rights and rights in accordance with land policies developed in particular during the socialist era, which are reflected in the 1999 Land Acts. The *wageni,* to whom the Maasai belong, have, however, land endowments in their home area, in principle at least, but endowments in the immigration area only in accordance with the existing policies granting any citizen of Tanzania above the age of 18 the right to be assigned land if accepted as a member of a village community. However, as will be seen, pastoral land rights are in general not well provided for in Tanzania, neither under customary laws nor under formal legislation.

---

9 The way land rights are articulated in practice in Iringa is not very different from other rural areas in Tanzania. See for example Odgaard 1987; Kiwasila and Odgaard 1992; Odgaard 1994; Odgaard and Maganga 1994; Odgaard 1999.

10 The concept of 'local law' is discussed in, for example, Hellum 2000 and is defined as a mixed product and a hybrid form of law that has evolved in colonial and post-colonial countries in Africa. See also Le Roy 1985.

11 The word 'indigenous' here refers to the group of people who consider Iringa to be their home area, and should not be confused with the term 'indigenous peoples'. In Swahili such groups of people are referred to as '*watu wa asili*'. The term indigenous peoples is seen by many as very controversial in Tanzania and in Africa in general. For discussions related to this, see IWGIA 1998; IWGIA 2001 and the essays in IWGIA, Document No.74, 1993 for example.

To what extent *wawenyeji* and *wageni* (as groups or individuals) are able to derive the potential benefits from their land endowments, e.g. to have legitimate effective command (entitlements[12]) over such benefits (what can be produced from the land – food crops, cash from sales and so on) depends on a number of factors, and access to power and bargaining power are very important for the results they are able to obtain from participating in negotiation processes about land rights.

According to 'modern' land legislation and policies, people can *have access to land* through purchase and through allocation by the authorities. The involvement of local authorities in allocating land is not a new phenomenon,[13] but the form under which this takes place at present is very much influenced by policies introduced during the socialist era in Tanzania.[14] Under the New Village Land Act, the village authorities are still assigned a very crucial role in land allocation (URT 1999b).

Landed property has in the past, and is increasingly, changing hands across family and clan divisions, and a land market has existed for a long time.[15]

All these different forms of tenure are found in practice in the Iringa District, although land rights, based on customary rules and norms, as mentioned, are by far the most common. The type of rights especially relevant for the two examples below is firstly rights held by *wawenyeji* in the area – mainly the Hehe. Rights differ in accordance with age, status and gender.[16] Claiming 'indigenous' customary rights to seemingly unoccupied land has increased concurrently with increased competition for land. Customary rights are considered locally to be as secure as private title deeds,[17] and are associated with obligations to use the land.

The type of rights in focus in example II is *customary rights held by wageni*. Such rights are mainly held by immigrants who have lived in Iringa

---

12 For a discussion of the terms endowment and entitlement, see for example Leach *et al.* 1999.

13 Hehe headmen in the pre-colonial and colonial periods in Tanzania had the authority to distribute land to both members of the Hehe and to people coming from other groups.

14 See below and URT 1983; Fimbo 1992; James and Fimbo 1973; URT 1994.

15 See, for example, Iliffe 1979.

16 There are detailed analyses of the way indigenous Hehe customary rights historically have been allocated in practice in the area in accordance with age, gender and status, and how such practices have been changing over time in, for example, Brown and Hutt 1935; Mumford 1934; TNA Secretariat Files No's 7794 and 7794/3, 1925; Accession No. 157, file No.6/42, 1938 and Odgaard 1999.

17 For an in-depth discussion of the security in tenure of so-called traditional rights versus other types of rights, e.g. individual private rights, see also for example Migot-Adholla *et al.* 1991; Havnevik 1995; Sjaastad and Bromley 1997.

District for some time. Procedures followed to acquire rights have differed depending on the point in time of arrival in the area. Before and during colonialism immigrants approached local chiefs and headmen and were shown an area where they could build a house and cultivate or graze their animals. In very sparsely populated areas people often just settled down without further ado. Later, during the socialist era in Tanzania, village authorities were given a more prominent role in allocating land rights to newcomers. But in many cases the local 'indigenous' authorities were, and still are, quite influential in land matters. The rights *wageni* were and are granted are customary in nature, in the sense that they are normally unwritten[18] and are tied to various obligations related to use and management. They can be granted to individual families or groups of households and be held individually or communally.

The distribution of specific use rights to individuals and families is normally taken care of by internally recognised 'traditional' authorities of these groups in accordance with the way they interpret their own specific ethnic customary rules. The Maasai mainly manage land as a common property resource, but as shown below there is, however, a trend in the area that immigrants in particular, who base their livelihood mainly on cultivation, try to secure rights by adopting, for example, Hehe burial customs.[19]

Example no. I: The scramble for women's access to landed property among the Hehe

Disputes about women's land rights vis-à-vis those of men are not uncommon in Tanzania, and reflect a continuous reinterpretation of rules and norms depending on situational circumstances (for example Manji 2000; Koda 1998; Maganga and Odgaard 2002). Example I shows how different interest groups among the Hehe interpret indigenous customary rights very differently, and illustrates that elements from different normative orders can be used in manipulating games.

Among the Hehe there are very different accounts of the rights of women and men respectively to property, especially landed property. As will be seen below, the distinction between land as property and other types of property (e.g. cattle) is historically a fairly recent phenomenon in the communities in question.

The majority of Hehe women of all ages who were interviewed argued that by custom women have the right to acquire land in their paternal home area, and to inherit such land from their fathers. A large number of men,

[18] This has been the case until recently when some form of written documentation is often sought and obtained. See Odgaard 2003.

[19] See below and Odgaard 2003.

especially women's brothers, claimed that women (in their own right) have no rights whatsoever to land in their natal home area. According to these men, women only have use rights to their husband's land. Only if a woman gets into trouble, (e.g. divorce, or if widowed and chased away by children and/or the deceased husband's family) may she be allowed to borrow a piece of land from her father or a brother. But according to this group of men, she will not be able to consider such land as her property, and her children are not entitled to inherit it.

The version given by the women was, however, confirmed by the majority of the older men, e.g. men belonging to the generation of fathers of the women interviewed, and the conflicting views therefore do not reflect a conflict between men on the one side and women on the other, but rather conflicts between two parties, e.g. a specific group of women (daughters) supported by their fathers, and specific groups of men, especially women's brothers.

As the Hehe are patrilineal and patrilocal the general assumption is that women get access to land only through marriage, and only use rights.[20] However, it appears clearly from historical accounts that Hehe women were entitled to property in their own right and that they have inherited such property from their fathers. Brothers usually inherited the largest shares because they had the obligation to take care of the sick, parents in their old age, and so on. But it also appears that whatever property a woman inherited was usually left in her natal home area and taken care of by her brothers when she married and moved to her husband's village. Historical accounts also show that land was actually not looked on as property until in the latter part of the colonial period (Odgaard 1999). So the dispute about men's and women's rights to land seems to be more complicated than assumptions referred to above suggest. A number of questions arise from the different accounts given by the interviewees: Why did different groups have different perceptions about their rights? Why did many fathers support their daughters' views, and brothers in particular oppose them? What type of changes over time, if any, could explain this controversy?

It appeared in practice that quite a substantial number of women living in their natal home area have been assigned or have inherited land there (Odgaard 1999). They claim to have effective command over the land and the benefits derived from it, even though this command may be shared with a husband and/or other family members.

Some of the confusion about women's rights to land seems to be related to historical changes. The historical sources, as well as information from the elders interviewed, are in agreement on at least the following points in relation to the pre-colonial situation among the Hehe:

---

[20] For a discussion about assumptions related to women's land rights in patrilineal communities, see Odgaard and Weis Bentzon 2003.

1. Previously land did not have any value as such, because there was plenty of it, and more than enough to satisfy the needs of the people.
2. Land did not constitute individual property, and land users were not attached to any specific pieces of land.
3. The role of livestock keeping was as important, if not more important, for the livelihood of the Hehe than cultivation.
4. Major cultivation activities were undertaken by women.

But this situation has changed fundamentally, except for the fact that women still play a very important role in agricultural production.

There has been a continuously increasing emphasis on cultivation, starting very early during the colonial era and continuing ever since. It was in the interest of the colonial powers to make productive use of the land, and large areas were alienated and given to private companies, used for government purposes, turned into conservation areas, forest reserves and national parks, and given to settlers.[21] The policies implemented by post-colonial governments have also emphasised agricultural production, and many African farmers have over time invested in new crops and improved technologies, and accumulated large holdings.[22] From being quite mobile with their herds of livestock the Hehe are now more permanently settled cultivators, who in time have developed more and more intimate cultural attachments to the specific pieces of land they are using,[23] and new normative orders have emerged.

The emphasis on agriculture during and after colonialism was, among other things, caused by the need to produce a surplus to pay taxes, school fees and so on. In concurrence with the massive increase in population, both natural increase among the Hehe themselves and large-scale immigration,[24] there is now increased competition for land, both for cultivation and pastures, and, therefore, naturally enough an increased focus on land rights.

These developments combined with the increased influence of paternalistic and male dominated ideologies and resulting changes in norms and values have implied that women now, much more often than previously, find themselves in situations where they need to make use of their rights to claim land and property from their own clan. Many are divorced or single mothers, either by choice (Odgaard 1997), or because they do not have contact with the fathers of their children. Many men complained that their sisters are in-

[21] See for example Bagshawe 1929; James 1971; James and Fimbo 1973 and Mbilinyi 1991.

[22] See for example Raikes 1986; Odgaard 1986; 1997; Bryceson 1993; Spear 1996.

[23] This is dealt with in some detail below, but in more depth in Odgaard 2003.

[24] This appears clearly from the population censuses from 1978 and 1988 (URT 1978 and URT 1988).

creasingly coming home and trying to get access to land in their native villages, where, in the opinion of many of the men, women are only entitled to borrow land and not to acquire it as property.

Nowadays, cases where widows, instead of continuing to cultivate land in their husband's village, are chased away and have to go back to their native village are not uncommon. Manipulation and reinterpretation of customary rules on the basis of male dominated ideologies is confirmed by the way many brothers interpret the rules. While arguing that their sisters do not have land endowments in their native village, they claim that wives can only be allowed to use their husband's land during the course of marriage. In case of divorce or widowhood the women will, according to them, have to return to their own native family or village.

The obvious contradiction here illustrates that, in order to protect their own interests, and while still referring to customary rules, these men try to eliminate the connection between exercising a right and fulfilling obligations embedded in customary rules. It also reflects the fact that, like their sisters and fathers, they re-interpret customary rules in accordance with changing circumstances (e.g. increasing land pressure) with the important difference, however, that fundamental guiding principles of customary rules are not adhered to. So in fact they discriminate against their sisters, and their brothers' wives. This is not only against the principles of customary rules and norms, but also against the New Land Policy and the two new Land Acts.

In the Village Land Act part II (URT 1999b), one of the general principles of the Land Policy is spelled out as follows: 'The right of every woman to acquire, hold, use and deal with land shall to the same extent and subject to the same restriction be treated as the right of any man' (p. 26). This gender equality principle is further reflected in provisions in relation to land applications, for example (p. 107), and assignment of customary rights by villagers (p. 141).

In the Village Land Act, Part IV: Village Lands, A: Management and Administration, Law applicable to customary right of occupancy, there is the following provision (URT 1999b: 95-6):

> (2) Any rule of customary law and any decision taken in respect of land held under customary tenure, whether in respect of land held individually or communally, shall have regard to the customs, traditions, and practices of the community concerned to the extent that they are in accordance with fundamental principles of the National Land Policy and of any other written law and subject to the foregoing provisions of this subsection, that the rule of customary law or any such decision in respect of land held under customary tenure shall be void and inoperative and shall not be given effect to by any village council or village assembly of any person or body of persons exercising any authority over village land or in respect of any court or other body, to the extent to which it denies

women, children or persons with disability lawful access to ownership, occupation or use of any such land.

Although it is not so easy to 'get the message' from the quotation, it does in my interpretation provide important support for the safeguarding of the customary rights that men and women are exercising and/or are entitled to. At the same time it says that if women are discriminated against under customary laws, such laws are not to be applied.

However, the men having the position referred to above see land as forming part of property, but unlike the other group of men and the women, they distinguish between land as a special type of property, distinct from other types of property, and stress that a father's landed property can only be inherited in the male line. Moreover, instead of being concerned with succession like the fathers, who emphasise the connection between right and obligation, the sons emphasise their exclusive right (in a 'modern' meaning of the word) to inherit property.

It turned out during interviews that fathers, if alive, actively support their daughters' land claims when brought forward. The tendency of women to inherit land in their native village is claimed to be increasing. This is no doubt connected with changes in fathers' practices in relation to the distribution of land between children. Many fathers argued that nowadays they want to divide their land between all the children while still alive, and many had already done so in order to prevent conflicts from arising between them. In this way fathers are like a semi-autonomous social field, striving to acquire rule-making capacity and to coerce compliance, but challenged by their sons who are trying to do the same vis-à-vis their sisters.

But why are fathers so keen on the issue? This is because, as they argue, daughters are generally more caring towards their old parents than sons, many of whom, due to education and/or employment, live away from their home areas. Interpretations of rules and norms related to the question of the size of shares of a father's property that sons and daughters are entitled to respectively, differed a lot even among respondents who recognised women's rights of inheritance. A substantial number of both female and male respondents said that sons and daughters get equal shares.

Returning to historical accounts, they clearly show that in general the male heirs, in particular the eldest son, were entitled to the largest shares. However, it also appears that the right to inherit is tied to obligations to care for parents, small children and sick members of the family.

A father's strategy in practice when distributing his wealth reflects his concern for being assured of support during old age. As daughters have proved to be important in relation to that, fathers want to make sure that daughters are assured of a livelihood. Fathers, therefore, indirectly make use of rules of disinheritance for those children who otherwise would be entitled to the largest shares. Fathers' concern is the question of succession, and if sons are not likely to live up to responsibilities accompanying rights to property, fathers form their strategy accordingly.

Even though there seems to be a tendency that more and more Hehe women are successful in claiming land in their own right, it is hard to deny that more sons than daughters manage in practice to get their share of fathers' land in Iringa and in most other places in Tanzania.[25] But changes are taking place and recent studies clearly show that the Hehe women are not the only women in Africa who have rights to claim property, including landed property, and who manage to exercise such rights in practice.[26]

Example no. II: Conflicting perceptions about the land rights of Maasai pastoral immigrants in Iringa

This example illustrates both the issue of land rights of 'first-comers' and 'late-comers' (*wawenyeji* versus *wageni*) and competition between two different land use systems: One in which land is used mainly as a common property resource, and another based on the cultivation of individualised specific pieces of land. The dispute deals with a general problem in Tanzania and many other African countries,[27] namely that cultivation is expanding into areas used as pastures.

The Maasai are mainly pastoral but cultivate maize and a few other crops usually on scattered fields around their homesteads. When they first arrived in the mid 1950s they obtained permission from the local chiefs and headmen to utilise a specific area for grazing and for cultivation. The type of rights they have therefore fall within the category I have described as: Customary rights based on non-indigenous customary rules and norms, but also under allocation by local authorities. However, as other livestock keepers are also allowed to graze their livestock in the same areas there is also a de facto open access situation.

Maasai do not generally claim ownership to any specific pieces of land, but use rights to grazing areas and watering places. They are engaged in transhumance, and movements are determined by the need for pastures. Land is mainly managed as a common property resource as far as possible, taking into consideration the fact that other livestock keepers also use pastures and water sources in the areas where the Maasai live. They do not

---

25 URT/NAI 1994, the various contributions in CHANGE 1997; Koda 1998; Maganga (work in progress); Odgaard 2003; Odgaard and Weis Bentzon 2003.

26 See, for example, Rocheleau and Edmonds 1997; Makenzie 1989; Muteshi 1997; Manji 2000.

27 See, for example, Aarhem 1986; Lane and Pretty 1990; Odgaard and Maganga 1994; Cleaver 2003; Lane 1993; Mwaikyusa 1993; Mustafa 1993; IIED 1999; Woodhouse *et al.* 2000; Broch-Due 2000a and b.

establish permanent fields or plant trees to gain prescriptive rights to any specific pieces of land, because, as they argue, this would undermine the pastoral lifestyle. But it is also a conscious strategy to prevent cultivation in general from expanding into pastures. The Maasai are, however, familiar with the concept of 'homestead' – both a homestead at present in use, *ng'ang'ai* – mainly a settlement with houses of the extended family and cattle kraal, and a settlement used previously, namely *imming'aang*. Only close relatives are allowed to use such areas, and if people from outside want to use them they need the consent of the previous user, according to Maasai rules and norms, because the first user often returns to the same settlement during seasonal movements.

Securing land rights has, however, as discussed above, become more and more important for the Hehe and other groups cultivating in the area. The special term used to define Hehe customary rights is *lungulu*, which is actually a Swahili word. But for the Hehe it now refers to the land where forefathers used to live and where ancestors are buried, and much is done to make graves visible to demonstrate one's right to the place. The Hehe word for land held under Hehe custom is actually '*lilungulu*'.

'*Lilungulu*' means settlement – that is, an area with only a few houses – maybe between one to ten houses and usually inhabited by families bound together by kinship ties (Brown and Hutt 1935). Previously the Hehe lived in scattered settlements. Land was readily available and people moved very frequently because of the livestock and therefore did not associate themselves strongly with a specific territory. According to the interpretations of land rights, at the time people had the right to the place where houses were situated, and to cultivate as much land as access to labour and other resources would allow. The Hehe headman was authorised to distribute use rights to people living in their area, and to people from outside – both Hehe and people from other ethnic groups, who asked for it – as long as there was enough land available. The only condition was to keep a proper distance from neighbours.

As a matter of fact, *'lilungulu'* for the Hehe previously had more or less the same meaning as *ng'ang'ai* and *imming'aang* have for the Maasai today – that is, when land was plentiful and when the Hehe themselves were mainly livestock keepers. However, the developments described above combined with more permanent settlement among cultivators have finally led to the present pressure on arable land and pastures. From previously being the place where one lived at any given time – a settlement with scattered houses and fields belonging to close relatives – *lungulu* has now become the epitome of rights to land sanctioned by Hehe custom, an integral part of Hehe culture.

Changes in Hehe burial customs illustrate this. Before the European occupation, dead bodies were generally not buried but left in the bush. However, during the German period[28] an order was issued that all corpses should be buried. Since then the dead have generally been buried in their *lungulu,* and maintenance and cleaning of the graveyards has become an important aspect of Hehe customs related to ancestor worship. A small plantation is made to mark the position of the grave. Only people who are considered rightful heirs to the property of the deceased can be allowed to use land where ancestors are buried. In the eyes of the Hehe, the presence of graves is by itself a justification for legitimate land claims (Odgaard 2003).

Some of the other ethnic groups living in the area have developed similar burial customs. The presence of graves is therefore a strong justification for making land claims, and is not immediately disputed. Claiming rights to specific pieces of land with reference to the presence of graves is a much used – and misused – strategy (Odgaard 2003).

Customary rights can, in principle at least, generally only be retained if it clearly appears that the land is or has recently been used. Most villages have rules specifying the number of years land can be left fallow, and there are sanctions if rules are not obeyed. If there are no visible graves or tree plantations on fallowed land, it can be alienated by the village authorities and given to other people if the number of years permitted for fallow has been exceeded. Even though some powerful people with large holdings may be able to bend the rules, the fact that rules exist implies that people with large holdings are interested in letting others use part of their land, and at the same time being able to get extra income from the arrangement. Renting and borrowing arrangements are very widespread in the area.

Due to the increasing scarcity of 'empty' land and grazing areas, the rights of the Maasai to be in the area are increasingly being contested. Their seasonal movements are now confined to smaller and smaller areas also used by other livestock owners, and with many scattered fields. It is therefore becoming increasingly difficult to keep livestock away from fields with standing crops, implying that a lot of damage is done to the crops and tensions between the groups are increasing.

Some village government members even expressed a clear intention to do whatever they could to have the Maasai removed from the area. One of the strategies used by village authorities has been to allocate more and more land in the grazing zone to cultivators. During a period of three years, when I visited the area regularly, it was very clear that fields were increasingly being established in areas previously used as pastures. Cases were identified of village leaders having facilitated enterprising individuals based in the regional capital city, Iringa, being able to obtain private property rights to large parts of the pastures (Odgaard 2003).

---

28 The German Occupation lasted from 1894 to 1918. During this period Tanzania, then called Tanganyika, was a German Protectorate.

Why have the Maasai not adopted the same mechanisms as some of the other immigrants, in order to claim more permanent land rights? When this was discussed, the Maasai argued that to establish more permanent fields and to claim permanent rights was fundamentally against their principles for use of pastures. Moreover, if the Maasai started doing that, they said, then the village authorities could make it even more legitimate for other people to open new fields in the grazing zone, and through investments be enabled to get more permanent rights to specific pieces of land. And that, the Maasai argued, would mean the end to the pastoral way of life – and their livelihood.

But why is it so easy to undermine the land rights of the Maasai, first in their home areas and later also in areas they have migrated to and been settled in for quite a long time, when other immigrants are able to have *lungulu* rights recognised? Numerous studies illustrate that this is related both to perceptions about what type of land use is seen as a legitimate way to gain undisputed rights to land, and to the fact that the pastoral way of life and pastoralists have been looked on as less 'developed' or more primitive than people who are permanently settled and grow crops.[29]

It is clear from both written sources and from interviews with authorities at all levels in Tanzania that for a land claim to be successful there have to be visible signs of use or investment in the form of labour (cleared bush) and/or visible structures, planted trees, standing crops and so on. Pastoralists generally do not leave visible investments behind during their seasonal movements. There has therefore been a continuous marginalising process, which has forced pastoral peoples in many parts of Africa to leave their home areas because their lands have been taken and used for other purposes. The large number of Maasai living as immigrants in Iringa and other parts of the Southern Highlands in Tanzania illustrates this process. Although there are certainly some pastoralists who have managed quite well as migrants, they become generally more vulnerable when they live as *wageni* in areas where many cultivators from overpopulated neighbouring regions are also living as migrants.

As mentioned, pastoral land rights are generally not well provided for in legislation, either previously or today. The pastoral land use system is viewed both by customary laws, as interpreted by the court system and by non-pastoral groups,[30] and by formal legislation,[31] as inferior or less 'developed' than cultivation. Even though there are more references to pastoral land rights in the new land acts from 1999,[32] and also specific provisions for

---

29 IWGIA 1998 and 2001; Tenga 1992; Tenga and Kakoti 1993; Mwaikyusa 1993; Lane 1993; Aarhem 1986; Talle 1999 just to mention a few.

30 Except hunters and gatherers, of whom very few are left in Tanzania.

31 See for example Shivji 1994 and Tenga 1992.

32 See for example Village Land Act 1999b: 98.

communal land rights, it is still very unclear how pastoral rights should be defined and how they should be protected.

Conclusion

While only representing a minor part of the types of land dispute found in Tanzania and other African countries, the disputes dealt with above do illustrate a number of issues of general relevance for the land question in Tanzania. They reflect the dynamic interplay between different normative orders and the ability of customary rules and norms to adapt to changing circumstances, in some cases, as we have seen, for the better and in other cases for the worse. They also illustrate how some groups manage to manipulate rules from different normative orders depending on access to power and bargaining power. However, there is also a cultural dimension to the dispute between Maasai pastoralists and Hehe cultivators, namely that close ties to specific pieces of land, crop cultivation and permanent settlement are perceived, by settled cultivators and a majority of the population at large, to be superior to pastoralism and transhumance.

From the analysis presented here it has become evident that there is no equal access to land rights in Tanzania or equal access to justice in the true sense, as formulated by Benda-Beckmann (2001: iii). Women and pastoralists have been identified as especially vulnerable in cases of increasing pressure on land. But land is not distributed equally between other social groups in Tanzania either, and the poorest people among the cultivators have access to very little or no land of their own. They therefore depend exclusively on people with larger holdings from whom they can borrow or rent. As discussed elsewhere,[33] borrowing and renting is widespread, and the economic terms on which such arrangements rest can be very tough, ranging from paying rent in kind, money or labour, or having to put yourself and/or members of your family at the landowners' service twenty-four hours a day (working in their houses, running errands or providing political support). Nothing is free of charge in Africa, and the right to use land is no exception.

So how can the situation for the most vulnerable be improved? This question has given rise to much debate. Recommendations from the international donor community, IMF and the World Bank in particular have emphasised more formalisation and the registration of land rights. While land registration and land titling may in certain circumstances provide more security for some people (for example, some groups of pastoralists and hunters and gatherers), it is not a realistic strategy in general in Tanzania. The large majority of rural people in the more than 8,000 villages in the country hold land in accordance with customary rules and norms. Such rights are obtained through processes

[33] See for example Odgaard 1987; 1994; 2003.

of negotiation between various social groups, and the outcomes reflect the type of social relations existing between these groups.

Formal land registration and individual land titling need a completely different institutional set-up than exists at the moment in African countries, and it would take many years and a fortune to establish this. In the meantime the legal situation for the vulnerable might be even more fluid than it is at present. But even if such structures were there, it is hard to imagine how poor people, women and other marginalised groups (such as pastoralists, or hunters and gatherers) would be able to generate the necessary economic resources to access such institutional structures (e.g. land surveyors, authorities from the village to the district and national levels, lawyers in cases of conflict and so on).

In the opinion of many observers of African conditions it is also not a proper way forward for these countries. As Sara Berry has shown in the case of Ghana, for example, which also applies to the situation analysed above, '(...) where rights to productive resources have been subject to on-going processes of negotiation, access to prosperity and power depends on participation in these processes, rather than denying or suppressing them' (Berry 1997: 1226).

References

AARHEM, K. (1986) Pastoralism under pressure: The Ngorongoro Maasai, in: Boesen, J., Havnevik, K.J., Koponen, J. and Odgaard, R. (Eds) *Tanzania – Crisis and Struggle for Survival*, Uppsala: Scandinavian Institute of African Studies, pp. 207-24.

ARMSTRONG, A.K. (1992) *Struggling over scarce resources. Women and maintenance in Southern Africa*, University of Zimbabwe Publications.

BAGSHAWE, F.J. (1929) *Tanganyika territory: Land development survey, first report*, London: Iringa Province, 1928-1929.

BENDA-BECKMAN, F. VON (2001) Legal pluralism and social justice in economic and political development, *IDS Bulletin*, 32(1).

BERRY, S. (1993) *No condition is permanent: The social dynamics of agrarian change in Sub-Saharan Africa*, Madison: University of Wisconsin Press.

BERRY, S (1997) Tomatoes, land and hearsay: Property and history in Asante in the time of structural adjustment, *World Development*, 25(8): 1225-41.

BOESEN, J., F.P. MAGANGA and R. ODGAARD (1996 and 1997) Field notes, unpublished.

BROCH-DUE, V. (2000a) Producing nature and poverty in Africa: An introduction, in: Broch-Due, V. and Schroeder, R.A. (Eds) *Producing nature and poverty in Africa*, Uppsala: Nordiska Afrikainstitutet.

BROCH-DUE, V. (2000b) A proper cultivation of peoples: The colonial reconfiguration of pastoral tribes and places in Kenya, in: Broch-Due, V. and Schroeder, R.A. (Eds) *Producing nature and poverty in Africa*, Nordiska Afrikainstitutet, Uppsala.

BROWN, G. and B. HUTT MCD. (1935) *Anthropology in action. An experiment in the Iringa District of the Iringa Province, Tanganyika Territory*, International Institute of African Languages and Cultures, Oxford: Oxford University Press.

BRYCESON, D.F. (1993) *Liberalizing Tanzania's Food Trade*, UNRISD.

CHANGE (1997) Vol. 5, First Quarter, Dar es Salaam: Change Publications Ltd.

CHANOCK, M. (1998) *Law, custom and social order. The colonial experience in Malawi and Zambia*, Portsmouth, NH: Heinemann.

CLEAVER, F. (2003) Reinventing institutions: Bricolage and the social embeddedness of natural resource management, in: Benjaminsen, T.A. and Lund, C. (Eds) *Securing land rights in Africa*, London: Frank Cass.

FIMBO, G.M. (1992) *Essays in land law*, Tanzania: Dar es Salaam.

GULLIVER, P.H. (1958) Land tenure and social change among the Nyakyusa. An essay in applied anthropology in South-West Tanganyika, *East African Studies*, 11, Special Issue: 1-47.

GULLIVER, P.H. (1961) Land shortage, social change and social conflict in East Africa, *The Journal of Conflict Resolution*, V(1): 16-26.

HALL, R.Z. (1945) Local migration in Tanganyika, *African Studies*, 4(2).

HAVNEVIK, K. (1995) Pressing land tenure issues in Tanzania in the light of experiences from other Sub-Saharan African Countries, *Forum for Development Studies*, 2.

HELLUM, A. (2000) How to improve the doctrinal analysis of legal pluralism, *Retfærd 89, Nordisk Juridisk Tidsskrift*, 23(2): 40-63.

IIED (1999) *Land tenure and resource access in West Africa: Issues of opportunities for the next twenty five years*, London.

ILIFFE, J. (1979) A modern history of Tanganyika, *African Studies Series*, 25, Cambridge University Press.

IWGIA (1998) *The indigenous world 1997-1998*, Copenhagen.

IWGIA (2001) *The indigenous world 2000-2001*, Copenhagen.

JAMES, R.W. and G.M. FIMBO (1973) *Customary land law of Tanzania. A source book*, Nairobi, Dar es Salaam: East African Literature Bureau.

JAMES, R.W. (1971) *Land tenure and policy in Tanzania. East African literature bureau*, Dar es Salaam, Nairobi and Kampala.

JAMES, R.W. and G.M. FIMBO (1973) *Customary land law of Tanzania. A source book*, Nairobi, Dar es Salaam: East African Literature Bureau.

KIWASILA, H. and R. ODGAARD (1992) *Socio-cultural aspects of natural forest management in the Udzungwa*, Report prepared for Danida, Copenhagen: CDR.

KODA, B. (1998) Changing land tenure systems in the contemporary matrilineal social system: The gendered dimension, in: Seppälä, P. and Koda, B. (Eds) *The making of a periphery*, Seminar Proceedings No. 32, Uppsala: Nordic Africa Institute, pp. 195-221.

LANE, C. and J.N. PRETTY (1990) *Displaced pastoralists and transferred wheat technology in Tanzania*, IIED, Gatekeeper Series, No. SA20. IIED, London.

LANE, C. (1993) The state strikes back, in: Veber, H., Dahl, J., Wilson, F. and Wæhle, E. (Eds) *Never drink from the same cup*, IWGIA Document No. 74, Copenhagen.

LASSTARRIA-CORNHIEL, S. (1997) Impact of privatization on gender and property rights in Africa, *World Development*, 25(8).

LEACH, M., R. MEARNS and I. SCOONES (1999) 'Environmental entitlements: Dynamics and institutions in community-based natural resource management', *World Development*, 27(2): 225-47.

LE ROY, E. (1985) Local law in Black Africa. Contemporary experiences of folk law facing state and capital in Senegal and some other countries, in: Allot, A. and Woodman, G.R. (Eds) *People's law and state law*, Dordrecht: Bellagio Papers.

MACKENZIE, F. (1989) Land and territory: The interface between two systems of land tenure, Murang'a District, Kenya, *Africa*, 59(1).

MAGANGA, F. (Work in Progress), Resource conflicts and conflict management. Some insights from Iringa and Mbarali Districts.

MAGANGA, F.P. and R. ODGAARD (2002) *UTUMI: Planning and implementing community based forest management in Kilwa and Lindi Districts*, Report to DANIDA, December 2002.

MAMDANI, M. (1996) *Citizen and subject. Contemporary Africa and the legacy of late colonialism*, New Jersey: Princeton University Press.

MANJI, A. (2000) Her name is Kamundage: Rethinking women and property among the Haya of Tanzania, *Africa*, 70(3): 482-500.

MBILINYI, M. (1991) *Big slavery*, Dar es Salaam: Dar es Salaam University Press.

MEINZEN-DICK, R.S., L.R. BROWN, H.S. FELDSTEIN and A.R. QUISUMBING (1997) Gender, property rights, and natural resources, *World Development*, 25(8).

MIGOT-ADHOLLA, S.E., P. HAZELL, B. BLAREL and F. PLACE (1991) Indigenous land rights systems in Sub-Saharan Africa: A constraint on productivity?, *World Bank Economic Review*, 5(1).

MOORE, S.F. (1978) *Law as process*, London: Routledge and Kegan Paul.

MOORE, S.F. (1999) Changing African land tenure: Reflections on the incapacities of the state, in: Lund, C. (Ed.) *Development and right*, London: Frank Cass, pp. 33-49.

MUMFORD, W.B. (1934) The Hehe, Bena and Sangu peoples of East Africa, *American Anthropologist*, 36(2): 203-22.

MUSTAFA, K. (1993) *Eviction of pastoralists from Mkomazi Game Reserve in Tanzania: A statement*, unpublished paper, IIED, March.

MUTESHI, J.K. (1997) A refusal to argue with inconvenient evidence: Women, proprietorship and Kenyan law, *Dialectical Anthropology*, 23(1), June: 55-81.

MWAIKYUSA, J.T. (1993) Community rights and state control in Tanzania, in: Veber, H., Dahl, J., Wilson, F. and Wæhle, E. (Eds) *Never drink from the same cup*, IWGIA Document no 74, Copenhagen.

ODGAARD, R. (1986) Tea – Does it do the peasant women in Rungwe any good?, in: Boesen, J. *et al.* (Eds) *Tanzania – Crisis and struggle for survival*, Uppsala: Scandinavian Institute of African Studies, pp. 207-224.

ODGAARD, R. (1987) De tog til Usangu! – Bondemigration i det sydvestlige Højland, *Den Ny Verden*, 20(3): 69-90.

ODGAARD, R. (1994) Jordbesiddelsesformer og bæredygtig ressurseudnyttelse – eksemplet Tanzania, *Den Ny Verden*, 27(2): 50-67.

ODGAARD, R. (1997) The gender dimension of Nyakyusa rural-rural migration in Mbeya Region, in: Ngware, S., Odgaard, R., Shayo, R. and Wilson, F. (Eds) *Gender and agrarian change in Tanzania – With a Kenyan case study*, Dar es Salaam: Dar es Salaam University Press (DUP), pp. 46-70.

ODGAARD, R. and F.P. MAGANGA (1994) *Local informal land and water management systems in Ruaha River Basin*, Copenhagen: CDR.

ODGAARD, R. (1999) *Fathers, daughters and sons in the scramble for women's land rights: The case of the Hehe and Sangu peoples of South West Tanzania*, paper presented at SASA International Conference, Copenhagen, November 1999.

ODGAARD, R. (2003) Scrambling for land in Tanzania: Processes of formalisation and legitimisation of land rights, in: Benjaminsen, T.A. and Lund, C. (Eds) *Securing land rights in Africa*, London: Frank Cass, pp. 71-88.

ODGAARD, R. and A. WEIS BENTZON (2003) *Rural women's access to property in patrilineal communities in East Africa – In a web of norms*, unpublished paper.

RAIKES, P. (1986) Eating the carrot and wielding the stick: The agricultural sector in Tanzania, in: Boesen, J., Havnevik, K.J., Koponen, J. and Odgaard, R. (Eds) *Tanzania: Crisis and struggle for survival*, Uppsala: Nordic Africa Institute, pp. 105-42.

RANGER, T. and E. HOBSBAWN (Eds) (1983) *The invention of tradition*, Cambridge: Cambridge University Press.

RANGER, T. (1993) The invention of tradition revisited: The case of colonial Africa, in: Ranger, T. and Vaughan, O. (Eds) *Legitimacy and the state in twentieth century Africa*, London: The Macmillan Press, pp. 62-111.

REDMAYNE, A. (1968) The Hehe, in: Roberts, A. (Ed.) *Tanzania before 1900*, Nairobi: East African Publishing House, pp. 37-58.

ROCHELEAU, D. and D. EDMUNDS (1997) Women, men and trees: Gender, power and property in forest and agrarian landscapes, *World Development*, 25(8): 1351-71.

SHIVJI, I.G. (1994) A legal quagmire: Tanzania's regulation of land tenure (Establishment of Villages Act, 1992), *Pastoral land tenure series no. 5*, IIED.

SJAASTAD, E. and D.W. BROMLEY (1997) Indigenous land rights in sub-Saharan Africa: Appropriation, security and investment demand, *World Development*, 25: 549-62.

SPEAR, T. (1996) Struggles for land, in: Maddox, G., Giblin, J., and Kimambo, I.N. (Eds) *Custodians of the land*, Eastern African Studies, London: James Currey, Mkuki na Nyota, Dar es Salaam: Ohio University Press, pp. 213-40.

TALLE, A. (1999) Pastoralists at the border. Maasai poverty and the development discourse in Tanzania, in: Anderson, D.M. and Broch-Due, V. (Eds), *The poor are not us. Poverty and pastoralism in Eastern Africa*, Oxford: James Currey.

TENGA, R. (1992) *Pastoral land rights in Tanzania, a review*, IIED Drylands Programme: Pastoral Land Tenure Series.

TENGA, R. AND G. KAKOTI. (1993) The Barabeig land case, in: Veber, H., Dahl, J., Wilson, F. and Wæhle, E. (Eds) *Never drink from the same cup*, IWGIA Document no 74, Copenhagen.

TNA (Tanzania National Archives) (1925 and 1938) *Secretariat files*, No's 7794 and 7794/3, accession no. 157, file No. 6/42.

URT (United Republic of Tanzania) (1978) *Population Census*.

URT (1983) *Agricultural policy of Tanzania*, Government Printer.

URT (1988) *Population census*.

URT (1994) *Report of the Presidential Commission of Inquiry into Land Matters, Vol.I: Land policy and land tenure structure*, published in cooperation with The Nordic Africa Institute, Uppsala.

URT (1998) *The Constitution of the United Republic of Tanzania of 1977.*
URT (1999a) *The Land Act 1999.*
URT (1999b) *The Village Land Act 1999.*
WOODHOUSE, P., P. TRENCH and M.D.M TESSOUGUE (2000) A very decentralized development: Exploiting a new wetland in the Sourou Valley, Mali, in: Woodhouse, P., Bernstein, H. and Hulme, D. (Eds) *African enclosures? The social dynamics of wetlands in drylands*, London: James Currey, pp. 29-72.
WOODMAN, G.R. (1997) Progress through complexity: Options for the subjects of legal pluralism, in Mehdi, E. and Shaheen, F. (Eds), *Women's law in legal education and practice in Pakistan*, Copenhagen: New Social Science Monographs.

11

Traditional additional authorities in Uganda and the management of legislatively decentralised forest resources

Frank Emmanuel Muhereza

Introduction

Since 1993, Uganda has implemented a spectrum of decentralisation reforms as part of a broader process of democratization. The expressed intention of decentralisation reforms in Uganda is to ensure that representative and downwardly accountable local authorities hold decision-making powers over public affairs (Villadsen and Lubanga 1996; Republic of Uganda 1998). Decentralisation reforms involve the transfer of administrative and political authority from central government to semi-autonomous public corporations, autonomous local governments, and non-governmental organisations (NGOs). While reforms in Uganda are invariably termed 'decentralisation', they involve a combination of delegation, de-concentration, privatization, and devolution. Only the latter, devolution, approximates a popular definition of 'political' or 'democratic' decentralisation as the transfer of significant decision-making powers from central government to lower levels of elected government (Nsibambi 1997; Republic of Uganda 1998).[1]

---

1 Agrawal and Ribot (1999: 475) describe devolution as the 'creation of a realm of decision making in which a variety of lower level actors can exercise some

The manner in which these decentralisation reforms have been played out has helped to define the key players in the decentralisation of Uganda's forest sub-sector, who include the following: The first key player is the central government, which exercises its powers through the National Forestry Authority (formerly the Forest Department), responsible for managing Central Forest Reserves (CFRs). The District Local Government is a second key player, whose primary responsibility in the forest sector is the management of Local Forest Reserves (LFRs). The third category of players encompasses the private sector actors who include individuals (especially business-persons) as well as non-state actors like traditional or cultural leaders, who head traditional institutions that own large chunks of land with natural (but also sometimes plantation) forest estates.

This study examines the experience and outcomes of decentralisation in Uganda's forestry sector. Specifically, it critically explores outcomes of attempts to transfer powers to manage certain forest resources away from the centre, using field experiences from Masindi District, an area to the north and west of the Uganda capital Kampala that is richly endowed with natural wealth.[2] In Masindi District, the study uncovers some interesting complexities regarding the legislative transfer of powers to manage protected resources, including on the one hand central forest reserves, which are supposed to be maintained, managed and controlled by the central state, and on the other, local forest reserves, supposed to be under the preserve of the popularly constituted local authorities, one of the beneficiaries being a traditional authority institution.[3] As this discussion imparts, decentralisation is

---

autonomy'. They understand de-concentration as 'devolution of powers to appointees of the central state'. Political decentralisation, occurs when 'powers are devolved to actors or institutions that are accountable to the populations in their jurisdiction', whereas delegation is seen as a form of political decentralisation that involves de-concentration. Ribot (1999) defines privatisation as the devolution of central state assets and powers to non-state bodies including NGOs or other private groups and individuals.

2 Masindi is one of the fifty-six districts of Uganda. The district has the largest Central Forest Reserve in the country and is one of the few districts in the country where all five forest classifications specified in section 4 of the 2003 National Forestry and Tree planting Act can be found. In terms of its overall biodiversity rating, it is ranked third highest in terms of species diversity, rarity value and biodiversity importance. It is also the only district in Uganda which had has so far approved the creation of a community forest provided for under 2003 National Forestry and Tree Planting Act.

3 Constitutionally, Uganda is a republic although Parliament in 1993 passed the Traditional Rulers (Restitution of Assets and Properties) Statute, which allowed the restoration of traditional or cultural leaders, having been abolished in 1967. Chapter 16, section 246 (1) of the 1995 Constitution provides for the existence of traditional leaders or cultural leaders, who preside over authority structures called Kingdoms. Bunyoro-Kitara is one such Kingdom, which covers the

not a 'value-free' process, but is instead inseparable from a broader political process controlled by the state in which some powers shift downwards whereas others shift upwards. This process, on its own accord, also generates it own internal contestations. It will be shown that the interests of the state are of supreme importance to understanding Uganda's decentralisation experience. Indeed, the interests of the state permeate the process of decentralisation, which can be understood through the 'actors, powers and accountability' framework conceptualized by Agrawal and Ribot (1999).[4]

The central argument of this chapter is that only limited forest-managing powers have been legislatively transferred to the level of local government, and only to the extent that decentralisation serves the interests of the state to expand its control of forest resources. The study is guided by the assumption that the outcomes of decentralisation are determined by the way powers are transferred (which determines the security of powers), the forms of forest tenure resulting from the way those powers are transferred, and resistance to the re-apportionment of powers. The analysis developed brings out the complexities inherent in relations of accountability that arise through the transfer of powers, and how these translate into practical environmental and economic outcomes.

The study presented in this chapter was part of a broader research collaboration between the World Resources Institute (WRI), Washington and Centre for Basic Research (CBR), Kampala on 'Accountability and Power in Environmental Decentralisation in Africa', funded by USAID. The study employed a case study approach to understand decentralisation of forest management in Uganda. Research was carried out in Masindi District in western Uganda between 2001 and 2003. Extensive interviews were conducted with key informants in Masindi, as were discussions with focus groups in various parts of Masindi, and with actors in central government departments and ministries. Primary source documents, including correspondence and minutes involving district and sub-county councils, private sector user groups, and the Forest Department and other central government agencies and departments were closely assessed.

---

districts of Masindi and Hoima. In section 246 (3e), these traditional or cultural leaders are prohibited from joining or participating in partisan politics, and in section 246 (3f), they are prohibited from exercising any administrative, legislative or executive powers of government or local government.

4 This framework is considered relevant in as far as it makes it possible to identify the key shortcomings in decentralisation reforms in the forest sub-sector. Using the framework, one is bale to discern the nature of powers devolved, who the repositories of these decentralised powers are, and how they are held to account by those who are subject to the exercise of these powers, from which one can determine whether or not there has been substantive decentralisation in terms of transfer of real decision-making powers.

Theoretical considerations

There is substantial documentation of the origins, evolution and outcomes of decentralisation reforms in Uganda, as well as the various factors that hinder the effective transfer to and use of powers by local governments (Villadsen and Rubanga 1996; Nsibambi 1997; Republic of Uganda 1998; Wagaba 1998; Onyach-Olaa and Porter 2000; Wagaba 2002). Elsewhere, other studies emphasise the actors involved in decentralisation, the powers that are decentralised, the relationships between the various actors involved in the exercise of decentralised powers, and the corresponding relations of accountability between those wielding power and those 'countering' power (Samoff 1990; Webster 1992; Agrawal and Ribot, 1999; Ribot 1999).

Agrawal and Ribot (1999) outline an 'actors, powers and accountability'-conceptual framework to assess decentralisation outcomes. They caution that moves to decentralise powers through specific policies and legislation can be countered by moves to re-centralise powers elsewhere, reflecting the unwillingness of the state to relinquish control over resources. This study contributes to the 'actors, powers and accountability'-framework by bringing out other factors that shape the various socio-cultural, political, economic and environmental outcomes of decentralisation. These factors include: (i) the 'means of transferring' powers from the centre to other actors (for this study, in the forest sector); (ii) (forest) tenures resulting from the way in which powers were transferred, and; (iii) resistance by different actors and at different levels to the new balance of powers. This study shows, further, that the fiscal and legitimacy needs of the state, as well as the extra-legal social, cultural and political-economic relations in which the key actors of decentralisation are embedded, are important to any comprehensive explanation of the outcomes of decentralisation.

Conyers (2001) suggests that security of decentralised powers is determined by the 'means of transfer' through which powers are shifted or created at lower levels of government. Transfers may occur through principal or subsidiary legislation, executive directives, and administrative decisions or through forms of joint management. These means affect the exercise of powers because they determine whether decentralised powers are transferred as secure rights or as privileges that can be withheld indiscriminately and at will by central authorities.[5] Two considerations related to the means of transfer influence decentralisation outcomes in ways that are outside the 'actors, powers and accountability' framework. One way is that the extent to

---

[5] According to Ribot (1999), effective participation in forest management entails power-sharing in decision-making, and the existence of locally accountable representative bodies that enable local communities to wield real decision-making powers over valuable resources, is important in determining decentralisation outcomes.

which local actors exercise new powers is shaped by the means through which these are transferred. A second and related way is that because central actors in government can apportion and appropriate decentralised powers as political need dictates, local actors may be hesitant to participate in new institutional arrangements supporting decentralised powers. This chapter emphasises the uncertainty of powers, which are apportioned through politically contingent means of transfer. Assessments of decentralisation must establish the security of powers that are decentralised. Finally, security in tenure is important in shaping who uses resources and how, and is an important consideration to understand the outcomes of decentralisation. Wily and Mbaya (2001) found that secure tenure for user groups dependent on forest resources was one characteristic determining the success of decentralisation reforms.[6]

As indicated above, the exercise of some of the powers transferred away from the centre is contested by those who are subject to the exercise of these powers, a significant factor determining decentralisation outcomes. There are many forms of resistance that are important for the analysis of the decentralisation outcomes in this study. The nature of these contestations and their manifestations varies considerably, with some being contextual while others result from the implementation of decentralisation reforms. One form of resistance is inherent of the state by its very nature – it is characterised by attempts to resist the loss of power by undermining the very process of decentralisation. A second form is the resistance of representative local authorities to powers exercised by representative of central government departments and agencies in the districts. A third form of resistance is by private sector actors at the local level to the exercise of powers by locally elected representatives and field agencies. Finally, locally elected leaders resist the further transfer of powers to community groups. While resistance may be a response to the exercise of powers, as well as to new burdens placed on local authorities and actors to manage forests, elected leaders at the local level who wield new powers also resist sharing their powers with sub-county councils at lower levels. While it is recognized that the state, especially in the line ministries, occasionally resists relinquishing certain powers, this study shows that local level actors in some cases exercise counter-powers to challenge state decisions, as well.

It is important to give attention to the political process in which decentralisation reforms are embedded. Understanding the outcomes of decentralisation necessarily requires critical insight into how political dynamics articulate with the 'actors, powers and accountability' framework. The imperative of the state to strengthen its legitimacy also helps to explain

6 According to the 1995 Constitution (article 237, section 2 [b]), forests are a national resource that the Government holds in trust for the people and are protected for the common good of all citizens.

Uganda's decentralisation experience. Historically and today, the control and use of natural resources has been critical to the calculus of power in Uganda, a fact mirrored elsewhere throughout Africa. Under British colonial rule, the control of forests was distinctly centralized, with few usufruct rights granted to communities living near to the forest.[7] Control of forests, similarly, is an implicit objective of the current government's forest policy. It is instructive to understand how current decentralisation reforms in the forest sector have advanced the interests of the state to control forest resources, while at the same time consolidating its power base.

This study concurs with Ribot (1999) who shows that the state uses politico-administrative means to dominate authorities in local government, as well as local resource users, to maintain powers that were ostensibly decentralised. In Uganda, there is evidence that local powers are circumscribed even when there exists a supportive policy and legal framework, as well as tenure arrangements. Effective political or democratic decentralisation depends on the transfer of local discretionary powers. However, the instrumental value of decentralisation reforms to prolong state control over natural wealth contradicts the intent of policy and legal reform to widen local discretion in the management of natural resources.

The lack of discretionary powers at the level of local government delegitimizes authorities in local government who are rightly viewed with scepticism as impotent or as carriers of state interests. Local authorities are not always downwardly accountable, in spite of the existence of electoral mechanisms to ensure real representation of local interests in important decision-making processes involving natural resources (Villadsen and Rubanga 1996; Ribot 1999). Given that the state still relates to local peoples as subjects rather than as citizens, it is understandable that authorities in local government are reluctant or ineffective in their use of decentralised powers to manage natural resources. The contradiction between the need of the state to be politically expedient by appearing to decentralise real powers and its interest to maintain ultimate control over valuable forest reserves in the districts is the essence of Uganda's decentralisation experience. Ultimately, in order to fully understand the contradictions taking place, the analysis must look beyond the seemingly straightforward transfer of powers to local government actors to the extra-legal social, cultural and politico-economic relations through which policies and legislation for decentralisation are transmitted and acquire meaning.

---

[7] The Crown held statutory tenure to forests under British colonial rule. The Forest Produce (Free issues) Rules of 23 December 1930 entitled Africans to 'cut, take or remove' any forest products, including timber of 'reserved trees', they required for domestic use, on the understanding that forest products could not be bartered or sold. Exclusive rights to fell mahogany were granted to a European saw-miller under a ten-year license (Uganda Protectorate 1947).

Background to forest sector reforms

Policy and legislative reform

The National Forestry and Tree Planting Act, 2003, has classified forests in Uganda under the following five categories: (i) central forest reserves under central government; (ii) local forest reserves under local governments; (iii) community forests under local community; (iv) private forests under an individual, group or institution, including cultural or traditional institutions or leaders, and; (v) forests forming part of a wildlife conservation area declared under the Uganda Wildlife Statute of 1996. Local forest reserves are defined by article 237 of the Constitution and section 9(3) of the National Forestry and Tree Planting Act, 2003, as areas that are to be held in trust by the respective local governments for the common good of all citizens. Local Forest reserves are managed, maintained and controlled by local governments, which functions relate to maintenance of tree crops, establishing requisite social and physical infrastructure (including a forest office), developing a forest use and management plan and collecting and administering forest revenues. Technical staff with the district office of the Forest Department provide oversight to these responsibilities.

Under the 1995 Constitution, the state retained the responsibility of protecting natural resources on behalf of the people (objective xiii), as well as promoting sustainable natural resources development and the responsibility of making the public aware of a need for rational management and use of the natural resources. In so doing, the state has retained privilege, right, title and interest in central and local forest reserves, or the embodiments of absolute ownership. Article 191, section (1) and (2) give powers to local government to levy, charge, collect and appropriate fees and taxes, in accordance with laws enacted by parliament, and shall consist of rents, rates, royalties, stamp duties, personal graduated tax, cess, fees on registration and licensing, and any other fees and taxes that parliament may prescribe. The districts have powers to issue licenses for cutting, taking and removing produce from forests outside of central forest reserves, provided it is in accordance with a forest management plan approved by the Minister or a person appointed by the Minister for that purpose.

In 1993, the management of natural resources was decentralised to the district level under the Local Government (Resistance Councils) Statute. The Minister of Local Government issued a statutory declaration in 1995 that categorized forest reserves as Schedule I or Schedule II. Schedule I or central forest reserves were above 100 hectares in size, whereas Schedule II or local forest reserves were below 100 hectares in size.[8] The Local Govern-

[8] The Statutory Instrument No. 2 of 1995 was an amendment of the second schedule (No. 2) of the Local Governments (Resistance Councils) Instrument of

ment Act of 1997 effectively transferred most management functions over central and local forest reserves to districts and sub-county councils (Republic of Uganda 1997). District councils quickly took advantage of their new powers to exploit the forests reserves, leading the Forest Department to complain to the then Minister overseeing the Forest Department.[9] Responding to concerns that the district local governments were abusing their new powers to deplete forest reserves, the central government issued the Forest Reserves (Declaration) Order (1998), which limited district prerogative in the management of forests to those that were less than 100 hectares in size, or local forest reserves. Powers over forests above 100 hectares (central forest reserves) were shifted back to the central government. The Order affected management of seventeen forests in Masindi District that were classified as central forest reserves.[10] For the exception of local forest reserves that were returned to the Bunyoro-Kitara Kingdom, control of forests has since remained unchanged.

The Forest Reserves (Declaration) Order of 1998 designated eight forests in Masindi as local forest reserves. Initially only two local reserves, Kirebe (forty-nine hectares) and Masindi Port (eighteen hectares), were retained by the District Council after the control over several local forest reserves had been returned to the Kingdom of Bunyoro-Kitara in May 2000. In 2001, the Kingdom assumed control of the Masindi Port eucalyptus plantation, leaving only Kirebe Forest under the jurisdiction of Masindi District.[11]

District Councils contested sharing revenue generated from central forest reserves following the designation of Schedule I and II forests in 1995. In 1996, policy was changed to share revenue from licenses, fees, fines and other royalties generated from central forest reserves on a sixty-forty ratio between the state and district councils (Olet 1996). This was in response to a sentiment expressed in the districts that revenue generated from central forest reserves should be shared more equitably with the districts. The state summarily increased the responsibility of district councils to oversee exploitation of central forest reserves. This included lending material and logistical support to Forest Department personnel to check illegal pit-sawing.

1995. It included forest reserves, land, mines, minerals and water resources on Schedule 2 of the Resistance Councils Statute.

9 Frank Turyatunga, Director of the former EPED Project (Masindi), indicated that the state was concerned that the districts lacked forest management plans as well as scientific judgment in exploiting forests (E-mail communication, 11 June 2002).

10 Forests that were re-categorised as central forest reserves were Budongo, Fumbya, Kaduku, Kasokwa, Kasongoire, Kibeka, Kigulya Hill, Kitonya Hill, Masege, Masindi, Musoma, Nsekuro Hill, Nyabyeya, Nyakunyu, Nyamakere, Rwensama and Sirisiri.

11 Interview with Eriagu Alomu, DFO, Masindi, 10 April 2002.

Structural reforms in the forest sector

Structural reforms in the forest sector were implemented as part of a civil service restructuring programme, launched under the decentralisation reforms that started in 1992. To reduce operational costs, the size of the civil service was reduced significantly. In the Forest Department, all patrol officers and forest guards in central forest reserves were retrenched and recruitment of new staff was frozen. By July 2000, 154 forest rangers, 283 forest guards, 700 patrol persons and twenty-five forest officers were retrenched (Republic of Uganda 2000: 36). The Department reduced its presence in each county to one individual. Although before the reforms the forest department was not adequately staffed, its ability to manage the forest estates was reduced considerably. The remaining field staff started working under extremely difficult conditions. Wages were often delayed. By April 2000, field staff representing the Forest Department in Masindi had not received wages since November 1999.[12] Considering that forty-six per cent of land in Masindi is classified as protected areas controlled by the state, it is evident that the reforms crippled the ability of the Forest Department to manage forest resources effectively.

The National Forestry and Tree Planting Act, 2003 assented to on 17 June 2003 and commenced on 8 August 2003, provided for the creation of a National Forestry Authority (NFA) replacing the Forest Department (FD) as lead agency in the Forestry sub-sector. Under the 2003 National Forestry and Tree Planting Act, district forest offices are to be established by district councils, but funded by the central government [section 48(1)]. The DFO ceases to be a centrally appointed official. The District Forestry Officers (DFOs) are to be appointed by the District Councils [section 48(2)] and are charged with the duty of advising the district councils on all matters relating to forestry [section 48(3)(a)], and performing any such function as the district councils will prescribe [section 48(3)(i)]. Before, the DFO was appointed by and accountable to the Central Government. While the DFO is still largely answerable to the NFA [section 48(3)(b)], significant controlling functions over the district forestry office/officers have been transferred to the districts.

The public can now check the exercise of decentralised powers held by those to whom these powers have been bestowed in the following ways. Before a Minister issues an order declaring an area as a central forest reserve, the local councils and local community in whose area the proposed forest reserve is to be located have to be consulted and parliamentary approval obtained [section 6(1)(a)(b)]. In order to declare an area as a community forest, the Minister is required to consult with the District Land

[12] See correspondence from Eriagu Alomu, District Forest Department, to the Commissioner for Forestry of 6 April 2000, Brief on current trend of illegal activities in Budongo Forest Reserve, referenced MSD. 7/7a.

Board, local community and obtain approval by resolution of a district council [section 17(1)(a)(b)]. Before a Minister issues an order transferring the management of a local forest reserve to the NFA, a ninety-days notice is issued in writing to a local government, within which the local government takes remedial measures or makes representations as to why the responsibility for the local forest reserve should not be transferred to the centre [section 12(2)]. A local community, a local council in an area in which a local forest reserve is situated, or an interested person, can request the minister in writing to review the status of a central or local forest reserve with the object of seeking a reclassification as a local forest reserve or central forest reserve respectively [section 16(1)]. In the past, these powers were exclusively exercised by the Minister without any consultations.

While the Act introduces procedural checks on the powers exercised by the Minister, it does not significantly devolve powers and control over the management of the forest estate. It only takes away some limited powers from the Minister. All the different categories of forests are to be managed in accordance with generally accepted principles of forest management prescribed in guidelines issued by the Minister [section 13(3)], and in accordance with its management plan, approved by the Minister or by a person designated by the Minister for that purpose [section 28(3)]. The Minister is the lead agency for regulating access to forest genetic resources [section 29(3)]. The power to arrest a person suspected of committing an offence under the National Forestry and Tree Planting Act, 2003, rests with an authorized person [section 88(1)], namely, a forestry officer, an honorary forestry officer, a wildlife protection officer, or any person designated by the Minister (section 51). If there is no working relationship between owners of community forests and private forests with authorized persons, the latter may not help to prevent illegal activities in forests belonging to the former that the former may not be aware of, although they can bring an action against anyone whose actions/omissions have or are likely to have significant impact on the forest and on the protection of a forest [section 5(2)(a)(b)]. While in the past the Minister enjoyed considerable powers, under the New Act some limited powers have been withdrawn.

By retaining significant controlling and supervisory roles, accountability has remained essentially upwards to the responsible Minister, as the vanguard of 'public domain'. For example, while all forest produce from a private natural forest on privately owned land or plantation forest on privately owned land belong to the owner of the forest, and may be used in a manner that the owner may determine, the forest produce has to be harvested in accordance with a management plan approved by the Minister or an officer appointed by the Minister for that purpose. They also have to comply with regulations made under the Forestry and Tree Planting Act [section 21(2); 22(2)]. Harvesting in the past did not require adherence to a management plan. The Minister, like in the past, retained powers of appointing a licensing authority for the issuing of timber export licenses [section 44(1)]; and has powers to issue an order prohibiting or restricting the movement by any person of forest produce for such periods, in such areas and on such terms as are specified in the order [section 45], which gives the centre sweeping controlling powers over the generating of revenue from harvesting different types of forest produce.

Return of forests to the Bunyoro-Kitara Kingdom

Masindi District is one of the two district recognized in the first schedule of the 1995 constitution as comprising the Kingdom of Bunyoro-Kitara. In August 2000, government, in accordance with the Traditional Rulers (Restitution of Assets and Properties) Statute of 1993 and a Memorandum of Understanding between government and Bunyoro-Kitara Kingdom signed on 19 May 2000, returned to the Kingdom several forests which, had under the Forest Reserves (Declaration) Order of 1998, been transferred to Masindi District Local Government as LFRs, and a few others that had been re-centralised (Byarugaba, 2000).[13]

Even after the Kingdom regained possession of forest reserves, it was still weary of the capacity of the state to reclaim control over these forest reserves, as revealed by the exasperation of Kingdom officials following the handing-over of the forests. In acknowledging the return of forests, a Kingdom official noted:

> We (the Kingdom) have taken full control of the reserves and forest produce from them, including the issuing of licenses subject to Statutory Instrument No. 8/93 and the Memorandum of Understanding of 19 May 2000. It is hoped that Bunyoro-Kitara Kingdom will not be forced back to the negotiating table on this well-concluded matter (Byabazaire 2000).

However, the return was beneficial both for the Kingdom and the government. The Kingdom now held relatively secure legal tenure over local forest reserves. By supporting the return of the forests, the ruling National Resistance Movement (led by President Yoweri Museveni) cultivated patronage among a vital section of the electorate, increasing its own legitimacy.[14] The

---

13 Natural High Forests returned included Kaniyo Pabidi, Kasokwa (seventy-three ha) and Busaju. Eucalyptus plantations included Musoma CFR (178 ha), Masindi LFR (thirty-nine ha) and Masindi Port LFR. Hilla savannah plantations included Fumbya (425 ha), Kaduku (583 ha), Kasongoire (3,069 ha), Kibeka (9,570 ha), Kigulya (391 ha), Nyankunyu (466 ha), Nyamakere (3,898 ha), Sirisiri (492 ha) (see record of meeting between Onyango G., Deputy Commissioner FD, Mrs. Musoke, Assistant Commissioner, FD, Mr. I. Ndahura, *Katikiro* Bunyoro Kitara Kingdom, and Mr. Byabazaire Mathew, Deputy *Katikiro*).

14 Traditional authorities were restored in 1993 amid claims by critics of the ruling National Resistance Movement government that the decision was intended to

transfer of powers within the public domain to a private actor (the Kingdom) was used by the state to consolidate its control over a certain constituency (the kingdom and its supporters). Powers to control and manage the forests were shifted to the Kingdom as a result of the return. Before the return, powers to control and manage the forests belonged to the Masindi District Council under the Forest Reserves (Declaration) Order of 1998. Other forests in the district, as noted above, were re-centralised under the Order.[15]

The powers of the kingdom are nevertheless not absolute. Forest produce from kingdom natural forests on privately owned land or plantation forests on privately owned land belong to the kingdoms, and may be used in a manner the kingdoms determine. However, the forest produce has to be harvested in accordance with a management plan approved by the Minister or an officer appointed by the Minister for that purpose. Kingdoms also have to comply with regulations made under the 2003 Forestry and Tree Planting Act [section 21(2); 22(2)]. While all forest produce from a private natural forest on privately owned land or a plantation forest on privately owned land belong to the owner of the forest, and may be used in a manner that the owner may determine, the forest produce shall be harvested in accordance with the management plan and regulation made under the Forestry and Tree Planting Act [section 21(2); section 22(2)]. Traditional or cultural institutions or leaders hold, own or manage forests, subject to such directions as the Minister may prescribe [section 25].

Licensing of forest products

While government or a local government has no ownership over trees or forest produce situated on private land [section 27(1)], DFOs issue directions to the owner of trees or forest produce situated on private land, requiring the owners to manage the trees or forest produce in a professional or sustainable manner. Licenses for harvesting forest produce on such lands are issued by the respective bodies responsible for the management of the different categories of forests, but are subject to the respective forest management plans [section 41(1)] approved by the Minister or a person designated by the minister for that purpose [section 28(3)]. The terms, conditions, rights and fees for licenses prescribed by the responsible body are subject to regulation prescribed under section 92 of the Act [section 41(2)]. Those to whom powers to license are devolved should also have powers to sanction and enforce compliance. Practically this necessitates a mechanism for collabora-

---

promote support for the 'movement' system of the government as opposed to a multi-party system. See Kayunga 2000 and Barya 1997.

15 See correspondence from D.N. Byarugaba, Ag. Commissioner for Forestry, of 14 August 2000 to the District Forest Officers of Hoima, Masindi and Kibaale, referenced 3/2. Subject: the return of Bunyoro-Kitara Kingdom Forests Guidelines.

tion between the various responsible bodies, in the absence of which, the centre assumes the responsibility, and in essence functions like no power has been transferred downwards, other than maintenance and management functions.[16] The DFO can vary or cancel any conditions pertaining to issuance of licenses without providing guidelines to follow in considering whether a license should be issued in the first place, as well as whether it should be cancelled or varied. Permits issued by the DFO specify materials allowed to the permit holder, the period in which the permit is valid, the quantities to be removed and the part of the forest from which they should be taken. The powers to issue concessions were solely enshrined in the commissioner who was not required by the law to consult anyone before awarding a concession. These powers are often subject to abuse.[17]

Following the return, the DFO was directed to remit all revenues generated from the local forest reserves to the Kingdom, as well as to permit officials from the Kingdom to monitor revenue.[18] New powers bestowed on the Kingdom enabled it to determine the continued involvement of Forest Department staff in management of Kingdom forests. For example, the Kingdom could request that FD personnel be moved. Although control of the forests was 'decentralised' to the Kingdom, the Forest Department retained significant powers over how produce from Kingdom forests entered the market. Under the new rules governing Kingdom forests, the Forest Department clears any produce harvested within Kingdom forests before it is transported to markets and the DFO issues transportation fees. However, no provisions were included to ensure that Forest Department staff enforced these directives.

---

16 The Forest Produce and License Order of 2000, Statutory Instruments No. 16 of 2000, defining the fees and taxes that could be charged on forest products, was drawn by the FD through the Environment Ministry and passed by Parliament. It defined fees for all the different types of forest produce including timber, poles (plantation and natural forest bush) and faggots, and fencing posts.

17 The Parliamentary select that investigated the management of the Forest Department following the interdiction of several top officials recommended that the Commissioner, Mr. E.D. Olet be retired in public interest on many grounds, includeing among others, awarding concessions to companies in which he had shares, and allowing his subordinates to do likewise, which amounted to conflict of interest under section 10 of the Leadership Code of 1991 (see interim report on the select committee on forestry, p. 48).

18 See correspondence from Eriagu Alomu, DFO, Masindi to the Minister for Environment, Bunyoro-Kitara Kingdom, referenced MSD. 3/1 of 29 October 2000.

Accountability relations and outcomes in the management of Kingdom forests

Monitoring of illegal timber harvesting

The District Forestry Officer is charged with regulating the harvesting of timber within local forest reserves, including the issuing of licenses and the charging of fees for felling trees for saw-milling and pit-sawing, and can still change or cancel conditions for obtaining licenses, as well as award concessions, unilaterally.[19] In principle, the awarding of licenses to saw-millers and pit-sawyers is based on an accurate allocation of specific trees, of which details are recorded. At any one time, the Forest Department has to be aware of the precise volume of sawn timber, beyond which a licensed pit-sawyer or saw-miller is not permitted to fell trees. All felled trees are supposed to be measured for volume and the off-take of individual pit-sawyers that is on the market must correspond to his/her measured quota.[20] Harvesting is further monitored and controlled using Timber Declaration Forms and Forest Produce Movement Permits. There is a database at the FD-headquarters in Nakawa that tracks the amount of timber harvested and revenue collected. A Timber Monitoring Team (TMT) has been working closely with the Uganda Revenue Authority (URA), the Police and the Internal Security Organisation (ISO) to impound illegally cut timber,[21] and has been the cause of much acrimony in the forest sub-sector. Official reports from the FD availed to the Media showed that indiscriminate harvesting, which has destroyed hundreds of square miles of forest land, is orchestrated by government officials, Members of Parliament, senior army and Police officers, in connivance with some FD employees. Others involved include District Local government leaders, the ruling Movement government leaders and Internal Security Organisation (ISO) personnel.[22] This means that even timber from Kingdom forests has to be reflected in the FD-database, especially if it has to enter the market. Hence, the Kingdom, and those to whom they issue pit-sawing licenses, have to pay revenue to the government through timber movement permits.

---

19 The Forest Produce and License Order of 2000, Statutory Instruments No. 16 of 2000, established the fees and taxes that could be charged on forest products. It was formulated by the Forest Department through the Ministry of Environment and was passed by Parliament. It defined fees for different types of forest produce including timber, poles, and fencing posts.

20 See Forest Department, 'Issues on the proposed transfer of Budongo', *op. cit.*

21 See correspondence from E.D. Olet, Commissioner for Forestry of 17 February 1998, to the Permanent Secretary, Ministry of Natural Resources, subject: Mismanagement of Forestry Sector, referenced C.1., in response to letter referenced CPF.2347 of 16 February 1998.

22 See 'Ministers, army bosses named in timber scam', *New Vision*, 25 August 2003, p. 3.

Relations with the district forest department

After the Kingdom regained control over the forests, the King of the Bunyoro-Kitara Kingdom, appointed the Bunyoro-Kitara Cultural Trust to manage the returned forests. As managers of the forests, the Trust carried out the same functions as the Forest Department, including inventory and monitoring of forest resources, and establishing and reviewing terms under which forest resources can be exploited. Forest resource users must sign tenancy agreements with the Trust, which receives revenue generated from royalties, fees and licensing of pit-sawing.[23] As of 2001, the Kingdom has depended on its own technical experts to manage the forest.

The Trust has been accused of mismanaging the Kingdom forests, mainly by permitting increased pit-sawing in the hope of meeting the Kingdom's objective to increase revenue from the forests. There is an alleged conflict of interest between the Kingdom's powers to regulate pit-sawing in its forests and its own involvement in pit-sawing and trade in timber. Furthermore, the Trust did not formulate clear management plans for its forests, and it arbitrarily set royalties on forest products. Although the Forest Department issued guidelines to govern the management of the returned forests, the Trust relied on its own experts and rarely consulted with the Forest Department on complex technical-managerial issues (Alomu 2000a). An official in the Masindi Forest Department observed:

> The Kingdom was selling trees like cows. They sold standing trees without undertaking an inventory to establish the volume of wood. This had partly contributed to the current over-exploitation of trees in Kingdom forests. The Kingdom officials refused to allow field extension staff to access their [Kingdom] forests, and even issued their own licenses for harvested timber, which created a lot of confusion in the Department.[24]

The inability of the Forest Department to take concrete action resulted in proliferation of illegal harvesting in protected and non-protected forests, and the forest staff were incapacitated because those who were involved had good connections in government- and security forces-circles.

Relations with communities surrounding Kingdom forests

The Bunyoro-Kitara Cultural Trust comprised elders and loyalists to the Kingdom of Bunyoro-Kitara. While it was possible that Kingdom through the Trust, could become downwardly accountable by seeking constructive

---

23 Correspondence of 26 May 2000 from Bishop Albert Baharagate, Chairman Bunyoro Kitara Cultural Trust, referenced BKK/TRUST/2/2000 to DFO Hoima. Subject: Bunyoro Kitara Cultural Trust Office to Check Kingdom Forest Resources and Record an Inventory.

24 Interview with Eriagu Alomu, DFO, Masindi, 10 April 2002.

engagement in the management of forest with forest-edge communities, no such initiative had not been attempted, let alone to consult the communities on forest management.[25] Accountability by the Trust was mainly upwards to the head of the Kingdom and not communities surrounding kingdom forests who depend on the forest for survival. In reaching management decisions, the Trust made limited attempts to establish constructive dialogue with forest-edge communities, which led to resentment in these communities. Communities near Wampanga and Musoma Forests, in 2000 and 2001, expressed resentment at not being consulted on the establishment of the Trust, or in the formulation of policies to manage the forest, and showed their opposition by refusing to comply with entry restrictions imposed by the Trust. In an interview, the King admitted that individuals from forest edge communities were burning trees in Kingdom forests because Trust regulations restricted the local communities' access to the forests. One documented incident was in Musoma in April 2001.[26]

In September 2001, the King, through his Prime Minister, fired the Kingdom Estate Manager for mishandling the Kingdom's Forests. The King cancelled all licenses and *concessionaires,* telling them to vacate the forests or pay Ushs.10 million each to remain. The post of Estate Manager was eventually abolished and the forests were brought under the control of the Kingdom's Administrator General.[27] Some pit-sawyers evicted from the Kingdom forests have since filed civil cases in the High Court challenging their eviction and seeking damages for breach of contract and loss of income. In one high profile case, a pit-sawyer sought special damages amounting to Ushs.8.24 million. The claimant filed a civil suit in the High Court claiming that she was authorised to cut and saw 23.3 cubic meters of timber from the Wampanga forest belonging to the Bunyoro-Kitara Kingdom, and deposited Ushs.910,000 as payment. The claimant contended that she was legally permitted to cut and remove trees from the forest up to October 31, 2001. However, the contract was terminated before the contract-end.[28] The Kingdom has since been embroiled in legal battles that have dragged on and on.

---

25 King Solomon Gafabusa Iguru of Bunyoro-Kitara gave a go-ahead for a strategic planning process for the Kingdom to take place at the beginning of October 2003, through which issues of popularity and image of the Kingdom were discussed, and a vision and mission statement for the Kingdom formulated.

26 Interview with *Omukama* Solomon Iguru at Hoima on 5 April 2001.

27 See 'Pay up or quit forest', *New Vision*, 30 September 2001.

28 See Fred Kyobe, 'Iguru dragged to court over breach of contract', *New Vision*, 21 November 2002, p. 6.

Pressures on the forest estate in Masindi district

The Kingdom forests are contiguous to the Budongo Tropical High Forest ecosystem, that has undergone an extended history of environmental change. A large section of the Central Forest Reserve has gradually changed over the past sixty years from a tropical high forest to a mixed-type forest due to selective logging and widespread silvi-culture, which favoured the growth of valuable timber species such as mahogany. Most recently, larger tropical hardwoods were extensively removed throughout the Forest, leading to an opening of the forest canopy. Budongo Forest is endowed richly with valuable trees, especially mahogany. The annual off-take of timber by pit-sawyers and saw-millers averaged 11,522.82 m^3 of round wood between 1991 and 1996. This was in addition to large volumes of timber that were harvested illegally, peaking between 1992 and 1994 when there was a Forest Department ban on all pit-sawing in the Forest (Republic of Uganda 2002: 89). Budongo Forest is separated into zones for conservation, commercial use, community use, recreation and research.[29] Tree felling is strictly prohibited in the 8,000 hectares zoned as a Strict Nature Reserve for conservation of bio-diversity and to protect water catchments. A majority of the Forest (seventy-five per cent) is earmarked as a production zone where harvesting of saw logs is permitted. A buffer zone comprising fifteen per cent of the Forest separates the conservation zone from the production zone. Inhabitants from local communities are permitted to harvest in the buffer zone using low impact technologies.[30]

Budongo Forest is located in an area of increasing population. The population of Masindi District nearly doubled between 1991 and 2002, increasing from 260,796 to 466,204, an average annual growth rate of 5.0. The population of Budongo and Bwijanga sub-counties increased from 44,054 to 76,929.[31] Pressure on the forest is evident in a slow attrition of forest patches that form part of the larger Budongo Forest ecosystem. These patches are under continuous pressure due to other land uses, including sugarcane plantations, tobacco and food crop cultivation, and human settlement. Encouraged by corrupt local authorities, migrants are encroaching on fringes of Budongo forest to grow tobacco.[32] In return for voting certain local councillors during elections, the migrants are protected from police

---

[29] Budongo Forest has a plan that was prepared by the Forest Department with the help of funding and technical support from the European Community. Different stakeholders and local resource users were also consulted.

[30] See Forest Department, *Issues on the proposed transfer of Budongo and Kalinzu Forest reserves to National Parks*, Forest Department Headquarters, 1998.

[31] The figures for the 1991 census were obtained from NEMA (1998: 53), while the 2002 census figures are available at http://www.ubos.org/fullreport.html.

[32] See ACDI/VOCA (2000). See also Budongo MPA December 2001 Monthly report, p. 2.

harassment.[33] Other pressures on Budongo Forest result from charcoal production. Insurgency has cut off the supply of charcoal from the northern districts in Uganda, increasing pressure on Masindi and neighbouring districts as producer areas. A recent study of potential sustainable levels of charcoal production in Masindi showed that most sub-counties could support less than one lorry of charcoal per week on a sustainable basis, although current levels of production are much higher (Diisi and Ayongyera 2001).

However, the harvesting of mahogany and other tropical hardwoods is by the far the greatest pressure on Budongo Forest. The sale of illegally harvested mahogany is widespread in Masindi town in spite of a ban. The Forest Department and the District Council agree that market-demand for mahogany and other valuable tropical hardwoods is putting pressure on the Forest. Between 1997 and 1998, all trees in Budongo Forest were identified, assessed and mapped to determine the condition and growth of the overall forest. The forest was divided into blocks and each individual tree was allocated a reference number to be used by Forest Department personnel to monitor and control harvesting. With this information, a range of measures are used to enforce the ban, including joint forest-protection patrols with the Uganda Wildlife Authority, the police and district administration,[34] arrest and prosecution of illegal timber cutters, confiscation of tools and timber, and eviction of encroachers.[35] The Masindi DFO reports that there is an average of 200 cases annually that involve prosecution of illegal harvesting. However, prison sentences and prohibitively high fines for those found guilty of illegally harvesting timber from the Forest are not bringing the ongoing illegal removal of the most valuable trees to a halt.[36]

Illegal harvesting of timber

One of many explicit objectives of decentralisation of the management of forest resources was to reduce illegal harvesting of timber in forest reserves. The Forest Department reasoned that the enforcement of its ban on the felling of endangered and valuable trees species would be easier if local government and private sector actors were involved in monitoring and policing illegal pit-sawing. However, the decentralisation experience in

---

33 Interview with Eriagu Alomu, DFO, Masindi, 10 April 2002.

34 See paragraph four of the correspondence from Eriagu Alomu, District Forest Department, Masindi of 17 January 2000 to Ag. Commissioner for Forestry, referenced MSD. 4/1, *op. cit.*

35 See paragraph 4, in correspondence from Eriagu Alomu, *op. cit.*

36 In December 2001 alone, out of six *fundis* who were arrested by forest patrols and taken for prosecution at Budongo sub-county Magistrates Court, four pleaded guilty and were sentenced to six months imprisonment or a fine of 60,000 USh. They chose to pay the money. Two pleaded not guilty and were remanded back to prison (see Budongo MPA December 2001 Monthly report, p. 2).

Masindi District shows a failure in the control of the illegal harvesting of timber. For example, mahogany is commonly sold in timber yards in Masindi town. Despite involving local government and private actors in monitoring and policing activities, illegal harvesting is pervasive. Examples include harvesting above individual quotas permitted under licenses, as well as unlicensed pit-sawing inside and near the Strict Nature Reserve inside the Forest by 'mahogany diehards'.[37] Other pressures on the Forest include encroachment by subsistence farmers, sugarcane out-growers and migrant tobacco cultivators for land, as well as for charcoal. Illegal grazing inside the forest reserves is also common during the dry season.[38]

Illegal harvesting of timber is well-organised, defiant and carried through with confidence. It is common, for example, for harvesters to operate near to the management road running through Budongo Forest. Most illegal pit-sawyers operate with the help of insider information, possibly from within the Forest Department itself, in addition to well-connected traders and politicians in Kampala.[39] Many illegal pit-sawyers have access to new technologies such as mobile telephones that enable them to more easily detect patrols and the movements of Forest Department personnel, as well as of licensed pit-sawyers. Most patrols evidently are detected even before they take place. Illegal pit-sawyers also operate at night, so as to avoid patrols by the Forest Department.

If anything, the determination of illegal pit-sawyers to harvest timber in restricted areas increased as patrols of Budongo Forest were intensified, as is shown by the boldness of their actions, reported by the FD-field staff. A pattern emerged where illegal harvesting increased in the weeks before Christmas and other significant public holidays, when family expenditures increase.[40] However, without viable alternatives to generate income, pressure on the Forest by illegal pit-sawyers is unlikely to decrease, and local communities are not likely to collaborate with the Forest Department to stop illegal activities from which they (local communities) earn income. There is evidence that communities near to the forest reserves collude with illegal pit-sawyers. For example, school children are commonly used as spies to moni-

---

37 See Budongo MPA December 2001 Monthly report, p. 3. It was noted that Nyakafunjo Strict Nature Reserve was not under invasion by illegal pit-sawyers. The situation in Waibira Strict Nature Reserve was also checked by Department staff during the same month. They found that many pit-sawyers were operating illegally inside the Forest.

38 See Budongo MPA, Monthly report, July 2001.

39 See paragraph 2 (iv), correspondence from Martin Eriagu Alomu, *ibid.* A recent newspaper expose indicated that illegal pit-sawyers in Masindi have backing from inside the Forest Department (see 'Loggers bribe Budongo Rangers', *New Vision*, 27 August 2002), a claim denied by the Commissioner for Forestry in a statement to *New Vision* (of 30 September 2002).

40 See Budongo MPA December 2001 Monthly report, p. 2.

tor the movement of Forest Department personnel. The children use coded messages such as blowing windpipes to alert illegal pit-sawyers of an approaching patrol (Langoya 1999). Observers positioned near to the entrance of the Forest typically alert illegal pit-sawyers inside the forest as well, by ululating whenever a forest patrol approaches.[41]

Resistance to patrols is well documented.[42] Personnel from the Forest Department have been assaulted with bows and arrows, as well as with machetes.[43] In January 2000, a Ranger was cut in the stomach with a machete when he attempted to arrest an illegal pit-sawyer.[44] In addition, in January 2000, a patrol officer sustained a machete cut on his hand after his patrol encountered two people harvesting charcoal from a fallen tree at the Forest's edge. In July 2001, nails were scattered across a service road inside the Forest to trap a Forest Department vehicle after Department personnel confiscated two saws and five bundles of rattan cane.[45] Witchcraft, significant in this case because it is a 'weapon of the weak', was commonly practiced to psychologically scare away Forest Department staff. Towards the end of 1999, various witchcraft articles were thrown into the compound of the DFO.[46]

Conclusion

This chapter has critically reviewed the context and consequences of transferring powers to manage forests in Masindi District to local government and the private sector, implemented as part of the Government of Uganda's cross-sectored decentralisation policy. Discussions have hinged on three policy changes with the greatest affect on the management of forests in Masindi. Most prominently, these included the 1993 statute that decentralised the management of natural resources to district and sub-county councils. Another important policy bearing on the management of forests was the

---

41 See Budongo MPA December 2001 Monthly report, p. 2.

42 See paragraph 5 of the correspondence from Eriagu Alomu, District Forest Department, Masindi to Commissioner for Forestry of 17 January 2000, subject: Assault on Staff while on forest protection patrols in Budongo Forest.

43 This particular conflict was recorded in File No. BD 13/14A of Budongo Forest Office, December 1996.

44 See paragraph 2 of the correspondence from Eriagu Alomu, District Forest Department, Masindi of 17 January 2000 to Ag. Commissioner for Forestry, referenced MSD. 4/1 on the subject: Assault on Staff while on Forest Protection Patrols in Budongo Forest Reserve.

45 See Budongo MPA July 2001 Monthly report, p. 4.

46 See paragraph four of the correspondence from Eriagu Alomu, *ibid.* The importance of witchcraft as a weapon of the weak and oppressed is so informative that it warrants a discourse of its own.

designation in 1995 of forests as central and local forest reserves. This was followed in 1998 by a Ministerial declaration that returned powers over central forest reserves to the Forest Department, thereby limiting the powers of district councils to local forest reserves. In Masindi, significant changes resulted from the return of most local forest reserves to the Bunyoro-Kitara Kingdom. Before the return of the forests to the Kingdom, the District Council held powers over the management of the local forest reserves.

Rhetorically, the intent of decentralisation reforms was to devolve significant discretionary powers to the district and lower sub-county councils through which they could generate greater revenue to improve the overall delivery of services. As Agrawal and Ribot (1999) show, actual political or democratic decentralisation occurs when discretionary powers are transferred to popularly elected and downwardly accountable local authorities. However, powers to manage most forest reserves in Masindi were privatised, not decentralised. In Masindi, the centre ultimately retained control of larger central forest reserves, and privatised some limited powers to manage central forest reserves to licensed user groups. Initially, significant powers over few Local forest reserves were devolved to the District Council. These powers over most local forest reserves were however transferred further away from the Masindi District Council to Bunyoro-Kitara Kingdom, another form of privatisation. This left the District Council with significant powers, but over only one local forest reserve.

The limited transfer of forest management powers through decentralisation satisfied the interests of the state to increase its legitimacy and support among pivotal rural constituencies. To a large extent, the state transferred powers to manage forests as a form of patrimony and insofar as doing so gathered greater popular support and legitimacy. The shift of powers through decentralisation, therefore, was carefully measured to consolidate the base of support upon which the state drew its legitimacy and power. The instrumental value of decentralisation to strengthen the position and power of the state, however, seemingly contradicts the intention of decentralisation reforms to share powers more widely with local government actors. It is therefore understandable that actors in local government in some instances viewed their new powers with a degree of ambiguity and hesitation.

For its part, the state relied on a spectrum of policy and legal instruments to transfer powers, confusing rather than clarifying the new roles and responsibilities of different actors in central and local government. Different means used to transfer powers included principal or subsidiary legislation, executive directives, administrative decisions and forms of joint management. Different ways in which powers were transferred in some cases left actors in the local government uncertain and in a weak bargaining position compared to that of the state. It was therefore difficult for the local government to consolidate its new powers, because they were wondering whether these would persist or be transferred elsewhere.

Understandably, the means used to transfer powers in part determined the extent to which the recipients of these new powers were inclined to use them. Apart from the means through which powers were transferred, outcomes of reforms in the forestry sector were also shaped by: (i) the forms of forest tenure resulting from the manner in which powers were transferred; (ii) resistance by central and local government actors to the new balance of powers, and; (iii) the exercise of counter-powers by the recipients of the new powers.

The experience of the decentralisation of forest management in Masindi is uneven. At one level, decentralisation in the forestry sector has contributed to new opportunities for corrupt commercial exploitation of valuable timber inside forest reserves. It has also contributed to greater inefficiency to a certain extent, as the transfer of powers is mired in a confusing array of legal and policy changes. Analysts note that decentralisation is not a 'value-free' process, but that the transfer of powers creates winners and losers, a point supported in the case of the decentralisation of the management of forest resources in Masindi. The state ultimately retained significant powers over the management of forests, while selectively 'decentralising' limited powers to representative local governments. Over time, powers shifted upwards and downwards, with the Forest Department regaining control of the coveted and larger central forest reserves in 1998. The unsteady progression of the decentralisation reforms in Uganda points to an unwillingness to transfer real, discretionary powers with regard to the management and use of forest reserves to the district and sub-county councils. The importance of this paper is its explanatory offerings and insights into a specific decentralisation experience. This short narrative does not claim to address the broader achievements and shortcomings of environmental decentralisation in Uganda. Instead, it does bring out some important lessons to inform possible adjustments to policy that are reviewed here.

References

ANDERSON, K. (2002) *Explaining the mixed success of municipal governance of forest resources in Bolivia: Overcoming local information barriers*, draft paper for the Centre for Studies of Institutions, Population and Environment Change, Mimeo: Indiana University.

AGRAWAL, A. and J. RIBOT (1999) Accountability in decentralisation: A framework with south Asian and west African cases, *Journal of Developing Areas*, 33: 473-502.

BARYA, J.J. (1997) *The Ankole Monarchy controversy: Testing democratization and cultural revivalism*, paper presented at NURRU General Assembly, White Horse Inn, Kabale, 27-28 February.

CONYERS, D. (2001) *Whose elephants are they? Decentralisation of control over wildlife management through the CAMPFIRE Programme in Binga District, Zimbabwe*, draft paper for World Resources Institute, Mimeo.
DIISI, J. and J. AYONGYERA (2001) *Study to determine allowable cut for charcoal Production in Masindi and Nakasongola District*, report prepared for ACDI/VOCA-EPED Project, Masindi, Mimeo.
ENGBERG-PEDERSEN, L. (1995) Creating local democratic politics from above: The 'Gestion des Terroirs' approach in Burkina Faso, *Drylands Issues Paper*, No. 54, London: IIED.
FOREST DEPARTment (1998) *Issues on the proposed transfer of Budongo and Kalinzu Forest reserves to National Parks*, Forest Department Headquarters.
INSPECTORATE OF GOVERNMENT (1999) *Report of investigations in the Forest Department*, Kampala.
KAYUNGA, S. (2000) The Federo (Federalism) Debate in Uganda, *Research Working Paper*, no. 62, Kampala: Centre for Basic Research.
LANGOYA, C.D. (1999) *Forest resource conflict mitigation through eco-tourism development: Case study of Mabira Forest Tourism Project and Budongo Forest Eco-tourism Project*, paper prepared for the African Centre for Technology Studies, Nairobi, Mimeo.
MADONDO, A. (2000) Situating Zimbabwe's natural resource governance systems in history, *CIFOR Occasional Paper*, no. 32, Harare.
MAMDANI, M. (1996) *Citizen and subject: Contemporary Africa and the legacy of late colonialism*, Kampala: Fountain Publishers with David Phillip and James Currey.
MASINDI DISTRICT (Production and Environment) (2000) *Ordinance 2000* (draft).
MUHEREZA, E.F. (2003) Commerce, kings and local government in Uganda: Decentralizing natural resources to consolidate the central state, *Environment and Governance in Africa Working Paper*, No. 8, Institutions and Governance Program, World Resources Institute (WRI), Washington, D.C.
NSIBAMBI, A. (1997) *Making democratic decentralisation an instrument of poverty eradication: The Ugandan experience*, paper presented at the UNDP Development Forum, Kampala, 4 April.
ONYACH-OLAA, M. AND P. DOUG (2000) *Local government performance and decentralisation in Uganda: Implications for central governments and donors*, Kampala: Mimeo.
REPUBLIC OF UGANDA (2002) *Uganda forestry nature conservation master plan*, Forest Department, Ministry of Water, Lands and Environment, Kampala.
REPUBLIC OF UGANDA (2001) *The Uganda forestry policy*, Forest Department, Ministry of Lands, Water and Environment, Kampala.
REPUBLIC OF UGANDA (2000) *The Parliament of Uganda: Interim report on the Select Committee on Forestry Department*, Kampala: Mimeo.
REPUBLIC OF UGANDA (1998) *Ministry of Local Government: Decentralisation implementation road map*, Ministry of Local Government, Kampala.
REPUBLIC OF UGANDA (1997) *The Local Government Act*, Entebbe: Uganda Printing and Publishing Corporation.
RIBOT, J.C. (1999) Decentralisation, participation and accountability in Sahelian forestry: Legal instruments of politico-administrative control, *Africa*, 69(1): 23-65.

SAMOFF, J. (1990) Decentralisation: The politics of interventionism, *Development and Change*, 21: 513-30.

TENDLER, J. (1997) *Good government in the tropics*, Baltimore: Johns Hopkins University Press.

THE FOREST ACT OF 31 DECEMBER 1947 (Chapter 246 of the Laws of Uganda).

THE FOREST ACT OF 31 DECEMBER 1964 (Chapter 246 of the Laws of Uganda).

UGANDA PROTECTORATE (1947) *Working plan for the Budongo and Siba forests (1945-1954)*, Entebbe: Government Printers.

VILLADSEN, S. and F. LUBANGA (1996) *Democratic decentralisation in Uganda: A new approach to local governance*, Kampala: Fountain Publishers.

WAGABA, F.X. (2002) *The decentralisation system: Uganda's experience*, Kampala: Mimeo.

WAGABA, F.X. (1998) *The process of decentralisation in Uganda: Achievements and challenges*, paper presented at the Regional Policy Workshop on Decentralisation and Local Empowerment, Arusha, 28 September – 2 October, 1998.

WEBSTER, N. (1992) Panchayati Raj in west Bengal: Popular participation for the people of the party?, *Development and Change*, 23(4): 129-63.

WILY, L.A. and S. MBAYA (2001) *Land, people and forests in Eastern and Southern Africa at the beginning of the 21st century: The impact of land relations on the role of communities in forest tenure*, Nairobi: IUCN-EARO.

12

Participative approaches and decentralized management of the Samori forest in the Baye municipality, Mopti region (Mali)

Bréhima Kassibo

Introduction

Worldwide, the principle of participation has become the cornerstone of environmental management, stimulated by international institutions like the FAO, UNCDF(FENU), the World Bank and so on, which have made it their hobby horse in the spheres of rural development and good governance. In the wake of such different movements and theories as that of populism,[1] economic and political choice, democratic theory, and so on, the participation of local communities in the management of their resources is generally considered an essential precondition for the effective management of these (Ostrom 1990; Ribot 2001). Mali, in instituting one of the most progressive

[1] According to Olivier de Sardan (1995: 19) populism is 'a certain relationship between intellectuals (associated with privileged classes and groups) and the common people (that is to say, the dominated classes and groups) whereby the intellectual classes become aware of the common people, commiserate with them and/or admire their abilities, and decide to serve them and work for their good'.

decentralization reforms in Africa, has created a favourable institutional framework for the stimulation of local participation in public decision-making. It created several levels of local government comprising democratically elected councils and consultative bodies in 1999, implying competition between political parties and independent candidates. However, while in the context of environmental decentralization the transfer of the powers exercised by central government to these new authorities is strongly recommended by the existing laws, the legal provisions necessary for their enforcement (decrees of enactment) have not yet come into effect. With respect to natural resources, the relevant texts recommend the transfer of powers, tracts of land and resources down to the lowest level of the administrative echelon of the *commune*, or municipal council, but to this day no power of decision has been officially delegated to it.

The present chapter[2] is based on a case study of participative forest management in the framework of decentralization plans that are not yet fully operative in Mali. Within this fuzzy and coercive environment and in spite of the central administration's retention of the right of management of its forest and of exercise of the powers relative to it, the Baye municipality council has claimed its transfer as recommended by the law. Taking advantage of the new decentralization trend, the NGO SOS Sahel (Great Britain) attempted to mobilize the skills of the representatives of the local civil society (population and local associations) in managing their forest resources. Nevertheless, the failure to enforce the laws governing the decentralized management of forest resources represents a perpetuation of the situation before the new reforms, before March 1991, which was characterized by an autocratic legal atmosphere, and sanctioned the state administration's monopoly of the management of natural resources. The participative efforts by SOS Sahel on the basis of revitalization of the traditional forest management authorities are restricted to the desire to ensure recognition of the legal rights of these authorities, in such a way that they will be able to decide on the management of their resources. However, due to the fact that the legal environment is not adjusted, as well as because of SOS Sahel's methodological approach, based as it is on the 'project approach', these efforts do not permit the realization of non-exclusive and effective popular participation. According to Agrawal and Ribot (1999), the transfer of powers and resources from the central authority to authorities representing and responsible to communities at grass-roots level constitutes an essential condition for the efficacious and sustain-

[2] The chapter is an extract from a comparative study of environmental decentralization in six African countries. In Mali the work was carried out by a team of Mali researchers led by the author in the region of Mopti from July 2000 to May 2001. The study was wholly funded and supervised by the Institutions and Governance Program of the World Resources Institute in Washington, USA. The views expressed here are nevertheless solely the author's.

able management of these resources.[3] Looking at the different institutional arrangements for the management of forest resources in the Baye municipality, one can conclude that the conditions for realizing genuine, democratic decentralization are far from being satisfied. The study on which this chapter is based, focused on all local actors who do or do not enjoy a measure of power in the management of forest resources, the nature of the powers at their disposal, the modes of their transfer, the legal principles governing the exercise of these, the mechanism whereby these actors are held accountable, and the social and environmental consequences of the institutional arrangements.

The research location

The Baye municipality

Administratively, the Baye *commune*, or municipality, is part of the district of Bankass, located in the region of Mopti. The settlement of Baye is the main centre of the municipality by that same name, resulting from the regrouping of thirty-three villages. It is one of the twelve municipalities of the district that have come about as a result of the territorial division of 1996. The municipality covers an area of around 21,142 square kilometres, and ninety per cent of it comprises a vast agro-ecological zone known as the forest of Samori or Baye. Its population varies between 23,000 and 26,000, according to different estimates, and constitutes about eleven per cent of the total population of the Bankass district. It is composed mainly of Dafing, whose neighbours are minority ethnic groups like the sedentary Samogo and Dogon and the nomadic Peul, Bellah and Bozo. Agriculture, animal husbandry, and fishing are the principal pillars of the economy of this rural area. The construction of dams in the Sourou River upstream in Burkina Faso has allowed an increase in fishing and rice growing in the floodplains along the river. The Bankass district is the recipient of generous foreign development aid. The municipality of Baye has enjoyed the assistance of a variety of partners, such as the British SOS Sahel, which is still active, the *Projet de Gestion des Ressources Naturelles*, the German GTZ, the *Fonds d'Equipement des Nations Unie*s (FENU/UNCDF), the *Volontaires Français du Progrès*, and the *Programme National de Vulgarisation Agricole*, which at present have finalized their programmes, and have left Baye. Baye also receives aid from agencies supporting the development of decentralized organisations, such as the *Fonds d'Aide aux Initiatives de Base* and the

---

3 This corresponds to the Anglo-Saxon concept of democratic decentralization as defined by several other authors, such as Crook and Manor 1998; Manor 1999; Ribot 2000.

National Investment Agency. All this constitutes an appreciable aid package for development projects. The British NGO SOS Sahel is paying significant sums to provide financial as well as technical assistance for forest management, while the UNCDF has financed, to the tune of fourteen million CFA Francs,[4] preliminary research concerning the development of 300 hectares in the Baye plain for agriculture and market gardening. It has also presented its old office buildings to the municipality, which uses it as a town hall. Tax revenues in the year 2000 contributed 23,000,000 CFA Francs[5] to the municipal budget, in spite of the current difficulties disturbing the functioning of the municipality (see below), that is to say an eighty per cent fiscal cover. It received two financial grants from the state, one in 1999 and one in 2000, each to an amount of 4,800,000 CFA Francs,[6] in 1999 and 2000.

Following charges of reported fraud during the local municipal elections, a serious dispute erupted between militant members of the two dominant parties, *l'Alliance pour la Démocratie au Mali* (ADEMA) and the *Parti pour la Démocratie et le Progrès* (PDP), after the establishment of the municipal office and the appointment of the ADEMA candidate as mayor.

This appointment was hotly contested by the opposing party, which called into question the legality of the municipal office and boycotted its meetings. This conflict between the two political parties has even sown division within the family of the mayor herself, finding herself in competition with her half-brother and PDP candidate. It eventually also involved the principal municipal centre, as well as the villages of the locality, which became divided into opposing factions. The administration in the person of the sub-prefect (a former government representative and head of the municipality) took the side of one of the clans that happened to be in the PDP camp, backed by the clan of the village headman of Baye and his advisors, and attempted to destabilize the opposing party by fanning the flames of discord so as to take advantage and recover its former prerogatives, which in the framework of decentralization had passed to the municipality. This unsavoury political climate has not only poisoned the life of the municipality but has also disrupted its activities since the installation of the municipal council in 1999. The two dominant parties presented the conflict before the state courts in 1999; and the situation only relaxed after the judgement passed by the Supreme Court in June 2001, which confirmed the 1999 electoral results by pronouncing the ADEMA candidate as the winner of the elections.[7]

---

4 Roughly the equivalent of 23,300 Euro.

5 Roughly the equivalent of 38,300 Euro.

6 Roughly the equivalent of 8,000 Euro.

7 See judgement, no. 25 of 14 June 2001, of the administrative division of the Supreme Court of Mali. This verdict gave the municipal office back its legitimacy and helped ease the tensions within the municipal council and among the citizens.

The Samori forest

The Samori forest constitutes for the three municipalities which it encompasses, in particular for that of Baye, an important source of timber resources, a potentially valuable source of improvement of the living conditions of these rural communities, generating considerable revenues. With a surface area varying between 210,800 (Diakité 1993) and 245,000 (Ba 1999: 5) hectares, the forest covers thirty-seven per cent of the surface area of the Bankass district. It is a trans-frontier and trans-community forest stretching from the foothills of the cliffs in the Dogon area to the interior of neighbouring Burkina. It is officially classified as a non-controlled forest, and its management is beset with numerous problems because of the multitude of actors involved. Contrary to popular images of a tropical African forest, as represented by the vast tracts of tree-covered land in central Africa, that of Baye constitutes a simple Sudanese-type agro-ecological zone, principally consisting of tree-covered savannah and gallery forests along the watercourses, the most important of which is the Sourou. It represents one of the last of the Sahelo-Sudanese bush types at that particular altitude in Mali.[8]

The Samori forest has been inhabited since the high middle ages by groups like the Samogo, Bobo, Mossi, Maninka, Peul and Dogon, who originally came from other regions. A large part has been appropriated by settlers who in the process established rights to the land, effectively controlling it, in particular access to the mineral, wood, animal and water resources found on the land. The body of rules of ownership and management of the exploitable space has been subsumed under the term 'customary rights' and has been transformed into simple rights of usufruct by both colonial and post-colonial law. These rights are still in force and continue to inform management of natural resources. The legal status of the forest has undergone a number of changes from the colonial period to the present day. The decrees of 1904 and 1906 confirmed the ownership by the French State of all unoccupied and 'ownerless' land. These rules also applied to Samori, as part of the territory of French Sudan, even though the French state recognized the customary rights of the inhabitants.

In 1948 the French administration proceeded to demarcate and zone certain portions of the forest with a view to designating forest reserves. This was to culminate in the eviction of the communities living in the relevant zones and the restriction of particular activities. The classification of the forest reserves proved impossible to put into effect, a situation that lasted till

[8] As far as forests go, this definition far from reflects the actual situation, as considerable areas have been, and continue to be, permanently colonized by agriculturists and sedentary and transhumant stock breeders. The actual residual core of this forest, which has long been subject to human exploitation, is constituted by only a few forested mountain ranges and some gallery forests along the Sourou River.

the end of the Second Republic. Due to a relaxation in forest supervision after the events of March 1991, the inhabitants defied the law by such acts as establishing farming hamlets on the peripheries of villages adjoining the classified zone in order to torpedo the project of re-establishing forest reserves, as had been announced in 1972. The state accepts customary rights to the portion of the forest that is designated for residential (farming hamlets) or pastoral use (creation of pastoral camps/erection of shepherds' huts), while the forestry authority retains control over forest exploitation rights, issues tree-cutting permits for the forest as a whole, and is responsible for policing the forest.

The management of forest resources is thus under state control, while that of the land continues to be vested in the customary owners of the land, in spite of the promulgation of the *Code Domanial et Foncier* (law on state control and land ownership). Hence, the forest is exploited by a multiplicity of occupiers, in accordance with either rights of usufruct or official rules. These users are: Sedentary farmers and holders of rights of usufruct, Peul sedentary stock breeders and transhumant nomads, agro-pastoralists, cultivators, timber harvesters, collectors of forest products, artisans (blacksmiths and carvers), beekeepers, hunters, fishermen, healers, and gatherers. The conflicts that frequently occur between the different occupiers and users over the exploitation of natural resources are in most cases solved by recourse to customary mediation instruments.

Exploitation dynamics and an analysis of constraints

The multiplicity of actors in the Samori area and the diversity of management rules are having negative impacts on this resource. These impacts vary in nature.

Frequent conflicts range the traditional authorities of the sedentary village against agricultural migrants seeking to settle in farming hamlets on their land. If the host village grants them permission, they take their clearing permit to the Conservation Service and set up home. However, the *massa* (political chief, see below) then sends one of his representatives to serve as a hamlet chief to them, to report to the *massa* on the migrants' doings. The settlement permission is submitted for consideration to the representative of the administration, who may or may not confirm it. Once the hamlet is established, it becomes subject to the village rules and loses its autonomy.

The migrant finds himself borrowing land that is liable to be taken away from him at any moment by the original owner. This gives rise to permanent insecurity regarding land. The eviction of migrants gives the original settlers a chance to use newly cleared land.

The creation of new hamlets and new fields is a source of forest degradation, according to Konaté and Tessougué (1996: 15), who point out that – after the events of March 1991, which resulted in a relaxation of forest surveillance – twenty-three hamlets were established in the space of five years. The authors identified a total of eighty-six hamlets, seventy-three per cent of which have been established since 1970 and forty-nine per cent after 1985. The establishment of these hamlets, according to them, looks like a defence strategy against classification of the forest, which the inhabitants fear is aimed at dispossessing them of their land. The creation of new hamlets thus serves the wishes of the villages to demarcate their boundaries vis-à-vis their neighbours by establishing colonies in their peripheries (Konaté and Tessougué 1996: 15). As a result of demographic growth, the increased demand for land is forcing villages to consent to illegal land reclamation, without the authorization of the Forestry Service, which in turn is increasing the risk of deforestation.

The increase in the volume of water in the Sourou River in the Samori area, since the construction of the Léry dam in Burkina Faso, has stimulated expansion in a number of activities, such as fishing, stock breeding, and especially rice-growing in the floodplains. This has given rise to an influx of numerous migrant farmers, stockbreeders and fishermen. The development of the valley of the Sourou has exacerbated the conflicts between the newcomers and the original inhabitants, with some forest landowners and villages starting to demand restitution of parcels of land they have given on loan to other cultivators. The conflicts over land that have ranged the Karé against the Kawéré and the Baye against the Songoré (Tessougué *et al.* 1998: 117-8; Ba 1999: 40) are characteristic of this kind of situation.

The occupation of the banks of the Sourou by rice-growers is blocking the access of the herds to the river, as is the clearing of fields in grazing lands. The occupation of pastoral tracts is giving rise to numerous conflicts between agriculturists who hold customary title to the land and stockbreeders, who are considered as no more than temporary occupiers. Analysis of two aerial photographs taken by the PGRN in 1992 and 1996 shows a total deforestation rate of forty-eight per cent of forested surfaces (Ba 1999: 11). The forests concerned are the gallery forests on the riverbanks and the forested mountain ranges. It would seem, then, that deforestation is the result of traditional agricultural practices rather than of deliberate timber cutting, which, under certain conditions, is apt to stimulate natural regeneration of the forest. The original settlers are also responsible for the former type of deforestation by reclaiming forest tracts for agricultural purposes and setting up farming hamlets, exacerbating the inherent disadvantages of swidden agriculture – the main factor responsible for the rapid exhaustion of the soil and the clearing of new areas of land.

The main obstacles to the effective management of forest resources can be characterized as follows:

- Lack of material, financial, technical and human resources, depriving the government of effective means of intervention in order to ensure sustainable management of the forest;

• Absence of a consistent plan for the exploitation of the forest (inventorisation, classification, protection, subdivision) and for the realization of management activities, which is putting obstacles in the way of the valorisation of forest resources and prevents the participation of local actors in their commercial exploitation;
• Lack of qualified personnel for effective policing and enforcement of the regulations, which is encouraging large – scale evasion of rules on the part of those exploiting the forest;
• Failure to form elected bodies of community representatives to participate in the management of the forest and, in cases where these do exist, the tendency to sideline them, which is depriving them of prestige vis-à-vis their electorates;
• Absence of legal recognition for the role of neo-traditional associations in the management of forest resources by the Conservation Service, which is undermining the former's authority in forest policing;
• The exclusion of community authorities and village associations from the distribution of tax revenues and subsidies, which is promoting social inequality as well as forming an impediment to local development.

As far as local communities are concerned, the commercial exploitation of the forest by the state is a disaster, as the holders of official timber-cutting licences are not sparing village copses or even trees protected by customary law, thus undoing years of combined efforts to maintain the copses. The cutting of such trees is done for commercial purposes and represents a violation of private ownership, according to Diallo (1993: 14). The ambiguity of the law is rendering the status of these resources increasingly uncertain. While the *Code Domanial et Foncier* (law on state control and land ownership) only recognizes legitimacy of ownership where title to land is enjoyed, customary law tends to equate permanent and exclusive tenure of resources with ownership rights based on the historicity of its appropriation.

Meanwhile the announcement of a policy of decentralization is influencing the perceptions and attitudes of the actors, leading to the emergence of a sense of citizenship. In the management of the Samori forest, local conservation associations and agents find themselves obliged to conciliate a multitude of contradictory forces. Unable to openly oppose loggers armed with cutting licences issued by official agencies, the associations check the documents and reject all those they suspect of not being legally constituted. They decide on quantities and specify the species to be harvested and direct the applicants to the zones they have allocated to them. There is reason to believe that this constitutes a beginning of the zoning of the forest. To prevent all foreign exploitation, even pastoral, the associations have seen fit to designate certain portions as no-go areas with the agreement of the forestry authority and SOS Sahel, which has assisted them with the demarcation and zoning. The village of Minta, in the Zérémadougou region, thus has proceeded to set sixty-five square kilometres aside as a no-go area. Other associations are in the process of following suit. Diendougou, for instance, has also set aside a part of its forested area that is to become subject to similar conservation measures in future.

The creation of rural markets for timber is officially condoned as a form of private participation by village groups in commercial lumbering. Four villages – Tionou, Songoré, Lossagou and Ganida – have proceeded with the aid of the Local Conservation Service to inventory and demarcate their forested mountain ranges, and to establish forest management units, but so far have not received permission from the forestry agents for their official conversion into timber-cutting and selling areas. Only the latter are in a position to complete the entire procedure. By reserving the technical facilities for themselves, they are reinforcing their powers and control over the forested mountain ranges in the area. This has led some to say that technology may act as an excuse for government agents to maintain particular advantages (Ribot 2001a). While waiting for official permission, villagers often proceed to sell timber products illegally without the knowledge of the forestry agencies. What is more, certain village associations have taken steps, with the assistance of the British NGO SOS Sahel, to obtain their official certificates as private enterprises. At the time we travelled to Minta, the local association had just obtained its licence and one of its members told us that now they had finally obtained the bit of paper which would restore their right of exploitation and control of 'their forest'. This happy outcome, though, could prove a step in the direction of the imposition of restrictions on the use of their forest reserve following the example of Minta, and lead to the exclusion of other external users such as pastoralists and other forest users from a hitherto communal space, if care is not taken.

Institutional organisation

The multiplicity of actors and management rules has made managing the Samori forest quite a complex business and a potential source of conflict. Moreover, several types of institutional organisations are encountered. The key actors in the management process are, in the first place, the technical services, among which we should mention first and foremost the *Service Local de Conservation de la Nature* (SLCN). Then there are the neo-traditional management associations that the British NGO SOS Sahel has proceeded to revitalize, namely the *ton*; and finally the elected municipal officers representing the municipal council. Below I shall describe these different actors in terms of their roles and the powers they wield.

Precolonial traditional management of the Samori forest

The Samori forest has been subject to human habitation from early times onwards, according to the different written sources reflecting different versions of the oral traditions. Some authors locate the first human settlements, made up of Mandéka from the east and Mossi from the south, in the twelfth century (Tessougué *et al.* 1998: 34). Other researchers maintain that the fourteenth century marked the settlement of the first Pana or Samogo and Bobo farmers (Ba 1999: 13). The latter version seems most probable, since the name 'Samori' for the forest of Bayé means 'land of the Samogo' in the Peul language, according to most authors. These migrant communities supposedly acquired extensive rights over the land and the different natural resources by virtue of first occupancy. Hence, customary rights were simply the reflection of the social relations, which conferred certain prerogatives with respect to land and human management on specific groups. With leadership being based on the possession of religious, political, judicial and economic rights, traditional social organisation in the Samori area was historically articulated around socio-territorial units ruled by persons holding particular powers. These include the following.

The zora *or masters of the land*

Territorial rights, including timber cutting and burning rights (i.e. instrumental in the first reclamation of uninhabited bush), are a derivative of the right of first occupancy. This confers a religious sovereignty on the first occupant by virtue of the pact concluded between him and the spirit of the area and imparts an aura of exclusiveness that encompasses certain prerogatives transmitted within the lineage in the agnatic line, and in accordance with the principle of seniority. In the Samori area, the *zora*, or master of the land, represents the priest traditionally charged with the function of priest of the soil. He:

- officiates at ceremonies of purification of soil contaminated by a violation of a particular taboo (sexual intercourse in the bush or violent death from a falling tree);
- gives the starting signal for sowing, harvesting of crops and the gathering of wild fruits;
- gives the first swing of the axe when a new field is cleared and drinks the first mouthful of water from a new well;
- is the first to descend into the water and consecrates the start of the fishing;
- arbitrates in disputes concerning land and punishes offenders;
- distributes the land among members of his lineage, allies and foreigners;
- rules over a cluster of villages regrouped into socio-territorial and religious units.

There were three units grouped around the villages of Oula, Dien and Tionou in the Samori area. These were Ouladougou and Diendougou, inhabited by Samogo, and Tiendougou, inhabited by Marka and Bobo. The *zora's* succession is affected in accordance with gerontocratic principles in force within his lineage.

The massa *or political chief*
As a result of the numerous invasions, the Samori area has long been an unstable zone. The *zora* were conquered by the Mandéka, conquerors from the east, to whom they surrendered some of their territorial prerogatives: The function of masters of the land, and is some places their control of the religious cult as well. Other conquerors, the Massaké, also seized the political power and appointed *massaden* from their lineage as village headmen. The *massa*, in his capacity as holder of political and military power, in many places gradually replaced the master of the land with respect to the control of natural resources. He is chosen from among the members of his lineage.

The sariatigui *or judge*
Alongside the above mentioned two political figures, there is a third, neutral one, namely the judge. The *sariatigui* exercises the function of arbiter in internal conflicts, such as those arising from cases of adultery. He also exposes any irregular behaviour on the part of the *massa* and the *zora*, with whom he entertains confidential relations. He is a neutral figure, chosen from among the most senior members of his family, and does not come from the family of either the *massa* or the *zora*.

The traditional village council
The village council, which comprises the village lineage heads and the advisors of the *massa*, adjudicates on all problems bearing on the fate of the community and takes part in decision-making. It thus looks like a veritable counter-weight to the three previous authorities.

The village unit therefore appears as a pluralistic entity, in which the multiplicity of powers and counter-powers create a balance between the different bodies by preventing a concentration of power in one single hand.

The traditional police associations: The ton *or* kana
Opinions concerning the role of *ton* or *kana* vary. Konaté and Tessougué (1996: 5) hold the view that there were no special institutions for the traditional management of natural resources. This function was exercised by the *kana* or *ton* (bush police) by virtue of the powers that the *massa* delegated to them. Made up of designated youths and active adults, the *kana* or *ton* were in charge of the surveillance of the bush and applied the local rules of natural resource management (bush fires, clearing, collection of unripe fruits, and so on). Violation of these rules was checked by custom, and penalties ranged

from confiscation of the products taken to payment of fines in kind. Ba (1999: 22), on the other hand, attributes both environmental and social policing functions to the *ton* or *kana*. He reports that in the Samori region (Baye and Oula) the Kannas (a revival of pre-Muslim supra-village 'instruments') and the Tondéni (village 'instruments' reflecting the influence of the kingdom of Bamanan, in Ségou) were management instruments. These 'instruments', made up of age groups in the village, probably functioned under the aegis of the *zora* and the *massa*. Among them a number of subdivisions can be discerned, each charged with a precisely defined social function, such as traditional Tondéni chiefs of hunters, of the communal hunt, of wells, of village waters, and so on. The *massa* and the *zora* delegated to them certain social (protection of individuals and goods against theft, for example), economic (actions aimed at promoting village solidarity), and environmental (solution of problems in connection with the management of a given resource) police duties, in accordance with the powers devolved to each Tondéni.

The revitalization of traditional associations: The ton

The new directions reflected by the forestry laws of 1995 involve a boosting of powers, devolution of responsibility, expansion of the rights to resources, and conferment of powers of decision to the different managers and users of the resources. They equally recommend the use of a participative approach in the management of natural resources. The objectives of the laws are based on the principles of safeguarding private, collective or government rights of ownership, simplification of administrative procedures, and support for socio-professional organisations in the protection of their interests and elaboration of local and regional agreements regarding the exploitation of natural resources. These new directions are a corollary of populism. The resulting participative approach is centred on the promotion of village land management bodies. This participative approach has been adopted by NGOs and government agencies in their intervention at the local level.[9] Concerning local management of the Samori forest, SOS Sahel has shown itself most active by encouraging the revival of traditional forest resource management associations known by the old name of *ton*. Below I will present an analysis of this experiment.

---

9 The Baye forest has been the subject of large-scale intervention by various bodies promoting local development, such as the *Projet d'Aménagement et de Gestion des Terroirs Villageois du Seno-Gondo* (PAGT/SG; Seno-Gondo Village Land Exploitation regarding Land Management Project), the British SOS Sahel, the *Volontaires Français du Progrès*, the PGRN, and the PNVA, which are campaigning, in the absence of user and local decision-maker frameworks, for environmental protection and the promotion of local development (Ba 1999: 4).

According to SOS Sahel traditional management of the forest of Baye was effective, thanks to the activities of village bodies called *ton*. These associations fell under the authority of the *massaké*, to whom they were accountable, and fulfilled environmental policing functions that were instrumental in protecting the forest from destruction. The introduction of the colonial and post-colonial administration has resulted in undermining the customary management structures by depriving them of all powers of decision-making. The practice of cutting permits has dispossessed the villagers of their rights by indiscriminately opening their environment to the commercial exploitation of timber. In their view, this led to the most insidious form of environmental degradation (see also Diakité 1993).

This nostalgic representation of traditional management of the Samori region has led SOS Sahel to revitalize local bodies in an attempt to promote community management of the Samori forest resources. To this end it launched the *Projet d'Aménagement et de Gestion des Terroirs Villageois du Seno-Gondo* (PAGT/SG). This experiment proved to be an extension of that in the plateau region, where the NGO had organised traditional Dogon associations called *alamodiou* into forest surveillance brigades. SOS Sahel acted as an interface between the latter and the local nature conservation service by advocating the signing of tacit agreements regarding joint forest management. This experiment has not had the anticipated results because of certain legal and administrative restrictions stimulating officials responsible for forest management to protect their natural resource management privileges by hiding behind the letter of the law. Yet, a similar kind of experiment was conducted by SOS Sahel in he Samori forest, where, contrary to the Dogon *alamodiou*, the traditional forest management bodies, the *ton*, had disappeared from the scene and only existed in local oral traditions evoking memories of them. Although the customary headmen, the *massaké* and *zora*, were still present in the locality, they were stripped of all real powers of decision regarding the exploitation of forest resources, which were now held by the representatives of the government. At most they fulfilled a vestigial function with respect to rural land. SOS Sahel did some research, the results of which allegedly confirmed the vestigial existence of particular socio-territorial units which still possessed a traditional dynamic. The reconstitution of these socio-cultural units led to the recognition of six of these, each made up of a number of villages clustered around a 'mother village'. SOS Sahel reconstituted just four such units in the municipality of Baye, namely Ouladougou, Diendougou, Tiendougou and Zeremadougou, with as chief villages and seats of *massa* Oula, Dien, Tionou (Konaté and Tessougué 1996) and Zerema. The chief town, Baye (which historically has played the part of principal canton, sub-district, and is the centre for the Panadougou municipality as a whole), being already covered by the PGRN, and as a consequence already possessing territorial management instruments (that is, a management committee and a land use plan), was not included. Its place was taken by the neighbouring village of Minta, which played the part of 'mother village' in the Zérémadougou unit. The research for this report focused on Oula, Yira and Minta, the sites of the head offices of three of these entities excluding Tionou (Tiendougou), while the majority of villages were located in another municipality.

Next, a number of management associations were set up in accordance with a modern organigram. The legitimacy of the *ton* was supposed to be rooted in tradition, which endowed them with social legitimacy through cultural transposition, to the level of the system of collective village representation.[10] In the same way as the Dogon *alamodiou*, charged in former times with the traditional surveillance of forest resources, SOS Sahel encourages the institution of modern *brigades de surveillance* (surveillance brigades) in twenty-five of the thirty-three villages of the Baye municipality. They are responsible for surveillance and policing, as well as conservation of the forest. These brigades, who have few female members,[11] are made up of twelve to fifteen individuals appointed by the village executive committee. The twenty-five villages are spread over units which each have a 'mother village' and each are ruled by an executive committee comprising twelve members appointed by the village council. The brigades report to these committees during joint meetings. Made up of members serving as animators to the surveillance brigades, the executive committee may act as an interface between local and supra-village bodies like the directing committees. These bodies are intended for the management for the forest, and SOS Sahel is meant to act as an interface between them and representatives of the SLCN.

SOS Sahel tries to boost local natural resource management powers of the committees and the *ton* by means of various kinds of activities, such as:

- implementation of forest zonation projects (including setting aside 39,000 hectares of forest in Zérémadougou for protection);
- reforestation through the establishment of nurseries;
- establishing management structures for the forest tracts in Lossogou, Songoré, Tionou and Ganida, four pilot villages in the municipality of Baye;
- developing management plans for water pools;
- technical training courses in methods of management and exploitation;
- mobilization of local populations;
- environmental education;
- reading and writing courses for members;
- transfer of reforestation techniques and setting up nurseries.

---

10 For more details on the modes of organisation of neo-traditional associations, see Konaté 1992; Konaté *et al.* 1996; Dembélé 1995; Care Mali 1998; Diakité 1993.

11 The role of women in surveillance is in fact quite limited, not extending beyond forest areas reserved for domestic uses, such as the collection of dead wood for cooking and of fruit.

The committees and agents have acquired natural resource management skills that might lead them to co-operate with the municipal council in the long-awaited event of a delegation of environmental responsibilities to decentralized local government structures, so SOS Sahel believes. Hence it might be said that the activities of SOS Sahel have been concentrated first and foremost on the institution of management bodies, to which limited discretionary powers have been delegated. Unfortunately, the project is still coming up against innumerable difficulties because of a legal-institutional environment that remains basically unchanged as a result of failure to enforce the forestry laws of 1995. Before embarking on this new venture, SOS Sahel should have taken into account these restrictions, which provided, and continue to provide, the main obstacle to genuine participation of village communities in the management of forest resources, confronted as they are with a government that is holding on to its vested rights of ownership.

Among these numerous restrictions we might mention:

- The *ton*'s lack of financial autonomy; it is the NGO which initiates activities and finances them; local authorities have no control over decisions taken by the technicians of SOS Sahel;
- The *ton* lack representative authority with the grass-roots communities, which do not always identify with them, but also at the municipal level;
- They lack legal recognition; their status is illegal and subordinate, which obliges them to compete with the SLCN, which is in charge of forest resource management;
- They have no powers of amendment and enforcement;
- They lack the power to enact and enforce management regulations;
- They are excluded from levying taxes;
- They lack real technical skills, as well as the necessary means for sustainable, effective management of this resource.

Government management

There are several government services in charge of management and control of natural resources. With respect to forest resources, the SLCN (formerly *Service des Eaux et Forêts*, Water and Forest Service) plays a prominent role.

The Service Local de Conservation de la Nature (SLCN)

The Baye forest has the status of non-controlled forest, as it is not demarcated and no land use plan has been developed for it. This allows the government to delegate its management to the community (article 51 of law no. 95-004). At the same time, however, because of its non-controlled character, it is the property of the state, which continues to be its principal beneficiary, through the forestry service, which enjoys the benefit of the proceeds (article 8 of decree no. 98-402/P-RM). According to the rules, the municipality stands to enjoy a five per cent share in the proceeds where the forest is zoned, and a ten per cent one where it is of the classified and managed type, according to the formula used for the distribution of revenues. Actually, interviews with the different actors show that the state is solely in charge, via the forestry service, the SLCN, of the official management of the forest of Baye. Trespassers and offenders are arrested and punished by the police, which is the only body with authorization to enforce rules. Any offences are reported to them by specially appointed informers, who receive a ten per cent share in the proceeds from fines. The issuing of timber cutting, transport and clearing licences is controlled by the forestry police. Although a number of agreements have been signed between the *ton* and the SLCN, the latter only recognizes the former's right to keep the forest under surveillance and to report offenders violating the forestry rules. The forestry police are only accountable to their superiors in the hierarchy, on whom they are dependent. They tend to think that, in the absence of an official act transferring the forest to the municipality of Baye, the latter has no role to play in its management, and that they are not in any way accountable to the local communities, for whose education in forest protection they are officially responsible. Nevertheless, their numerical weakness and lack of resources, both financially and logistically, means that it is impossible for them to fulfil their public service mission properly. Furthermore, the stopgap measure of using civilian informers, who are often guilty of corrupt practices vis-à-vis users, is apt to tarnish even further their image with the rural communities, though they have been officially appointed to raise environmental awareness within these communities and train them in the sustainable management of the forest. Rural communities are not democratically participating in the management of forest resources, as the government arrogates all prerogatives in this sphere to itself in the absence of fully democratic decentralization that has been announced for some time, but not (yet) realized. Moreover, rural communities are obliged to participate in activities such as reforestation, surveillance, protection of trees, fire fighting and prevention (creation of firebreaks and extinguishing bush fires), construction of improved housing, anti-erosion measures, and so on. This is the kind of participation imposed on its rural partners by the government through the concept of the participative approach.

The municipal council

As a consequence of the creation of decentralized bodies from 1999 onwards, the municipality has become the basic administrative unit. It is the lowest territorial echelon, as the village does not enjoy legal personality. Consequently it should benefit from the delegation of natural resource management powers. As no transfer of government forestland has been forthcoming, the municipal council still lacks all power of decision-making. It denounces what it calls the commoditisation of the forest, the indiscriminate cutting – because of its non-controlled status – as a result of licences issued to foreign loggers by other administrative authorities that are based in areas beyond the Baye municipality. Moreover, the councillors cannot avoid noticing what they call deforestation as a result of the clearing of forest for the establishment of new agricultural hamlets, which were authorized by the sub-prefect, without their consent. In spite of the efforts of development partners to work out an environmental plan, the council claims it still lacks the necessary facilities for an efficient management of forest resources. Although it is receiving technical and financial support from NGOs like SOS Sahel and other partners in environmental management schemes, the neo-traditional associations have benefited most from the improved technical facilities in forest resource management. This might provide a starting-point for fruitful co-operation between the main protagonists. It may also stimulate demands on the part of rural communities for ownership of natural resources as well as the facilities for their sustainable management, against the backdrop of an institutional legality that confers powers of decision-making on elected representatives of the municipality. Private individuals, associations and other socio-professional groups will not be able to benefit directly by an immediate transfer of powers and ownership rights on the part of the state (MDD 1997). Although the law advocates the institution of conventions between them and the municipal authorities for purposes of natural resource utilization, the failure to enforce the law renders all these arrangements null and void. The solution would be to proceed to a reclassification of the territorial patrimony of the municipal villages in such a way as to eventually effect hereditary ownership of the land by the municipality, which will be subject to consensual management to ensure the traditional owners full participation in all decision-making with respect to its management.

Legitimacy and responsibilities of the actors

After identifying the various actors by describing the different kinds of arrangement, I will now take a look at the nature of the powers they wield and the kinds of responsibilities they have.

The traditional management actors

The institution of executive and controlling associations in the form of the *ton* has been encouraged mostly by SOS Sahel. The process of establishing the associations differed in each of the three units visited by me. In Minta I was told that for the establishment of the village executive council for the six village neighbourhoods, all the neighbourhood headmen who are members of the village council directly nominated 'their people' for the surveillance brigade, which consisted of twenty members. The interviewees were not specific about who these people were. After nominating the brigade, the twelve members of the village executive committee were chosen. Oula showed the same scenario, with the members being nominated by the village chief and his advisors. Then 'some people' were chosen to elect the executive committee, called *tonba* or Sabu Nyuma ('the great association' or 'the Good Cause'). In Diendougou I was told that there is only a village executive committee, which also acts as surveillance brigade, at the village level. The names of the candidates for the village executive committee were put forward by the village head. Then 'people' were put forward for membership of the executive committee of units called *tonba* or *benkadi* ('good feeling'). In spite of the non-transparent procedure whereby candidates are put forward, it appears that all choices are submitted to the village assembly for approval and that certain criteria are respected. For instance, the treasurer has to be a trustworthy person and the administrative secretary has to be literate. Appointments are supposed to be made on the basis of the candidates' intrinsic abilities, regardless of their age. Representatives of SOS Sahel recommended inclusion of the *massaké* or one of their representatives in the unit executive committees as honorary members. For the election of these, twelve members are chosen from among the delegates sent by the villages (five per village). After a number of village executive committees had been set up, SOS Sahel recommended representation of all socio-professional levels in the village. Surveillance personnel had to be devoted individuals. CEV or brigade chairmen were supposed to figure at the committee level also. The surveillance brigades are accountable for their actions to the members of the CEV, who in turn are obliged to keep the members of the CDE informed, and these then report to SOS Sahel. As an example of popular control, we were informed that some members of these associations had been dismissed by the village assembly or denounced by their peers for various reasons, for example apathy, indifference, and so on. According to some SOS Sahel animators, the associations are accountable to the village, which is involved in all their activities, and use what is known as 'assisted auto-diagnosis' with regard to the budget for the past campaign and the projected budget for the next one. SOS Sahel is encouraging the *ton* to bring their statutes more into line with the spirit of modern organisations (periodical renewal of members, integration of women into their structures, elaboration of their internal rules and regulations). It has become clear in the course of our interviews that SOS Sahel had very specific goals, and has solicited the backing of village communities for its project of the creation of forest management structures with the aim of preventing deforestation and desertification and ensuring sustainable management of forest resources. A number of people we interviewed viewed the stakes of such measures in terms of recovery of their lost patrimony (the forest) and the possibility of managing it in accordance with the inherited norms of their tradition. SOS Sahel's actions are based on a community participation approach. They are intended to be continuous, but participation remains no less externally provoked.[12] This is the result of SOS Sahel's thematic approach, which is aimed at increasing management powers by rural communities only in the field of environmental protection, without looking at the necessary legal powers or indispensable facilities communities need to take decisions concerning the management of natural resources. Moreover, the associations instituted are run in a way that is far from being genuinely indigenous or autonomous, with the *ton* being dependent on paid SOS Sahel animators. With the anticipated announcement of SOS Sahel's withdrawal from the forest of Baye a crucial phase of evaluation of the actual long-term impact of its actions on the population, institutions and resources is in sight. The post-project phase is crucial, as it may lead to a real evocation of consciousness in the beneficiaries who could then appropriate the project while maintaining the initial synergy. On the other hand, it may also lead to disenchantment if no appropriate indigenous mechanisms are found to ensure real autonomy and guarantee the permanence of forest resources.

Representative authority and social legitimacy of the ton

Is the neo-traditional association truly representative and does it enjoy genuine social legitimacy? To answer this question we need to make a comparison between traditional and modern structures. With regard to the traditional mode of management described above one may postulate that the precolonial *ton* enjoyed a certain social legitimacy and representative authority. Sponsored as they were by customary authorities, their legitimacy had its roots in the traditional system of belief with respect to the relation of man to nature and the public utility associated with their function. As a consequence they enjoyed particular powers delegated to them by the whole of the social body, and exercised their function under the supervision of the entire social group in a context of abundance of resources that was less conflictual than the present situation, subject as it is to increasing needs and demographic pressure.

What is the present situation?

The village social configuration has changed a lot from the precolonial period to the present day as a result of state control, whereby a government monopoly has been imposed on the management of land and natural resources, excluding the local population. Moreover, the nature of village

---

12 Meister (1977) distinguishes several types of participation, namely provoked, imposed, voluntary, planned or spontaneous. SOS Sahel's actions correspond to the category 'provoked' and in no way fit what we have defined in terms of the concept of democratic or political decentralization.

authority has changed considerably. The village headman at present is appointed by councillors elected by the population, and his choice is very often the object of bitter quarrelling on the part of other candidates from his own lineage who compete with him for the post. Besides, the nomination is submitted to the scrutiny of the responsible administrative authority (the prefect), which may reject it. The village council is officially regarded as the auxiliary of the state administration, and in the eyes of the people it is a body that carries out the orders of the state apparatus, without much power of decision-making. It therefore enjoys but a limited degree of legitimacy where forest management is concerned, being subject to official legal rules in whose formulation it has no say. Moreover, we should underline the fact that the legitimate customary authorities (*zora, massaké*) in the old days used to collectively exercise the supervision of the *ton*, which supposedly boosted their legitimacy. The members of the executive committees, whose composition varies, no longer possess the same degree of representative authority. It should be borne in mind that the choice of members of these executive committees and of the surveillance brigades has often come up against the weight of a tradition that tends to lend the exercise of power a gerontocratic character. To achieve a relative democratisation of existing structures, SOS Sahel has had to compromise. This way traditional authorities have had honorific functions bestowed on them, while other functions have been conferred on the basis of the intrinsic abilities of the individuals concerned. Thus a young person may exercise responsible functions if he has the necessary capacity. Responsibility for surveillance of the forest has been given to Peul pastoralists and hunters in consideration of their forestry experience and practices. Furthermore, it was necessary to adapt these associations to modern needs and bring them into line with the legislation concerned. In short, it has been necessary to free them from the traditional village yoke, and modernize and at the same time revitalize them. Nevertheless, associations conceived externally and subject to a dynamic generated externally have difficulty in acquiring true autonomy and ensuring their representative authority in the eyes of the population. This attempt at neo-traditionalisation (the creation of modern structures inspired by custom) may be seen from a theoretical point of view as a measure aimed to provide SOS Sahel's participative approach with an ideological and political legitimisation. SOS Sahel has been anxious to put the precepts of the neo-populist philosophy that serves as basis for its development approach into practice. However, the methodological approach it has adopted seems to lack analytical solidity, as the relevance of former homogeneous socio-cultural entities, if they ever existed at all, in modern conditions has not been proved. What is more, they no longer possess the same content, nor the same significance in the system of popular representation of which the Dafing and Samogo *ton*, unlike the Dogon *alamodiou*, have become vague reflections in the course of time. The fragmentation of the national territory into geo-administrative and political units by the different, successive hegemonic powers in the area over time has failed to take into account existing ethnic, cultural and economic groups. These divisions have been effected in the cause of safeguarding the political, economic and strategic interests of those who happened to be in power at the time. Thus one passes here from mediaeval provinces to cantons, subdivisions, districts, sub-districts, and finally municipalities, bearing in mind that this last, most recent territorial unit is simply an offshoot of the total redivision of the old *arrondissement* (sub-district), resulting from an earlier redrawing of administrative boundaries, which is far from constituting an indigenous socio-cultural unit.[13] The character and the seats of power have changed over time and space as a consequence of these political upheavals, not to mention the socio-cultural influence of inter-ethnic marriages.[14]

Conclusion

The principal result we have observed is that none of the institutional arrangements, past or present, analysed by us can be qualified as democratic by reference to the criteria for popular participation, as defined in the introduction. None of these systems is stimulating a genuine process of delegation to lower levels calculated to give local actors more responsibility. The nature of the powers handed down is making it impossible to establish a field of discretionary powers at the local level, which is robbing local institutions, at the level of the municipal council as well as neo-traditional associations, of all representative authority. SOS Sahel's mode of intervention, modelled on the village approach or form of territorial management advocated by the

---

13 Tessougué *et al.* (1998: 35-6), referring to Konaté and Tessougué 1996, observed a change of ethnic identity in this area, occasioned by inter-ethnic matrimonial alliances between Dogon, Bobo, Mossi and Pana, or Samogo. This has resulted in the emergence of a hybrid cultural group called Dafing. The majority of Islamized Samogo, besides those from Diendougou who have preserved their dialect, recognize this new identity as Dafing.

14 In spite of SOS Sahel's arguments for the continuity of socio-territorial units in the municipality of Baye and in Samori, it has been obliged to introduce some substantial modifications in its operational schema, for a variety of reasons. In the first place, the borders of the municipality of Baye no longer correspond to those of the former socio-territorial unit of Pana. Then, the social centre of the unit of Tiondou has been transferred to Ganida, which is the base of the executive committee of the unit instead of the 'mother' village, Tionou. The same is true of Minta, which has been put in the place of the 'mother' village of Zéréma in Zérémadou, as of Yira, which replaces Dien in Diendougou. They have been given the leadership in forest management, contrary to custom, for practical reasons such as demographic and economic importance, financial capacity, infrastructure, and so on.

PGRN, has long since shown its limitations (Mathieu and Laurent 1995; FENU 2000; Utting 2000).[15] Based on techniques of inclusion, experimental mobilization and often instrumentalisation, it is unable to ensure genuine democratic participation by local populations in the management of their resources.

One last point to which attention should be drawn is the residual existence of a repressive regulatory and legislative framework that in fact still sanctions the government's monopoly in environmental management, to the detriment of other actors, in spite of the decentralization and end of nationalization as announced by the new legal texts. There is a wide gulf between the government's continued ideological discourse on decentralization in Mali – mainly for the benefit of financial backers – and the current practice. In other words, the government of Mali is saying what it isn't doing and is doing what it isn't saying. In fact, it has a duty to accelerate the processes of delegation of powers and transfer of land to decentralized bodies to foster the development of genuine democratic decentralization.

The activities of SOS Sahel, like those of other development partners, should be directed in the new decentralization context to the development of institutions that are really representative of the general public interest; and no other unit than the municipality is better qualified to play the role of privileged partner in local development. The application of criteria considered to be indispensable to the realization of democratic decentralization, namely transfer of powers, responsibility and accountability, seems to be an appropriate analytic method for the definition of participation. It is not exhaustive concerning responsibility, as one could conceive of forms of control other than through democratic elections, which may oblige those in authority to answer to their electoral base by such means as information, transparency, social pressures, public education of the people, and so on (see

---

[15] The main criticisms levelled at these approaches by these authors concern:

- the persistence of the technical services' directional and technocratic attitude to projects;
- a desire to safeguard the interest of all parties by giving non-controversial matters priority;
- the lack of communication between external management organisations implementing projects and local institutions wielding authority over the rest of the village;
- the preference given to physical management, to the detriment of conflictual matters bound up with the stakes of local powers;
- the inferiority of a contracted interventional hierarchy (village land) to the more relevant supra-village one;
- the non-replicability of organisational models, suffering as they do from too great a degree of specificity; and
- the accentuation of social hierarchisation by a strengthening of the power and status of the wealthiest.

Ribot 2001a). It nevertheless marks an important step forward in the understanding of environmental decentralization processes thanks to the deconstruction and deflation of the concept of participation, which nowadays is so discredited and used as a banner for the most controversial interventions in environmental management and rural development.

Effective participation by decentralized bodies and local communities can only be realized if the government is prepared to transfer powers and consequently resources to local representative authorities. Hence the government should proceed to a rapid redistribution of forest and other lands to local communities and involve them more closely in their management. However, the new discourse of the representatives of the Conservation Department suggests that what is envisaged at present is a simple transfer of rights of management of government-owned land, instead of a transfer of the land itself, to decentralized bodies. What is still required to guarantee sustainable management of natural resources, however, is a simplification of procedures aimed at facilitating access to state forests by its users, and the initiation of genuinely consensual forestry policies on the basis of environmental education of rural communities. It would be a good idea to restore equity and weaken the government monopoly by creating neutral instruments for settling conflicts facilitating arbitration between all parties involved in the management of forest resources. One problem that is currently impeding decentralization in Mali is linked to the introduction of local democracy. A transfer of powers and resources to local democratic bodies alone will not be enough to automatically achieve democratic decentralization. An efficacious means of strengthening control of the actions of municipal authorities and of initiating downward accountability should be worked out as soon as possible. Likewise, the relations between the municipal council and village communities should comprise a delegation of powers of natural resource management to grass-roots organisations and communities in an appropriate form (institution of local assemblies, joint management, elaboration of specifications of the responsibilities of all parties involved under the supervision of the conservation authority, and so on). Law no. 98-066 of 30 December 1998 relative to territorial groups in the Republic of Mali, in article no. 72 provides for local partnerships in that it urges municipal councils to compulsorily consult the village, sub-village and neighbourhood councils in all matters that come within their purview, such as the organisation of rural activities, environmental protection, natural resource management, disputes about land and land ownership, and so on. Over and above mere consultations, will these bodies be able to effectively oppose the decisions of the municipal council, seeing that they do not have the same rights in terms of taking decisions, which nevertheless affect them first and foremost?

The actions of NGOs like SOS Sahel are justified in that they recognize the legitimate right of rural communities to decide about the way their resources are managed. However, the debate should focus especially on their theoretical approach, so that the ways and means of initiating genuine popular participation, without excluding any party, may be identified. The village community approach is open to reproach on a number of points, which constitute as many obstacles to true democratic decentralization. For example, whereas the designation of forest tracts as protected areas by the *ton* may look like an attempt at conservation, encouraged by official environmental policies, the unilateral closure of these to exploitation by other users (pastoralists, loggers, artisans, and so on) tends to lend them a exclusionist character, sanctioned by local police practice. Paradoxically, these associations, made up for the greater part by sedentary agriculturists, scorn all notions of conservation where their own interests are at stake. The current example of illegal clearing bush by their followers in order to extend the arable land area is a good illustration of the nature of what is at stake for the local communities. The village, in spite of its character as a community centre, is traditionally responsible for excluding marginal groups (women, members of certain castes, foreigners, and so on) from access to resources. Local custom is based on particularism and is not applicable to everyone everywhere; while the communal area officially constitutes a legally homogeneous administrative unit for all human inhabitants and resources which are subject to the authority of the council. The problem is to proceed from a form of participative management to a decentralized natural resource management model, which Ribot considers as 'a change from democratic forms of inclusion orchestrated from without, to representative forms of locally elected democratic authorities' (Ribot 2000: 5). In other words, to achieve democratic decentralization it is necessary to proceed from a project approach to legally institutionalised popular participation by legitimising local actors and giving them environmental management responsibilities. These are the reforms that should be affected in the relations between the state and rural communities before the latter can be allowed responsible management of their resources with a view to sustainability.

Abbreviations

ADEMA	*L'Alliance pour la Démocratie au Mali* (Alliance for Democracy in Mali)
CDE	*Comités Directeurs des Entités* (Unit Executive Committees)
CEV	*Comités Exécutifs Villageois* (Village Executive Committees)
CFA	*Communauté Financière Africaine* (African Financial Community)
FAIB	*Fonds d'Aide aux Initiatives de Base* (Aid Fund for Grass-Root Initiatives)
FAO	Food and Agriculture Organisation

PAGT/SG *Projet d'Aménagement et de Gestion des Terroirs Villageois du Seno-Gondo* (Seno-Gondo Village Land Management and Exploitation Project

PDP *Parti pour la Démocratie et le Progrès* (Party for Democracy and Progress)

PGRN *Projet de Gestion des Ressources Naturelles* (Natural Resource Management Project)

PNVA *Programme National de Vulgarisation Agricole* (National Program for the Popularisation of Agriculture)

SLCN *Service Local de Conservation de la Nature* (Local Nature Conservation Service)

VFP *Volontaires Français du Progrès* (French Volunteers for Progress)

References

AGRAWAL, A. and J.C. RIBOT (1999) Accountability in decentralisation. A framework with South Asian and West African cases, *Journal of developing areas*, 38 (Summer 1999): 473-502.

CARE MALI (1998), *Ogokana, agriculture and natural resources*, Technical report series, Mopti, Projet d'agro sylviculture villageoise de Koro, unpublished report.

CROOK, C. and J. MANOR (1998) *Democracy and decentralisation in South-East Asia and West Africa: Participation, accountability and performance*, Cambridge, Cambridge University Press.

DEMBÉLÉ, E. (1995) Care et la renaissance des Ogokana en milieu dogon, Bamako, *Les Cauris*, no. 50.

DIAKITÉ, M. (1993) *Etude primaire sur les aspects socio-économiques dans la problématique de la gestion de la forêt de 'Samory'*, Bamako: SOS Sahel (GB), unpublished report.

DIRECTION NATIONALE DE LA CONSERVATION DE LA NATURE (1999) *Recueil des textes législatifs et réglementaires en matière de gestion des ressources forestières, fauniques et halieutiques*, Bamako: Ministère de l'Environnement et de l'Eau/Intercoopération suisse, pp. 1-87.

FENU/UNCDF (2000) *Développement local et gestion décentralisée des ressources naturelles*, rapport général de l'atelier de Cotonou, New York: FENU/UNCDF, pp. 1-96.

KONATÉ, A.B. (1992) *Contribution au séminaire atelier sur la décentralisation dans la gestion des ressources naturelles. Les Allamoudiou Garou*, Mopti: Unpublished report.

KONATÉ, A.B. and M. TÉSSOUGUÉ. *La gestion durable des ressources naturelles dans la forêt du Samori, éléments de reconnaissance de la forêt du Samori,* vol. 2, Bankass: Unpublished report.

LAURENT, P-J. and P. MATHIEU (Eds) (1995) Actions locales, enjeux fonciers et gestion de l'environnement au Sahel, special issue of *Cahiers du Cidep*, n° 27, Paris: L'Harmattan.

MEISTER, A. (1997) *La participation pour le développement*, Paris: Les Editions Ouvrières.

OSTROM, E. (1990) *Governing the Commons: The evolution of institutions for collective action*, Cambridge: Cambridge University Press.

RDM (1986) Loi No. 86-42 /AN-RM du 24 mars 1986, portant code forestier qui se substitue à celle antérieure No. 68-8/AN-RM du 17 février1968, *Journal officiel de la république du Mali*, Bamako: Sécrétariat général du gouvernement.

RDM (1995) Loi No. 95-003 portant organisation de l'exploitation du transport et du commerce du bois, *Journal officiel de la république du Mali*, Bamako: Sécrétariat général du gouvernement.

RDM (1995b) Loi No. 95-004 fixant les conditions de gestion des ressources forestières, *Journal officiel de la république du Mali*, Bamako: Sécrétariat général du gouvernement.

RDM (1996) Loi No. 96-050 portant principe de constitution et de gestion du domaine des collectivités territoriales, *Journal officiel de la république du Mali*, Bamako: Sécrétariat général du gouvernement.

RDM (1996b) Loi No. 96-050 portant principe de constitution et de gestion du domaine des collectivités territoriales, *Journal officiel de la république du Mali*, Bamako: Sécrétariat général du gouvernement.

RDM (2000) Ordonnance No. 00-27/P-RM du 22 mars 2000 portant code domanial et foncier, *Journal officiel de la République du Mali*, Bamako: Sécrétariat général du gouvernement.

RIBOT, J.C. (2001) *La nature de la décentralisation démocratique en Afrique Saharienne, étude sur la gestion de l'environnement et des ressources naturelles*. Paper presented at the FENU/UNCDF Workshop 'Decentralisation and Governance in Africa', Cape Town, March 2001.

RIBOT, J.C. (2000) Science use rights and exclusion: A history of forestry in francophone West Africa, *Issue Paper*, No. 104, Drylands Program, International Institute for Environment and Development, London: IIED.

SARDAN, J.P.O. DE (1995) *Anthropologie et développement, essai en socio-anthropologie du changement social*, Paris: APAD-Karthala.

UTTING, P. and R. JAUBERT (1998) *Discours et réalité des politiques participatives de gestion d'environnement, le cas du Sénégal*, Genève: IIED/DNRISD.

13

Insiders out: Forest access through village chiefs in Senegal

Sagane Thiaw and Jesse C. Ribot

Introduction

When asked why village chiefs allow outsiders to cut forests against the will of local people, Makacolibantang's Deputy in Senegal's National Assembly, Kabina Kaba Jakhaté, stated 'the chief is only a pulley – he facilitates but has no authority' (Interview, July 1994 in Ribot 2000: 147). Chiefs are often approached by environmentalists and other development agents as if they represent and act on behalf of local people (Ribot 2004; Ntsebeza 2004). They are approached as if their legitimacy – that is their continued presence and reign – is based on respect from local people rather than on fear or a lack of options. Observations in Senegal and elsewhere bring into question some positive assumptions about these so-called 'traditional' authorities (Ntsebeza 2004; Van Rouveroy van Nieuwaal 1997; Ribot 1999). In the cases discussed in this chapter, chiefs usually work for their own profit, the interest of government and other elite, and against the interests of villagers.

This study focuses on two Senegalese Rural Communities: Makacolibantang and Pata. The Rural Community of Makacolibantang is located in the Region of Tambacounda, in eastern Senegal. This forested region produces most of the charcoal (cooking fuel made from partially burning wood) for Senegal's urban centres. The Rural Community of Pata is in the southeastern part of Senegal, in the Region of Kolda. Migrants from the peanut basin, further north in Senegal, have been illegally clearing parts of the forest reserves in this region. Patterns of forest access in this chapter will be explored through two cases: Charcoal production in forests around villages within Makacolibantang, and forest clearing for farms in the Pata forest reserve. These two cases explore the relations among village chiefs, government authorities, other elite and migrants concerning land and forest access.

In both areas, village chiefs currently exercise authority in allocating forest access to forestry merchants, woodcutters, and migrant farmers. In many areas in rural Senegal, particularly in the centre and north (Senegal River Valley), outsiders' or migrants' access to land or resources claimed by insiders is opposed by insiders (Diop 1992: 28).[1] But in this part of the country (East and South East), the opposite is found. Chiefs have facilitated forest access for outsiders, while excluding insiders from natural resources exploitation and from the significant incomes that this generates.

Chiefs seem to be acting as clients of and administrators for the central government as well as political and commercial elite. The chapter poses the questions: Who are village chiefs? Where does their chiefly authority come from? Why do chiefs prefer to privilege outsiders instead of the local villagers? How do insiders view the decisions their chiefs make? The chapter concludes with a few reflections on the implications of uncritically privileging chiefs.

The material presented in this chapter is based on interviews and surveys conducted in August and September 2002 by Sagane Thiaw in the Rural Communities of Pata and Makacolibantang in Eastern and South East Senegal. Village chiefs and villagers were interviewed in ten villages in each Rural Community. In each village the village chief and five men and five women were interviewed. In each Rural Community a sample of rural councillors, the sub-prefect and prefect and local forest officers were also interviewed.

Chiefly authority

Villages of approximately 100 to 1,500 people are common settlement units in the West African Sahel. Each village typically has a chief and some have specialised chiefs who oversee forest use. Additional authorities at village level include land priests, sorcerers, marabouts, Imams, non-village-based pastoral chiefs, griots, merchants, heads of certain castes (e.g. hunters in Mali), and chiefs of the young (*maasamari* in Niger) (see Ouédraogo 1994;

---

1 Repeated conflicts between agriculturalists and pastoralists in Senegal Valley in the late 1980s, case of bloody conflicts between agriculturalists and pastoralists in the 'groundnuts basin' of Senegal (DIOP 1992: 28).

Bassett and Crummy 1993: 6; Roberts 1997; Kini 1994: 21). Pre-colonial chiefs derived their authority from multiple sources: Rights of conquest, control over land, direct descent from ruling ancestors; and membership of a particular ruling family (see Alexandre 1970; Crowder and Ikime 1970: xi; Fisiy 1992; Fortes and Evans-Pritchard 1987 [1940]: 10-11; Schumacher 1975: 87). The institute of village chieftaincy has existed across Africa since the pre-colonial era. Most European colonisers recognised traditional African chiefs and subordinated them. These chiefs continue to hold authority in the post-colonial era despite changes in their legal and jurisdictional status and their own form of rule. Village chiefs typically have some authority over land and natural resources.

Village chiefs in the colonial period

While village chiefs were important, most of the literature on chiefs focuses on the canton, district, or paramount chiefs, operating on larger territorial-administrative scales. The French did, however, work with, depose, appoint and regulate village-level authorities, deeply shaping the current legal standing and powers of village chiefs. The position of chiefs at all levels has been established or deeply transformed by the process of state formation in the colonial period (Geschiere 1993: 151,165; Bayart 1991: 78; McIntosh 1990: 27; Cowan 1958; Van Rouveroy van Nieuwaal 1987; Fisiy 1992; Alexandre 1970a: 24; Suret-Canal 1966; 1970; Ranger 1993; Roberts 1997). Chiefs were heavily tainted by the colonial experience which had at once strengthened their powers through subjugation followed by European backing, and had undermined their legitimacy through the excesses and contradictions that external backing and the exigencies of colonial administration produced (Cooper 1996: 12; Mahwood 1983; Van Rouveroy van Nieuwaal 1987).[2]

Village chiefs have been integrated into the State as an administrative extension through the colonial periods to the present (Alexandre 1970a; Suret-Canal 1966; Lund 1998: 67). This role has been fraught with ambiguity and tension due to the dual allegiances of chiefs downward to their people and upward to the central state, the competing sources of chiefly power and legitimacy within local culture, and the role of chiefs as links to and agents of the outside world.

As the French worked through and began to back local chiefs, they chose them – 'as far as possible' – by 'custom' (Alexandre 1970a: 52-3). But this was not very far. 'In general, the first "chiefs" [recognised by the French]

---

[2] Chiefs were given a meagre salary and expected to collect taxes, recruit *corvée labor* and soldiers, etc. Chiefs often were in conflict therefore with both their *Commandant de Cercle* and their own people. (Van Rouveroy van Nieuwaal, 1987). For an example from French Soudan, see the case of Mademba Sy (Roberts, 1991).

were people who had served or entered into other relationships with the European authorities' (Bayart 1993: 135-6) (cf. Buell 1928: 990; Foltz 1965: 12-3). Under French colonial rule, Africans (such as cooks, translators, soldiers and so on) could become chiefs, even if they were not from the region in which they were appointed (Van Rouveroy van Nieuwaal 1987: 6-7). In some cases the pre-colonial authorities sent captives or other caste persons to work with the Europeans (Bayart 1993: 135-6; cf. Geschiere 1993). In the 1930s, due to resistance to colonial rule, the French made a greater effort to align the appointment of chiefs with what they believed was local custom (Van Rouveroy van Nieuwaal 1987).

In 1934 a French decree covering Guinea required that village chiefs be '(...) designated by the authority of family heads' (Alexandre 1970a: 52-3).[3] Then from 1936 the colonial French West African government required that 'the people' be consulted through the medium of village chiefs about the choice of a canton chief (Cowan 1958: 177), reflecting presumed representativity and legitimacy of village chiefs.[4] In 1947 the colonial government issued a decree on 'Indigenous Rule in Senegal,' stating that 'Village chiefs and commissions are elected by direct universal suffrage by the electors, male and female (...)' for a four year term (Alexandre 1970a: 58).[5] But in 1957 the colonial government of French West Africa introduced legislation again limiting suffrage to household heads (as in 1934) and a specified list of notables, while limiting candidacy for the position to those from '(...) families who have a right to the chieftaincy (...)' (Alexandre 1970a: 61).[6] No limits were set on their term.[7]

---

3 Governor General J. Brévié proposed such a policy for the West African colony in 1932 (Cowan, 1958: 44). By the 1940s the British also emphasized the need to introduce elections (Geschiere, 1993: 163). Chiefs were to be replaced by elected 'native authorities'. In the 1944 a district officer in an area with '(...) four times as many "strangers" as natives' argued for elections: 'Here you are, the Bakweri Native Administration receiving approximately 1,500 pounds sterling a year in tax money of which the strangers in your midst pay almost exactly half. You benefit by their money and you decide how their money shall be used (...). This is absolutely contradictory for the things we British believe in and it is against the very things for which we are now fighting a war' (in Geschiere 1993: 163). Ironically, as Geschiere points out, the British adage became 'no taxation without representation'. The Bakweri opposed elections for fear of being outnumbered in their own region. They blocked elections until 1958.

4 Proposed canton chiefs then had to be approved and appointed by the administration. *Arrêté du 28 Décembre 1936* (Cowan 1958: 177).

5 It would be worth digging through the colonial record to find the story behind this short reign of universal suffrage and limited terms at the village level. One can find the reasons evocated by colonial government to stop this first local democracy experience.

6 In the late colonial period twenty-nine of thirty heads of village households elected a chief who was '(...) not of aristocratic origins, nor was he even from

Chiefs, as instruments of French rule, were backed by the French military, allowing them to make and enforce 'native' laws through the system of 'native' tribunals, *l'indigénat*, gather and deliver tax revenues, and recruit workers for *corvée* and soldiers. During the 1940s, however, chiefs lost much of the power given to them by the French colonial state. Powers shifted away from chiefs as the cadres of professional administrators and specialists within the bureaucracy grew and Africans were elected to political office. At the same time the authority of chiefs was weakened as they lost the power to recruit and use forced labour, with the increased role of technical services and with the activities of political parties among rural constituencies. As Cooper (1996: 276) writes of French West Africa, 'the ultimate sign of a shift in the nature of authority was that "traditional chiefs" in the 1950s tried to organise themselves into trade unions, to be set up regionally and regrouped under *Union Fédérale des Syndicates des Chefs Coutumiers de l'A.O.F*'. By the end of the colonial period chiefs had risen to and fallen from the peak of their power.

Post-colonial village chiefs

Although French educated leaders such as Boigny, Touré, Senghor, and Keita turned against chiefs during independence in the new West African nations, the role of the chief in local communities persisted. Chiefs in the new independent states were incorporated into the administration as civil servants, in pursuit of national unity in a manner similar to their role in the French colonial administration (Van Rouveroy van Nieuwaal, 1987: 9-21). Despite these transformations, the village chief remains a principal authority for the great majority of rural West Africans (Alexandre 1970a: 24; Fisiy 1992; Ouali *et al.* 1994: 16; Van Rouveroy van Nieuwaal 1987: 23). However, Ouali *et al.* from Burkina Faso's Decentralisation Commission (1994: 16) noted that their legitimacy is 'full of ambiguity'. The awareness that chiefs were often creations of the administration caused '(...) the *évolué* ['evolved' – meaning the French-educated Africans] to look upon the chief not as a representative of a way of life that is essentially African, but as a tool in the hands of the administration' (Cowan 1958: 186). While chiefs cannot force governments to take any positive action, everywhere in Africa they possess the power to hinder government policies by showing – as discretely as they like – that they do not favour popular cooperation. Consequently, although it is seldom mentioned in speeches and development

that region (...).' and he was not the customary inheritor of the chieftainship. Unfortunately, the administrator objected on the grounds that it would be '(...) a blow to indigenous authority (...)' (Cowan 1958: 178).

plans, government officials in most countries make special efforts to obtain the local chief's consent on various initiatives (Mahwood 1983: 231).[8]

In independent Senegal, there are still laws in force that structure processes for choosing village chiefs. Village chiefs (usually the head of the hereditary male line) are elected by heads of households, who are virtually all male. Generally consensus is required, but in the absence of consensus, elections are organised (RdS 2003: 161, 165). This system is identical to the colonial system first instituted in Guinea in 1934 and later institutionalised throughout the French West African colonies (Alexandre 1970a: 52-3). The household's choice of their village chief in Senegal must be ratified, by nomination, by the *préfet* after the *sous-préfet*'s proposition. But the *préfet*'s decision will be final after the approval of the Minister of *Intérieur* (RdS 2003: 165).

Village chiefs in these Sahelian countries are not necessarily representative of the populations over whom they preside. The official processes in Senegal systematically exclude women. They are not representative – in any procedural sense. Further, in the presidential decree that specifies their roles, there is no formal downward accountability imposed on them (RdS 2003). While villagers may not be able to remove them directly, the government administration can. Disability, serious breaches in exercising administrative functions, condemnation for crimes and offences, or refusal to carry out laws are the primary conditions for terminating a chief's mandate (RdS 2003: 166).

Apart from the systems of chief selection and administrative removal, there are various social mechanisms that can hold village 'customary' authorities or elites locally accountable (see Fisiy 1992: 213; Spierenburg 1995; Mamdani 1996; cf. Hirschman 1970; Scott 1976; Thomson 1995: 14). Hirschman (1970) observed for instance that the negotiating position of subordinate classes was strengthened by their 'exit options' (cf. Scott 1976). In Bayart (1993: 22) it is noted that dependents were not without a voice within either lineage or central societies. They were (more or less) represented in a range of councils, associations and societies in which they often had important functions. Over a third of the monarchies and the chiefdoms that were investigated included councils of commoners who were involved in political decision-making, and more than three-quarters of the chiefdoms,

---

[8] Indeed, as Van Rouveroy van Nieuwaal (1987: 23) states: 'When we speak of chiefs in Africa in the present context we are not speaking about an extinct or even a dying species. We are speaking at most about a threatened one, threatened by the intervention of the legislator and the administration, who are all too often of the opinion that through legal reforms, institutions such as that of chieftaincy, still firmly entrenched in African society, can be blotted out or robbed of their legitimacy'.

and the quasi-totality of the monarchies, had created lay courts of justice. These figures provide some indication of the limitations that the subordinate actors were able to impose on the leaders.

Bayart then gives the example of how village chiefs imposed by the powerful Yatenga monarchy were not forced on the population. Chiefs named by the king, but unwanted or unliked, may be met by silent resistance and obfuscation until '(...) a new assignment will be found for the unfortunate chief' (Bayart 1993: 23). These structures, however, still do not guarantee the accountability of chiefs. Some are despots, and others responsive community leaders, depending on the personality of the chief, the specific history of the village in question, and its location in a larger political economy.[9] International development agencies still, nevertheless, often establish and facilitate their ties to local populations through chiefs, without questioning whether they represent or are accountable to the local population.

In Senegal, chiefs are not always an alternative to the State, but are usually a particular manifestation of state intervention in the rural arena. Current village chiefs are chosen through state-sanctioned processes in which they typically come into the position through inheritance via a patrilineage tracing back to warriors, the founding family of the village, or families chosen by colonial powers to replace antagonistic local leaders. 'The village chief is appointed by the *préfet* [regional administrative authority] upon being proposed by the *sous-préfet*, after the latter has consulted with the chiefs of the village's subdivisions (*carrés*). The decision becomes definitive with the approval of the Minister of the Interior' (article 34, RdS 2003: 165). The chiefs are then administrative authorities in their village under the supervision of the *sous préfet*. Chiefs are charged with – among others tasks – the collection of rural taxes, and the implementation

9 The notion that indigenous African chiefs were despots was used during the early colonial period to justify subjugating them to European standards of conduct. For example: 'When the French undertook the occupation of West Africa they were confronted with a number of native tyrants who cruelly exploited their subjects. Life and property were insecure; slavery and human sacrifice prevailed in many areas. In a few cases, local Almanys had imposed a form of discipline, maintained by terrorism, upon thousands of unwilling subjects' (Buell 1928: 987). Much of this view was probably European projections that served to justify the 'civilizing' mission of colonization. It was clear, however, that under the French, indigenous chiefs were despotic when they could hide behind their French backing. This latter problem helped justify the curtailing of chief's powers over '(...) judicial matters, land and tribute' and more direct control by the French administration (Buell 1928: 987). But these criticisms of chiefs by no means constitute a comparison with or excuse for French colonial administrative practices, which were certainly also despotic, cruel and violent, and fostered despotism among chiefs (Buell 1928; Suret-Canal 1966).

and enforcement of law (Sissokho 2002; RdS 2003). To view chiefs as purely indigenous, 'traditional', local, and accountable representatives of rural populations is to assume too much. Intervening through chiefs may be, as Mamdani (1996) suggests, the continued encapsulation of individuals within community through the administratively driven empowerment of these so-called 'customary' decision makers to 'represent' local people.

The Makacolibantang and Pata cases

The choice of the Makacolibantang Rural Community is based on the history of forest access in this area that was marked, in the early 1990s, by a schism between chiefs and villagers concerning charcoal production by migrants in village forests (Ribot 2000; 1999: 134-5). In the late 1990s, the forest reserve of Pata was the site of a famous and bloody conflict over land between local and migrant farmers. The land in Pata is in a protected forest. Pata was chosen as a comparative case illustrating a struggle over forest access for agriculture.

The Makacolibantang case

In the Makacolibantang Rural Community – a Rural Community being the lowest level of political-administrative jurisdiction usually made up of five to thirty villages – migrant labourers from Guinea and elsewhere in Senegal are engaged in commercial forest exploitation for the production of charcoal. Charcoal is made from wood by partial, oxygen-deprived burning, and is produced to supply the capital city, Dakar, with cooking fuel. Among the ten villages[10] we surveyed, only two villages (Makakoto and Ndoussouan) had autochthonous charcoal makers.

For migrant charcoal makers to work in the forests around villages which are within the 'community forest' domain of the Rural Community, the 1998 Senegalese Forestry Code (article L.4: 8) requires commercial charcoal producers to obtain the authorisation of the President of the elected Rural Council of the Rural Community prior to obtaining wood-cutting permits – delivered by the forest agents. Further, because charcoal makers live in the forest villages, this disposition of the forestry law was extended to village chiefs. The President of the Rural Council is required to obtain the approval of chiefs before allowing authorisation for commercial producers.[11]

---

[10] The ten villages are: Makakoto, Ndoussouan, Maka Cissé, Saré Diamé, Saré Niana, Saré Mala, Manigui Kolikassa, Yorodondé, Missirah Seydou and Yoli Souma.

[11] This requirement is not a written in the new forestry law, but is an informal agreement between Forest Service, merchants and local elected governments. It

Most of the village chiefs we surveyed in the Rural Community of Makacolibantang welcomed charcoal makers in their villages (Makakoto, Ndoussouan, Saré Diamé, Saré Niana and Saré Mala). In some villages (Yoli Souma, Manigui Kolikassa), chiefs want charcoal makers in their villages – stating that the African tradition dictates that foreigners must be welcomed. But they still do not want them to cut wood in the surrounding forests. Chiefs of these villages give their permission to outsiders, in the name of, and despite the opposition of the villagers. In these villages, chiefs see themselves and are seen by villagers as the 'owners' of the villages. So 'the right to make decisions concerning village life and the surrounding forests belongs only to him', according to a Saré Diamé villager (interview, August 2002). Unfortunately, there are no laws or regulations requiring consultation with the population under the chief's authority, and even if they existed, an opposing voice might be stifled, in this socio-cultural context, by the predominant voice of the chief.

There are also chiefs in the Makacolibantang Rural Community who are deeply against charcoal makers lodging in their villages and cutting surrounding forests. These villages are Maka Cissé, Yorodondé and Missira Seydou. The chiefs of these villages followed the wishes of villagers, with whom they collectively made their decision, and on behalf of whom they are now acting against charcoal production in surrounding forests. Among the reasons advanced by the Yorodondé village chief (interview, August 2002): 'It is not in our practices to cut a tree in order to make fuel. We are agriculturalists; we need the forest in order to have our rainy seasons, so we reject everything that could destroy the rainy season'.[12] Even if most village chiefs allied with outsiders, allowing them to exploit forest resources, there still remain three out of ten villages around which chiefs are following the desires of the villagers and are against migrant outsiders producing charcoal.

The Pata case

In the Rural Community of Pata, agriculture is expanding by the clearing of the Pata forest reserve. This is being done by Wolof and Serere farmers moving from the middle of the country in search of land to farm. When settling new lands, these migrant farmers benefit from the cooperation of local and higher political and religious authorities. Despite even violent opposition by most villagers in autochthonous villages in this area, many new villages were founded in 1990s by migrants who left earlier migrant villages founded in the 1970s and 1980s. These new village founders are

---

may have been the subject of a circular or decree, but we have not seen the circular or decree.

[12] This discourse that connects the rains to the forests was likely appropriated from various development and environmental agents who have been saying this for years - whether or not it is a demonstrated link.

supported by the chief of the village to which they first migrated. After settling in a new site, the founder is then joined by migrants – who are generally his relatives – coming from the middle of the country. This is the common pattern. As the village chief of Darou Khoudoss explained (in September 2002): 'I came from the area of Paoskoto [in the Sine Saloum region]. After I first settled in Darou Salam [in the forest reserve of Pata], I founded this village [Darou Khoudoss] in 1993. Then my relatives from Sine Saloum joined me'.[13]

According to the Senegalese forest legislation, clearing is forbidden within a forest reserve unless it is done with an official farming contract given by the Forest Service (Code Forestier 1998: 10, art. L15). In the case of the Pata forest reserve, all official farming contracts have to be signed by both the Forest Service and the Rural Community of Pata, whether for autochthons or migrants. None of the migrants had farming contracts at the time of our fieldwork (September 2002). Despite this, autochthon villagers from Kéréwane, Kohel, and Saré Yoro have witnessed, powerlessly and against their will, the foundation of migrant villages (Sinthiou Telli, Darou Thiendou, Darou Salam, and Sinthiou Abdoul) in the forest reserve over the last twenty-five years.

How can the migrants settle in the forest reserve of Pata and remain there without being expelled? An official of the Regional Forest Service of Kolda (just next to Pata), (interview, September 2002) said:

> They [migrant farmers] benefited from complicity between autochthon populations and administrative, political and even religious authorities, including village chiefs, rural councillors and council presidents. And all these authorities had not failed to use their powers and influence so that persons at fault would not be punished when cases of infringement were brought against them by forest agents.

But he mentioned that during this occupation of the forest reserve his office had been inconsistent and he lacked the means to play his role.

The past inconsistency of the Forest Service and the Rural Council was confirmed by the migrants' attitudes towards the forest reserve when these institutions resolved, in the end, to forbid any new clearing in September 1999. About the ban on clearing a migrant installed in Darou Khoudoss explained (interview, September 2002):

> When I arrived in 2000, I was informed by the village chief about the decision of the Rural Council of Pata and the Forest Service to forbid any new clearing in the forest reserve. Since this date, I have had no land to cultivate. I always

---

[13] Franchette (1999: 7) observed two waves of migration: 'the first villages founded by migrants coming from Sine Saloum (in the 1970s and 1980s) become real jumping-off points for the foundation of new satellite settlements'.

> borrow from the first comers who have land. But I wish to have my own land because those who lend their lands to me today may need it back tomorrow.

This migrant is one of the few latecomers without land who still lives in the villages within the forest reserve. Most of those who came after the clearing ban had to return to their region of origin, the Saloum in the Region of Kaolack.

In both Makacolibantang and Pata there was discrimination over access to land and forest resources. Outsiders from the areas had been privileged by the organisation of the charcoal production establishment, the administration, the technical services (agriculture and forestry), and especially by village chiefs, while the insiders were excluded from forest decision-making processes and, more significantly, from the commercial exploitation of these forests.

Analysis

How can we understand chiefly authority over forest access in these two Rural Communities? What are the main reasons that chiefs privilege outsiders to the detriment of insiders? How do outsiders see the chief's position on forest access? How does the chief retain his authority locally when his actions are contrary to local needs?

Chiefly authority over forest access

Chiefly authority over forest access in both Pata and Maka Rural Communities comes from at least three sources: The first is the traditional identity as descendant of the village founder. Being the descendant of the village founder, the village chief considers and is considered by the villagers as the owner of the village and the only local authority with whom one must deal in order to gain access to the land and forest resource around the village. This conception about the chiefly authority over forest access comes from the widespread rural notion (often evoked in discussions with villagers and chiefs) of 'right of foundation', especially in the South East and Upper Casamance regions of Senegal. Founding a hamlet in a deep forest area is a common investment that a farmer or a herder can make. When this hamlet grows, via arrivals of other farmer or herder families, the founder automatically gains authority over allocation of housing space in the village, and surrounding land and forest. His authority is first recognised by the families that join him, and later by the administrative officers. After he dies, his oldest descendant inherits the position and authority over villagers, land and forests. Access to land and forests depends only on his will. For a typical example, in the village of Saré Diamé (Rural Community of Makacolibantang) when we asked the opinions of the villagers about the chief's decisions on forest access, one villager said 'I cannot disagree with our chief's decision on forests because he is the boss, the owner of the village' (interview, September 2002). The chief in this village was a direct descendant of the founder of the village.

A second source for chiefly authority is their location in a network of higher political-administrative and social authorities who use them for access to village resources (human and natural): Chiefs in most of the charcoal production villages in the Rural Community of Makacolibantang claim to be great friends with local and regional political leaders (based on interviews with chiefs in Makakoto, Saré Diamé, Manigui Kolikassa villages). These leaders also have close relations with charcoal merchants, who use chiefs to gain access to the village and to the forests for their migrant labourers. By influencing local and regional political leaders, merchants gain the chief's approval to lodge their employees in the village and to cut the surrounding forest. This network of influence has worked well because political leaders, outsiders and chiefs share the same political party and sometimes the same religious brotherhood. In March 2000, when the *Parti Socialiste*'s long rule came to an end, most merchants and chiefs changed parties, maintaining the same convenient alliances. In the Rural Community of Pata, this network of political and religious relationships helped chiefs to found new villages in forest reserves. The higher political and religious authorities protected these chiefs – against the sanction of foresters and the judiciary – during the settlement process and while their villages expanded.

A third and final source can be recognised in the fear on the part of villagers of being excluded from the village or of having bad relations with the village owner/chief: In each village of these two areas studied, particularly in the Rural Community of Makacolibantang, villagers continuously fear being excluded from the village by the chief if they go against his will. He is the chief, the 'owner' of the village, and so he has the 'right', according to himself and to the other villagers, to expel any villager. The expelled villager has no chance to refer the chief's decision to higher administrative authorities – such as the *sous-préfet* – because these authorities, often, back the chief's decisions. If a villager protests against a chief's decisions, he risks exclusion from the chief's network of access to the outside world – such as access to commercial opportunities – and loss of the chief's social assistance and support based on his outside sources of income. In a context of widespread rural poverty, this network of access represents a significant source of income for each household head and the chief's assistance and support are wanted and welcomed. However, in the Makacolibantang case, the chiefs who welcome only outsiders in their villages and not in the forest around have no authority over forest access. They recognised that the forests around their villages are under local Forest Service authority. Here chiefly authority covers only village people, dwelling area and land for farming.

Why chiefs privilege outsiders

The cases above show that chiefs usually privilege outsiders in forest access. Two main reasons lead chiefs to do this. First, pressures from multiple actors within the state and religious hierarchies: This pressure comes mainly from the local elected authorities – rural councillors and the deputy from the national assembly – and the local appointed civil servants – *sous-préfets*, foresters. The local elected bodies sometimes participate, physically, by standing next to the merchants and the forest service agents in the process of requesting the chief's approval for charcoal makers' lodging in the villages. Chiefs do not see or talk with them frequently and when they make requests, chiefs are unable to refuse any request coming from these local elected rulers.[14] For example, in the village of Saré Niana the chief revealed that in 1996 the former president of the elected Rural Council of Makacolibantang met him twice in order to ask him to welcome and give lodging to charcoal makers who would be arriving in the near future. The chief did so, and since this insistent request, charcoal makers have been living in the village and cutting the surrounding forest. Many of the village chiefs were faced with the same situation. Sometimes it is the administrative state agents (*sous-préfets* and their assistants) who pressure village chiefs to allow their dependants (merchants or migrant farmers) to harvest forest products or to farm. Faced with such pressures, chiefs conform to the will (and interests) of State agents. And there is a well-rooted and shared sense that the governed can do little against these State powers.

The second reason is the pursuit for personal material interests: When allowing merchants' workers access to forests or giving forest land to clear to migrant farmers, the chief expects some financial bonus or gifts or project from the outsiders. In some cases he expresses his expectations. In the villages of Saré Mala and Ndoussouan (Rural Community of Makacolibantang), before allowing outsiders to lodge in the villages and to access the forests around them, the chiefs demanded that the outsiders bore a well (Ndoussouan) or redig the existing one (Saré Mala). If in Ndoussouan the chief's demand was satisfied while the outsiders were cutting the forest, it was not yet the case eight years later in Saré Mala village, and despite all this, the chief allowed the merchants to stay. Some chiefs receive or demand money or food (bags of rice or millet) from the charcoal merchants in exchange for their approval for forest access. In most of the villages, merchants accepted the deal, and then it was established as a tacit rule for access to the forest. In the village of Saré Diamé, for example, the chief revealed that 'a sum of 15,000 FCFA[15] was given to me by the merchant who

[14] In most of these villages, it is only in the electoral period that chiefs see these local leaders. The leaders come to ask for the votes of villagers, in turn, the chiefs express some grievances of their people.

[15] Around 23 Euro (Approx. US $28, at 13 August 2004).

led the first charcoal makers to the village'. 'Since this first arrival,' continued the chief, 'once a year each merchant who has charcoal makers here gives me between 10,000 and 15,000 FCFA' (interview, September 2002). The material interests of the chief are usually small, but significant in the context of rural livelihoods.

In the villages of Yoli Souma and Manigui Kolikassa, the chiefs declared that their decision-making power did not extend to the forests, and therefore they have no reason to allow access to outsiders or not. This neutrality could be due to the chiefs' ignorance of new forestry laws, or to their powerlessness in front of State agents and outsiders. They have been told for years that the forests belong to the forest service.

Insiders and forest access

While chiefs are balancing political and materials interest in forest access control, what do villagers gain and what do they think of their chief's authority over forest access? In the Rural Community of Makacolibantang, villagers living near the forests, except those of the two villages, Makakoto and Ndoussouan, obtained only indirect income from charcoal production. Villagers' income is from services offered to the charcoal makers, like renting out rooms (around 3,000 FCFA per month), selling meals (around 6,000 FCFA per month), and renting their horse drawn wagons (around 1,500 FCFA per day). These expenses are considerably less than the charcoal makers' income – nevertheless, in some cases the charcoal makers leave without paying for the villagers' services. Further, insiders' access to the commercial benefits of charcoal production is delegated by chiefs and merchants (who control production permits) for the above mentioned functions – providing lodging, food and local transportation – that bring in little income. And in return they see others profit from surrounding forests, while they are left to bear the ecological and economic consequences. This makes villagers unhappy with the chief's decisions.

In the Pata forest reserve, the villagers from autochthonous villages of Kéréwane, Kohel and Saré Yoro were unhappy to see the forest that they had protected for at least fifty years damaged in the last twenty years by outsiders pursuing commercial interests. The migrants farmed large areas of groundnuts for significant cash incomes. The vast migrant farms signifycantly disrupted traditional livelihoods in the forest reserve. So autochthon villagers are resentful and fearful of migrants and are angry with the local elected and appointed authorities and higher political and religious leaders who facilitated forest clearing by migrants.

Conclusion

The discourse of outsiders is consistent. Rural councillors and administrative agents, foresters and development agents claim that the chiefs are legitimate and represent the village. But villagers tolerate chiefs out of a sense of tradition and fear. Their legitimacy does not derive from the good deeds they do or their accountability to the population, but is exerted by dint of their position of power reinforced by outside authorities and tradition. The chiefs are caught in a contradictory double role – as agents of the outside world and as ostensible representatives of the population – so often evoked as a source of double resentment in the post colonial literature. Despite this double resentment, chiefs are still privileging outsiders while the forests are being exploited and the anger of the insiders is growing. Despite this resentment, outsiders, such as development agents, NGOs, foresters and others still empower chiefs by using them as instrumental intermediaries – pulleys – for gaining access to the forest well.

Village chiefs can hardly be said to represent or be accountable to the village population. But villagers are, as Mamdani (1996) describes, 'encapsulated' in tradition by a set of outside actors whose interest is to maintain villagers as subjects so as to facilitate access to forests for their own clients. Requiring elected councillors to consult village chiefs before permitting forest access further extinguishes the voices of rural people by the legitimisation of these non-representative local authorities. This looks suspiciously like a modern reproduction of micro-indirect rule.

If chiefs do not represent local people, why do environmental and development agents like them so much? If local people do not like them, how can the idea that they are 'legitimate' justify working with them? Weber (1982) did not place a moral spin on legitimacy. He viewed it as *status quo* – things are legitimate when there is no open conflict. But are intervening agents aware that they are supporting authorities whose legitimacy often stems from fear, backing by the state (as under indirect rule), lack of alternatives, or lack of any sense that there are other options? Legitimacies based on different forms of coercion should be viewed differently from legitimacies based on appreciation, respect or representation. Environmentalists and other development agents and practitioners should take a critical view of customary, traditional, indigenous and other such local authorities if their interventions are to be emancipatory.

References

ALEXANDRE, P. (1970) Chiefs *commandants* and clerks: Their relationship from conquest to decolonisation in French West Africa, in: Crowder, M. and Ikime, O. (Eds) *West African Chiefs: Their changing status under colonial rule and independence*, New York: Africana Publishing Company, pp. 2-13.

BASSETT, T.J. and D.E. CRUMMEY (Eds) (1993) *Land in African agrarian systems*, Madison: University of Wisconsin Press.

BAYART, J.-F. (1993) *The state in Africa: The politics of the belly*, London: Longman.

BUELL, R.L. (1928) *The native problem in Africa*, Volumes I and II, New York: The MacMillan Company.

COOPER, F. (1996) *Decolonization and African society: The labor question in French and British Africa*, Cambridge: Cambridge University Press.

COWAN, L.G. (1958) *Local government in West Africa*, New York: Columbia University Press.

CROWDER, M. and O. IKIME (Eds) (1970) *West African chiefs: Their changing status under colonial rule and independence*, New York: Africana Publishing Company.

DIOP, M. (1992) *Sénégal: Trajectoires d'un état*, Paris, Khartala.

FISIY, C.F. (1992) *Power and privilege in the administration of law: Land law reforms and social differentiation in Cameroon*, Research Reports 1992/48, Leiden: African Studies Centre.

FOLTZ, W.J. (1965) *From French West Africa to the Mali Federation*, New Haven: Yale University Press.

FORTES, M. and E.E. EVANS-PRITCHARD (1987) *African political systems*, London: KPI Press.

FRANCHETTE, S. (1999) *Colonisation des terres sylvo-pastorales et conflits fonciers en Haute Casamance*, Collection tenures foncières pastorales N° 13, London: IIED.

GESCHIERE, P. (1993) Chiefs and colonial rule in Cameroon: Inventing chieftaincy, French and British style, *Africa*, 63(2): 151-75.

HIRSCHMAN, A.O. (1970) *Exit, voice and loyalty: Responses to decline in firms, organizations and states*, Cambridge: Harvard University Press.

KINI, R. (1995) An evaluation study of natural forest management for wood fuel production in the Sahel: A Burkina Faso case, submitted to Michigan State University in Partial Fulfillment of the Requirements for the Degree of Master of Science, Department of Resource Development.

LUND, C. (1998) *Law, power and politics in Niger: Land struggles and the rural code*, Hamburg: Lit Verlag.

MAHWOOD, P. (1983) The place of traditional political authority in African pluralism, *Civilisations*, Vol. XXXII, No. 2 1982-Vol. XXXIII, No. 1 1983, pp. 209-37.

MAMDANI, M. (1996) *Citizen and subject: Contemporary Africa and the legacy of late colonialism*, Princeton: Princeton University Press.

MCINTOSH, A. (1990) Rethinking chieftaincy and the future of rural local government: A preliminary investigation, *Transformation* (Durban), 13: 27-45.

OUALI, F., P. KIEMDÉ and D. YAMÉOGO (1994) *Etude de base sur l'état de la décentralisation au Burkina*, summary report, Commission Nationale de la Décentralisation, Primature, Burkina Faso, June 1994.

OUÉDRAOGO, H.M.G. (1994) Les coutumes relatives à la gestion des ressources naturelles au Burkina Faso, FAO, Programme de Coopération Technique, FAO-LEG: TCP/BKF/2352, Rome, March 1994.

RANGER, T. (1993) The invention of tradition revisited: The case of colonial Africa, in: Ranger, T. and Vaughan, O. (Eds) *Legitimacy and the state in twentieth-century Africa: Essays in honour of A.H. Kirk-Greene*, Oxford: MacMillan Press, pp. 62-111.

RDS (2003) Décret no. 96-228 du 22 mars 1996 modifiant le décret no. 72-636 du 29 mai 1972 relatif aux attributions des chefs de circonscriptions administratives et chefs de village, *Le Recueil des textes de la décentralisation*, Edition Novembre 2003.

RIBOT, J.C. (1999) Decentralization, participation and accountability in Sahelian forestry: Legal instruments of political-administrative control, *Africa*, 69(1).

RIBOT, J.C. (2000) Rebellion, representation and enfranchisement in the forest village of Makacolibantang, Eastern Senegal, in: Zerner, C. (Ed.): *People, plants and justice. The politics of nature conservation*, Columbia University Press, pp. 134-58.

RIBOT, J.C. *Decentralization of natural resources: Encountering and countering resistance*, Washington, DC: World Resources Institute.

ROBERTS, R. (1997) Conflicts over property in the Middle Niger Valley at the beginning of the twentieth century, *African Economic History*, 25: 79-96.

SCHUMACHER, E.J. (1975) *Politics, bureaucracy and rural development in Senegal*, Berkeley: University of California Press.

SCOTT, J.C. (1976) *The moral economy of the peasant: Rebellion and subsistence in Southeast Asia*, New Haven: Yale University Press.

SISSOKHO, O. (2002). Cas de l'exploitation du bois dans la zone de Makacoulibantang, Aspects Juridiques, draft report prepared for World Resources Institute, May 2002.

SPIERENBURG, M. (1995). *The role of the Mhondoro cult in the struggle for control over land in Dande (Northern Zimbabwe): Social commentaries and the influence of adherents*, Center for Applied Social Sciences, University of Zimbabwe, Harare, and Amsterdam School for Social Science Research, Amsterdam, October 1995.

SURET-CANALE, J. (1966) La fin de la chefferie en Guinée, *Journal of African History*, VII(3): 459-93.

THOMSON, J. and C. COULIBALY (1994) Decentralization in the Sahel: Regional Synthesis, *SAH/D*, 94(427), Regional Conference on Land Tenure and Decentralization in the Sahel, Praia, Cape Verde, CILSS, OECD, Club du Sahel, January 1994.

VAN ROUVEROY VAN NIEUWAAL, E. (1987) Chiefs and African states: Some introductory notes and an extensive bibliography on African chieftaincy, *Journal of Legal Pluralism*, 25-6.

14

Fighting over crumbs? Small valleys in West Africa as a new locus of land claims

Mayke Kaag

Introduction: Small valleys in West Africa

> *Senegal, January 2003.*
>
> *It is already two months into the dry season and the fields have turned into brown and grey. In the small valley stretching out along the village, however, everything is still green and fresh. Looking at it from the plateau, it resembles an ancient Italian landscape painting: Dispersed over the valley, people, men and women, old and young, are weeding their small plots, taking water from the small bore holes they have made here and there, while others are sitting in the shadow of a tree, enjoying the view of their green gardens. It makes a peaceful and harmonious picture, one of calm prosperity. In this chapter it will, however, become clear that the agricultural activities in the valley are not only a sign of prosperity but also tell a tale of poverty and marginalization. Furthermore, it will be shown that behind the apparent peace hides an ongoing history of competing land claims.*

All over Africa can be found small valleys, such as the *dambos* in central and eastern Africa, the *vlei* in Zimbabwe, the *fadama* in Nigeria, and the *boli* in Sierra Leone. From a geological perspective, a distinction can be made between different types in this kind of landscape, based on form, soil hydrology and so on. However, as this chapter is not concerned with technical aspects, I will use 'small valleys' as a generic term to indicate shallow grassy depressions found in the headwater zones of drainage systems that are inundated annually for at least some days and that have hydromorphic soils. This corresponds closely to what Zeppenfeld and Vlaar (1990) call *bas-fonds* in French.

Until now, small valleys in Africa and their uses have received only scant attention from researchers and policy-makers. While the droughts of the 1970s and 1980s reinforced interest in agriculture and livestock keeping, most attention has been directed to problems such as the low productivity of the main cereal crops, the decline in world market prices for main cash crops like peanuts and cotton, and overgrazing. Most often, large-scale solutions have been proposed, for example large-scale irrigation works or mechanization. From this perspective, small valleys evidently do not have much to offer, for they are small (mostly varying in width from a few metres to over one kilometre) and are not suitable for mechanized agriculture and large-scale exploitation. However, taken together the area they cover is substantial. In Zimbabwe, for instance, it is estimated that there are 1.3 million hectares of *vleis* (Whitlow 1989); Turner (1986) estimates that on average, *dambos* occupy two per cent to thirty per cent of the total land area with an average of ten per cent over extensive areas. Furthermore, they have specific interesting characteristics: Many small valleys are very well suited for small-scale agricultural and horticultural uses utilizing superficial water sources, meaning that their use is not restricted to the rainy season only. Further, because the areas cultivated are most often not very large, their exploitation can be rather intensive and adapted to the characteristics of the different parts. Small valleys are also important for cattle keeping. At the start of the dry season, the cattle can feed themselves from the leftovers of the harvest that remain in the fields. But at the end of the dry season and at the beginning of the rainy season, herding in small valleys may be important to overcome fodder shortages. One of the main problems is that small valleys generally are very susceptible to water erosion. They may also dry up and lose their capacity to retain water. (Turner 1986: 343-6).

The limited literature that is available on small valleys in Africa is mostly composed of articles on their geomorphology and more or less technical works on their agricultural possibilities and the best ways to put them into use (Raunet 1984; 1985; Vernier and Hamasselbe 1988; Berton 1988; Whitlow 1989). Lavigne Delville, Bouju and Le Roy (2000) stand out in combining a focus on improved management of small valleys through irrigation schemes with a perspective on land tenure issues. Bell and Hotchkiss (1991) should also be mentioned, as theirs is one of the few studies that analyse the use of small valleys in the context of people's livelihood strategies. Apart from these publications, there are a number of reports and studies, for example by agricultural services or students, that not have been made available on a large scale.[1] Among them there are a few that examine the use of small valleys in their local context and that pay some attention to diverse historical developments that have had an influence on the use of these valleys. Most studies, however, fail to pay attention to farmers' strategies and only point to economic and demographic factors explaining the use made of small valleys. The effect is that the use of valleys is depicted merely as part of a unilinear process of agricultural development, fuelled by economy and demography only, while the interaction between people's agency and longer term processes in the use of these valleys remains hidden from view. This is a pity, as small valleys constitute a particularly fascinating study subject in this respect.

More specifically, in this chapter it will be argued that small valleys are particularly interesting in terms of emerging dynamics of claiming control over land. Many of them have only recently been taken into agricultural use. As they do not usually constitute part of the agricultural land traditionally controlled by local families and will often be used for purposes other than traditional crops and agricultural activities, they are being subjected to new strategies of land claims. People invent new ways of claiming control over land in such valleys by combining old and new rules, by building new alliances or by revitalizing old ones, and by referring to different authorities. These authorities, customary rulers and state agents alike, have to position themselves in this dynamic in a way that offers them chances to enhance their power, but that also often puts their legitimacy to the test.[2]

I will investigate these emergent dynamics of claiming control over land with the case of a small valley in southern central Senegal. In addition to analysing the strategies of the users of the valley, I will pay particular attention to the role of different authorities, especially the village chiefs as traditional power holders, and the rural council which is the state representative at the local level. At the end of the 1980s and the beginning of the 1990s in a couple of years the valley was cleared and put under cultivation by local farmers. This can be considered an anarchistic act, as nobody asked permission from the rural council, the administrative body in charge of land allocation. The rural council, however, certainly had an influence on the clearing process – but so did the village chiefs. Furthermore, women, who according to local custom have no rights over land, started to claim rights in the valley on the basis of this same customary law. Cattle-holders who saw their customary rights in the valley being violated turned to the rural council, which tried to settle their claim by evasion, a strategy that is often associated

---

1 Zeppenveldt and Vlaar (1990) offer a synthesis of a number of these studies.

2 It follows that I consider power as a means used by actors in order to act and to adopt a position; but power at the same time sets the baseline and the margins for actions and the positions of actors, in the sense that it is an expression of larger processes and phenomena.

in particular with customary authorities and conflict settlement (Cf. Berry 1993; Mathieu 1996; Lund 1998).

The case shows that the dynamics of claiming land can fruitfully be studied in areas that constitute a new locus of land claims, as it reveals how old rules are reinvented and how new ones develop in the interaction between land users and authorities, against the background of ecological, economic and political change. I will argue, however, that the importance of what happens in the valley is not restricted to this small area alone. Studying the dynamics of claiming land in the valley may enhance our understanding of land claiming dynamics and social transformations in (local) society at large. For land claiming practices and strategies may be considered as an expression of people's livelihood strategies. Studying land claims may thus offer a means for obtaining an insight into these strategies. Moreover, many authors have stressed the fact that land tenure in Africa is strongly embedded in social, political, and economic relationships and processes (Bassett and Crummey 1993; Berry 1989; 1993; 2001; Blundo 1996; Hesseling 1992; Juul and Lund 2002). Consequently, studying land claims and how these are pursued means gaining a better idea of these relationships. New claims and new strategies for pursuing these claims may be an indication of how relations are changing, not only between groups of people in society, but also between different authorities, because with traditional village authorities and decentralized state representatives both claiming a say in land matters, often nothing less than the (re)definition of their respective competencies and areas of control is what is at stake.

Case: The clearing of a valley in southern central Senegal

Context: A brief history of land tenure and agrarian change

My case concerns the rural community of Kaymor in southern central Senegal, some twenty km north of the Gambian border in the department of Nioro du Rip. Here, between the end of the 1980s and the mid 1990s, a small valley, stretching between a couple of villages in the community that always had been bush and was only in use as a cattle path, was taken into agricultural use. Elsewhere (Kaag 2001), I have discussed in greater detail how the valley became attractive to the inhabitants of Kaymor as land for farming by the coincidence of economic, ecological and political processes.[3] In this

[3] The history of this small valley and its interlinkages with larger processes of economic, ecological, political and social change in the area constituted the main focus of my Ph.D. research. The fieldwork data used in this chapter were collected during field research from October 1995-November 1996, September-November 1998, and during a short visit paid to the research area in January 2003.

chapter, I will instead focus on the process of clearing and the way in which land claims were asserted in this process. But for a good understanding of these dynamics and the importance of the valley, I think it is useful to outline firstly local land tenure arrangements and national land law and the developments that contributed to the valley being taken into cultivation.

According to the customary rule, land belongs to those families that have cleared it. Underlying this system is the basic territorial rule that is the right of the founding family of a village or clan, normally represented by the village chief. Land inheritance is based on the patrilineal transmission of rights. In former days it was the eldest male, most often a younger brother of the deceased, who was the first inheritor. Only when there were no male representatives of one generation left were rights transmitted to the next generation. This system has been transformed by the increased influence of Islamic law (Venema 1978), and nowadays rights are transmitted from a father to his sons. Women traditionally are not allowed to inherit land. This is justified by the fact that upon their marriage they normally leave their family home.

Apart from these hereditary rights, several forms of temporary rights to land developed. Firstly, a family could lend a piece of land for a period of time that was limited but not agreed beforehand. The one who received the plot was not obliged to pay. This situation occurred when a family had more land than it could cultivate at a certain moment. The practice was called *dink*. Another form was called *dogal*. In this case, the duration of the loan was clearly determined beforehand, most often one year, and some form of payment was implied. Apart from these practices, land is also distributed within the family. The land that is distributed each year by the head of the family or household to his dependents (the women in the family, the children who have reached the age of being able to till a plot themselves, and other adults who form part of the household) is given in *abal* (Venema 1978).

The Law on the National Domain of 1964 made virtually all rural land state property, which in turn is given in usufruct to the farmers. In practice, the families that already cultivated the land are allowed to continue as before, although under the ultimate supervision of the state. Only when land is not exploited sufficiently can it be taken away and allotted to another. In addition, one can claim rights to a piece of land when one has cultivated it for more than three years. This means that local land rules are recognized, although within the limits set by national law: Families can claim rights to their land as long as they continue to till it, but fallow periods of more than a few years as well as longer term lease contracts such as *dink* may create problems, in that the rural council or the temporary tenant may claim the land on the basis of national legislation. An additional problem in this respect is the fact that the criteria of 'putting into use' (*mise en valeur*) are not well defined (Traore 1991).

The Law on the National Domain implied a total revision of the Senegalese administrative infrastructure with the creation of rural communities consisting of a number of adjacent villages. The administration of these new entities is in the hands of a rural council, made up of elected locals with a five-year mandate. Its tasks are the application of the Law on the National Domain by allocating and re-allocating land, and the execution of modest development projects. The council has its own budget, supplied mainly from the taxes of the rural population.[4] This does not prevent the village chief from continuing to play an important role at village level. However, his position inevitably changes with the introduction of a new layer of administration. In the following, we will see that both authorities had an important part in the clearing of the valley that constitutes this chapter's case-study. But before broaching this topic, I will outline the developments that contributed to the fact that at the end of the 1980s the local population became interested in the valley as farming land.

Some 100 years ago, peanuts were introduced into the area as a cash crop by the French colonial power, in addition to crops such as millet and sorghum that had already been cultivated for centuries as a food crop. The millet was cultivated in the vicinity of the village. On the higher plateau, farmers started to practise a rotation of millet and peanuts. At that time, the valley was still virgin, densely wooded bush; the soil was more or less like a swamp, because of its poor situation. Women used to collect fruits and other bush products around its edges, and men hunted game. During the dry season, the valley was used as a watering place for cattle and as a cattle-track, but during the rainy season it was too damp and too densely wooded. In that time, the farmers were not yet interested in the valley as an agricultural area, because there was still farming land in abundance, and because the priority of most farmers was peanuts. This crop needs relatively sandy and dry soils; the moist and clayey soil of the valley is too heavy for growing peanuts.

But times changed. The population increased. From the 1950s onwards, the government promoted the use of animal traction and chemical fertilizer. This was intended to bring about an intensification of agriculture, so that the farmers would not increase their area under cultivation, but instead could get

---

4 The installation of the rural communities administered by a rural council from 1972 onwards was the first phase in the Senegalese decentralization process. The second step was taken in 1990, when the president of the rural council was given greater authority to the detriment of higher levels of administration, in particular with respect to budgetary matters. The third stage was set in motion in 1996, when some competencies that previously had been the domain of the central state were delegated to the rural communities, which were given greater responsibilities in several areas such as health care, education and natural resource management.

a higher production from their present fields (cf. Benoît-Cattin 1986). It turned out, however, that while the farmers did adopt these innovations, they frequently used them to increase their area under cultivation (Yung 1992). This had to do with the fact that from the 1970s onwards economic and climatic circumstances became progressively more insecure. Prices for peanuts went down and there were years of severe drought. In this situation of insecurity, extending the areas under cultivation instead of trying to achieve as high as possible a production on a small piece of land was a rational strategy.

The extension of the areas under cultivation contributed to an increasing scarcity of agricultural lands. At the same time, the fertility of the soils declined as a consequence of the cultivation of one sole crop and the absence of rotation (mono cropping), and because of the fact that the fields were no longer left fallow but were cultivated every year. In this way, the soil did not have the time to recover. Erosion had always been a problem, but got worse over time. Because most vegetation cover had been removed for agriculture, no plants were left to protect the soil from the rains and the wind. In the 1970s, periods of drought aggravated the situation. Many of the problems, however, could still be eased by the use of fertilizer. The farmers could obtain fertilizer on credit, from the co-operatives that were set up by the government. During times of food shortage, the state also offered food free.

In the framework of a structural adjustment program, however, the state retreated from assistance to the agricultural sector in the mid-eighties, having as a consequence that the farmers could no longer obtain seed and fertilizer on credit (Freud *et al.* 1997). This made it less attractive for them to keep growing peanuts, also because the prices for peanuts continued to decline (Duruflé 1994). Instead, they began to focus on food crops such as millet and maize and to diversify as much as possible to spread the risks of bad harvests and of low prices on the market. People got interested in new crops like melons and vegetables as sources of income.

It was in the context of these changes that the valley became attractive as an agricultural area, because in the valley there was still virgin land that was indeed fertile, did not need any chemical fertilizer and was well suited for cultivating crops such as maize, rice and vegetables for the sake of diversification. Besides, in the valley the soil used to stay moist for a long time after the rainy season had ended, while because of the climatic changes of the last thirty years it had lost most of its swampy character.

The clearing process

The coincidence of macro-economic, political and ecological processes described above constitutes the background for the massive clearance of the valley. The exact process and pace of clearing, however, are to a large extent the product of local political and social developments. It is precisely by means of a study of this process that much can be learned about the theme of customary authority versus decentralized state authority, as we will see in the following. The process of clearing can be divided into two phases. The first, in which clearing is still sparse, is to be considered as the preamble to the second phase that can be characterised as 'the great rush'.

The first phase started in about 1977 and went on until 1989. The village chief of Kaymor, the main village of the rural community, was the first to clear in order to start a garden. He had been a combatant in the Second World War and after that had served as a policeman in many parts of Senegal, before returning to Kaymor to succeed his brother as village chief. He had seen gardening in other parts of Senegal and thought that the soil of the valley would be very suitable for this. He recounts that in the beginning the people in the village thought that it was just the odd idea of a former combatant, but when they saw that the garden was doing very well, they became interested as well. One year later, a big trader, politician and the deputy of the imam of the grand mosque at the time,[5] followed the village chief's example. But after that clearing occurred only sporadically until the end of the 1980s. One of the reasons for this was that the rural council claimed that the valley was intended to be a cattle path. Another reason was that until the mid 1980s, before the New Agricultural Policy that was part of the Structural Adjustment Programme, most farmers were still very much involved in peanut growing, and the soil of the valley was not very suitable for this.

In Passy Kaymor, a small village situated on the other side of the valley, clearing also started in this period. Here too it was someone who had travelled a lot and at the same time belonged to the village elite as a member of one of the oldest families of the village who started to clear a plot. He judged that the valley was very suitable for cultivating rice, as he had seen in the Casamance in southern Senegal.

It is evident that the local initiators are local notables. They have sufficient room to do as they please, and they have the courage to pursue their goals without bothering too much about the ideas of others. We will see below that people who have a more marginal position in society, such as immigrants, people of low birth and adherents of the opposition party, only start clearing when they are 'backed' by similar actions of people who have a more secure position in local society.

In addition to these local initiatives, during this period some interventions by non-locals also contributed to a start of clearing the valley. Two women's groups, one in Passy Kaymor and one in another village, started gardening in the valley under the guidance of some outsiders, a Peace Corps volunteer and later on a French priest setting up development activities in the zone. Gardening can be considered a new activity in this area. Women were used to growing vegetables such as okra, hibiscus and peppers behind their huts.

---

[5] He was appointed imam in 1987.

They used these for the sauce when it was their turn to prepare the meal. Off-season gardening, however, which is the case here, is something very different. Not only were new species introduced, such as lettuce, carrots and cabbage, but also new techniques, such as growing in beds and the use of chemical products for fighting plant diseases. These all were easily adopted, however. As someone remarked: 'It is not so difficult to teach an agriculturalist to practise agriculture'.

Let us consider the role of the rural council, as it has as a major task the allotment of rights to land that has not yet been put to use. In fact, the village chief and the deputy imam in Kaymor had not asked for an allocation. However, they had done this later on at the beginning of the 1980s when the sub-prefect had promised to finance a well in their gardens but for this demanded that their rights to the plots be officially recorded. The women's groups had also ultimately asked for an official allocation at the instance of their donors. The rural council had approved of these demands. At the same time, however, it had also warned against further clearing of the valley. Certainly during the period 1986-1990, when more farmers showed an intention to clear in the valley, the council officially stated that the valley was intended as a cattle path and should not be put to agricultural use. This was frequently repeated after the Friday prayers at the Kaymor mosque. These warnings appear to have had an effect, as massive clearings did not take place during this period.

The rural council was able to enforce its view, as during this period the councillors acted firmly as an unity. Their unity was based on their all being local notables and all members of one political party, the *Parti Socialiste* that was the ruling party at the national level.

This was going to change at the end of the 1980s, when factionalism sprang up in the community.[6] Factionalism has always been a characteristic of Senegalese politics and often took the form of rivalry between two factions within the PS, mainly concerning access to the resources available at the national level. A strong vertical political organization was thus constructed, linking the local to the national, a logic from which the newly created rural councils could not escape (see, for example, Blundo 1998). In the rural community of Kaymor, however, the political family was rather homogeneous and tied to only one politician at the national level. Here, factionalism only became a reality at the end of the 1980s as a result of the 'parachuting' of national politicians in search of clients. The rural council became divided into two factions, each having relations with a different PS politician at a higher level. This fact contributed strongly to the second phase of clearing the valley. As the rural council no longer acted as an unity, it could no longer prevent farmers from clearing. As a result, during this phase

---

6 See for a more extensive treatment of the appearance of factionalism in Kaymor and its effects on politics and social life, Kaag 2001; Kaag and Venema 2002.

(1990-1996) massive clearing occurred, until in 1996 virtually all of the valley had been taken into agricultural use. By this time, the valley had been transformed in a patchwork of small plots, claimed by a diverse range of local inhabitants: Autochthonous people, migrants, family heads, younger people, women, people from high and low birth, rich and poor people. None of these late clearers had permission from the rural council. The rural council still claimed that the valley was a cattle path and should not be cultivated. The factionalism that had taken hold of the rural council had, however, seriously weakened its position vis-à-vis the local population. The farmers profited from this situation and could pursue their own goal of having a plot in the valley without fear of being punished.

Claiming land

A more detailed examination reveals that land claims were advanced in different ways and with reference to different rules and authorities. A distinction can be made between the individual level, referring to the claims made by the different farmers to a piece of land, and the communal level, at which level farmers and cattle holders contested each other's land claims. After an analysis of the practices of making claims on both levels, the observations made will then be screened with attention to the role of rules and authorities.

The individual level: Claiming plots

In 1995/1996, I investigated all plots in that part of the valley that was adjacent to the villages of Kaymor and Passy Kaymor. I found that out of the 54 plots, 37 belonged to men, fifteen to women and two to women's groups. Most plots were 0.25 to 0.5 ha. Most people practised one or more forms of diversification: Diversification of crops, diversification of plots, or diversification of activities. For some of them, their plot in the valley meant a diversification of the totality of their plots or of their activities; in addition, most people practised a diversification of their crops and/or varieties in the valley. Rice, millet, maize and melons were popular among the men, while the women often grew rice, maize and vegetables.

This diversification was partly on purpose, in a deliberate attempt to spread risks: When one crop or one variety did not produce well, there were always the others that might do well. But the diversity is also an expression of a lack of means. The people sow the seeds they have at their disposal; when the seeds of one variety are not available to them at a certain moment, they are obliged to adapt their plans and strategies. Added to this is the fact that farming in the valley is a rather risky affair: Often, for instance, one loses one's first sowing because of water erosion or water that remains stagnant in the field. It can be concluded that cultivating in the valley requires much flexibility and adaptation, and a great deal of hard work, but that it also offers the farmers the opportunity to be flexible and to adapt to changing circumstances.

Apart from the village chief and the imam in Kaymor and the women's group of Passy Kaymor, no one had an official allocation from the rural council, but they claimed that their plot was theirs because they had cleared the land. At the end of the 1990s the lending of plots started to occur, but remained relatively rare. Despite the illegal status of their plots, people invested much in them, for instance by planting trees, building fences, and combating water erosion by setting up ridges of stones.

The land claims laid by diverse women are particularly interesting. While in Wolof society women traditionally do not control land and were only given a plot of land each year by their husband to cultivate peanuts, this practice became less common in the course of the 1970s and 1980s with the growing scarcity of land and seed for sowing. This meant that progressively more women came to be without a piece of land to cultivate. When the great rush to the valley set in, some women eagerly seized the opportunity and also started to clear a plot in the valley. Some of them told me that they had done the heavy work of removing the tree trunks with their own hands. And because they had cleared it themselves, they claimed that the land was theirs, and that it would still be theirs when they were dead. There were also some women who had paid others to do the clearing; they considered themselves as the proprietor of their plot as well.

It seemed that the men did not have problems with this 'hijacking' of the customary rule that whoever clears a piece of land may consider himself as the owner of the land. A woman told me that her husband had even recommended that she clear a plot for herself, when she asked to be allowed to use a part of his parcel. As long as the men had no additional costs or work, they were in favour of their women clearing a plot. Another benefit is of course that the women's production from their plot contributes to the overall food security of the family. It must be said, however, that not all women who cultivate a plot in the valley have cleared their piece of land themselves. Some women have a part of their husband's plot to cultivate vegetables, or they use a piece of land on the basis of a kind of *dogal* agreement.

All villages situated along the valley have one or more women's groups, informally or more formally organized associations that engage in different activities, such as running a millet mill or tilling a collective field. As mentioned earlier, the women's group of Passy Kaymor was one of the first to start a garden in the valley with the help of a French priest. At his urging, they asked for an official allocation of the plot they cultivated. Some other women's groups that started to work with external donors in the course of years did the same. Other women's groups received a plot from someone in the village. The women's group of Kaymor, for instance, received a plot on loan from the husband of the chairwoman of the group. But when because of tensions within the group the women did not become very productive and he wanted to cultivate melons on the plot himself, he started to cultivate the plot again himself. The women were left empty-handed.

Within the gardens of the women's groups, different methods of organization are found. Some groups do all the work in the garden collectively, and share the money after the produce has been sold. In other cases, the women each have their own individual bed with vegetables. They can claim a share because of their membership of the women's group.

In 1996 a large project for the communal management of natural resources (PCGRN – *Projet Communautaire de Gestion des Ressources Naturelles)*, financed by USAID, was started in the community. The project's policy was only to work with groups that had officially registered and that had a piece of land that was officially allotted by the rural council.

Conflicts between the farmers over land in the valley started to present themselves as the valley was taken into agricultural use more and more. Some cases were reported of farmers who tried to claim other people's land in the valley by simply enlarging their area under cultivation, or by moving the signs of demarcation between the plots. These conflicts could still be settled without interference; some conflicts continued to exist, but went on without direct clashes.

The communal level: Competition between agriculture and animal husbandry

The valley had always been used as a cattle path to lead the cattle to the watering places and from the one grazing area to another. The progressive clearing of the valley increasingly caused problems for the passage of the animals, and cases were reported of animals that caused damage to the plants when entering a plot in the valley. Most farmers took this for granted and tried to protect their crops with fences, keeping watch at times when the herds were expected to pass. Their modest attitude was inspired by their having no permission for clearing from the rural council. They claimed, however, to have a right to cultivate in the valley because, they said, the agricultural possibilities of this part of the community's territory are much more important than the activities of the cattle holders.

The cattle holders, for their part, were not so demanding either; they only wanted to have some space for their animals to pass. In fact, most cattle holders are also agriculturalists, and thus there was no clash between two opposing social groups. What frustrated them, however, was the fact that they felt that their problems were not being taken seriously and that animal husbandry was being marginalized in favour of agriculture. When the valley was progressively taken into use for agricultural purposes, the cattle holders in the community decided to take action and asked the rural council to officially delineate a cattle path in the valley. This was granted and the cattle holders collected the money that was necessary to have the officials of the rural extension service delineate the circuit. But the rains came before anything had happened, and when the cattle holders asked the rural council for an explanation, the president answered that they had to wait another year because it would be a pity to destroy the seedlings. Due to the continued pressure by the cattle holders, the following year the case was again considered by the rural council, and after lengthy deliberation it was decided that a cattle circuit of fifty m would be delineated. Such a circuit is called a *parcours d'arrangement*. This is a rather informal arrangement between farmers and cattle holders in which the rural council plays the role of arbiter. As well as this kind of circuit, there is the more official circuit that has a width of 100 m. But for this form, a more official procedure has to be followed, with the approval of the prefect and so on, and delineation by the rural extension service.[7]

It can be concluded that the council first tried to let go, and after that tried to solve the matter by fixing a *parcours d'arrangement*, in view of the delicacy of the affair. With this arrangement, they also wanted to preclude the interference of higher levels of the administration and to keep the affair local. This solution, however, did not prove to be a real solution. First of all, it appeared that the farmers did not adhere to the decision taken; they moved the marking pegs or they sowed within the limits of the circuit. Secondly, a cattle path of 50 m is simply too narrow for allowing the animals to pass without causing damage to the crops, if the fields are not well fenced.

Rules and authorities

When considering the above with an account of the different rules and authorities playing a role, it can be concluded that at the individual level farmers base their claims merely on customary rules and avoid the rural council. At the communal level, the rural council is indeed consulted by the cattle holders. Its strategy is, however, not so much to give more clarity and to fix claims to land, but to evade clear measures and to invent temporary solutions that will not offend anybody too much. This is certainly not the attitude expected by those outside intervening agencies that encourage people to settle claims to land at the office of the rural council in order to be able to invest in a secure way! It shows that it is wrong to differentiate rigidly between customary and national law, and between customary and state authorities. State authorities may pursue strategies that are normally associated with customary tenure, and vice versa (cf. Nijenhuis 2003). In addition, it is wrong to assume that when people base themselves on customary law, as a consequence national rules and state authorities do not play any role whatsoever. We have already seen that the strength of the rural council indeed played a role in people's decisions to clear a plot in the valley. In fact, with respect to the current dynamics of land tenure in Kaymor, the

---

[7] Source: interview with the *sous-préfet* and minutes of rural council meetings, archives of the *sous-préfecture*, Médina Sabakh.

working of customary law and national law, as well as the role of customary authorities and the rural council, can no longer be understood in isolation from one another. This is also illustrated by the following.

When looking at the process of the great rush to the valley, it appears that this process went into top gear earlier in Passy Kaymor (1990) than in Kaymor (1993). Because the villages were comparable in terms of land scarcity, there have to be other reasons. A clue can be found in the relative importance of the rural council in both villages. Kaymor is the chief village of the rural community. The headquarters of the rural council is in Kaymor and four of the 32 councillors are from Kaymor. Passy Kaymor, by contrast, has no councillors among its population. This makes it plausible that the inhabitants of Passy Kaymor were less influenced by the warnings of the rural council than the people from Kaymor.

The picture becomes all the more interesting when the roles played by the village chiefs are included in the analysis as well. It is remarkable that in Passy Kaymor the son of the village chief prepared the big rush by clearing a piece of land in the valley in 1989. In the following years others followed his example. The village chief of Passy Kaymor was a cattle-holder himself and was strongly opposed to clearing the valley for agricultural use. The clearing by his son served as a justification for others who formerly had been held back by the village chief's authority.

By contrast the village chief of Kaymor, who, as we have seen, had his garden in the valley from a very early stage, played a stimulating role with regard to the agricultural use of the valley in his own village. Inhabitants of Kaymor told me that they had gone to the village chief because they were in need of land, and that he had replied that the valley was there and that they could clear and cultivate over there, on condition that they built a good fence at the same time. But it is clear that the village chief of Kaymor, more than his colleague in Passy Kaymor, had to reckon with the rural council. This coincidence meant that the process of massive clearing manifested itself at a slower pace in the chief village of the rural community.

Apart from showing that the positions and actions of the village chief and the rural council cannot be comprehended in isolation from each other, this analysis also illustrates that land claiming dynamics can often better be understood in terms of people's actions and power relationships than in terms of competing jurisdictions. Taking competing jurisdictions as the entry point for an analysis of land conflict may easily lead to a static picture of opposing judicial systems. Starting from people's actions offers the opportunity to see the dynamic of the 'social working of law' (Hesseling 1994). People interpret the circumstances they are in (including the sets of rules with which they have to reckon) and react to them, using the rules available to them. In this process, rules may change. This implies that jurisdictions should not be considered as given, but as moulded in the interplay between land users and authorities. Jurisdictions indeed play a part in the dynamics of claiming land, although not as a determining reality, but as a means in the hands of people.

Such a perspective opens up the possibility for a more layered analysis than would be possible from the perspective of a jurisdiction. Hence we have seen that local people pursuing a claim in the valley reported to those authorities and rules that most suited their interest, that is, in their particular situation and as they perceived it. The authorities, the village heads and the rural council (and within the rural council, also the different councillors) may also want to use the situation for their own sake, although also bounded by the situation and the power relationships they find themselves in. The rural council avoids clear solutions and tries open-ended measures in order not to lose (possible) clients, as they depend on them for their re-election. The village chiefs try to push their own agenda, that is, they want the valley to be used as they perceive best. In the meantime, they also know that more is at stake: The result of the claiming process will also reflect and further influence their positions of power. The power struggles between the different parties are, however, not pursued very openly and directly. Cultural codes that stress the importance of not defying another's dignity and of defending one's own also influence the claiming process and contribute to the fact that rivalries are often not played out very openly.[8]

Claiming land in the valley as a reflection of social dynamics in local society at large

As I suggested in the introduction, what is happening in the valley is interesting in its own right, but its importance is not restricted to this small area alone.

Firstly, the very clearance of the valley points to increasing land scarcity, scarcity of fertilizer and other inputs that is linked to the retreat of the State from the agricultural sector, and, in this context, to changing livelihood strategies of farmers. Peanuts are no longer the dominant focus, and farmers increasingly try to diversify their crops. Having a plot in the valley allows them to diversify and to be flexible, and this is part of a deliberate strategy of spreading risks, but on the other hand it is also a reflection of many farmers' precarious situation.

Secondly, the form that the clearing process took points to social dynamics at work in local society and offers a view of local social relationships and how they are changing over time. Thus we have seen that the valley offers the have-nots the opportunity to possess a piece of land. Immigrants and

---

8 Unfortunately, this chapter does not offer scope to elaborate further on this aspect. I therefore refer to Kaag (1999), which deals with the influence of cultural codes on trust and co-operation in the area of research.

people of low birth can, however, only start clearing when others have paved the way. What is interesting is that there are no open conflicts between locals and immigrants concerning land in the valley – in fact nobody is denied land in the valley because he is a stranger. As in fact there is a situation of illegality, all farmers making a claim feel that they cannot push too far to the detriment of others. Another contributing factor is the fact that recent migrants do not constitute a large group in the community and are not felt as a collective threat to the autochtonous community – which, certainly in the chief village of Kaymor, is constituted for a large part of migrants who came some generations ago.

Also for the women, the valley constitutes a chance for them to gain control over land. Some women profit from the situation and clear a plot for themselves, and following local custom, clearing means that the plot belongs to them. This could be considered a real revolution, as in Wolof society women traditionally are not allowed to claim land. How is this change made possible? It seems that the position of women in this respect changes when, by the coincidence of different processes, at a certain moment this is also advantageous to the men. There is a shortage of land – if the women have their own plots, the men are no longer obliged to provide a plot for their wives. There is a shortage of seed – if the women grow crops other than peanuts, their husbands are freed from the obligation to provide them with seed. In addition, the women's plots contribute to diversification within the household and in so doing help the family to face the insecurity of the food supply that is never far off. One could further argue that this access to land according to customary rule that the women have gained does not have much value, as this apparently goes together with a shift of importance away from customary rules to national legislation, to a large extent stimulated by external interventions. Finally, in fact few women have seized the opportunity to clear a plot for themselves; the others have not done so because they are not used to it, because they fear the hard work, or because they are deterred by their husbands who fear that the women will neglect their other duties. Therefore the revolution should rather be considered as an essential opening for eventual further and more specific changes. In this respect, the power that is displayed by several women's groups on the basis of their profitable garden is more real. The garden of the women's group in Passy Kaymor, for instance, benefits the entire village, but also means that the women are a force to be reckoned with because of their economic importance, but also because they are organized around a common goal. Thus, in certain respects, the position of women remains unchanged: They only get chances when the men are not interested or when they see a profit for themselves in including women. In other respects, however, the power relations between the sexes seem to be changing structurally, albeit slowly. This happens through individual women seizing the opportunities that they find, through economically successful women's groups, but also through women participating in the rural council or in projects such as the USAID-project mentioned earlier (for a more extensive treatment of these issues, see Kaag 2001).

Finally, the case of the valley also offers food for thought concerning the shifting importance of rules and authorities. While most agricultural land is still solidly in the hands of the families that claimed it under customary rules, land in the valley becomes an area of contestation, in which claims are made on the basis of both customary and national rules and arrangements, but also of the alleged importance of the activities undertaken. Local rules till now have sufficed to make people feel secure about their rights to land, at least at the level of the plots. A sign is that they invest in their plots by planting trees, building fences and so on. National legislation is applied mainly when outside interventions demand this. It is likely, however, that its importance is going to increase because donor interventions at the level of the rural communities are very much on the increase, stimulated by the decentralization policy of the Senegalese government.

Conclusion

The case illustrates the importance of small valleys for people in West Africa in the current economic, political and ecological context. Most rural areas in West Africa have experienced increasing ecological problems and climatic variability, the effects of structural adjustment measures, and unstable and low producer prices for their commercial crops. In this situation of insecurity, small valleys offer opportunities for diversification and for having a harvest with few material requirements. The increased use of small valleys for agriculture may thus be seen as a deliberate strategy of diversification, as well as the expression of the precarious situation of many West African farmers today.

While the background of clearing small valleys may be quite similar in many West African cases, the exact process of opening up these valleys and the actors and land claiming dynamics involved may differ, depending on specific local conditions, such as farming preferences, social relations, political dynamics, and relations with the 'outside world'.

The case illustrates that often a sharp distinction between a customary and legal realm cannot be made. State authorities may pursue strategies that are normally associated with customary tenure, and vice versa. In addition, it is wrong to assume that when people base themselves on customary law, national rules and authorities do not play a role in their thoughts and actions. Claiming rights to land is increasingly taking place at the crossroads of customary and national law. We have seen, for instance, that the very existence of plural jurisdiction makes people hesitant to press their claims too forcefully.

It is probable that the increasing interference of projects and donors at the local level that is promoted by current decentralization policy in Senegal, but also in other West African countries, will lead to a growing importance of national legislation at the local level. It is, however, not at all certain what form and content this will take in practice, as this to a large degree depends on the norms, goals and strategies of the different actors and on the power relations between them. The rural council may for instance continue to avoid clear-cut solutions in a context marked by factionalism and by local norms of not offending others in a direct way. Competing jurisdictions play a part in the dynamics of claiming land, although not as a determining reality, but as a means in the hands of people.

References

BASSETT, J. and D. CRUMMEY (1993) *Land in African agrarian systems*, Madison: University of Wisconsin Press.

Bell, M. and P. HOTCHKISS (1991) Garden cultivation, conservation and household strategies in Zimbabwe, *Africa*, 61(2): 202-21.

BENOÎT-CATTIN, M. (Ed.) (1986) *Les Unités Expérimentales du Sénégal. Recherche et développement agricole*, Montpellier: CIRAD.

BERRY, S. (1989) Social institutions and access to resources, *Africa*, 59(1): 41-55.

BERRY, S. (1993) *No condition is permanent. The social dynamics of agrarian change in sub-Saharan Africa*, Madison: Univerisity of Winconsin Press.

BERRY, S. (2001) *Chiefs know their boundaries. Essays on property, power, and the past in Asante, 1896-1996*, Portsmouth, Oxford, Cape Town: Heinemann, James Currey, David Philip.

BERTON, S. (1988) *La maîtrise des crues dans les bas-fonds: Petits et micro-barrages en Afrique de l'Ouest*, Paris: Gret.

BLUNDO, G. (1996) Gérer les conflits fonciers au Sénégal: Le rôle d'administration locale dans le sud-est du bassin arachidier, *Cahiers Africains/Afrika Studies*, 23-24: 101-19.

BLUNDO, G. (1998) Logiques de gestion publique dans la décentralisation Sénégalaise: Participation factionnelle et ubiquité réticulaire, *APAD bulletin*, 15: 21-47.

DURUFLÉ, G. (1994) *Le Sénégal peut-il sortir de la crise? Douze ans d'ajustement structurel au Sénégal*, Paris: Karthala.

HESSELING, G. (1992) *Pratiques foncières à l'ombre du droit: L'application du droit foncier urbain à Ziguinchor, Sénégal*, Leiden: African Studies Centre.

HESSELING, G. (1994) Legal and institutional conditions for local management of natural resources: Mali, in: Bakema, R.J. (Ed.) *Land tenure and sustainable land use*, Amsterdam: Royal Tropical Institute, pp. 31-46.

JUUL, K. and C. LUND (2002) *Negotiating property in Africa*, Portsmouth: Heinemann.

KAAG, M. (1999) Trust and co-operation in a Senegalese rural community, in: Smets, P., Wels, H. and Loon, J. van (2000) *Trust and co-operation; Symbolic exchange and moral economies in an age of cultural differentiation*, Amsterdam: Het Spinhuis.

KAAG, M. (2001) *Usage foncier et dynamique sociale au Sénégal rural. L'histoire d'un bas-fond et de ses défricheurs*, Amsterdam: Rozenberg.

KAAG, M. and L.B. VENEMA (2002) Local manifestations of a globalizing donor regime: 'Good governance' in a Senegalese rural community, in: Kooiman, D., Koster, A., Smets, P. and Venema, L.B. (Eds), *Conflict in a globalizing world. Essays in honour of Peter Kloos*, Assen: Van Gorcum.

LAVIGNE DELVILLE, PH., J. BOUJU and E. LE ROY (2000) *Prendre en compte les enjeux fonciers dans une démarche d'aménagement. Stratégies foncières et bas-fonds au Sahel*, Paris: Gret.

LUND, C. (1998) *Law, power and politics in Niger. Land struggles and the rural code*, Hamburg: LIT Verlag.

MATHIEU, P. (1996) Pratiques informelles, gestion de la confusion et invention du foncier en Afrique, *Cahiers Africains*, 19-20: 64-87.

NIJENHUIS, K. (2003) Does decentralisation serve everyone? The struggle for power in a Malian village, *The European Journal of Development Research*, 15(2): 67-92.

RAUNET, M. (1984) Les potentialités agricoles des bas-fonds en régions intertropicales: L'exemple de la culture du blé de contre-saison à Madagascar, *L'agronomie tropicale*, 39(2): 121-35.

RAUNET, M. (1985) Bas-fonds et riziculture en Afrique. Approche structurale comparative, *L'agronomie tropicale*, 40(3): 181-200.

TRAORE, S. (1991) Sénégal, la plus ancienne reforme foncière d'Afrique francophone doit s'adapter aux nouveaux enjeux. Communication au colloque de l'IPREFA/LAJP: Repenser la mobilisation de la terre dans les stratégies de développement rural en Afrique noire, Paris, 9 et 20 avril 1991.

TURNER, B. (1986) The importance of Dambos in African agriculture, *Land use policy*, 3(4): 343-7.

VENEMA, L.B. (1978) *The Wolof of Saloum. Social structure and rural development in Senegal*, Wageningen: Pudoc.

VERNIER, P. and A. HAMASSELBE (1988) Amélioriation de la riziculture sur nappe phréatique: Cinq années de recherche au Nord-Cameroun, *L'Agronomie Tropicale*, 43(1): 3-17.

WHITLOW, R. (1989) A review of Dambo gullying in South-Central Africa, *Zambezia*, XVI(ii): 123-50.

YUNG, J.M. (1992) Innovation et monétarisation; Le bassin arachidier, Sénégal, in: Bose, P.M., Dollé, V., Garrin, P. and Yung, J.M. (Eds) *Le développement agricole au Sahel. Tome III: Terrains et Innovations*, Montpellier: CIRAD, pp.3-21.

ZEPPENVELDT, T. and J.C.J. VLAAR (1990) *Mise en valeur des bas-fonds en Afrique de l'Ouest; Synthèse préliminaire de l'état des connaissances*, Ouagadougou: Comité Interafricain d'Études Hydrauliques/Université Agronomique de Wageningen.

List of contributors

Dr. Taylor Brown
A political scientist, Taylor Brown's work focuses on how politics shapes the lives and livelihoods of poor people. His recent work has examined policy formation and administration in developing countries with particular reference to the gaps between policy as designed, its implementation and its local-level impact. He has carried out long term research into land tenure and community-based resource management in Zambia and Nepal. Taylor is a staff consultant for the UK-based IDL group, an organisation that provides advisory, applied research, training, and project management services to international development agencies and partner institutions throughout the world.
taylor.brown@theidlgroup.com

Aninka Claassens
Aninka Claassens worked as a land activist in the anti-apartheid struggles for many years and is currently an independent consultant on land issues. She has published extensively on land restitution and tenure reform in South Africa.
Africa.aninka@icon.co.za

Prof. Ben Cousins
Ben Cousins currently holds a Chair in Development Management at the University of the Western Cape (UWC), South Africa, and has directed PLAAS (Programme for Land and Agrarian Studies at UWC) since its inception in 1995. His research and many publications have focused on land reform and rural social dynamics in Zimbabwe (1986-90) and South Africa (1991-2005).
cousins@uwc.ac.za

Dr. Sandra Evers
Sandra Evers is Assistant Professor and senior researcher at the department of Social and Cultural Anthropology of the Vrije Universiteit Amsterdam. She specialises in Southwest Indian Ocean Studies, with a particular focus on the Seychelles and Madagascar. She has studied and lived among the Betsileo people of Madagascar over a period of fourteen years. Her publications examine frontier societies within the context of globalization,

natural resource management, poverty and sustainable development. She is author of the book 'Constructing History, Culture and Inequality: The Betsileo in the Extreme Southern Highlands of Madagascar' (Brill, 2002).
sjtm.evers@fsw.vu.nl

Dr. Dereje Feyissa

Dereje Feyissa is a post doctoral research fellow at the Department of Conflict and Integration of the Max Planck Institute for Social Anthropology in Halle/Saale, Germany. In his work he focuses on conflict and identity politics in the Gambella region, western Ethiopia. He obtained his Ph.D. in 2003 on a work entitled 'Ethnic groups and conflict: The case of the Anywaa-Nuer relations in the Gambela Region, Western Ethiopia'.
dfeyissa@yahoo.com

Dr. Mayke Kaag

Mayke Kaag is a social anthropologist with an interest in processes of change and continuity in West and West Central Africa. She did a PhD on land use and social dynamics in Senegal (2001), and conducted research on transnational Islamic NGOs in Chad (2004). Currently, she is doing research on transnational livelihood networks of the Senegalese Mouride brotherhood.
kaag@ascleiden.nl

Dr. Bréhima Kassibo

Bréhima Kassibo is director of research in social anthropology at the Institute of Sciences and the Humanities in Bamako, Mali. From 1986 to 1999, he worked in the department of Rural Development of the Mali Institute of Rural Economics, focusing on organization of freshwater fisheries production and management. From 1998 to 2002 he was director of the research program 'Democratization, Migration and Access to Resources' focusing on Malien migrants across West Africa. From 2000 to 2002, he has directed a team of Malien researchers in the World Resource Institute (WRI) Decentralization and the Environment project. Bréhima Kassibo is the author of several articles dedicated to rural development, migration, the management of natural resources and local governance. He is currently working in Japan at the National Museum of Ethnology of Osaka as senior associate.
bkassibo@idc.minpaku.ac.jp

Dr. Bill Kinsey

Bill Kinsey works at the Faculty of Economics of the Vrije Universiteit Amsterdam and holds an honorary appointment at the Institute of Development Studies, University of Zimbabwe. He has been conducting a longitudi-

nal study on the social and economic effects of land reform and resettlement in Zimbabwe since 1983.
bkinsey@feweb.vu.nl

Prof. Carola Lentz
Carola Lentz is Professor of Social Anthropology at the Johannes Gutenberg University, Mainz (Germany), and was a fellow at the Netherlands' Institute for Advanced Studies in 2000-2001. Following her doctoral research on labour migration and ethnicity in Ecuador, she has conducted research on ethnicity, elite formation and history in Northern Ghana. She is author of 'Ethnicity and the Making of History in Northern Ghana' (Edinburgh University Press, forthcoming) as well as many related articles. Her current research focuses on mobility, land rights and the politics of belonging in North-Western Ghana and South-Western Burkina Faso, and has resulted in a number of publications, including the edited volume 'Land rights and the Politics of Belonging in West Africa' (Brill, forthcoming).
lentz@uni-mainz.de

Mr. Frank Muhereza
Frank Emmanuel Muhereza has a first degree in Political Science from Makerere University, Kampala, Uganda. He obtained a diploma in Development Studies from Cambridge University and has also studied a Masters of Science in Environment and Natural Resources Management from Makerere University. He is currently a senior research fellow at the Centre for Basic Research in Kampala, finalising the design of an Integrated Disarmament and Development Programme for Karamoja, on behalf of the Danish International Development Agency (DANIDA) and the Office of the Prime Minister (OPM) of Uganda. His publications include 'Case studies into commercial livestock ranching and pastoral institutions', together with Peter Otim.
fmuhereza@cbr-ug.org

Dr. Lungisile Ntsebeza
Lungisile Ntsebeza is Associate Professor in the Department of Sociology at the University of Cape Town, South Africa. He has done extensive research on democratisation, traditional authorities, local government and land rights in South Africa. His book 'Democracy Compromised: chiefs and the politics of land in South Africa' has just been published with Brill, Leiden.
Ntsebeza@humanities.uct.ac.za

Dr. Rie Odgaard

Rie Odgaard is an anthropologist working as Project Senior Researcher at the Department of Development Research, Danish Institute for International Studies (DIIS) (former Centre for Development Research) Copenhagen, Denmark. She is also coordinating a research network on 'Custom and Conflict in Land and Water Management in Africa'. Her research focus is now mainly on land rights and land conflicts (with special emphasis on the gender and ethnic dimensions), agriculture and rural development, especially in Eastern and southern Africa. Recent publications include 'Scrambling for Land in Tanzania. Process of Formalisation and Legitimisation of Land Rights' (2002) (*European Journal of Development Research*, 14(2)) and Bill Derman, Rie Odgaard and Espen Sjaastad (eds), 'Citizenship, Identity and Conflicts over Land and Water in Contemporary Africa' (James Currey, forthcoming).

rie@diis.dk

Dr. Jesse Ribot

Jesse Ribot is Senior Associate at the Institutions and Governance Program of the WRI in Washington. Currently he is associated with the Woodrow Wilson International Center for Scholars in Washington, D.C., doing research on 'Divisive Politics of Recognition: Institutional Choice and Belonging in Natural Resource Decentralizations'. His expertise is in the fields of rural enfranchisement; social structure of markets; theories of access and household vulnerability, especially in Africa.

RibotJ@wwic.si.edu

Dr. Marja Spierenburg

Marja Spierenburg is Assistant Professor at the Vrije Universiteit Amsterdam, Department of Culture, Organisation and Management. She has worked on land reforms and resistance in Zimbabwe. Currently she is working on the co-operation between environmental organisations, development NGOs and state agencies in relation to transfrontier conservation initiatives. Her publications include 'Strangers, Spirits and Land Reforms, Conflicts about Land in Dande, northern Zimbabwe' (Brill 2004).

mj.spierenburg@fsw.vu.nl

Sagane Thiaw

Sagane Thiaw, a human geographer, is currently teaching at the *Lycée Cherif Samsidine* in Velingara, Senegal. He is also doing research focused on forest resources management in the context of decentralization in Senegal.

saganethiaw@yahoo.fr

Dr. ir. Bernhard Venema

Bernhard Venema is Associate Professor at the Department of Social and Cultural Anthropology of the Vrije Universiteit Amsterdam. In his research, he focuses on rural transformations and development policy in Africa, investigating for example political and social transformations in rural areas of Senegal and Morocco. His publications include (together with Hans van den Breemer) (eds) 'Towards negotiated co-management of natural resources in Africa' (Lit Verlag 1999).

lb.venema@fsw.vu.nl

Dr. Harry Wels

Harry Wels is Associate Professor at the Vrije Universiteit Amsterdam, Department of Culture Organisation and Management. He has worked on issues of private wildlife conservation and community development in Zimbabwe and South Africa. He is currently working on structures of organisational cooperation within the Great Limpopo Transfrontier Conservation Area in southern Africa. His publications include: 'Private wildlife conservation in Zimbabwe. Joint ventures and reciprocity' (Brill 2003).

h.wels@fsw.vu.nl

Index

A

access · 1-4, 12-13, 15, 22-23, 27, 29-30, 33-34, 37, 49, 51-52, 65, 92, 98, 103-105, 109, 116, 122-124, 142-143, 158, 162, 168, 174, 177, 179, 181-186, 188, 191-199, 209, 212-213, 216, 223, 238, 243-244, 246, 249-251, 253-256, 259-261, 263, 274, 279-280, 283, 293, 295, 311-312, 315-316, 322, 325-329, 341, 348, 350
administrator · 319
advocacy · 3, 7, 8, 12
agricultural extension · 109, 111
agricultural production · 29, 33, 63, 74, 103, 109-110, 113-114, 123, 147, 168, 170, 185, 188-189, 204, 211, 230, 243-245, 249-250, 252, 255-256, 258-260, 281, 334-335, 337-339, 344, 350
ancestral spirits · 11, 18, 116-126, 139, 156-157, 173, 179
apartheid · 7, 17-19, 23, 27, 29, 31, 33-34, 43, 45, 51, 53-54, 58, 69, 76, 177
autochthony · 112, 114, 157, 183, 206-207, 324, 328

B

boundary · 7, 22-23, 26-28, 37, 39, 41, 45, 50, 88, 113, 116, 122, 130, 136, 145, 157, 160-161, 163, 167-168, 171, 175, 177, 184, 187, 196-197, 203-204, 206, 210, 221, 247, 295, 309, 350

C

capitalism · 53, 101, 182
cash crop · 245, 334, 338
centralisation · 5, 14, 18, 123, 126
chief · 12, 15, 26-27, 30-32, 39, 42, 51, 53, 83, 85, 88, 90-91, 94-98, 103, 106, 120, 122, 124, 130, 135-139, 142, 146-148, 151-152, 156, 162, 165, 192, 294, 299, 301, 306, 308, 315-316, 318-321, 323-328, 337-338, 340-341, 343, 346, 348
  and government · 23-24, 30, 83, 107, 187, 329
chieftaincy · 29, 36, 52, 87, 92-93, 95, 174, 317-318, 320, 330-331
churches · 12, 55-76, 84
civil society · 30, 38, 40, 44, 46, 51, 80, 84-85, 153-154, 290
claiming natural resources · 1, 3, 10, 93, 110, 116, 130, 151, 158, 161-162, 166, 169-172, 174, 182, 196, 199, 209, 211, 214-215, 219, 223, 226-228, 230, 232, 235, 237, 251-253, 255, 258, 283, 286, 326, 329, 335, 337, 344, 347-348
clan · 22, 135, 157, 183, 207-208, 246, 249, 252, 292, 337
colonial · 2-5, 7, 10-13, 16-18, 21-25, 28-31, 35, 39, 43-44, 49, 51-58, 60-61, 64, 67, 73-74, 76, 81-83, 87, 101-102, 104-105, 110, 123, 126, 130, 135, 150, 158-161, 163, 165, 171, 175, 177, 180, 182, 186-191, 193, 199-200, 211, 226, 228, 243-245, 248-249, 251-252, 256, 260-263, 270, 281, 293, 301, 307, 317-321, 329-331, 338, 351
commodification · 93
common pool resources · 22, 81, 92, 95, 100, 142-143, 148
commons · 13, 53, 92, 131, 141, 179, 181-182, 184, 186, 188, 193-195, 197-199, 212
communal land · 12, 18, 21, 38, 41-42, 49, 51, 55, 103-110, 112, 120-121, 123, 125-126, 132-133, 136
communal tenure · 3, 5, 12, 21-23, 26-31, 33-34, 38, 43, 48-49, 83, 86, 91, 103-104, 108, 159-160
complicity · 8-10, 324
conflict · 1, 7-8, 13, 16-17, 23, 25-26, 29-31, 43, 50-51, 53, 56, 64, 66, 69, 76, 80-81, 84, 93-94, 97, 102-105, 111, 115, 117, 120, 122-124, 126, 130, 153,

158, 160-163, 165, 167-168, 170, 173, 178, 181, 183-184, 187-188, 191, 192, 194, 199, 205, 209, 210, 212-213, 216, 218-219, 221-222, 224, 239, 243, 251, 260-263, 267-269, 277, 279-280, 284, 286-287, 292, 297, 317-318, 321-323, 329, 331, 336, 340, 346, 349, 351
control · 2-5, 11, 14, 16, 22, 25, 27, 29-32, 35, 48, 83, 87, 103, 105, 108-109, 115, 117, 121-122, 124, 126, 130, 140, 143, 149-150, 153, 160-161, 163, 171-172, 174, 177, 191, 193, 213, 219, 223, 230, 233, 238, 262, 267-268, 270, 272, 274-277, 279-280, 282-283, 285-287, 294, 296-297, 299, 303, 306-307, 310-311, 317, 321, 328, 331, 335-336, 343, 348
corruption · 32, 79, 94, 97, 99, 137
crown land · 27, 82-83
customary law · 13, 25, 38, 47, 106, 120, 136, 160, 177, 182, 190, 193, 199, 224, 246, 248, 253-254, 258, 296, 335, 345, 349
customary management and tenure · 297, 299-305, 307-308, 312

D

democracy · 1, 5, 17, 30-31, 36, 40, 42, 45, 49, 52-53, 55, 59, 61-62, 64-65, 75, 84, 150-151, 196, 218, 265, 270, 285, 287, 289, 291, 304, 307, 309-312, 318
descent · 5, 116, 157, 161, 185-186, 197, 199, 206-207, 226-230, 232, 234-238, 241, 317
discourse · 6-7, 11, 13, 16-17, 19, 103, 124, 158, 161, 164-165, 167, 169-171, 173-176, 178, 204, 206-207, 209-211, 217, 220, 237, 239, 263, 284, 286, 310-311, 323, 329
discourse, counter-narrative · 3, 7-8, 121
displacement · 81, 90

E

elite · 18, 81, 192, 201, 315-316, 340
ethnicity · 3, 39, 87, 133, 157, 161, 164-165, 168, 170, 181, 196, 199, 204-207, 209-213, 217-219, 221, 245-246, 250, 256-257, 291, 309
eviction · 35, 90, 146, 280, 282, 293-294
exclusion · 4, 6, 14, 22, 58, 81, 100, 107, 178, 193, 195, 198-199, 213, 218, 223, 227, 229-230, 296-297, 314, 326
exploitation · 10, 31, 189, 272, 279, 286, 293-294, 296, 297, 300-302, 312, 314, 316, 322, 325, 331, 334

F

farm labourer · 24, 34, 63, 105
farming · 24, 33-34, 81, 83, 87-88, 94, 95, 104-105, 110, 112-114, 122, 211, 230, 294-295, 324, 326, 336, 338, 342, 349
forestry · 165, 266, 273-274, 277, 286-287, 294, 296-297, 300, 303-304, 308, 311, 314, 316, 322, 325, 328, 331

G

gender · 14, 36, 44, 48, 244, 248-249, 253, 261-262
grazing · 22-24, 37, 91-95, 109, 116, 123, 131, 136, 141-146, 151, 193, 199, 243, 255, 257-258, 283, 295, 344

H

headmen · 25, 27-28, 81, 91, 94-96, 100, 103-104, 107, 114-124, 130, 135-137, 140, 147, 149, 207, 222, 249-250, 255-256, 292, 299, 301, 305, 308
household · 22, 33, 63, 66, 92, 111, 117, 131, 142-143, 154, 229, 318, 320, 326, 337, 348, 350

I

identity · 3-4, 39, 87, 133, 142-143, 157, 161, 164-165, 168, 170, 181, 196, 199, 204-207, 209-213, 217-219, 221, 229, 245-246, 250, 256-257, 291, 309
ideology · 14, 16, 104, 175-176, 205-206, 209-211, 218, 228, 239
illegal · 15, 35, 57, 113, 146, 272-274, 278-279, 282-284, 295, 303, 312, 343
inclusion · 178, 198-199, 208, 210, 217-218, 306, 310, 312
Independence · 12, 104-105, 107-108, 116-118, 121, 123, 132, 190
  struggle for · 25, 30, 36, 95, 103-104, 110, 113, 116-118, 121, 125-126, 132, 211, 218, 220, 318
indigenous · 4, 22-23, 56, 83, 85, 129, 159-161, 163-164, 175-176, 192-193,

203-204, 248-250, 255, 261, 307, 309, 319, 321-322, 329
insiders · 15, 142, 316, 325, 328-329
institution · 36-37, 49, 57, 107, 155, 190-191, 194, 266, 271, 302-303, 305, 311

L

labour · 5, 13, 19, 23-24, 28-31, 34-35, 54, 83, 122, 133, 172, 182, 199, 230, 256, 258-259, 319
  migration · 19
land
  acquisition · 57, 76, 226
  agriculture · 15, 65-69, 72, 74, 89, 136, 145, 154, 171, 177, 335, 339, 349
  allocation · 5, 21-22, 28, 31-32, 52, 81, 83-84, 87, 102, 105-108, 110, 121, 124, 131, 141, 151, 172-173, 215-216, 218, 249, 255, 278, 325, 335, 341, 343
  claim · 1, 3, 10, 93, 110, 116, 130, 151, 158, 161-162, 166, 169-172, 174, 182, 196, 199, 209, 211, 214-215, 219, 223, 226-228, 230, 232, 235, 237, 251-253, 255, 258, 283, 286, 326, 329, 335, 337, 344, 347-348
  degradation · 2, 27, 53, 112-114, 117, 144, 294, 301, 304, 334, 342-343
  invaders · 104
  ownership · 13, 36, 74, 84, 93, 158, 175, 237, 239, 294, 296, 311
  redistribution · 12, 34, 40, 51, 63, 74-75, 104
  reforms · 12, 21, 32, 34-36, 38-40, 45, 48-53, 55-56, 60-81, 84, 86, 93, 100, 106, 109, 121, 125-126, 153, 177, 270-271
  residential · 22, 63, 65-68, 73, 109, 111, 116, 132, 136, 143, 151, 181, 294
  right · 3-4, 7, 14, 16, 18, 21-28, 30-42, 44-45, 47-59, 61-63, 65, 68, 71, 74-75, 80-81, 83, 85-86, 88, 90, 92-93, 95, 96-97, 101, 103-105, 122, 124, 130-131, 141-143, 145-146, 148, 157-166, 168-172, 174-179, 185, 191, 193, 195, 199, 212, 214-215, 221, 224, 230, 243, 245-263, 268, 270, 276, 290, 293-294, 296, 298, 300-301, 303, 305, 311, 314, 335, 337, 341, 349
  security · 16, 22, 27-29, 32, 35-36, 38, 41, 44, 47, 49, 51-52, 55-56, 62-63, 70, 79-80, 90, 96, 107, 129, 154, 176, 205, 213, 220, 249, 259, 263, 267-268, 279, 343
  shortage · 25, 56, 60, 72, 75, 79, 104, 111, 114, 116, 123, 132, 230
  speculation · 89-90
  tenure · 2-3, 5-6, 8, 11-12, 14, 16, 18, 21-28, 30-33, 34-36, 38-41, 45, 47-53, 55-56, 62-63, 65, 70, 74-75, 79-81, 83-87, 92, 95-99, 101-102, 104, 108, 125-126, 131-132, 141, 154, 158-161, 163, 175-177, 179, 188, 198, 224, 249, 253, 261-263, 267, 269-270, 275, 286, 288, 296, 334, 336-337, 345, 349-350
  use · 5-6, 8, 11-12, 14, 31, 41, 45-46, 73, 109-111, 122-123, 125, 145, 155, 157, 243-244, 252, 255, 258, 281, 301, 303, 336, 346, 350
  use policy · 13
landless · 25, 56, 60, 72, 75, 79, 111, 116, 123, 132, 230
law · 3-4, 6-8, 12-13, 15-16, 18, 21-59, 61-66, 68, 71, 74-75, 79-110, 116, 118, 120, 122, 124, 129-130, 134-137, 139-143, 145-146, 148-155, 157, 158-172, 174-179, 182, 185, 190-191, 193-196, 198-199, 212, 214-215, 221-224, 230, 234, 238, 243, 245-264, 266, 268-276, 280, 285-288, 290, 293-296, 298, 300-301, 303-304, 307-308, 310-311, 314, 317, 319-320, 322, 329-330, 335, 337, 340-341, 343, 345-346, 348-349
leasehold · 80-82, 84-88, 91, 93-94, 96, 98, 100
licence · 296, 304-305
livelihood · 2, 10, 21, 23, 31-34, 48, 53, 80, 91, 94, 102, 328
livestock · 15, 23, 25-26, 33, 73, 74, 91-93, 109-110, 113, 118, 123, 133, 137, 141-143, 162, 184, 193, 197-198, 209-212, 227, 230, 245, 250, 252, 255-257, 334, 336, 338, 340-346
livestock production · 23, 73
local government · 44, 46-48, 58, 69, 97, 101, 106-109, 111, 113, 115, 120-122, 135-136, 138, 146-147, 155, 244, 272, 276, 282, 285, 292, 305, 308, 316, 322, 324, 327, 331, 341, 345

M

migrant · 25-26, 28-30, 33, 227, 232, 240-241, 283, 294-295, 298, 316, 322-328
migration · 33, 109, 115, 158, 161, 163-164, 166, 168-169, 171, 175-176, 183-184, 208, 214, 245, 261-262, 324
mobility · 4, 13, 85, 89, 158, 163-164, 169, 171, 177, 200, 207, 211, 214, 245, 252, 283

N

narrative, see *discourse* · 6, 11, 13, 16, 103, 124, 161, 169-170, 173, 286
nationalism · 83, 104
natural resources · 2, 4-5, 14, 19, 22, 34, 53, 83, 103, 116, 124, 129, 136, 139-140, 145, 148, 162, 176, 209, 219, 262, 270-271, 284, 287, 290, 293-294, 298, 299-300, 303, 305, 307, 311, 313, 316-317, 331, 344, 350
NGO · 44, 64, 73, 75, 176, 290, 292, 297, 301, 303

O

outsiders · 15, 22, 69, 71, 90, 93, 95-96, 99-100, 141-145, 181, 184, 194, 198-199, 209, 315-316, 323, 325-329, 340

P

participation (community) · 45, 106, 150, 154, 226, 260, 268, 287-290, 296-297, 300, 303-305, 307-312, 314, 331
pastoralism · 94, 191, 204, 211, 259, 263
peasant · 30, 102, 153, 262, 331
policy · 3-4, 7-12, 14-15, 17-18, 21-32, 36, 38, 43, 48-51, 53, 60, 62-64, 75-76, 80, 82-84, 88, 99-102, 104, 106, 116, 121, 123, 125, 134, 154, 159, 177, 179, 182, 187, 192, 199, 211, 218, 224-225, 227, 238, 243, 246, 248-249, 252, 261, 263, 268, 270, 272, 280, 284-287, 296, 311-312, 318-319, 334, 344, 349-351
political capital · 213, 218
politics · 4, 7-8, 16-17, 19, 21, 48, 52, 79, 101, 125-126, 154, 158, 163-164, 167, 173, 178, 182, 192, 201, 203, 205, 211-213, 216-218, 221, 267, 287-288, 330-331, 341, 351
poverty · 2, 14, 16, 33-34, 48, 52-53, 80, 153-154, 198, 223-225, 260, 263, 287, 326, 333
project · 6, 12, 39, 44, 65, 71, 76, 91, 94, 105, 108-120, 122-124, 154, 163-164, 209, 213, 215, 218-219, 221, 290, 294, 303, 306, 312, 327, 344, 349

Q

quitrent · 24-25, 28

R

racial discrimination · 36, 55, 75
religion · 26, 55-62, 64-68, 70-75, 77, 126, 158-161, 166-168, 170, 172, 174, 178-179, 197, 208, 228-229, 232-236, 239, 241-242, 257, 299, 331
representation · 10-11, 16, 27, 40, 89, 132, 140, 152, 215, 270, 301-302, 306, 308, 318, 329, 331
reserve · 15, 23-24, 26, 28-30, 34-35, 83, 252, 266, 270-273, 275, 277-278, 281-283, 285-287, 293, 316, 326
resettlement · 13, 104, 112, 116, 126, 130-137, 140-154, 204
riverine cultivation · 13, 110, 114, 116, 122-123, 211-212, 220, 333, 351

S

settlement · 1, 13, 26, 50, 56, 82, 96, 105, 111, 136, 151, 158-159, 163-164, 166, 168-170, 173, 175-177, 188, 191-194, 198-199, 204, 207, 209, 213-215, 219, 226-228, 256, 259, 281, 291, 294, 298, 316, 326, 336
settler · 4, 17, 185, 199
slavery · 57, 167, 226, 228, 238-239, 262, 321
State · 6, 16, 27-28, 35, 88, 98, 110, 137, 181, 205, 211, 221, 224, 293, 317, 321, 327-328, 330, 345, 347, 349
stranger · 84-85, 88-89, 133, 153, 162, 167, 170, 182, 185-186, 189-190, 193, 195-197, 208, 213, 298, 312, 318, 323

T

tax · 25, 64, 69, 224, 271, 296, 318-319
territoriality · 206-208, 219-220
tomb · 14, 223, 232, 239

traditional authority · 12, 15, 23, 25-28, 30-32, 35, 38-40, 42-49, 51-53, 79, 81, 83-85, 88, 90-91, 94-98, 100, 103-107, 115-124, 130, 134-139, 142, 146-149, 151-152, 155-156, 162, 165, 187, 192, 207, 222, 228, 230, 234, 244, 249-250, 255, 266, 294, 299, 301, 305, 308, 315-316, 318-321, 323-328, 337-338, 340-341, 343, 346, 348
tribal · 3, 24, 26-27, 30, 37, 81-83, 104, 175, 182-195, 199-200, 208, 245

V

valley · 109, 114, 122, 156, 295, 333, 335-336, 338-349

W

war · 25, 30, 36, 95, 103-104, 110, 113, 116-118, 121, 125-126, 131-132, 211, 218, 220, 318
witchcraft · 120, 284

www.ingramcontent.com/pod-product-compliance
Lightning Source LLC
Chambersburg PA
CBHW071415230926
51846CB00001B/94
9789004147805